ALSO BY JAN JARBOE RUSSELL

Lady Bird: A Biography of Mrs. Johnson
They Lived to Tell the Tale (editor)

THE TRAIN TO CRYSTAL CITY

FDR's Secret Prisoner Exchange Program
and America's Only Family Internment Camp
During World War II

JAN JARBOE RUSSELL

SCRIBNER

New York   London   Toronto   Sydney   New Delhi

SCRIBNER
A Division of Simon & Schuster, Inc.
1230 Avenue of the Americas
New York, NY 10020

First Scribner hardcover edition January 2015

SCRIBNER and design are registered trademarks of The Gale Group, Inc.,
used under license by Simon & Schuster, Inc., the publisher of this work.

For information about special discounts for bulk purchases,
please contact Simon & Schuster Special Sales at 1-866-506-1949
or business@simonandschuster.com.

The Simon & Schuster Speakers Bureau can bring authors to your live event.
For more information or to book an event contact the Simon & Schuster Speakers Bureau
at 1-866-248-3049 or visit our website at www.simonspeakers.com.

Interior design by Erich Hobbing
Jacket design by Mark Melnick
Jacket photograph © Myron Davis/The LIFE Picture Collection/
Time & Life Pictures/Getty Images

Manufactured in the United States of America

1   3   5   7   9   10   8   6   4   2

ISBN 978-1-4516-9366-9
ISBN 978-1-4516-9368-3 (ebook)

Photograph credits appear on page 393.

This book is in memory of Maury Maverick Jr.,
heroic civil rights lawyer, politician,
fearless newspaper columnist, and my mentor.
Before he died on January 28, 2003, he would often call to ask,
"What have you done for your country today?"
This book is my attempt at an answer.

Enemies are people whose stories you haven't yet heard and whose faces you haven't yet seen.

—*Irene Hasenberg Butter,*
Holocaust survivor, during an interview at her home
in Ann Arbor, Michigan, June 13, 2013

Contents

CONTENTS

PART THREE

THE EQUATION OF EXCHANGE

PART FOUR

THE ROAD HOME

THE TRAIN TO CRYSTAL CITY

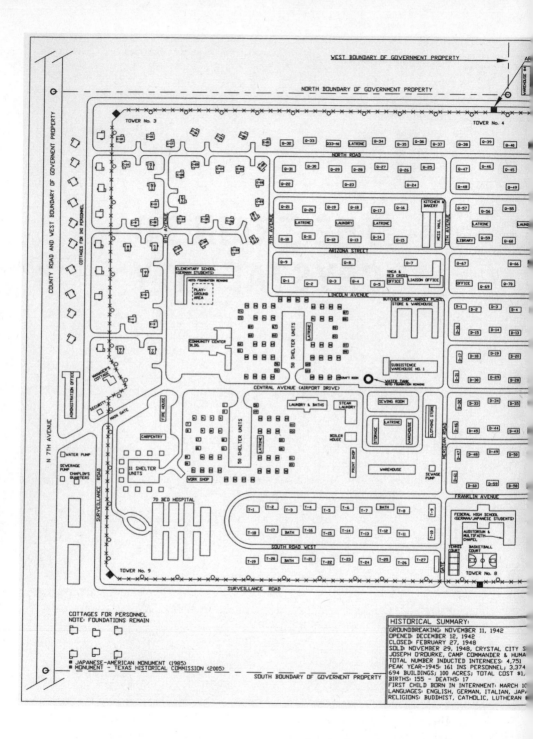

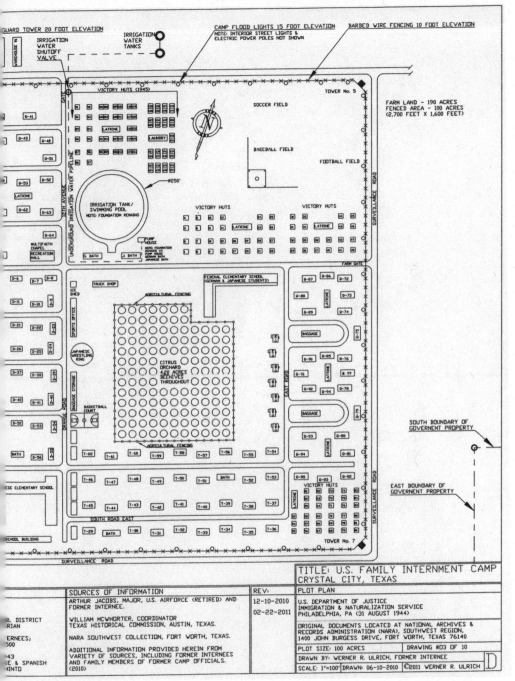

The camp map was drawn by former internee Werner Ulrich, with details supplied by other former internees and camp officials, as well as Ulrich's own research from records at the National Archives and Records Administration.

Used by permission of the University of Texas at San Antonio Libraries Special Collections.

Preface

Trains are a primary symbol of World War II. During the war, life and death revolved around the arrival and departure of trains. American troops boarded Pullman cars with signs on them that said HITLER HERE WE COME and ON TO TOKYO. Along the tracks, American workers, who saved rubber tires and tin for the war effort, waved their arms to the troops, saluting them with smiles. Trains led soldiers to ships and to battle. Women waited at train stations for the return of their husbands and lovers and kicked up their heels when their men disembarked. In Germany, more than 6 million Jews were shipped in cattle cars, floors strewn with straw, to concentration camps.

And then there were the trains that transported people to Crystal City, Texas. Week after week, month after month, from 1942 to 1948, trains with window shades pulled shut carried approximately six thousand civilians from all over the world across miles of flat, empty plains to the small desert town at the southern tip of Texas, only thirty miles from the Mexican border.

The trains held Japanese, German, and Italian immigrants and their American-born children, and many families from Latin America. The Crystal City Internment Camp, administered by the Immigration and Naturalization Service under the Department of Justice, was the only "family" internment camp—on either side of the Atlantic or the Pacific—that operated during the war. It opened in 1942 for the official purpose of reuniting immigrant fathers who'd been arrested and imprisoned as "dangerous enemy aliens" with their wives and children. The length of their internment was indefinite. Internees poured into Crystal City under the veil of government secrecy, dusty trainloads and buses of men, women, and children arriving tired and confused, with tags around their necks that displayed family identification numbers and symbolized that they had been torn away from the lives they had known.

The government's official name for the facility was the Crystal City Enemy Detention Facility. Surviving internees had their own distinctive terminology, based on their culture and experience. Japanese survivors, who later erected a granite monument on the site of the camp in November 1985, called it the Crystal City Concentration Camp. On that monument, no mention is made of the Germans, Italians, and other nationalities also interned in Crystal City. The Germans, sensitive to the Nazi extermination camps in Germany, never referred to it as a concentration camp. They generally called it the Crystal City Internment Camp. Some, however, describe it more harshly, as a kidnap camp.

Sumi Utsushigawa, born in Los Angeles to Japanese immigrants, was a shy teenager when she came to Crystal City. Her first glimpse of the city was of whirls of dust moving down a deserted main street lined with dozens of one-story buildings made of adobe. Before the outbreak of World War II, Sumi lived near downtown Los Angeles, a center of business, entertainment, and international trade. In Crystal City, she found herself in the American equivalent of Siberia, as small and isolated a place as she could imagine.

A bus took Sumi and her parents inside the front gates of the 290-acre Crystal City Internment Camp. A ten-foot-high barbed-wire fence surrounded the camp. Guards with long rifles were positioned in six guard towers at the corners of the fence line. Other guards, who wore cowboy hats and chaps made of cowhide, patrolled the perimeter of the fence on horseback. At night, the searchlights from the camp could be seen across the border in Mexico.

Paul Grayber, born in Elizabeth, New Jersey, to German immigrants, was only four years old when he arrived with his mother, two brothers, and a sister in Crystal City to be reunited with their father, who was arrested shortly after Pearl Harbor. Paul's first clear memory in life was of the camp's barbed-wire fence. One afternoon, while on a walk with his father, Paul pointed to a small cabin beyond the fence where the officer in charge of the camp lived.

"Why is the man who lives there fenced in?" Paul asked.

"Son," his father replied, "it's us who are fenced in."

The popular history of America's internment of its own citizens during World War II has long been focused on the incarceration of 120,000 Japanese, 62 percent of them American-born, who were forcibly evacuated from the Pacific coast after the bombing of Pearl Harbor. On February 19, 1942, President Franklin D. Roosevelt signed Executive Order 9066, which permitted the secretary of war to arrest and incarcerate Japanese, Germans, and Italians who had been declared "enemy aliens." Not only could they be arrested and held without charges or trials, but their homes and businesses could be seized without warning. The day before Roosevelt signed the order, FBI agents had arrested 264 Italians, 1,396 Germans, and 2,209 Japanese on the East and West Coasts. The hunt for perceived enemies was on.

Virtually unknown, even to this day, is that the arrests of suspected enemies extended far beyond our national borders. Over the course of the war, the US government orchestrated and financed the removal of 4,058 Germans and 2,264 Japanese and 288 Italians from thirteen Latin American countries and interned them in the United States, many in Crystal City. Carmen Higa Mochizuki was eleven years old when her father, a poor farmer in Peru who made his living selling milk from his cows, was arrested. The government seized her father's assets. They lost everything in an instant. Her mother, father, and nine siblings were transported to the United States, under American military guard, from Callao, Peru, to New Orleans. Their passports and visas were confiscated.

At the port in New Orleans, the women and children were marched to a warehouse, forced to strip, and made to stand in line naked. "Then we were all sprayed with insecticide that stung our skin," remembered Carmen. "Since we had no passports or proof of identity, we were arrested as illegal aliens and put on a train to Crystal City. During the train ride, my sister thought we might be killed there."

I first learned of the Crystal City Internment Camp more than forty years ago when I was an undergraduate at the University of Texas at Austin, a young reporter on the student newspaper. One of my sources was Alan Taniguchi, a professor of architecture and prominent Japanese American. During a meeting, I asked Alan how he got to Texas.

"My family was in camp here," he said.

"Church camp?"

"Not exactly." He laughed. Taniguchi told me that his father, Isamu Taniguchi, then an old man with a weatherworn face who stood five feet two inches tall and weighed less than a hundred pounds, had been interned as a dangerous enemy alien in Crystal City, Texas.

I met Isamu, who had been an innovative farmer in the San Joaquin Delta of California at the outbreak of the war. In addition to tomatoes and other row crops, Taniguchi grew almonds and apricots on his farm. The FBI arrested him in March 1942 when he was forty-five, and in that moment of arrest he lost his farm and everything he owned.

In Crystal City, Isamu continued his work as a gardener, but grew much more reflective and philosophical. He claimed that during his time in Crystal City he came to understand that World War II represented what he called the "beast heart in mankind." After his release from Crystal City, stricken with grief and shame, he decided to devote the rest of his life to peace. At seventy, he created a Japanese garden in Austin with his own hands. It took him over two years to build. The Taniguchi Garden, a small, green oasis near downtown Austin, still exists and is dedicated to peace.

The raw intensity of Isamu's face stayed with me as the decades passed and America fought wars in Vietnam, Iraq, Afghanistan, and elsewhere. One day a few years ago, I was in Austin and went by the Taniguchi Garden. I remembered the story about Crystal City. I stopped by Alan's office and discovered he had died. His son, Evan, also an architect, greeted me. Evan shared his father's file on Crystal City. The last time I'd seen Alan, he had told me that something about Crystal City was unresolved: a mystery needed to be unraveled, a story to be told.

I opened the file and saw a list of names, written in Alan's meticulous hand, of many children who were incarcerated in the Crystal City Internment Camp at the time his father was interned. The children were now old men and women, who lived all over the world. The next day, I started telephoning them.

Alan's hunch had been right. Slowly, the secrets of the camp and its sorrowful inhabitants began to unfold. The experience of their internment lay embedded in their memories, driven into them like spikes into the ties that held the rails beneath the trains that had brought them to South Texas. "During the war, there was no place like Crystal City," said Ingrid Eiserloh, who had been a teenager in Crystal City. "So many families living behind the barbed wire, many of us born in America, humiliated and betrayed by our government."

Living now in Honolulu, Hawaii, Eiserloh agreed to talk to me after I contacted her. On February 12, 2012, I arrived at her house. She was eighty-one years old and not in good health. She greeted me in her kitchen, ran her bony fingers through her short hair, picked up a pack of cigarettes, and poured a cup of coffee. We walked outside to the back porch, surrounded by black mountains folded into deep-green cliffs. Ingrid's breath was quick and raspy. She seemed glad that I had found her. Time was short and she had a story to tell.

PART ONE

WITHOUT TRIAL

CHAPTER ONE

New Enemies

On January 8, 1942, one month and one day after the surprise Japanese attack on Pearl Harbor, America's entry into World War II, Ingrid Eiserloh's world changed forever. At six that morning, Ingrid's father, Mathias Eiserloh, a German-born immigrant, left the family's Strongsville home, a square, concrete box made by his own hands, for his job in nearby Cleveland, Ohio. Then forty-six years old, Mathias was fair-haired with gray-blue eyes. Five feet eight inches tall, stocky, he had the ruddy skin of a man well accustomed to hard labor. A structural engineer, Mathias worked for the Pittsburgh Plate Glass Company for $60 a week. He was in charge of constructing lime plants for the chemical division of Pittsburgh Plate, a company that made glass. His large hands carried a scent of sour chemicals that Ingrid did not find unpleasant, as the smell meant her father was with her.

Ingrid had been born on May 8, 1930, in New York. Her parents, Mathias and Johanna, had immigrated to America from Germany seven years before. In the midst of the Depression, they had purchased in Strongsville a heavily wooded, five-acre lot, which sloped down to a creek. There Mathias built a tent on a wooden platform, and Johanna, a slim, green-eyed beauty with chestnut hair and fair skin, raised chickens. Johanna took a lot of pride in her chickens. They yielded eggs at a rate that astonished her and added to the family's meager income. Over the years, German-born friends and relatives who lived nearby helped Mathias and Johanna mix the concrete that was used to add on

3

to their large, sturdy house. They built their home one room at a time. They had no indoor plumbing or electricity for years.

Ingrid lived her early life like a woodland nymph, roaming the forest and collecting animals. On her third birthday, her father gave her a raccoon. On her fourth, she was given a German shepherd puppy which she named Tire Biter, because biting tires came so naturally to him. Other dogs followed: Senta, another German shepherd, and a collie mix named Pal, with long golden hair.

As a child, Ingrid had long hair, red as a penny, which trailed down her back, and a gift. Her young soprano voice, while still immature, had the potential to rival the opera stars she listened to on the family's Victrola phonograph. She babied her voice and knew better than to scream. Her voice teacher, a neighbor who lived down the road, regularly told her to protect her voice. The child had a rare four-octave range and an unusually disciplined disposition. If Ingrid had to cough, she coughed gently to avoid strain. In smoky environments, Ingrid breathed through her nose, not her mouth, to protect her throat. Her middle name, chosen at birth by her adoring father, was Goldie. That was the name her teacher had given to her voice: Goldie, the teacher called it, a treasure to be prized.

Even in tiny Strongsville, the unbearable news of Japan's crippling strike at Pearl Harbor (3,581 casualties, 188 planes destroyed on the ground, 8 battleships sunk or run aground) rolled off newspaper drums and hummed across radio signals. On the morning of December 8, 1941, the headline of the *Cleveland Plain Dealer* was: "Japs War on U.S., Britain; Bomb Hawaii, Philippines; Congress to Hear F.D.R." The newspaper printed instructions for responding to blackouts. Air-raid sirens shrieked fifteen miles away in downtown Cleveland. The *Plain Dealer* printed instructions for responding to blackouts. Terms such as *spies*, *saboteurs*, and *Fifth Column subversives* were alive on editorial pages. Suddenly in America there arose an entirely new lexicon—*krauts*, *Nazis*, *yellow devils*, and *Japanazis*—all new words deployed to categorize enemies in the contest between the forces of good and evil.

German immigrants to the United States, such as Ingrid's parents, had long been subjects of suspicion. In 1936, President Franklin D. Roosevelt secretly issued an order to J. Edgar Hoover, director of the Federal Bureau of Investigation, to investigate not only suspected members of the Nazi movement, but anyone who might pose a security risk in the event of war. Hoover had earlier instituted a sweeping surveillance program that proved much more far-reaching than his commander in chief had in mind. In just four years, from 1932 to 1936, the FBI swelled from three hundred to six hundred agents. Hoover's coast-to-coast team wrote daily reports of real and imagined subversive activities, wiretapped suspects, and developed an extensive file of secret dossiers, built on the word of anonymous informants.

Within a few hours after the first Japanese bombs were dropped on Pearl Harbor, FBI agents, working from a list of thousands of names already compiled into its secret Custodial Detention Index, arrested an estimated 2,000 Japanese and German immigrants on the West and East Coasts. Fourteen days later, the FBI held under arrest 1,430 Japanese, 215 Italians, and 1,153 Germans in the continental United States and Hawaii. All of this news inflated the public's fear of immigrants. The pursuit of enemies was on—even in such places as rural Ohio.

In Strongsville, half of Ingrid's neighbors had either been born in Germany, like her parents, or were first-generation, born in America, like Ingrid and her two younger siblings. With the news of arrests of Germans, a worried hush fell over the neighborhood as every family of German descent came under suspicion. Mathias and his German friends stopped meeting at the neighborhood beer hall. They stopped speaking German in public. Agents came to town to interview their non-German neighbors. As had happened during World War I, anti-German sentiment was everywhere. Sauerkraut became "liberty cabbage" and hamburgers were renamed "Salisbury steak." In nearby Cleveland, the city orchestra stopped performing the works of Beethoven.

Two days after the attack on Pearl Harbor, Ingrid rode the bus to school. She was a small girl, not even five feet tall, and scrawny as a shadow. Fueled by the anti-German influence of the day, four boys held her down on the bus, pulled her hair, and jeered, "Hotsy-totsy Nazi!" When the driver finally called off the boys, Ingrid picked herself up. Flushed and angry, she willed herself not to show fear. She had her father's pride.

That year, 1941, Christmas came and went. Her mother sent no *Weihnachtskarten*—Christmas cards—and the house seemed silent and sullen. As an escape Ingrid went outside into the woods and sang arias to the trees, as if the high, crystal notes could chase away the oppressive gloom. When confined to the house, she felt claustrophobic and hummed softly to console herself.

Day by day, Ingrid sensed her father's growing anxiety. When he came home from work, usually after dark, he threw himself into a kitchen chair and grumbled about the coworkers he thought might be his enemies. "Perhaps the FBI was interviewing them?" he wondered aloud. "Who knows what they might say?"

During family dinners he called them anonymous accusers. "What's fair about that?"

Obsessed by fear and worry, he talked too fast and was incapable of staying on a single subject for more than a few minutes. Before Pearl Harbor, Mathias smoked two packs of cigarettes a day. Now he was never without a cigarette. Ingrid's mother, Johanna, complained that Mathias was up to four packs a day. When, wondered Ingrid, would her father next draw a clean, easy breath? And when would she have to stop holding her breath in his presence to protect her voice?

January 8, 1942, was a Thursday and a cold winter's day. Ice had formed on the surface of the creek behind the Eiserloh house. Ingrid and her six-year-old brother, Lothar, were away at school. Their baby sister, Ensi, only one year old, was quiet in the crib.

Two FBI agents pulled up in large black cars and parked in front of the house. They walked to the front door and knocked. Johanna opened the door, Mathias by her side.

The agents walked in and presented their identification. They were dressed in dark suits and hats, like characters in a movie. Both carried guns. They asked for permission to make a search of the premises. Mathias said yes. He was eager to comply but the agents didn't need his permission. They had an authorized search warrant, signed by the attorney general of the United States, Francis Biddle.

Mathias fumbled through his pocket and finally produced from his wallet his alien registration card, which he carried with him everywhere. He pointed to the number on the card—4772829—in a desperate attempt to prove his legitimacy. Though born in Germany, he explained to the agents that he was a legal resident of the United States. His papers were in order. Johanna produced hers as well, along with both of their passports. Johanna explained that all three of her children were American-born. Didn't that count for anything?

Over the next few hours, the agents moved from room to room, looking for dynamite, shortwave radios, cameras, and any other suspicious items, which they did not find. They confiscated ordinary letters and photographs from relatives in Germany. Paintings of German landscapes were taken from the walls. Other items seized that night were a black leather book with names and addresses of other German legal aliens who lived near them in Strongsville; twelve hardcover books in German that Mathias had recently purchased during a book sale at the German consulate in Cleveland to raise money for winter relief; and a list of shortwave German radio programs from the month of January 1941.

The agents opened drawers and inspected closets. They examined bank records from the Cleveland Trust Co. and noted the small amount of money in Eisleroh's account, a mere $700. Among the postcards they took was one Ingrid had written to her father during a recent trip to Chicago to visit relatives. The card was written in English, Ingrid's first language, but she also knew German. "I forgot my promise to write this in *Deutsche*," she wrote, each letter neatly formed, "but I'm tired of writing now and won't start all over."

Finally the agents snapped handcuffs on Mathias's wrists and placed him in what they called "custodial detention," which meant that he could be held in prison indefinitely. The word *arrest* was not used. No one read Mathias Eiserloh his rights because as a legal resident alien from Germany, an ally of Japan's and Italy's in the war against the United States, Eislerloh had no rights under US laws. He was not allowed a lawyer. No charges were filed, and he would never be convicted of any crime. Yet from that moment on, Eiserloh was officially branded a "dangerous enemy alien."

The agents instructed Johanna to pack a small bag for her husband. Eager to comply, she gathered a toothbrush, a shirt, a pair of pants, and pajamas and placed the items a small bag. "He won't be gone long," the agents told Johanna. This was the standard line designed to soothe anxious wives and used by FBI agents all over the country during arrests of Germans, Japanese, and Italians.

When Ingrid returned home from school, she found Ensi safe in her crib but both of her parents vanished. She walked outside to the garage and saw her uncle, Mathias's brother-in-law, spread-limbed on the floor. He was drunk, and Ingrid shook him by the shoulders to wake him. Once on his feet, her uncle told Ingrid that FBI agents had arrested her father. He described how humiliated Mathias looked in handcuffs, eyes downcast as he slipped into the backseat of the black car. Johanna had taken the family car and driven to the jail in Cleveland to find out how long Mathias would be gone.

Ingrid left the garage, collapsed on the cold ground, and stared into the sky. Her father had vanished. She filled her lungs, and then out came an unwilled, painful roar to the sky. The high wail of her voice was so raw it made the hair on the back of Ingrid's neck rise. Her legs came up to her chest and she rolled back and forth like a wounded animal. Then there was silence.

Like the moment captured by the artist Edvard Munch in his iconic painting *The Scream* almost fifty years before, Ingrid's shriek was a life-changing moment. Munch's painting expressed a moment from his walk in 1892 in which the sky turned bloodred and the expressionist artist sensed "an infinite scream passing through nature." For many years after her father was snatched, Ingrid felt a similar massive disorder in her environment and in the depths of herself. The particulars of her life at home—the chicken coop, the woodburning stove, the dogs, the daily bus ride to school—all seemed blurred, no longer certain. That day, lying in the woods, Ingrid's shriek left her silent and spent. "My God," she thought to herself. "What will happen to us?"

After that day, Ingrid no longer sang to the trees or hummed during her household chores. Life as she had known it was finished. By the time that she next saw her father—two long years later in what seemed the other side of the world in Crystal City, Texas— Ingrid's golden voice, along with a great many other things, had been lost.

On the morning of December 7, 1941, Sumi Utsushigawa, a thirteen-year-old American girl, rested her elbows on the windowsill of her second-story apartment on East First Street in Little Tokyo, the commercial and cultural enclave for Japanese in Los Angeles. In the neighborhood, filled with Shinto shrines, judo and kendo schools, and many Japanese restaurants, the culture of Japan was everywhere. The weather was in the high seventies and sunny, and the light streamed through the windows into the apartment. It was the kind of shiny California winter day, set among green hedges and eucalyptus trees, that seems improbable anywhere else.

Below Sumi's apartment window was a traffic jam. Cars filled with angry white American men lined the street. Horns honked. Radios blared. Voices shouted. The surprise attack on Pearl Harbor unleashed panic and alarm at the possibility of additional attacks on American soil. After the worst naval disaster in American history, the Japanese might strike anywhere next. Fear of the "yellow peril," racism toward anyone of Japanese ancestry, swept the country. The white men who crowded into Little Tokyo that day carried guns, ammunition, and baseball bats. They were on patrol to see if any of the Japanese in Little Tokyo had the temerity to celebrate their countrymen's attack on Pearl Harbor. A few of these men carried posters with an enraged message: JAP HUNTING LICENSE, GOOD FOR DURATION OF HUNTING SEASON, OPEN SEASON NOW. NO LIMIT.

Crossing First Street, a Japanese businessman hurried toward Sumi's building. He wore a dark suit, white shirt, and a broad-brimmed hat and carried a Christmas package tucked under one arm. Two small children walked by his side, each clutching one of his hands. The man's gaze was lowered and his children's faces were blank.

Sumi's mother, Nobu, shouted at Sumi to stay away from the window and to stay indoors. "It's very dangerous," her mother told her in Japanese. Her mother need not have worried; Sumi had no desire to leave the apartment. The sight below had the dark, unreal quality of a Martian invasion, something impossible to believe.

Meanwhile, Nobu and Sumi's father, Tom Utsushigawa, a photographer who owned the apartment building at 244½ East First Street, moved quickly through the two-story building. They went door-to-door—to the beautiful Japanese dancer on the first floor, next door to the somber Japanese lawyer. They pounded on doors and in feverish Japanese shouted to tenants to remove portraits of the Japanese emperor and the royal family from the walls of their apartments. Inside, the residents were just learning the news from Hawaii. "Quickly," Tom warned. "Protect yourselves." Suddenly, being Japanese in America was dangerous.

None of it made any sense to Sumi. She found herself on the other side of an invisible line that she had not drawn. While her parents were issei, immigrants born in Japan, Sumi was a nisei, born in America. In every way, she fit the stereotype of the nisei, the second-generation Japanese who worked hard to become "100 percent American." Unlike her mother, Nobu, who wore her long sheet of black hair in a chignon at the back of her neck and took small, delicate steps through the apartment, Sumi wore her hair in bedraggled pigtails and had the gait of an awkward pony. She talked in California slang: "What you guys this and what you guys that?"

She had been born on August 14, 1928, in Los Angeles. That was the year Walt Disney debuted Mickey Mouse, the madcap cartoon character that became Sumi's childhood hero. Her teenager's closet was filled with Mickey Mouse T-shirts, caps, and sweaters. Her friends gave her Mickey Mouse pins for birthday presents. She said the Pledge of Allegiance at Central Junior High School, located only six blocks from her apartment. She celebrated the Fourth of July. A young American teenager, she had, until this day at least, been naturally optimistic. Now Sumi tried to make sense of the uncomfortable reality that her own country—America—was at war with the homeland of her parents.

Within two hours of the bombing of Pearl Harbor, FBI agents had swarmed through the narrow streets of Little Tokyo and placed Japanese leaders in handcuffs, leading them away from their friends and families. A physician who lived in Sumi's building was among the first arrested. His wife, known as Battleship Mama, had entertained members of the Japanese navy in their tidy apartment, decorated with furniture from Japan. When young Japanese seamen, far from home, visited Los Angeles, she invited them to her home and performed the tea service, stirring green tea into exquisite small cups. These events for sailors were an innocent act by a traditional Japanese woman well schooled in hospitality. But what once seemed a courteous, sympathetic tie to her homeland was now perceived as subversive, reason enough for her husband's arrest.

Over the next few days, the Japanese bank branches in Little Tokyo closed. Suddenly, Sumi's parents were penniless because the US Treasury had frozen all bank accounts of anyone born in Japan. The vegetable markets along Central Avenue were shut down. Even Fusetsu-do, a Japanese sweetshop, where Sumi and her friends bought fortune cookies, was padlocked. Rumors flew through the streets. People were picked up by the FBI for having feudal dolls or playing Japanese music. Families buried ancient Japanese swords, jade jewelry, and other family heirlooms on the banks of the Los Angles River.

The day after the attack, the *Los Angeles Times* declared California "a zone of danger" and said it was the duty of alert citizens "to cooperate with the military authorities against spies, saboteurs and 5th columnists." The term *5th columnist*, which originated during the Spanish Civil War, was used to describe domestic disloyalty, and applied to anyone suspected of sympathizing with enemies. By the early 1940s, it was shorthand for sedition. The *Rafu Shimpo*, a Los Angeles Japanese newspaper founded in 1903, closed that day; however, on the next day, the newspaper resumed publication, publishing two pages in English only. The inside pages, usually in Japanese, were now blank. The government officially censored news printed in the Japanese language. In an editorial in English, the newspaper called upon Japanese Americans to fully support the war effort. "The treacherous infamy of Japan's attack upon the United States has united the minds of all Americans, regardless of race, color or creed," wrote the editors. "Fellow Americans, give us a chance to do our share to make this world a better place to live in!"

The next day Sumi was frightened as she walked to Central Junior High School. She worried that the angry white men might return to her neighborhood and take out their rage against her and her friends.

Her school was a melting pot of blacks, Caucasians, Japanese, Chinese, the children of immigrants from all over the world. Sumi's best friends were whites, blacks, and other Asians. She had never felt uncomfortable at Central Junior High School. Many students had parents who were from some place other than America.

On this day, inside the halls of the school, the white girls shot her lethal looks and turned their backs. Sumi willed herself to take it in stride. After all, she was an American citizen, born in Los Angeles. On the walk home, a group of Filipino boys spit at her shoes, wrestled her to the ground, and pinched her ears. "Dirty Jap," they said. On the same day as Pearl Harbor, Japanese forces had also attacked Hong Kong, Wake Island, Guam, Malaya, and the Philippines. In retaliation, the Filipino boys struck back at Sumi, who covered her face and picked herself up from the ground. Her first thought was "Why are they calling me a Jap?" Then it dawned on her: in their eyes—and in the eyes of other Americans—she was one.

Japan was the country of her parents, a series of tiny islands, far from the grid of Los Angeles's crowded streets and the sparkling coastline of Southern California. Sumi understood her parents were torn between their mother country, Japan, and the country they had chosen as their own. They were born in Japan, but by law were not allowed to become US citizens. In 1924, concerned about the competitive threat of Japanese workers in the California agricultural industry, the United States passed the Asian Exclusion Act, making it illegal for Japanese immigrants to be citizens.

Sumi's father's first name was Tokiji. His memories of Japan weren't happy. He was born on April 25, 1877, in Miyagi-ken, Japan, to a farmer. His mother abandoned the family when he was only three years old. His father, unable to bear the sound of his son's cries for his mother, soon left him on the doorstep of a Buddhist temple. The punitive monks fed him scraps and beat him with sticks when he disobeyed. When Tokiji was sixteen, he set his sights on a better future and came to the United States. He brought only what he could carry, a knapsack with a change of clothes.

His first job was as a janitor for the famed Belasco Theater, a historic twelve-hundred-seat playhouse with a huge gilded dome at 337 South Main. He worked for Edward Belasco, the manager of the theater, who gave Tokiji a nickname that was easier for Belasco to pronounce: Tom. Belasco considered Tom a hard worker who was much smarter than the usual janitor, someone who might have other uses. One day Belasco gave Tom a box camera. Soon, Tom mastered the art of taking and developing photos and Belasco put him to work as the theater's publicity photographer. In those days, the Belasco was popular among Hollywood actors, and many of the plays and musicals performed on its stage later became movies. Tom photographed Lionel Barrymore, Joan Bennett, Tallulah Bankhead, and other famous actors of the day. Some of the photos appeared in the *Los Angeles Times*.

By the early 1900s, Tom was well established in Los Angeles and wrote to his father to help him find a wife. His father made the necessary arrangements with Nobu's father, as was the custom in Japan. After a series of letters back and forth with his father, Tom went back to Japan, met Nobu for the first time, and was married. He returned to Los Angeles alone to prepare for his wife's arrival. In a few months, he sent money back to bring Nobu to America. She arrived at Terminal Island, an isolated beach located across from San Pedro, a suburb south of Los Angeles that served as the immigration point for first-generation Japanese in California.

In Nobu's first glimpse of America, women were tanning themselves on the beach to the sound of the surf. Nobu, whose skin was pale white, wanted to fit in, so she placed a white towel on the sand and warmed herself with the rays of the sun.

In a few hours, Tom arrived on the beach with a bouquet of flowers and a box of candy. He'd expected Nobu to have beautiful white skin, so highly prized among Japanese men. Instead, her face and arms were bright red. Disappointed and angry, Tom threw the flowers and the candy into the sea. Nobu picked herself up off the beach and followed Tom. Thus began her marriage.

Tom also expected his wife to be subservient, but Nobu was independent-minded and found ways to successfully navigate her new world. Once settled in Little Tokyo among the safety of other Japanese immigrants, Tom, already successful as a photographer for Belasco, bought the building. But it was Nobu who swept the floors, arranged for repairs, collected rent, and resolved disputes among tenants. She kept the books. When Tom decided to open a photography studio of his own in their apartment, Nobu recruited clients and made appointments. During photo shoots of families, Nobu shyly dangled puppets and other toys in front of children to make them smile.

Although Little Tokyo had seven other Japanese photographers,

Tom was the pioneer and the most in demand. He was short—only five feet three inches tall—but he was strong and carried himself with the demeanor of a dandy. His suits were handmade specifically for him by the tailors in Little Tokyo, who used the finest wool for suits and Japanese silks for shirts. Nobu packed away her Japanese robes and soon began to wear American-style A-line skirts and dresses with sleek lines and square shoulders. On a shelf in her closet was a row of hats with broad brims and sturdy shoes with square heels. Their apartment was filled with fine antique porcelain objects, Oriental rugs from Japan, and expensive furniture. They owned a 1930 black Hupmobile, a flashy, four-cylinder roadster that sold for about $80 and was advertised as "the best car in America for the smallest amount of money."

Before Pearl Harbor, the only shadow over the Utsushigawa family was that Tom wanted a son, but Nobu had produced three daughters. Sumi was the last of the three, ten years younger than her oldest sister and eight years younger than her second sister. A proud Japanese man who considered himself the emperor of his own house, Tom was angry that he had no heir, no "number one son," to take over his business. He was occasionally dismissive of his daughters and did his best to ignore them by staying busy with his photography. On the day war was declared, Sumi's two older sisters were on a trip to Japan, visiting grandparents. Sumi was the only girl at home. As a young child, Sumi understood that when her father looked at her, all he could see was his desperate wish for an heir. On the other hand, her mother treated her as if she were an only child, lavishing affection. But in the eyes of Tom and her two sisters, Sumi was too American in her manners and demeanor, not submissive enough—or, in a word, spoiled.

In the three months after Pearl Harbor, many Japanese men from Little Tokyo were arrested. Still, no one came for Sumi's father. Mistakenly, her father believed he would avoid arrest.

"I haven't done anything wrong," he told Sumi, speaking in Japanese. "This is America. They don't put innocent people in jail here. Don't worry."

Nonetheless, Sumi began to listen for the sound of shoes on the steps to the family's apartment. The knock on the door finally came on March 13, 1942—Friday the thirteenth, an unlucky day in America and perhaps an omen. Sumi was in school, going through the motions of her seventh-grade classes. Little did she know that it would be her last day at Central Junior High School.

At the end of the day, Sumi shuffled up the iron steps of the apartment building. On the second floor, she noticed that the front door was open. She paused. Her mother was seated at the dining-room table with her head in her hands. When Nobu looked up, she had a frozen smile on her face. Nobu was almost always cheerful. She laughed easily and never complained. Even at thirteen, Sumi could see through her mother's mask—she was terrified and disoriented.

Sumi walked through the plundered apartment. Drawers had been dumped onto the living-room floor. Chairs were toppled. Piles of photos were everywhere. Her father's good clothes were strewn in the bedroom; the contents of the kitchen cupboards were spilled on the counter.

"Mama," said Sumi. "Was Papa arrested?"

"Yes," said Nobu. "Five FBI men came. They took Papa away."

Nobu spoke no more. Eventually, Sumi learned that her father had walked to the vegetable market to buy some produce. When he came home, the five agents were waiting and arrested him immediately. As was the case in most arrests of enemy aliens, there were no charges, no reason given for his arrest except that Nobu had donated $200 to a Japanese school, Dai Ichi Gakuen, in Little Tokyo. After his arrest, Tom was given an internment serial number: 25-4-3-610.

On the street, notices announcing forced evacuation were stapled to telephone poles and on the backs of bus-stop benches. Nobu read only Japanese. Sumi studied the tiny black-and-white English print on the notices and took charge of preparing to leave. Mother and daughter worked side by side silently, packing kitchen goods, clothes, and family photographs. The frozen smile never left Nobu's face. They sold some of the furniture to junk dealers and put most of the rest of their belongings into one room before hammering the door shut. They packed one suitcase each. All the while they waited for word of where they would be relocated and word from Tom.

Four weeks after his arrest, Sumi learned her father was in a detention station in Tujunga, a thirty-mile drive north from Little Tokyo. Though they still had the Hupmobile, neither Sumi nor her mother knew how to drive; Tom had done all the driving in the family. A friend volunteered to take them to Tujunga. When they arrived at the detention center, operated by the Immigration and Naturalization Service (INS), Sumi saw a prison surrounded by barbed wire. Outside the center was a long line of women and children waiting to visit their incarcerated husbands and fathers. Sumi and Nobu took their place in line and waited.

Finally, after more than an hour, it was their turn. A guard with a gun on his hip and a rifle with a bayonet explained to Sumi that her parents would have to stand on opposite sides of the fence—five feet apart—and that they could speak only English to each other. Though Nobu knew a few words in English and Tom knew a few more, they spoke to each other only in Japanese. The rule would be a problem.

"But they speak Japanese," Sumi said.

"English only!" replied the guard.

Her mother and father faced each other, one on one side of the fence and one on the other. At first, they stared into each other's eyes, both of them afraid of making further trouble for themselves.

Finally Tom said, "Mama okay?"

Her mother nodded. "Papa okay?" she asked weakly.

That was the only English they could manage. For ten minutes they faced each other in silence. In desperation, Nobu asked Tom a question in Japanese about where he might be sent next.

The guard quickly stepped between them. "English only!" He pointed the bayonet at Nobu's throat.

"Take that gun away from my mother's face," Sumi said. The sight of the guard with his fixed bayonet and the look of helplessness and humiliation on the faces of her parents filled her with rage. Her favorite class in junior high school had been civics. She'd been taught that every American had a right to freedom and justice, and whatever happened, Sumi vowed to claim hers.

"I told them they could only speak English," replied the guard, but he looked away from the fierce gaze of a young teenager and slowly lowered his weapon to the ground. In that moment, Sumi became not only the interpreter for her parents but their protector.

"Let's go back home, Mama," said Sumi. "Leave everything to me."

That was the last day Sumi's father was referred to as Tom. In government files he was listed as Tokiji, and from then on he answered only to his Japanese name.

CHAPTER TWO

Eleanor vs. Franklin

Neither Ingrid nor Sumi realized it, but they had an ally in Eleanor Roosevelt. On Monday, December 8, the day after Pearl Harbor was attacked, Eleanor left the White House for an overnight trip to Los Angeles and San Francisco. She took New York's mayor, Fiorello La Guardia, with her. As part of his declaration of a national emergency, FDR named La Guardia director of the Office of Civilian Defense. The goal of Eleanor and La Guardia that day was to encourage the Army, the Navy, and civilians on the West Coast. This mission, while similar to her past travels across the United States, signaled a shift in Eleanor's role as first lady.

The country had 950,000 people enrolled as air-raid wardens, fire fighters, and medical technicians. Now that America was involved in history's greatest armed conflict, the powerful first lady's job was to support her husband in readying for war. However, she also wanted to protect the rights of immigrants. La Guardia, a charismatic Italian American, was an important ally. As La Guardia snarled to Eleanor before the trip began, "Hell, this isn't a pinochle party we're having. It's *war*."

Once they were airborne, the pilot sent word back to Eleanor that thirty Japanese airplanes were bombing San Francisco. La Guardia was in the rear of the airplane, taking a nap. When Eleanor woke him with the news, the response of the feisty mayor was immediate: "If the report is true, we will go directly to San Francisco." It lifted her spirits that La Guardia gave no thought to retreating to Washington.

The rumors, however, were false, an indication of the country's sudden jitteriness. Eleanor and La Guardia went as planned directly to Los Angeles.

On the ground, they met with a group of press and public officials in downtown Los Angeles, not far from Sumi's apartment in Little Tokyo. Standing six feet tall, with grayish-brown hair and cobalt-blue eyes, Eleanor spoke to the work at hand, her imposing appearance lending weight to her words: "I am not here to give you any message. I am here to get down to work. I came here to find out from you what are the most helpful things we in Washington can do to help you. Tell me what you found lacking and what you want." The statement summed up her approach to her job as first lady: duty first.

After Los Angeles, Eleanor traveled up the West Coast to Tacoma, Washington, where she had photographs taken with a group of American-born Japanese students—teenagers with foreign-born parents like Sumi and Ingrid. The students in Tacoma told the first lady about the FBI's arrest of key Japanese leaders hours after the attack on Pearl Harbor. They described the government confiscation of cameras and radios, the establishment of 9:00 p.m. curfews for anyone of Japanese ancestry, and the closing of Japanese-owned businesses. The students were bewildered and frightened. In a statement given after the photograph was taken, Eleanor issued a warning that reflected her deeply held commitment to civil rights: "Let's be honest. There is a chance now for great hysteria against minority groups—loyal American-born Japanese and Germans. If we treat them unfairly and make them unhappy, we may shake their loyalty, which should be built up. If you see something suspicious, report it to the right authorities, but don't try to be the FBI yourself."

Despite mob attacks on Japanese businesses in California and on German and Italian businesses on the East Coast, and the growing fear of immigrants, Eleanor continued to call for patience and tolerance. In her weekly newspaper column, "My Day," she wrote, "We know there are German and Italian agents, Japanese as well, who are here to be helpful to their own nations. But the great mass of people stemming from these various national ties must not feel they have suddenly ceased to be Americans."

These were not popular arguments, but unlike her predecessors as first lady, Eleanor did not worry if she was popular. She was forty-eight when she became first lady and spoke her mind, even when her opinion differed from her husband's. For instance, in February 1933, one month before Franklin Roosevelt's inauguration as president, Eleanor ghostwrote a column arguing that taxes should be lowered and that Franklin should insist on more public spending from Congress. In private, she regularly disagreed with Roosevelt, who was not threatened by opinionated women. His mother, Sara Delano Roosevelt, was demanding and outspoken as well.

Since FDR's election as president in 1932, Eleanor had relied on her own judgment and her convictions. Politics was the bond that defined the marriage. Eleanor served as his mobile surrogate, his chief champion for the New Deal's relief and social policies, traveling more than 280,000 miles in his first two terms. Bound to a wheelchair because of his paralysis due to polio, Franklin used Eleanor as what he called "my eyes and ears," to visit people and places he could not easily reach and gather the knowledge he needed to lift the country out of the Great Depression. During Eleanor's first summer as first lady, Franklin asked her to go to Appalachia and report to him on the poverty there. "Watch the people's faces," he told her. "Look at the conditions of the clothes on the wash lines. You can tell a lot from that."

Dressed in a miner's clothes, Eleanor went down into the mines with workers to report on conditions. A celebrated 1933 *New Yorker* cartoon by Robert Day captured the miners' surprise. The cartoonist depicted two miners shoveling coal in a dark shaft, with their faces looking up to the light. The breathless caption read, "For gosh sakes, here comes Mrs. Roosevelt!" Wherever Eleanor went, she spoke her mind.

But that day on the West Coast, the character of this political partnership changed. Eleanor was spitting into the winds of war. She and Franklin had two different visions of the way forward for the country, as well as two competing visions for their complicated life partnership. Eleanor was focused on conditions at home—the fight against poverty, the press for social reform, and the protection of the civil liberties of German, Italian, and Japanese immigrants. To her, the assurances of the First Amendment were nonnegotiable. Even before the attack on Pearl Harbor, as Roosevelt watched Hitler annex Austria, occupy Czechoslovakia, and march into Poland on September 1, 1939, the president's attention shifted away from the home front to the events in Europe, leaving Eleanor out of many decisions, especially the ones related to the fate of American immigrants from Germany, Japan, and Italy.

Even in the aftermath of a disaster as large as Pearl Harbor, Eleanor felt the guarantees of the Bill of Rights must be protected. Roosevelt did not agree. He believed the threat from saboteurs and spies was real and took aim against enemies at home, real and imagined. Again and again, Eleanor tried to make her case to him that the problem with immigrants was grossly exaggerated. "These people were not convicted of any crime," Eleanor wrote in an unpublished magazine article for *Collier's*, "but emotions ran too high, too many people wanted to wreak vengeance on Oriental looking people. There was no time to investigate families or to adhere to the American rule that a man is innocent until he is proven guilty."

Although history would later prove her right, on the day after Pearl Harbor, Eleanor was in a distinct minority. Walter Lippmann, the most influential journalist in America, published a column in the *Washington Post* on February 12, 1942, titled "The Fifth Column on the Coast." Lippmann insisted national security preempted civil rights. "It is a fact that the Japanese navy has been reconnoitering the Pacific Coast more or less continually and for a considerable period of time, testing and feeling out the American defenses. It is a fact that communication takes place between the enemy at sea and enemy agents on land." He argued that the arrest of Japanese

Americans would not violate their constitutional rights. "Nobody's constitutional rights include the right to reside and do business on a battlefield. There is plenty of room elsewhere for him to exercise his rights."

Three days later, Westbrook Pegler, a conservative columnist who did not usually agree with Lippmann, expressed similar views in his column in the *Washington Post*: "The Japanese in California should be under armed guard to the last man and woman right now and to hell with habeas corpus until the danger is over."

The entire political establishment applied pressure on Roosevelt to act not only against Japanese immigrants but also against Germans and Italians. All the military figures—General John DeWitt, Provost Marshal General Allen Gullion, and Secretary of War Henry Stinson—supported the arrest and incarceration of anyone suspected of disloyalty to the United States and the total evacuation of the Japanese from the West Coast. California's attorney general, Earl Warren, later immortalized as a civil rights champion on the US Supreme Court, urged Roosevelt to intern all Japanese on the West Coast. Warren called the threat of Japanese subversives "the Achilles heel of the entire civilian defense effort" and warned, "Unless something is done, it may bring about a repetition of Pearl Harbor."

No one was as influential in the decision to uproot thousands of Japanese and Japanese Americans from their homes—as well as thousands of German and Italian immigrants on the East Coast—and incarcerate them without charges as DeWitt, the Army's West Coast commander. In testimony to a subcommittee of the House Committee on Naval Affairs in April 1943, DeWitt said, "I don't want any of them here. They are a dangerous element. There is no way to determine their loyalty. It makes no difference whether he is an American citizen, he is still a Japanese. American citizenship does not necessarily determine loyalty. But we must worry about the Japanese all the time until he is wiped off the map."

Later, DeWitt made clear that he also wanted Germans and Italians removed as well. "I include all Germans, all Italians, who are alien enemies," he said to a fellow military officer. "Evacuate enemy aliens in large groups at the earliest possible date; sentiment is being given too much importance. Get them all out."

Roosevelt's decision to arrest and intern about 120,000 Japanese, two-thirds of them American citizens such as Sumi, and thousands of other immigrants, mainly Germans such as Ingrid's father, had its roots in his experiences as an ambitious young man at the start of his political career. On March 17, 1913, at the age of thirty-one, Roosevelt was appointed assistant secretary of the Navy, a position he held for seven years. In his new post with the Navy, he had access to secret intelligence, and he approached it with bravado. "I get my fingers into everything," he said, "and there's no law against it." He oversaw the Office of Naval Intelligence, which was in those days a small operation. Roosevelt threw out the sleepy bureaucrats and replaced them with several of his Ivy League friends who, like Roosevelt, believed that America was in danger from German assassins.

Their fears were confirmed by an act of sabotage in New York known as the Black Tom incident on July 30, 1916. Just after midnight, a small band of Germans set off a large explosion. The force of the blast turned the night sky over New York bright orange. Its epicenter was a small island called Black Tom. The bang jolted people from their beds. The Brooklyn Bridge shook, and the Statue of Liberty, less than a mile away, was damaged by shards of red-hot steel. The most important loading terminal in New York Harbor, then used to send munitions to Britain, was destroyed. The largest explosion ever in the United States, it convinced Roosevelt of two things: that America must enter the war, and the nation was at risk from a vast network of undercover German agents.

A few days after the Black Tom incident, Roosevelt burst into the office of his boss, Secretary of the Navy Josephus Daniels, and said, "We've got to get into this war." The following year, President Woodrow Wilson, then a frail, elderly man and newly reelected, declared war. In a speech in Washington, DC, Wilson warned listeners that the Kaiser had sent German agents to America "to spread sedition among us" and to "undermine the government with false professions of loyalty to its principles." By the fall, Germans and German Americans were barred from strategic areas, including harbors, canals, railroad depots, and wharves.

Roosevelt feared he was personally a target of German spies. He told his friends in Naval Intelligence that the Secret Service had found a safe in the German general consul's office in New York with a document headed "To Be Eliminated." Roosevelt's name was on the list. For about ten days after the discovery, Roosevelt, shaken by the threat, carried a revolver in a leather shoulder holster.

On February 15, 1933, a few weeks before Roosevelt was inaugurated as president, his life was threatened by Giuseppe Zangara, an Italian immigrant and out-of-work bricklayer. Roosevelt arrived that day in Miami after a cruise from Jacksonville on Vincent Astor's yacht. Zangara met the boat at the dock and then followed Roosevelt's entourage to Miami's Bayfront Park. From the backseat of a convertible, Roosevelt delivered a short speech. After he finished, people gathered around the car to shake the president-elect's hand. Zangara, only five feet tall, stood on a chair to get a closer view of Roosevelt and opened fire with a .32-caliber pistol, purchased at a pawnshop for $8. The shots missed Roosevelt but hit several bystanders. Anton Cermak, the mayor of Chicago, was wounded in the chest.

When Secret Service agents swarmed Roosevelt, the president-elect motioned for them to place Cermak in the back of the car and ordered the driver to rush to the nearest hospital. He talked to Cermak all the way to the hospital. "I'm glad it was me instead of you," Cermak told Roosevelt in the car. Three weeks later, on March 6, Cermak was dead.

But it wasn't just Roosevelt—the entire country was gripped in a social paroxysm surrounding German, Italian, and Japanese immigrants. In March 1933, the following headline appeared in the *New York Times*: "Nazi Units in United States List 1,000 Aliens; Admit Their Aim Is to Spread Propaganda." Other headlines followed:

"Nazis' Hand Seen in Activities Here" and "Hitler's Men Said to Be Ready to Send Report of Sabotage to Reich Authorities." By 1934 the House Un-American Activities Committee (HUAC), led by US representatives John McCormack and Samuel Dickstein, was investigating Nazi propaganda and secret agents in the United States.

Novelists also reflected the general dread of dangers at home. In his bestseller *It Can't Happen Here*, Sinclair Lewis told the story of a native-born, Hitler-type character named Berzelius Windrip, whose nickname was Buzz. In the story, Buzz deploys his own private army, the Minute Men, to storm the White House. Ernest Hemingway's play, *The Fifth Column*, published in 1938, was about the threat to liberty in Spain, but it powerfully reinforced fears of Fifth Column influence in the United States.

At the White House, Roosevelt and a small cadre of advisers, including Secretary of State Cordell Hull, a tall, white-haired Tennessean, well respected by both liberals and conservatives on Capitol Hill, became convinced that Nazis and Fascists would attack the United States from within, using immigrants as Fifth Column forces. On May 8, 1934, Roosevelt issued a secret directive to authorize J. Edgar Hoover's FBI to investigate Nazis and Nazi sympathizers in the United States. The spy hunt began.

On that day, Roosevelt called Hoover to the White House. In a memorandum that is the only written record of the meeting, Hoover wrote that Roosevelt asked him to work in collaboration with the Secret Service and the INS to conduct "a very careful and searching" investigation of Nazi and Fascist organizations. In particular, Roosevelt asked Hoover to find "any possible connection with official representatives of the German government in the United States."

Roosevelt had in mind a limited investigation and impressed on Hoover that the operation must be secret. Under Hoover's direction, Roosevelt's modest directive soon ballooned into a vast and illegal national campaign of targeting hundreds of thousands of politically defenseless immigrants, including the fathers of Ingrid and Sumi, who if left to their own devices would have continued to live quiet, harmless lives as their children joined the mainstream of American life.

On August 24, 1936, Roosevelt again called Hoover to the White House for a private meeting. He told Hoover he wanted a "broad picture" of subversives in the United States. The following day, Roosevelt and Hoover met with Hull, the normally sanguine secretary of state. On this day, Hull was in a frenzy over the political activities of foreigners at home. "Go ahead," said Hull, "investigate the hell out of those cocksuckers."

By the end of the year, Hoover had built his own bureaucratic empire. Moreover, Roosevelt's directive allowed Hoover unlimited public resources to spy on the FBI director's list of his personal enemies, including—of all people—Eleanor Roosevelt. It's a measure of the general delirium of the times that the first lady was not immune from FBI surveillance.

Hoover's covert investigation of Eleanor initially targeted her ties to the American Youth Congress, an organization including members of the YMCA, the American League for Peace and Democracy, and the Popular Front—in other words, liberals like Eleanor. Eleanor believed that money spent on arms and military buildup would be better spent on education and medical care. She knew that some of the young people in the AYC were self-proclaimed Communists, but she thought the numbers were few. After a speech by Eleanor to the AYC, noted in her FBI file, Hoover scrawled in his own hand, "Shut her up."

With his new power, Hoover instructed his agents to illegally monitor Eleanor's movements and tapped her telephone without a warrant. In time, case file 62-62735 grew to more than four thousand pages—one of the largest in the FBI's history. Neither Eleanor nor Franklin knew that Hoover had Eleanor in his sights. However, Eleanor made no secret of her dislike of Hoover. When she learned that FBI agents had investigated two members of her staff—Edith Helm, her social secretary, and Malvina Thompson, a personal aide—she complained to the attorney general and to her husband.

Franklin asked Hoover to explain the matter to Eleanor. Hoover then wrote a confidential letter to Eleanor claiming it was a mistake, that the FBI agents did not realize Helm was her social secretary. "Had the FBI known, the inquiry would not have been initiated," Hoover lied.

Two days later, Eleanor fired back: "This type of investigation seems to me to smack too much of Gestapo methods."

For her candor, Eleanor made an enemy of Hoover for life. No one challenged Hoover the way Eleanor did. In Washington, his position was impregnable. He continued to monitor Eleanor until the day she died.

As had World War I, the run-up to World War II brought more disagreements to the marriage of Eleanor and Franklin. Eleanor continued to focus on conditions at home while Franklin monitored events in Europe. He realized that America would eventually have to get into the war, but isolationism gripped the nation. Even after Hitler invaded Poland, polls showed that 90 percent of Americans favored neutrality, although 80 percent wanted the Allies to win the war. The country wasn't ready for war. At best, the Army could muster five fully equipped divisions, and the munitions industry in the United States was practically nonexistent.

On September 1, 1939, the day German tanks, infantry, and cavalry invaded Poland with 1.5 million troops, Roosevelt created a highly secretive division within the Department of State called the Special Division. He ordered this division to identify American civilians: businessmen, physicians, and government officials who were currently in Japan and Germany and who would be in danger when the United States joined the war. The State Department estimated that, as of January 1, 1939, 80,428 US nationals resided in Europe, 12,111 in the Near East, and 17,138 in the Far East. More than 100,000 US civilians were in harm's way.

A few months later, Roosevelt authorized the Special War Problems Division to find Japanese and Germans in America and in Latin America who could be used as hostages in exchange for the more valuable of the Americans. Once the United States joined the war, Roosevelt knew that American soldiers, many of them wounded, would be captured and held as prisoners of war, and that he would need a ready source of exchange. Slowly and secretly, the vast machinery of internment and prisoner exchange sputtered to a start. The Special Division's exchange program was informally known as "quiet passage."

In 1940, Hoover installed the first group of FBI agents in Latin America. Based on the FBI reports, Roosevelt was convinced that Germans and Japanese in Latin America were a direct threat to hemispheric security. His primary fear was of the Germans. Beginning on April 9, 1940, Hitler's forces overran Denmark, Norway, Belgium, and France, leaving Britain alone to fight against Germany's domination of Europe. America's involvement in the war was now a matter of time. Again and again, Roosevelt warned his advisers to keep their eyes on Hitler: "Germany first!" became his battle cry. Isolationists had vanished—now a majority of Americans favored war. As *Time* magazine reported on June 3, 1940, one way that citizens demonstrated patriotism was to become informants for Hoover. "Hundreds of gossips wrote to the FBI volunteering to spy on their neighbors," noted the magazine.

In September 1941, Roosevelt took to the airwaves to declare that "Hitler's advance guards" are readying "footholds, bridgeheads, in the New World to be used as soon as he has gained control of the oceans" and warned that German agents "at this very moment" are carrying out "intrigue, plots, machinations, and sabotage." To secure the Panama Canal from sabotage, Roosevelt reached an agreement with the government of Peru that allowed the forcible detention in American internment camps of eighteen hundred Japanese Peruvians—men, women, and children with no ties to the United States.

Roosevelt pressured other Latin American governments, so-called good neighbors, to comply. Only Argentina, Mexico, and Brazil refused Roosevelt's demands to deport Germans.

On September 5, 1941, three months prior to the attack on Pearl Harbor, Francis Biddle, a short, slim man whom both Eleanor and

Franklin knew well, was sworn in as the new attorney general. Like the Roosevelts, Biddle was born an American aristocrat into an old, rich East Coast family from Philadelphia. Francis was a half cousin four times removed from James Madison. Like Roosevelt, as a boy Biddle went to Groton, the elite Massachusetts prep school, and later graduated from both Harvard and Harvard law school. The motto of Groton—*cui servire est regnare*, "to serve is to rule"—was part of his and Roosevelt's DNA.

On Sunday, December 7, 1941, Biddle was at a luncheon in Detroit to sell defense bonds organized by the Slav-American Defense Savings Committee. After lunch was served, as Biddle rose to speak, his assistant Ugo Carusi handed him a note: "Japanese today attacked Pearl Harbor, great U.S. Naval Base in the Hawaiian Islands, and are also bombing Manila from planes probably released from aircraft carriers. The President made the official announcement at 2:20 p.m. The raids are still in progress."

Biddle rubbed his balding head and sighed. He steadied himself at the podium and faced the large audience of Slavic immigrants. "Even as I was speaking," recalled Biddle in his memoir, *In Brief Authority*, "Japs were bombing our country." He looked at his audience and explained that Pearl Harbor had been attacked. After a few gasps, everything fell to a hush. Biddle described the Nazi ruthlessness in Czechoslovakia, Poland, and Yugoslavia, now matched by the Japanese surprise attack on American battleships. "From now on," said Biddle to the crowd, "we will be at war with the dictatorships." Then he excused himself and abruptly left to return to Washington.

That night at 8:30 p.m. Biddle and the other cabinet members gathered in Roosevelt's study. The president sat silently at his desk. One by one, they filed in. Biddle later described the president's face as "gray, even ashen, and graver than I had ever seen him."

Finally the president spoke: "I'm glad you all got here." Not since the outbreak of the Civil War, Roosevelt said, had any cabinet faced such a crisis. A proud Navy man, Roosevelt could not bear to describe the details of the attack on America's unsuspecting fleet.

By 10:00 p.m. congressional leaders had joined the cabinet. More chairs were brought into the now-crowded study. The president told them that the Navy ships and airplanes had all been lined up, one after another. "On the ground, by God, on the ground," Roosevelt moaned. The idea that the battleships were not at sea and the planes not in the air seemed incomprehensible.

Everyone was in shock. The room was completely silent.

Finally, Senator Tom Connally of Texas, chairman of the Foreign Relations Committee, sprang to his feet, his face red with rage, and banged the desk with his fist. "How did they catch us with our pants down, Mr. President? Where were our patrols?"

Roosevelt bowed his head. "I don't know, Tom. I just don't know."

Roosevelt told the group that he would appear before a joint session of Congress the next day and declare a state of war between America and Japan. His statement would be short.

At noon the following day, Eleanor and Franklin left the east gate of the White House by car. They drove to the Capitol under heavy security. When Roosevelt took his place at the podium, he looked out into the audience and said, "Yesterday—December 7, 1941, a date that will live in infamy—the United States was suddenly and deliberately attacked by naval and air forces of the Empire of Japan." He enumerated the assaults on the Hawaiian Islands, Guam, the Philippines, on Wake and Midway Islands. To a standing ovation, he asked Congress to declare war so that "this form of treachery shall never endanger us again." It took only thirty-three minutes for the House and Senate, sitting separately, to declare war, with only one dissenting vote. Jeannette Rankin of Montana, a pacifist and the first woman elected to the House, sobbed, "No," as she answered the roll call.

Prior to Pearl Harbor, Biddle had been Eleanor's strongest ally in the battle to protect the rights of legal immigrants and their children. About a month before Pearl Harbor—on November 5, 1941—Eleanor, concerned in particular about the threat to Japanese immigrants on the West Coast, wrote a letter to Biddle asking about the "possibility of loyal Japanese aliens of many years' good standing becoming naturalized citizens." In his reply on December 1, Biddle explained that Japanese aliens could not "enjoy the privilege of naturalization." State and federal laws prohibited them from becoming citizens. They were also banned from owning land. For Japanese to become naturalized citizens would require amendments to both federal and state laws. "However," continued Biddle, "they should be reassured by the knowledge that their alien status will not prejudice them in any way or deprive them of scrupulously fair and just treatment, so long as they remain loyal and engage in no activities hostile to the United States or inimical to its welfare."

Only six days later, the attack on Pearl Harbor forced Biddle to take the very steps against Japanese, Germans, and Italians that he had assured Eleanor in his letter would never be taken. Biddle had been naive to think that he could stop it. Though Biddle repeatedly pressed Roosevelt not to carry out internment orders, he was the newest member of the cabinet and he did not have the power to overcome public opinion.

Roosevelt's position was clear: the war could not be lost. Shortly after the president and first lady returned to the White House after the speech to Congress, Biddle reluctantly took over an executive order authorizing the attorney general—that is, himself—to intern enemy aliens previously identified on Hoover's black list. By the next day, 1,212 Japanese enemy aliens had been taken into custody, along with 620 Germans and 98 Italians. They came from all parts of the United States. "I do not think Roosevelt was much concerned with the gravity or implications of this step," Biddle later wrote. "He wasn't theoretical about things. What must be done to defend the country must be done."

Three days later, Germany and Italy declared war against the United States. Roosevelt called Biddle to come at once to the White House, this time with an appropriate proclamation of war. Biddle arrived in the afternoon. The president was in his study with Admiral Ross T. McIntire, the White House physician. Roosevelt was suffering from a sinus attack, brought on by the stress of the events of the last few days. When Biddle entered the room, the doctor was bent over the president, swabbing out FDR's nose.

Roosevelt looked up, motioned for Biddle to take a seat, and asked, his voice hoarse and harsh, "How many Germans are there in the country?"

"Oh, about six hundred thousand."

"And you're going to intern all of them," said the president angrily. "I don't care so much about the Italians. They are a lot of opera singers, but the Germans are different: they may be dangerous."

"Please, Mr. President," the doctor pleaded. FDR sank back into his chair, and McIntire resumed the swabbing as Biddle quickly withdrew. When he looked back, he noted that Roosevelt's color had returned, his cheeks were ruddy. Biddle later wrote that the prospect of war, so long in coming but now here, had revived Roosevelt.

James H. Rowe, who was Biddle's assistant and a confidant of Eleanor's, continued to press the first lady's case. On February 2, 1942, in a private memorandum to Tully, Roosevelt's private secretary, Rowe warned that the president would soon receive a proposal by the military to relocate and intern all Japanese and Japanese Americans in California. Rowe opposed the proposal. He believed it was unconstitutional and driven by public hysteria.

"Please tell the President to keep his eye on the Japanese situation in California," wrote Rowe. "It looks to me like it will explode any day now." He told Tully that "public pressure" to move all Japanese out of California—citizens and legal aliens—was "tremendous." If that happened, Rowe wrote, "It will be one of the great mass exoduses of history." He also warned the mass arrests would require the suspension of the writ of habeas corpus, the ancient right of detained prisoners to seek relief from unlawful imprisonment.

Rowe's admonitions went unheeded. Seventeen days later, on February 19, Roosevelt accepted the argument of military leaders and the increasing public demands for evacuation of all Japanese from the West Coast states. On that day, Roosevelt signed the War Department's blanket order—Executive Order 9006. The order required the forced removal of all people of Japanese descent from a "military zone" that included the entire state of California, the western half of Washington and Oregon, and the southern part of Arizona. Germans and Italians who lived in the zone were also subject to evacuation and internment, but because of their larger numbers were not evacuated en masse.

When Eleanor heard of Franklin's decision, she was disappointed. Even though the country was now at war, Roosevelt's order, signed in his own hand, seemed to her a violation of democracy at home. For more than one hundred thousand people to be taken from their homes without any charges or chance to defend themselves against accusers seemed intolerable.

Eleanor went directly to Roosevelt and asked if they could discuss the issue. "No," he told her coldly. And then he asked her never to mention it again.

When the novelist and humanitarian Pearl Buck, Eleanor's friend, wrote to her protesting the "inhuman and cruel treatment" of the Japanese, an action Buck compared to the actions of the Nazi Gestapo, Eleanor replied, "I regret the need to evacuate. But I recognize it has to be done." All through the war, Eleanor and Franklin would maintain their different stances. In the end, the president's decision was the only one that mattered. However passionate an ally Eleanor was to families such as Ingrid's and Sumi's, her duty was to support her husband's decision, and she did.

CHAPTER THREE

Strangers in a
Small Texas Town

Earl G. Harrison, Roosevelt's new commissioner of the Immigration and Naturalization Service, stood, on the morning of November 6, 1942, in a place so strange that it might have appeared imaginary to him. Before him stretched a desolate prairie of dusty soil, dry cactus, and a variety of wild, dense shrubs. The small town of Crystal City was named for a vast stretch of artesian springs, now dangerously dry due to a drought. The landscape was incongruous to the town's name. Thirty-five miles to the west, the flat, bleached-out land emptied into the Rio Grande, and across that river the land stretched wide into Mexico. Locals called the region the Wild Horse Desert. It had a between-worlds feeling, not quite Mexico, not quite America.

Sixty-five million years before, in the Late Cretaceous era, this desert was the floor of the ocean. When the waters receded, deposits of oil and salt domes were left, grown over by grasses, plants, and trees. Small, peaceful groups were the first to live on the land. For sustenance, they gathered roots, hunted deer, and fished in the Gulf of Mexico. Apache and Comanche, warring tribes, followed them. The first European—Cabeza de Vaca—didn't arrive until the sixteenth century. De Vaca was so struck with the loneliness of the land, so vast and so barren, that he named it El Desierto de los Muertos, the Desert of the Dead.

When Anglo settlers streamed into Texas in the 1820s, most colonists steered cleared of this forbidding brush landscape, calling it "heartbreak country." Stephen F. Austin, the father of Texas settlement, preferred the rich, wooded lands of East and Central Texas. After a trip to Matamoros, Mexico, Austin wrote of the land near the future Crystal City, "It is generally nothing but sand, entirely void of lumber, covered with scrubby thorn bushes and prickly pear cactus." On March 2, 1836, Austin and other Texas colonists, many of them slaveholders and secessionists, formed an independent republic. The new Republic of Texas had its own Texas Constitution, capital in Austin, and flag. Texas was its own nation—unto itself. Nonetheless, South Texas, where Crystal City was located, continued to function as it always had—as a direct channel into Mexico. As late as 1839, the Texas maps described South Texas this way: "Of this section of country little is known." In those days, maps of Texas stopped in San Antonio, even though Texas extended farther south, all the way to the Rio Grande River and into Mexico.

One hundred and twenty miles from San Antonio sat the small Texas town of Crystal City. Large ranches dominated the border area. On both the US side and the Mexican side, *vaqueros*, Mexican cowboys, worked cattle on horseback. In 1905, two bankers from San Antonio, Carl Gross and E. J. Buckingham, bought a ten-thousand-acre ranch and platted the town site of Crystal City. They subdivided the ranch into ten-acre farms and set about selling the area to unsuspecting outsiders as a Garden of Eden. With other owners of large ranches, Gross and Buckingham invested $345,000 to build a rail line to connect San Antonio, Uvalde, and the Gulf of Mexico. The SAU&G line originated in 1909 in Crystal City and Uvalde, and by 1914 was extended between San Antonio and Corpus Christi. By 1914, the line, nicknamed the Sausage, was completed. Before the railroad arrived, Crystal City had a less-than-thriving population of 350 souls and no reliable connections with the outside world. The culture was built around cattle. With the arrival of the railroad, small farmers, many from the Midwest, made their way to South Texas. Most of the new residents brought farming methods and equipment unsuitable to the arid land. They introduced sheep, which ate closer to the ground than cattle, causing overgrazing and ferocious conflict between the ranchers and the sheep owners. Yet over time, progress came to Crystal City. Fields of Bermuda onions and spinach were planted. Cotton gins hummed. In 1928, Crystal City became the county seat of Zavala County. The train was a lifeline for the tiny town. In 1930, 3,959 train cars of spinach, 443 cars of onions, 214 cars of vegetable plants, and 140 cars of cattle were shipped from Crystal City.

Twelve years later, when Harrison arrived in Crystal City, the population had climbed to six thousand, 90 percent Mexicans and their children, most born in America. The town was divided into two segregated neighborhoods. Mexicans lived to the west, many of them in fifteen-by-twelve casitas made of adobe. In the morning, women hosed down their porches and watered their trees and plants. In the late afternoon, men gathered in backyards under the merciful shade of pecan, orange, and tangerine trees. They pulled chairs around small tables and listened to Spanish-language radio and played dominoes. To the east lived the Anglo population, farmers, small-business owners, doctors, teachers, and police officers. Though Anglos were newcomers to a land that was originally part of Mexico, they nonetheless saw themselves as dominant and viewed the Mexican Americans as outsiders. Schools were segregated, as were hospitals and funeral homes. The language spoken on the streets was a hybrid: English, Spanish, and both languages rolled into one, a mixture called Tex-Mex. In so vast and isolated a region, identity was confused and complex.

From his house in Rose Valley, a bucolic suburb of Philadelphia, it took Harrison three days on the Baltimore and Ohio Railroad to arrive in Crystal City. At forty-three, Harrison made a striking impression—grave blue eyes, wavy blond hair, strong jaw, broad shoulders, a face animated with thought. His friends called him an "indefatigable worker" and marveled at his capacity for long hours on the job. His secretary, Miss Margaret Paul Parker, who worked by his side six days a week for twenty-five years, described him as "always industrious," a "real doer." Harrison traveled to Crystal City that day to consider the town as a possible location for the only family camp for internees and their families during World War II. This much Harrison knew for sure: the future camp would be busy and require enough space and facilities to house as many as four thousand internees and their families at any given time during the war. Not many places in the United States offered enough empty space to accommodate Harrison's needs, but Texas, a state larger than Spain, certainly did.

As commissioner of the INS, which in 1940 had become part of the Department of Justice, Harrison had jurisdiction over twenty-two district offices and ten internment camps that housed the aliens of enemy countries. During the war, the US government operated more than thirty camps, some administered by the Army; others by the War Relocation Authority, a civilian agency created by Roosevelt; and others as federal prisons, where prisoners of war were held in isolation.

The camp at Crystal City would be the largest INS camp, used to intern a wide variety of prisoners of war, including Germans, Japanese, and Italians, from the United States and thirteen Latin American countries—and their wives and children, many born in America. Many of these men were leaders in their respective communities—Buddhist and Shinto priests, German and Japanese businessmen, men of great wealth and influence from Peru, Bolivia, Honduras, Panama, and other Latin American countries. All of these enemy aliens had been separated from their bewildered families upon their arrest.

In Harrison's mind, the need for a camp to reunite families was a humanitarian step, one of many reforms he hoped to make as commissioner. He had his hands full, especially with the Latin American phase of the internment. In 1938, Roosevelt became convinced that in the event of war, Axis nationals living in Latin America would engage in pro-Axis propaganda and espionage. In October

1941 the State Department had reached secret agreements with Panama, Peru, Guatemala, and the other countries in Latin America to restrict Axis nationals living in their countries and to prepare for their arrest and deportation. The FBI station agents, known as legal attachés, were stationed at US embassies throughout Latin America. As early as July 1941 newspapers in Latin American countries published La Lista Negra—the black list—of Axis nationals. Hours after Roosevelt declared war on December 8, Guatemala froze the assets of Japanese, Germans, and Italians, and restricted travel. Costa Rica ordered all Japanese interned. Police in practically every Latin American country, except Mexico, Venezuela, and Brazil, which had their own internment camps, arrested fathers first, held them in jail, and deported them to the United States on American troop ships. Their families were then arrested and deported as well. Those arrangements had been made by the Special War Problems Division of the Department of State. The justification for the arrests, from the point of view of the United States, was to protect national security. The media reported nothing about the deportations. Some of the countries—including Peru, which arrested 702 Germans, 1,799 Japanese, and 49 Italians—deported Axis citizens for economic motives. In return for delivering Axis nationals to the United States, the governments seized their homes, businesses, and bank accounts.

Once the Latin Americans set foot on American soil in ports in New Orleans or California, the INS was in charge. Officers arrested them for "illegal entry." They were deloused with strong showers, sprayed with DDT, and loaded on trains bound for internment camps. Jerre Mangione, an Italian American writer who worked for Harrison at the INS and helped decide where to locate the family camp, later wrote in a memoir about why Latin Americans were deported to the United States: "The rationale for this international form of kidnapping was that by immobilizing influential German and Japanese nationals who might aid and abet the Axis war effort in the Latin-American countries where they lived, the United States was preventing the spread of Nazism throughout the hemisphere and thereby strengthening its own security." According to Mangione, many in the INS, including himself, opposed the arrest of Latin Americans. One of the officers in charge of an INS camp told Mangione, "Only in wartime could we get away with such fancy skulduggery."

In the wake of all that had occurred, Harrison wanted the camps under his jurisdiction to be as efficiently and humanely administered as possible. By law, interned civilians were not officially subject to Geneva Convention protocols that dictate treatment of prisoners of war, but the policy of the US government was that the treatment of enemy aliens should follow the principles of the convention. In most US internment camps the principles were loosely applied. In a manual he wrote for INS officers Harrison insisted that INS "humanize" immigration laws. "Immigration laws often appear to work a hardship on aliens. Officers can humanize these laws at the same time carrying out the intent of Congress and the will of the people. Officers should always keep in mind that their decisions may spell future happiness or despair for those affected by such decisions."

With Harrison in Crystal City that day were two other people, Willard F. Kelly, Harrison's number two man, who served as assistant commissioner for alien control, and Dr. Amy Stannard, the officer in charge of the INS internment camp in Seagoville, Texas, a small town near Dallas. Stannard was the incarnation of Rosie the Riveter, a wartime symbol on posters of a woman laborer performing what previously was a man's work. A graduate of the University of California medical school with a specialty in psychiatry, Stannard was the only woman in charge of an internment camp, or any type of POW camp, during the war. The Seagoville camp opened in 1941 as a federal minimum-security prison camp for women. In the spring of 1942, Stannard's facility was adapted to an alien detention camp for women and children, and she was named officer in charge. "I was surprised," she later told an interviewer. "We didn't have much advance notice, so I didn't much dwell on the novelty of being the only woman with this kind of job. I had to get to work."

The women's camp in Seagoville was built on eighty acres and was surrounded by a six-foot, woven-wire-link fence topped by barbed wire. The guardhouse was manned at all times by agents of the Border Patrol. Guards also patrolled the perimeter of the camp, sometimes on horseback. The women and children lived in Victory Huts, prefabricated, small dwellings built during World War II, and six dormitories. Many of the women were Japanese, including fifty Japanese-language teachers from California. In addition, there were women and children from Latin American countries sick with flu, some with tuberculosis.

"We began admitting women and children from Central and South America. They were the families of male aliens, of enemy nationals—Germans, Japanese, and a few Italians who had been interned in other camps in the States. They had been caught up in a sort of dragnet because they were thought to be potentially danger-ous to the security of the United States," Stannard said. "It isn't clear to me why the State Department came to work that out. Apparently it was the result of some fear that Japanese, Germans, and Italians in Central and South America might rise up in some way to endan-ger the United States. I know of no episodes where that happened, however."

It was November and the temperature was about eighty degrees as Harrison, Stannard, and Kelly walked around a 240-acre Crys-tal City site that was used as a migrant-worker camp for Mexican laborers. Later, an additional 50 acres was acquired to the south of the existing camp, enlarging it to 290 acres. Due to the mild winter climate, landowners in Crystal City had four growing seasons a year, much of it devoted to spinach. In March 1937, a statue of Popeye, built of shiny fiberglass, was erected in front of the tiny, one-story city hall in Crystal City. It was dedicated to "the children of the world." City leaders, all Anglo, proclaimed Crystal City the Spin-ach Capital of the World. Spinach was referred to as green gold. In 1945, the Del Monte Corporation bought the town's cannery and produced 2.5 million cases of spinach a year. Popeye became the city's iconic symbol, a totem with mixed messages. On the Anglo side of town Popeye meant prosperity, a tribute to the thriving spinach industry. But on the Mexican side of town, where a majority of the citizens of Crystal City lived, the statue symbolized poverty. "We hated that statue," said Jose Angel Gutierrez, who grew up in Crystal City and later became a civil rights leader in Texas. "The statue symbolized our servitude to the spinach and the Anglo owners of the company."

On this day, only a few Mexican workers still lived on the migrant-worker site, which was owned by the Farm Security Administration. When war broke out, many Mexican migrant workers who came to Crystal City from the Northwest and Midwest each winter stopped coming for fear of being arrested. The federal government had doubled the number of agents patrolling the Mexican border, which was in effect closed.

It wasn't only rock-ribbed Texas conservatives such as Congressman Martin Dies, chairman of the feared House Un-American Activities Committee, who stirred anti-immigrant sentiment. In San Antonio, liberal mayor Maury Maverick, who had served two terms in Congress as a loyal Roosevelt New Dealer, called on the chief of police to arm every officer with a submachine gun to defend against German spies who might cross the border from Mexico. Maverick's edict alarmed San Antonio's large German population.

At that time, one in every six persons who lived in San Antonio was of German heritage. The central street in town was King William Street, known by German Texans as Kaiserwilhelmstrasse. The street was lined with stone mansions built by the wealthy Germans in San Antonio who formed the mercantile class. Until 1942, San Antonio had a German newspaper, the *Freie Presse für Texas*, which was closed when war broke out. German Texans in San Antonio who were involved in German cultural and singing societies became afraid when they learned that the FBI had arrested several hundred German Texans. Newspapers in San Antonio and Dallas asked their readers to be on the lookout for German agents. The readers responded. An FBI agent in Dallas stated that citizen reports had led to the arrest of sixty-one Germans, thirty-six Italians, and seventeen Japanese.

On the day that Harrison arrived in Crystal City, the internment of enemy aliens was well under way. Unlike in some less conservative towns and cities on the East Coast, Texas welcomed the idea of incarcerating suspected spies. Five internment camps were in Texas. The camp in Seagoville was occupied by single women and a few families, and the camp in Kenedy incarcerated only men. In San Antonio, a prisoner-of-war camp at Dodd Army Airfield at Fort Sam Houston held primarily German and Italian men. In El Paso, German and Italian prisoners of war were held at Fort Bliss. If the proposed family camp were to be located on the East Coast, opposition would be strong. Harrison understood political nuances and recognized that the establishment of a multinational family internment camp would not provoke hostility in Crystal City. Indeed, it would be welcomed. The farmworkers would be moved out, replaced by Japanese, German, and Italian enemy aliens and their families.

Surveying the site of the migrant-labor camp, Harrison noted what amenities existed. The site had been used to confine Mexican migrant laborers during their work stays, as well as illegal aliens arrested for border violations, and the facilities were stark. None of the 41 cottages or 118 one-room shelters had running water. The workers used outdoor privies. They slept on cots and hung their work clothes on nails.

The land itself was an expression of the American frontier. There were no paved roads. Most of it was farms and ranches, far from large cities. The social setting was western: intolerance, vigilantism, with economic competition the rule. When Mexican laborers at the camp failed to produce, some ranchers resorted to locking them in tiny chicken coops. Mexicans were viewed by Anglos as a subservient class, cogs in the wheels of business and daily life. Mexicans, despite their majority status and historic ties to the land, played the role of strangers in town.

From Gutierrez's point of view, the camp fit into the political and economic patterns that were already in place in Crystal City: "Before the war and after, Zavala County existed as a kind of stable dictatorship with the Anglos in charge of the majority population, which was Mexican. As a boy, I understood that I lived in a city in which my Mexican heritage was being subtracted from me, slowly and surely. The Anglos called this process 'assimilation.' It did not occur to them that we Mexicans were perfectly happy the way we were. Assimilation meant: We learn to act like Anglos. We don't get to be ourselves. We were, in effect, subjects on land that was native to us." The irony was that the majority of German, Japanese, and Italian nationals and their American-born children who were later interned in Crystal City welcomed assimilation. Indeed, they wanted desperately to be Americans. But for the accident of their countries of origin, they would never have found themselves in Crystal City.

Harrison had many practical issues to consider: how many miles of roads would need to be built, how many more cottages erected, the cost of a barbed-wire security fence and a guard tower suitable for twenty-four-hour surveillance. The Farm Security Administration had offered to donate the land, but Harrison realized it would take a million dollars or more to build and maintain the family internment camp.

A precedent existed for converting a government-owned facility to an internment camp. Earlier in 1942, the INS established the camp for single men in Kenedy, Texas, on land owned by the Civilian Conservation Corps, one of FDR's New Deal programs. On the day Harrison visited Crystal City, the camp in Kenedy was overcrowded with more than a thousand German and Japanese men, and conditions were harsh. Swiss inspectors, acting under the terms of the Geneva Convention rules, found the German internees "in an uproar." Upon their arrival, seven hundred German internees were lassoed by Texas Rangers on horseback and herded into a stockade. Their living quarters were primitive as well, with internees sleeping in four-men Victory Huts that offered little shelter from the weather. Snakes slithered through the cracks in the walls. Following the protocols of the Geneva Convention, which required that nationalities be segregated in prisoner-of-war camps, Ivan Williams, the officer in charge in Kenedy, packed the Japanese internees en masse into dormitories notorious for the stench of the communal toilet.

In Crystal City, at least the Victory Huts were secure and the site dotted with a few existing buildings. Still, much of the family camp would have to be built from the ground up. Utilities wouldn't be a problem. Electrical service could be purchased from the Crystal City Power and Light Co. Natural gas was plentiful and cheap in oil-rich Texas. Telephone service might be a challenge in such a remote location, but there was a local carrier.

From Harrison's point of view, the isolated location of the camp was also a positive. Crystal City, situated fifteen hundred and eighteen hundred miles from the East and West Coasts, areas that were considered vital to the war effort, was not a likely target for sabotage. It was geographically close to Latin America, from which many families would be transported. By the next day when Harrison boarded the train to make his journey back home to Rose Valley, he'd made his decision. Crystal City would be the location of the family camp.

Harrison's trip to Crystal City had been a long time coming. He was born on April 27, 1899, in the Frankford section of Philadelphia, to Joseph Layland Harrison and his wife, Anna. His formal name was Earl Grant Harrison. Grant because he shared his birthday with Ulysses S. Grant.

Both of his parents were foreign-born. The immigrant experience was the primary lens through which Harrison viewed the world. His father, Joseph, was born in England and was brought to the United States as a child by his parents. He settled in Philadelphia and became a moderately successful wholesale grocer. Harrison's mother, Anna, came from Northern Ireland with her three sisters, all of whom worked in the textile mills in Philadelphia, and died before the age of thirty-five.

Physically, Harrison resembled his father, a robust man who

thought nothing of riding a bicycle from Philadelphia to Atlantic City, a round-trip of 130 miles, on Sundays, his only day off. But Harrison's strongest memories were of his mother, an amateur actress who performed in stock companies around Philadelphia. In temperament, he shared Anna's Irish charm and good nature. Like his mother, Earl made a point of rising each day with a smile. The idea of wasting time was anathema.

He grew up solidly middle class and attended Frankford High School, where he was president of his freshman, sophomore, and senior classes. He played all sports in high school, except cricket. Anna died before Earl graduated from the University of Pennsylvania as valedictorian of his class in 1920. After college, Harrison went to law school at the University of Pennsylvania, where he graduated in 1923. That year, he played the role of a hero in a play put on by Mask and Wig Productions, the university drama club. The heroine in the play was a pretty, dark-eyed student named Carol Sensenig, who, like his mother, was outgoing. Carol's family came from Mennonites who had emigrated from Germany in 1690 and settled in Pennsylvania in search of religious freedom. The two married after graduation, and Harrison joined the law firm of Sawl, Ewing, Remick and Saul, a distinguished downtown Philadelphia firm. It was exactly the future his mother had in mind for him.

Before the surprise attack on Pearl Harbor, Harrison lived a quiet life with Carol and their three sons. Their only daughter, Carol Hope, died of influenza in 1931. An independent liberal Republican like his father, Harrison was civically engaged. In 1937, he organized an effort to consolidate city and county government in Philadelphia. Two years later, he helped found a Democratic Fusion ticket, combined of Republicans, who held a majority in Philadelphia, as well as Democrats and independents, to campaign for consolidated government. It was not successful. He ran the United Way and helped start a local Boys' Club.

He and Carol bought a large house in Rose Valley in 1932. It was in foreclosure, and they got it on twenty-four acres for a steal—only

$18,500, according to their son J. Barton Harrison. Earl had grown up playing tennis on public courts in Frankford, and in the yard of his home he built a large tennis court. He and his young sons played regularly. Carol brought them platters of hefty sandwiches and gallons of lemonade. In the run-up to the war, Carol planted a large victory garden. She had chickens and several cows. In 1939, as Jews streamed out of Europe, Carol and Earl sheltered several Jewish refugees behind the hedged lawn of their family compound.

Barton was only eight when his father visited Crystal City in 1942. Back home in Rose Valley the threat of another attack from either the Japanese or the Germans was a tangible part of their everyday life. "German submarines had been spotted off the Atlantic coast," recalled Barton. "In our house we had long-handled shovels with buckets of sand nearby in case incendiary bombs were dropped. In our neighborhood, we set up a system of fire spotters. I was one. At eight p.m. I would light a flare outside our house. And then a spotter would write down the moment he spotted my flare. Everybody took the threat very seriously."

Before the war, Harrison carried little political weight and had nothing obvious about him to attract the attention of Francis Biddle, then the solicitor general of the United States. On June 28, 1940, Congress passed the Alien Registration Act, and Biddle decided to persuade Harrison, whom he knew from legal ties in Philadelphia, into public service. The act made it mandatory, for the first time in American history, for every alien living in the United States to register and be fingerprinted.

Biddle agonized over the passage of the law, which he believed was a reflection of irrational congressional fears that would alienate millions of foreign-born residents who were not citizens. That this program would be administered by the Department of Justice—normally charged with prosecuting criminals—particularly rankled him. As Biddle later wrote, "The very word *alien* suggested those who had been estranged and excluded." With the passage of the act, Biddle wrote, "The beginning of the witch hunt was on."

Biddle had only two months to put the bureaucratic machinery in place. He was worried about how to administer the program with skill and tact and chose Harrison as the director of alien registration. Of Harrison, Biddle later wrote, "He understood how important it was to make foreigners here understand how much they had contributed to us. He did not want to melt out the richness of their own cultures."

Harrison accepted the job and turned his attention to how to convince aliens that the registration law was not something to fear, not a trick by the government to force their deportation. He decided to sell the program to noncitizens as an initiation into an "American club." He argued that while registration didn't mean citizenship, noncitizens who complied would demonstrate loyalty to America's rule of law.

It was a grim sell. The fears of aliens were well founded. Attorney General Robert H. Jackson called the new law "a phase of our national defense program," a mechanism for weeding out spies. Foreign-born immigrants knew that Hitler registered the Jews in Germany as a first step to stripping them of all their rights. Most approached the idea of national registration with panic and dread.

Harrison assembled a staff of twenty young lawyers, many of them his friends, and set up an office in an abandoned ice-skating rink in Washington, DC. It became the official headquarters of the Alien Registration Division of the Justice Department. The rink was not air-conditioned, and in the sticky summer heat the battalion of lawyers, briny with sweat, prepared the complicated apparatus for registering every noncitizen. It was like putting together a giant jigsaw puzzle, with an unknown number of pieces and no clear pattern of how to solve the puzzle.

According to the statute, all noncitizens aged fourteen or over, including those in the process of naturalization, had to register with local authorities and be fingerprinted by December 26. Harrison and his team had only six months to register every noncitizen in the United States.

It wasn't just a matter of a simple signature. All aliens were required to answer fifteen primary and twenty-seven secondary questions, including when they first entered the United States and how many trips they'd made abroad. They had to state religious affiliations and provide employment records. The questions had to be answered under oath, and violations were punishable by a fine of $1,000 or imprisonment or both. To lessen the aura of criminality associated with fingerprinting and the threat of imprisonment, Harrison insisted that registrations be done not at police stations, as the law directed, but at local post offices.

Within days after the implementation of Harrison's plans, cities all over the country began to purge aliens from county relief rolls and denied them charity. Many employers fired aliens who were not citizens. In Texas, Mexican nationals, and even some naturalized and native-born Latinos, feared the plan was a deportation scheme. Some voiced their concerns to local authorities. In offices in Dallas, Houston, and San Antonio, Mexican American civil rights leaders from LULAC (League of United Latin American Citizens) directed registration of Mexican aliens in an attempt to avert fears. In the face of hostility and rising unemployment, many Mexican nationals and even US citizens chose to return to Mexico.

Convinced that aliens would trust foreign-born Americans more than those born on American soil, Harrison built his staff from a wide array of ethnic backgrounds. For his deputy, he chose Donald Perry, born in Yugoslavia, a trusted classmate of Harrison's at the University of Pennsylvania. As director of communications to design a publicity campaign, Harrison chose M. E. Gilford, a Jew. Gilford's assistant was the writer Mangione, an Italian. The choice of Mangione for such an important position was strategic. At the time, more aliens living in the United States were from Italy than from any other country.

Harrison urged his staff to think of the good that registration might do. The data gleaned from the questionnaires might dispel the ignorance and racism that characterized the average American's concept of aliens as saboteurs. Moreover, it might avert the passage of more anti-immigrant laws. As Mangione later wrote, "With a degree of empathy which at that time of my life I found remarkable in one who called himself a Republican, Harrison understood the fears of aliens and did everything within his administrative powers to calm them."

Harrison made the deadline. Six months after the start of the program, almost 5 million noncitizens, including the fathers of Ingrid and Sumi, were registered. Out of all immigrants in the United States only 1,061 were prosecuted for failure to comply with the act, which Harrison argued proved that most were loyal to the United States and that the threat of traitors was exaggerated.

He resigned his position, cleared out his office at the rink, and on January 21, 1941, returned to his law practice in Philadelphia.

To honor Harrison for his service, the month before, Eleanor Roosevelt had invited Harrison and Carol to dinner at the White House. Though Harrison was a Republican, Carol was a liberal Democrat and utterly devoted to Mrs. Roosevelt. The first lady, still at odds with her husband over the treatment of foreign-born immigrants, wanted to talk to Harrison firsthand about registration. She had received a lot of mail from frightened noncitizens. In addition to the Harrisons, Mangione was a guest, and he wrote about the dinner party in his memoir, *An Ethnic at Large*.

The president, on a Navy cruise to inspect American and British military bases, was not present at the party. The Harrisons and Mangione were ushered into a blue room with gilded chairs. An attendant explained that Mrs. Roosevelt would join them shortly and showed them a diagram of where they should sit at the table.

To Harrison's dismay, the first guests to arrive were a well-known Chinese couple, Dr. T. V. Soong, the brother of Madame Chiang Kai-shek's banker, and his wife. Their presence might make it difficult to talk frankly about alien-registration problems. Since 1882, the Chinese had been excluded from US citizenship.

Henry Morgenthau Jr., the secretary of the treasury, arrived with his wife. To make polite conversation, Carol told Dr. Soong that one of her favorite writers was Lin Yutang, whose translations of classic Chinese texts into English were bestsellers. Soong reciprocated that he admired the work of Pearl Buck about China.

Then Eleanor made her entrance into the room and offered apologies and warm greetings. She ushered them into a large dining room on the ground floor. The plates were rimmed with gold and etched with the Roosevelt family crest. After everyone took their places, Eleanor described to Harrison some of the mail she had received from frightened aliens. In one letter, she told him, a woman expressed fears that she would have to reveal embarrasing information about herself that her husband did not know. Prior to her marriage, the letter writer had been convicted of theft and served a prison sentence. Another letter told how a respected member of a community, who had been voting for years because he thought he'd fulfilled all the formal requirements of the nationalization law, learned that in fact he had not fully completed them. He had been voting illegally. What should the man do?

The rest of the table sat in silence. Harrison quietly explained that nothing in the Alien Registration Act required aliens to register in the communities where they lived. Both of the letter writers could avoid embarrassment by registering in any city where the registration clerks did not know them. That the man had voted illegally wouldn't be known in his home county.

The presence of the Chinese couple did not prevent Eleanor from talking about the law. She spoke her mind, offering a window into how much she disagreed with Roosevelt and the Congress. What, she asked Harrison, about all the aliens who had never learned English, who lived in immigrant enclaves and knew only enough English to get by in their jobs and on buses? She was angry at the law because it discriminated against groups of foreign-born people, an idea she considered un-American.

Harrison, who also believed the law was flawed, adopted a diplomatic stance. He reassured the first lady that his office was doing all it could to reach non-English-speaking immigrants through the foreign-language press and radio.

Coffee and cake arrived and Eleanor shifted to the subject of race relations. Earlier in the week, she'd visited a high school in Texas. WHITES ONLY signs were on all public restrooms, cafés, movie theaters, and swimming pools. Texas schools were all segregated. NO MEXICANS signs were as common in Texas as NO NEGROES. A young Latino in the high school crowd told Mrs. Roosevelt that in Mexico, where his family came from, Negroes weren't segregated from society and racial intermarriage was accepted. The boy wanted to know how Mrs. Roosevelt, a powerful figure, could tolerate racial segregation.

That night Eleanor told her guests that the boy's question put her on the spot and made her feel ashamed of the country. While she expressed disapproval of racial inequality to friends and confidants, she had been reluctant to speak against existing laws in public. Finally, she told her guests, she decided the boy deserved an honest answer. She told him that she agreed with him and said, "A democracy which does not serve all its people could not long survive." The Latino students in Texas gave her a standing ovation.

Harrison asked if the statement had attracted press coverage. "Not yet," Eleanor said. "Sometimes newspapers don't print ideas they don't like."

When Eleanor signaled the end of the dinner party, she kissed Carol good-bye on the cheek and shook Earl's hand.

Harrison was praised for his work as director of alien registration. The *Survey Mid Monthly*, an influential journal edited by Paul U. Kellogg that published essays on social reform, wrote that Harrison had carried out the registration program in such a way that anxieties were allayed, and what might have been a witch hunt became an "orderly experience in sound public administration and compliance with the law." While many enemy aliens would not have agreed, Biddle was pleased with Harrison's work. "I hope that the temptation towards public work will keep simmering in you," Biddle wrote to Harrison in a private letter. "Once you have yielded to it, nothing else can be as good."

When Biddle became attorney general in 1941, he recommended to Roosevelt that he appoint Harrison to the position of commissioner of immigration. Roosevelt knew that Harrison was an independent Republican, an idea he did not much like, but he was willing to follow Biddle's recommendation. However, Roosevelt wanted to know if Harrison had voted for him.

"Dear Earl," wrote Biddle to Harrison on August 27, 1941. "Did you vote for the President and when?"

"I voted for the President in 1940 but not before," Harrison replied to Biddle. "Which indicates how long it takes me in some situations to reach the proper conclusion."

Roosevelt was amused by the answer. He told Biddle to go ahead with Harrison's nomination, but to clear it with Senator Joseph Guffey, an old-line Democrat from Pittsburgh. Guffey, who held a grudge against Biddle from a previous ruckus over another presidential appointment, told the new attorney general that he would claim senatorial privilege and block Harrison's appointment. Guffey quickly filed a "blue slip," signaling his opposition, with the Senate Committee on Immigration and Naturalization.

On March 24, 1942, Roosevelt ignored Guffey's opposition and nominated Harrison to the position. Guffey told reporters he would ask his fellow senators to reject the nomination as a courtesy to him. The fight was on.

"A first class row is in the making in the Senate," the *Washington Post* said that day. "Biddle Dares Guffey on Harrison: Assails Senator as Inconsistent," said the headline in the *Philadelphia Inquirer.*

In private correspondence with Biddle, Harrison offered to withdraw his name to spare embarrassment to Roosevelt but Biddle would have none of it; the fight was now personal. Guffey had taken aim directly at Biddle. In April, the *Evening Bulletin* in Philadelphia wrote, "Guffey today assailed Attorney General Francis Biddle as the ringleader of a 'silk stocking' move to gain control of the Democratic Party in Pennsylvania."

A few days later, the *Philadelphia Record* responded with a defense of Harrison: "Earl G. Harrison is an excellent example of a new type of public servant attracted to government work in the last decade. The politicians now throwing eggs at Harrison seem to forget that the Democrats would never have carried the country and would not have come close to carrying Pennsylvania, were it not for Roosevelt Republicans."

Finally, Biddle persuaded Roosevelt to intervene, and the president wrote a letter to Guffey: "Dear Joe: As one old friend to another I want to ask you to forgo your fight on the Harrison appointment. I know how deeply you feel about it, but I do not believe that the matter is one of sufficient importance to make an issue out of it that is bound to embarrass a lot of your and my good friends. Will you do this for me? F.D.R."

The following day, Guffey withdrew his opposition, and the Senate quickly confirmed Harrison. As a condition of accepting the appointment, Harrison insisted that the national headquarters of the INS be transferred from Washington to Philadelphia for the duration of the war, as he did not want to be separated from his family. Biddle agreed and Harrison took over as commissioner six months after his nomination.

When Harrison returned to his office in Philadelphia from Crystal City in the fall of 1942, he wrote a report recommending the small South Texas town as the site for the family internment camp. On December 12, 1942, thirty-five German families, who had all been in custody at Ellis Island and Camp Forest, Tennessee, arrived in Crystal City. Most of these families, which totaled 130 people, had agreed to be repatriated to Germany in exchange for Americans being held there. They were under the jurisdiction of the Special War Problems Division of the Department of State, not the INS, and eligible for quiet passage. From the beginning, the two sides of

America's internment policy—detention and exchange—were intertwined at Crystal City.

The Germans entered a primitive camp that was unfinished. A planned ten-foot-high perimeter fence with floodlights and guard towers did not yet exist. So few guards were in Crystal City that Border Patrol agents were sent from San Antonio to guard the German internees.

Nick Collaer, whom Harrison had chosen to be the officer in charge of the family camp, was a career US Border Patrol officer who had the year before established the all-male internment camp in Fort Missoula, Montana. He, his wife, and three children arrived in Crystal City by train from Fort Missoula five days after the German internees and took up residence in one of the forty-one government-owned cottages. Collaer paid $15.17 a month in rent.

In a nearby roped-off section, the German families were crowded into twenty-nine of the same style of cottage as the Collaers lived in, except the German families shared cottages and the Collaer family had its own.

Before leaving Ellis Island and Tennessee, the male German prisoners promised to construct housing for internees, but changed their minds when they arrived and discovered the camp was conceived as primarily for Japanese enemy aliens and their families, the first of whom were scheduled to arrive on March 17, 1943. In a memo to Harrison on January 1943, Collaer explained that the Germans refused to do work that would benefit the Japanese. When pressed, the German men arrived to work sites late, complaining that they had no alarm clocks or other means of awakening. "Some of this work does not require journeyman carpenters—merely men who can handle hammers," wrote Collaer. "There should be a considerably greater number of these in the present group of internees than have been working recently." Collaer's memo was a precursor of future disputes between German and Japanese internees.

A warm front arrived in Crystal City, and by midday in January 1943, the temperature rose from eighty to ninety-six degrees.

Rattlesnakes were everywhere. S. F. Oliver, the camp doctor, issued an order to employees and internees regarding rattlesnake bites: "A tourniquet should be applied above the bitten area and as much of the poison sucked out of the bite by mouth as possible. It is imperative that these cases be gotten to the hospital as soon as possible because delay may mean loss of life. Treatment with serum will be available at the hospital. Whiskey is of no value in this condition—it may even be harmful."

Both the internees and Collaer's staff of eight INS employees suffered with the monstrous heat and the isolation. Collaer's daughter, Christine, who was five when the family moved to Crystal City, said her only memories of Crystal City were "the heat and the terror of rattlesnakes." She remembered her father was anxious and overworked. His requests for fencing, lighting, and guards took a long time to be answered. Once when Christine didn't move fast enough for him, he looked her in the eye and said, "You know, I could trade you for a yellow dog—and then I'd shoot the dog." She knew he didn't mean it; it was the tough talk of the frontier.

Little by little, more German prisoners arrived and construction progressed. The ten-foot-high security fence topped with barbed wire was completed and lit at night by searchlights. The lights from the camp could be seen for miles in every direction. Border Patrol agents manned the watchtowers twenty-four hours a day. Every detail of the camp's growth was noted by Collaer and sent to the INS in Philadelphia. For instance, on February 13, 1943, Harrison sent a radiogram from Philadelphia authorizing Collaer to buy one hundred board feet of lumber from Mexico. A few weeks later, he gave Collaer permission to conduct transactions that did not exceed $50.

That summer Harrison named Collaer acting assistant commissioner for alien control, and the Collaer family moved to Philadelphia. In Collaer's place, Harrison named forty-seven-year-old Joseph O'Rourke, an Irishman who had served as Stannard's assistant at the Seagoville camp, as officer in charge at Crystal City.

A tall man with wavy hair and a rugged face, O'Rourke was born in Brooklyn, New York. He completed four years of high school in Poughkeepsie, but records show he did not graduate. Instead, he joined the Army during World War I and served for two years. In 1924, he became a Border Patrol agent with the INS and made a career of it. He consistently received high marks from his superiors within INS. One report in 1933 praised O'Rourke for his "loyalty, integrity and efficiency" and singled out his "fine manner of handling personnel under his supervision and inspiring loyalty, respect, and affection in his subordinates." Before his post in Seagoville, O'Rourke had worked at a detention camp in Hot Springs, West Virginia, where Japanese ambassador Kichisaburo Nomura and Special Envoy Saburo Kurusu were interned after the Japanese attack on Pearl Harbor.

In Crystal City, O'Rourke's experience in dealing with Japanese, German, and Latin American internees, and his knowledge of how to manage people, would serve him well. He spoke halting Spanish, enough to know that the term *Agent Pancho*, which he heard regularly on the streets of Crystal City, was a slur used by Mexican nationals who feared deportment.

Despite his record and charismatic personality, O'Rourke was lonely when he arrived in Crystal City to assume control of the camp. He was separated from his wife, Loretta, a strict Irish Catholic woman, who lived in their small house on Cleveland Street in Buffalo with their only daughter, Joan. According to his granddaughter, Pamela Smith, it had been O'Rourke's decision to end the marriage. He left Loretta embittered and Joan confused.

In Crystal City, his staff and others described O'Rourke as a "jolly Irishman" who paid particular attention to the children, who followed him like a Pied Piper.

One night Mangione, Harrison's special assistant, visited O'Rourke at Crystal City. The two drove the short distance of less than two miles into town and spent the evening at a beer joint. Mangione asked O'Rourke how he tolerated the isolation of the area and demands of his work. "The only way I can keep my head straight is to do a little drinking now and then and try to find some loving woman," O'Rourke said. He related that he'd recently picked up a woman in the beer joint: "She was in her forties, and so damn grateful."

O'Rourke transformed Crystal City from a migrant camp to the largest and busiest internment camp of the war, a place of constant coming and going of internees and their families. Eventually the INS spent more than a million dollars to construct 500 buildings on 290 acres, including a hospital with 70 beds, administrative buildings, and separate barber and beauty shops for Germans and Japanese. The three schools included one for Germans, another for Japanese, and the Federal Grammar and Federal High, which offered an American-style education to any child in camp. O'Rourke's staff grew to 150 INS personnel and 200 additional employees who served as construction workers and laborers. On December 23, 1943, O'Rourke sent administrative order no. 9 to his staff and the INS offices in Philadelphia: "Effective this date, the auditorium in the Federal High School will be known as Harrison Hall, in honor of the Commissioner of Immigration and Naturalization, Mr. Earl Harrison." The auditorium became a central gathering place in the camp.

After O'Rourke was named officer in charge, Harrison paid another visit to Crystal City and saw the changes. During a tour, Harrison and O'Rourke encountered a group of small children. O'Rourke asked what they were doing. "Playing war," a young boy said.

"Okay," said O'Rourke. "But I hope nobody gets killed." He and Harrison continued their tour.

On the way back, they stopped at the same spot. The children were seated on the ground, looking glum.

"What happened to the war?" O'Rourke asked.

"It ended," they explained. "Nobody wanted to be the enemy. We all want to be the Americans."

PART TWO

DESTINATION: CRYSTAL CITY

CHAPTER FOUR

Internment Without Trial

On the morning of January 9, 1942, the day after Mathias Eiserloh was arrested, Ingrid woke to the familiar sound of guinea hens cackling in the bare linden tree at the corner of the house. For a moment, it seemed like an ordinary day. Then Ingrid remembered events from the night before—the inexplicable look of confusion on her mother's stricken face, her father arrested by the FBI.

She got up, dressed quickly, and slipped out the back door to feed the farm animals before her mother saw her. As usual, Senta, her German shepherd, was by her side. Pal, the golden collie, was tied up in back by the outhouse. She fed both dogs, then went to the chicken coop and gathered eggs. Even at eleven years old, Ingrid was conscious that without the $60 per week from her father's job in Cleveland, her mother would need egg money now more than ever.

Ingrid walked to the garage. Several months before, she'd found three wild owls, two small ones and a single large one. Mathias had built a cage for them and the owls were now in the garage. Johanna had scolded Mathias for indulging Ingrid's habit of collecting wild animals. Often the child brought home green frogs from the creek and she rescued lame birds. Once she trapped a family of otters. But Johanna's complaints were too gentle to make much of an impression, so great was the whole family's pleasure in the woods and wildlife around their homestead.

Now Ingrid decided she should liberate the owls. The idea of her father behind bars made the sight of the incarcerated owls unbearable.

She swung the door of the cage wide and stepped aside. The owls beat their comblike wings and made a muffled, almost silent, ascent into the cold, gray January sky.

After Ingrid returned to the house, Johanna left to go to Cleveland, a drive of a little more than twenty miles, to find out what she could about the fate of her husband. If Johanna harbored the hope that Mathias's problems could easily be resolved, she soon found out otherwise. Mathias and several other German-born men were behind bars at the Seventh Precinct Station of the Cleveland Police Department. Upon her arrival, officials confirmed that Mathias was there, but wouldn't tell Johanna why. She pressed for answers. They only said that her husband's status was "under investigation."

"For what?" she asked.

He wasn't charged with anything, but all her questions were turned aside. At least Johanna knew where Mathias was. All over the country, FBI agents had seized German, Japanese, and Italian immigrants without notifying their families. According to one State Department memo, some suspected enemy aliens had "disappeared for as long as two weeks, leaving businesses in operation, cars parked on the streets which were taken by the police for over-parking and families totally without knowledge of their whereabouts." Johanna left the station, not knowing when or if she would see Mathias again.

Over the next few weeks, Johanna carried baskets of eggs to her usual customers. Neighbors spoke to her through cracked doors, mumbling rejections. Many refused to talk to her. No one believed an innocent man could be jailed, much less be held in jail without charges. The coldness of her neighbors astonished her. Already a subtle, but important, aspect of American internment was embedded in Johanna's mind. She believed that her husband was innocent. As an immigrant, she still believed in the integrity of American justice. She understood that the Fifth Amendment to the US Constitution guaranteed that no one could be deprived of liberty or property without "due process of law." But the arrest of Mathias, without charges, defied that guarantee. She didn't yet understand that these two beliefs—in her husband's innocence and in the American right to due process—were unrelated. It was wartime and Mathias was a citizen of Germany, not America.

In her first effort to formally defend her husband, Johanna sat at the kitchen table and typed a letter to Biddle, the attorney general of the United States. "My husband has too much character to be un-American," she told Biddle. "I am sure that the agents who have taken many things from our home that were dear to me have seen nothing there indicating that anyone in our family sought to, and could or would, engage in activities against the interest of the United States, because none of us ever entertained any such thoughts."

Within a couple of months after his arrest, the family was destitute. When Mathias was arrested, his $700 account at the Cleveland Trust Co. was frozen. Johanna was unable to pay the mortgage of several hundred dollars a month. The bank threatened foreclosure. Johanna tried to find work as a seamstress, but the stigma of her husband's arrest kept away potential customers. To help her mother with the chores, Ingrid stopped going to school and stayed home. It was just as well to not have to endure the taunts of her classmates. In the mornings, she cared for her younger brother, Lothar, and infant sister, Ensi. Ingrid continued her studies on her own. She practiced arithmetic and read novels. *Little Women* was a favorite.

One day Ingrid walked over to her nearest neighbor's house, owned by Ernie and Helen Hoelscher, to ask if she could buy a loaf of day-old bread. Ernie had a small bread business.

"Don't let the dogs loose," Johanna had warned Ingrid as she headed out the back door. Ingrid heeded her mother's warning. She placed Senta and Pal on a long rope and tied them to a tree at the end of the driveway.

Ernie was not at home, but Ingrid found Helen, a slim woman with red hair, who was in her forties, about the same age as Ingrid's mother. To her surprise, Ingrid also saw a small company of circus performers camped on Helen's property. In her younger years, Helen had worked in the circus as a trapeze flier. The sight of several horses, caged monkeys, and a solitary elephant filled Ingrid with pleasure. The pleasant scene momentarily distracted her from the loss of her father.

Helen stood outside in her yard and called out to Ingrid, "Come on over." Ingrid was relieved by Helen's friendliness. Like her mother, Ingrid now feared being snubbed by people she'd assumed were family friends.

Helen pointed to a trapeze and a trampoline set up for practices. Ingrid asked if she could try the trapeze. "Sure," Helen told her. "But do it before Ernie gets back." She immediately understood that for some reason Helen didn't want Ernie to see Ingrid. She didn't know why, but the trapeze was too exciting a prospect to ignore.

She hopped on the seat of the trapeze and pumped her legs. She swung, back and forth, higher and higher. On a high pass, she opened her eyes and looked behind her to a nearby field and saw a streak of Pal's golden hair, followed by Senta nipping at his heels. Her two dogs were off their rope and running at full gait.

Then she heard the sound of two shotgun blasts.

Heart racing, Ingrid jumped off the trapeze and ran toward the sound of the shots. She saw a bloody path through the tall grass at the edge of the field. She followed the trail and saw her dead dogs. She broke into a sweat. Slowly, shock rising in her like nausea, she turned and walked home.

When she got to her house, she told her mother what happened. Johanna's face was stern. She showed no emotion, as though her body's nervous system failed to register the news. It frightened Ingrid that her mother was so disengaged from the tragedy, as if Johanna was in a spell of sorrow, too distracted by her own problems.

What Ingrid did not know, but is made plain in her father's declassified FBI files, was that Helen and Ernie were among those jittery neighbors who'd smeared Mathias as a potential German spy.

The FBI file reveals that Mathias and Ernie had been involved in a long-running dispute over the boundary between their two properties. Part of Ernie's motive for providing information to the FBI may have been to settle that dispute. Ernie may have wanted to prove his own loyalty by accusing his neighbor of disloyalty. The dogs were also a point of contention. Ernie had a kennel filled with dogs of his own. He'd warned Mathias to keep Ingrid's dogs on the Eiserlohs' property. When he saw them running that day, he fired and killed both dogs.

Helen was a particularly aggressive accuser. Helen told one of the agents that Mathias had placed a large cement cistern in his basement, which she thought might be used as a secret room for saboteurs. According to Eiserloh's FBI file, "She advised further that in her opinion the cistern might be filled with quicklime used to dispose of dead bodies in the event of war." Ingrid explained that the cistern was simply used to collect extra water for her family.

Agents interviewed Robert Poots, the chief of police in Strongsville, who knew about the excessive amount of cement that Eiserloh had used to build his home. Poots told the agents there was "no indication that the subject was building a secret room there," much less a containment system for dead bodies. Though Poots disputed Helen's claim, it nonetheless became part of the dossier used against Mathias.

Helen also told FBI agents that the flat roof that Mathias had built on the top of his house might have been constructed "with the idea in mind of using it as a landing place for a gyro-plane in the event of war with Germany." The truth was far more mundane and sprang from an engineer's mind: Mathias had plans to add a second story to the home. Mathias told Ingrid and Lothar he had designed a swimming pool for the roof: "Americans love swimming pools. I'll build you one someday soon. If we ever the sell the house, it will add to the value."

Not long after after Ingrid's dogs were killed, Johanna received an offer on the house and property. Without income, she had no choice but to accept it. She contacted her sister-in-law Emily, who lived in nearby Cleveland and was a real estate agent. Emily was married to Johanna's younger brother, Ludwig. Johanna explained that she needed to move out of the house soon and the sale had to be in cash—otherwise, the bank would freeze the proceeds. Emily arranged for resale. The offer—$4,000—was lower than she expected. On a tally of assets that Mathias gave to the FBI after his arrest, he listed the value of his house at $5,000. Still, Johanna realized that the opportunistic buyer had the best of her. Realizing that the family would have to move anyway, she took the money.

The morning after the sale was completed, Ingrid woke early to the sound of Ensi fussing in the crib in her parents' bedroom, next to Ingrid's room. She pulled herself from bed, walked down the hall, and poked her head into Johanna's bedroom. Her mother lay under the sheets, still and silent. Ensi stood in the crib and cried for milk.

Ingrid checked on Lothar, who was sound asleep in the living room, and went to the kitchen and turned on the stove to heat a bottle of milk. She wondered why her mother had not awakened and fed Ensi, but assumed that Johanna had just overslept.

Ingrid gave Ensi her bottle, sat down in the rocker, and watched the baby suck down the warm milk. Happy to see Ensi's eyes droop, Ingrid placed her back into the crib in her parents' darkened room. As Ingrid walked toward her mother's bed, her foot slid on something sticky. She reached for her mother's hand, but Johanna didn't move. Now Ingrid was scared. When she tried to find her voice, it came out as a croak.

"Mom," she said, shaking her mother gently. "Are you all right?"

Her mother, who was curled on her left side in a fetal position, groaned.

Ingrid backed away from the bed to find the light switch on the wall. When she went back to her mother's side, she saw blood on the floor. She shook her mother and Johanna opened her eyes.

"What happened?" asked Ingrid.

"I'm okay," said Johanna, groggy.

"Mom, can you sit up?"

Johanna didn't move. Ingrid pulled the bedcovers back and saw that her mother's nightgown was torn and blood was on the sheets.

Ingrid wasn't sure where the blood had come from—it could have come from the back of her mother's head, her pelvis, or her legs. All Ingrid knew was that her mother was injured and needed help.

The house had no telephone. Ingrid raced about an eighth of a mile down the hill to a farmhouse owned by the McGoverns. Pat McGovern was in the same grade as Ingrid, and the Eiserlohs knew the family well.

Rosemary McGovern came to the door but would not let Ingrid enter the house. Through the screen door, Ingrid explained that her mother was hurt. She asked Mrs. McGovern to call the sheriff. Then Ingrid handed her the phone number for her aunt Klara, Mathias's oldest sister, in Cleveland.

"Please tell Aunt Klara to come right away," said Ingrid. "Please, Mrs. McGovern, Mom is hurt. We need help."

Ingrid ran home and took a bucket and a mop and cleaned the blood off the floor. Later, she regretted destroying what could have been evidence, but it made no difference. The sheriff never came and there was no investigation. Mrs. McGovern never called him. Even if the sheriff had arrived, Johanna would never have reported a rape or a burglary. Why borrow more trouble? All through that morning, Ingrid nursed her mother. She heated water on the stove, made her coffee, and in the afternoon helped Johanna up from the bed to take a shower.

Later, Johanna told Ingrid and Lothar that a man wearing a mask and dark clothes broke into the house and appeared at her bedside. He demanded cash, saying he knew the house had sold. Johanna denied it.

While no guns were in the house, Johanna had a lead pipe hidden underneath her pillow because she was frightened living without her husband. Sleepy and confused, she'd reached for the pipe and swung at the intruder's face. She heard a crack and thought she might have broken the intruder's nose. He turned and ran out of the house.

Ingrid became convinced that her mother had been raped. Although she believed Johanna may have used the pipe to fight off the man, she also thought the man might have wielded the pipe against her mother. For months after the attack, Johanna was confined to bed. Much of the left side of Johanna's body was paralyzed. She couldn't use her left arm and dragged her left leg. Johanna blamed the injury on "shock" and later told INS authorities that she had suffered a stroke. When Ingrid asked Johanna for more information, her mother refused. Later she told Lothar she had been "assaulted" and that the man had attempted to rape her. Lothar did not ask his mother for details, but remembered that his mother was focused on how the intruder knew she had cash in the house. Had her sister-in-law Emily inadvertently told someone? At least the man did not get the cash, as Johanna had hidden it well.

Later that day, Ingrid's aunt Klara and her husband, Frank, arrived at the house. While Mrs. McGovern had not called the sheriff, she had called Klara and asked her to check on the Eiserloh children. Johanna told Klara she no longer felt safe in the house. Klara and Frank packed bags for all three children and Johanna and drove them to their house in Cleveland. Over the next few months, Klara made space for them in her home. She nursed Johanna and cared for the children.

Meanwhile, Mathias, jailed at the Cleveland Police Department, remained unaware of the FBI file that Hoover's special agents had gathered against him. A warrant for his arrest had been issued on January 3, 1942. He was on the custodial detention list, informally known as Hoover's black list. The FBI's ranking system categorized suspects such as Eiserloh according to the danger they posed. Class A was considered the most dangerous, Class B indicated suspects who would be arrested but subject to conditional release, and Class C indicated suspects about whom the FBI did not have sufficient information to indicate need for investigation. The headings were subjective, based on an investigator's judgment, but as a German man living legally in the United States who was employed in a business heavily engaged in defense work, Eiserloh was classified Class B.

As an engineer with the Pittsburgh Plate Glass Company, Eiserloh had designed many bridges in Ohio, including the first iron drawbridge across the broad span of the Cuyahoga River. On the day the bridge opened, Johanna christened the bridge with a bottle of champagne, as if she were the queen. It was one of Ingrid's favorite childhood memories. Now that the United States was at war, FBI agents concluded that since Eiserloh designed bridges and had access to dynamite, he also had the capability to blow them up.

By comparison with the FBI's investigation of suspected Class A subversives and primary German targets such as the leaders of the German American Bund in New York, known as the American Nazi Party, the field investigation of Mathias Eiserloh was routine and the case against him unremarkable. No illegal wiretaps were used against Eiserloh, no "black bag jobs," meaning no home or office break-ins.

The investigation of Eiserloh began in October 1941, before the attack on Pearl Harbor, when one of his coworkers at the Pittsburgh Plate Glass Company anonymously dropped his name to the special agents in the Cleveland field office. As Hoover later put it in official correspondence to Edward J. Ennis, director of the Alien Enemy Control Unit of the Immigration and Naturalization Service, "The informant believes that the subject [Eiserloh] is dangerous to the security of the United States because of his skill and knowledge of structural design." Hoover's letter to Ennis was written on January 5, 1942, only three days before Eislerloh was arrested. Eiserloh did not know it, but he was already enmeshed in the machinery of government internment—a carefully prepared paper trail existed that sealed his fate.

During the investigation, agents compiled a comprehensive biography of Eiserloh. He was born on July 4, 1895, in Plaidt, Germany, in the Rhineland. As a boy, he worked alongside his father, who was a building contractor. Eiserloh was drafted into the German army in 1915 during World War I, served as an infantry officer, and was discharged in 1917. He was wounded in November 1917, leaving a scar down the right side of his back and damaging the hearing in his left ear. In 1921, Eislerloh graduated from the Technical College for Civil Engineering in Idstein with a degree in structural engineering.

While in Idstein, he met Johanna, who lived there with her parents. Mathias had an older sister, Anne, who had immigrated to the United States. Johanna and Mathias decided to marry and immigrate there as well. Ensi, their youngest daughter, said, "My mother was crazy about America. As a girl, she thought the streets were paved with gold. I believe one of the reasons she married my father was to get to America."

Mathias left Germany on the *Reliance* steamship and arrived in New York on March 29, 1923. He traveled to Williamson, West Virginia, and stayed with Anne, his sister, and her husband, a World War I veteran who worked as a coal miner. For two months Mathias worked in the mines with his brother-in-law. In October, Mathias went to work for the Mingo County Road Department as an engineer.

Johanna followed him to the United States later that year. On Christmas Eve 1923, Mathias and Johanna were married. In their wedding photograph, Johanna wears a knee-length, pale silk dress, white stockings and shoes, and holds a large bouquet of roses. Mathias is dressed in a double-breasted, pin-striped suit. They both display hopeful smiles and already look as prosperous as they had dreamed of becoming—the image of shiny new immigrants to America. If they worked hard, the couple believed, they would become American citizens in due time.

In the 1920s, it took Germans living legally in the United States five years to obtain citizenship. Applicants had to report every year to the Immigration and Naturalization Service and provide references. If applicants missed a step, they would have to start anew.

In 1924, a year after they married, Mathias and Johanna moved to Cleveland, Ohio. Mathias secured a job with the Cleveland Electric Illumination Company, and both he and Johanna finally felt settled in America. They filed their applications in Cleveland to become citizens. In a signed document, they pledged their intention to "renounce forever all allegiance and fidelity to any foreign potentate, state or sovereignty and particularly to The German Empire." With their signatures, they officially transferred their loyalty from Germany to America. The document required Mathias and Johanna to certify that they were not anarchists or polygamists, which were automatic disqualifiers for citizenship. Their pledge to the government and to themselves was "in good faith to become a citizen of the United States of America and to permanently reside therein: SO HELP ME GOD."

But Mathias was careless about meeting the requirements for citizenship. Five years after he filed his application, he was required to file additional documents, but he failed to meet the deadline. In the summer of 1929, he and Johanna went on a prolonged trip to Germany to visit Johanna's ailing parents. The missed deadline meant they had to start the process all over again.

The trip to Germany had other negative consequences as well. Prior to leaving America, Mathias worked as a structural engineer for the New York Central Railroad in Cleveland and earned a decent wage. When the Eislerohs returned to the United States in the fall of 1929, the country was in the depths of the Depression and he was unable to regain his former position. Mathias took a series of low-paying jobs in Cleveland, and he and Johanna lived in an upstairs room of an old hotel in the city's downtown for $5 a week. After Ingrid was born on May 8, 1930, Eiserloh paid $50 down for an isolated property on Albion Road in Strongsville. He put up a tent on the land and moved in with Johanna and Ingrid. "With just sand and cement and a few steel bars, the cheapest material to be had, but the hardest to work with, I managed to build four walls with a floor and a roof over them to live in," he later wrote. "But it was very primitive."

During all these years, Mathias lived as an unremarkable new immigrant. "I was a graduated civil engineer when I entered this country, 28 years old and in prime condition," Eiserloh explained in his own letter to Biddle after his arrest. "My only ambition was to work hard, to live an honest and decent life, to be among my family, and give my children happiness and an education as my father gave me."

Though they struggled financially, Mathias and Johanna were resourceful, worked hard, and built a reasonably stable life in Strongsville. Mathias was arrested only once, in 1927, when he was working for the New York Central Railroad in Cleveland as an engineer. On the way home from work, he ran a red light and did not have the money to pay the fine. He spent three hours in jail until Johanna could arrive and bring $30.

For six weeks in 1934, Mathias was unable to find work, but he received help from the local relief headquarters in Cuyahoga County. Proud, and by his own description a "stubborn German," Mathias was embarrassed to accept charity. "I cannot and do not want to live on somebody's sweat," he told authorities.

In early 1935, he finally secured a job with the White Motor Company in Cleveland as an automobile body designer. It paid $45 a week, less than Eiserloh thought he deserved, but at least his family was off the dole, which lessened his shame. "The job hardly allowed me to buy the materials that I wanted but I worked hard in my spare time. "By 1937, there were five rooms in the house," wrote Eisleroh. "It was a period of relative contentment."

A year later, the White Motor Company suffered an economic setback and Eiserloh lost his job again. He applied for a job with the Works Progress Administration, one of Roosevelt's New Deal projects, but he was not eligible. Only citizens of the United States could apply, a requirement that prompted Mathias to file another application for citizenship. Nine months later, on the day he was supposed to appear at the INS, he had a job interview and failed to make the appointment. For the second time, his citizenship application was put on hold. The more jobs he lost, the more setbacks he suffered, the more he felt like an outsider in America.

By September 1939, Hitler had seized power in Germany, rolled across the Polish border, and seemed unstoppable. In response, France and Britain declared war on Germany, and America stood at the brink. As a result, the US economy had improved and companies were hiring more engineers. Nonetheless, month after month Eiserloh looked for jobs without success. As he explained to Biddle, "a certain question always spoiled my chances"—that of his nationality. "As a husband and now father of two children, I could not see why they and my wife should starve, just because I was born in Germany." Ashamed, he took a chance. He told an employment agent that he was Swiss and his scheme worked. In the late fall of 1939, he got a job that paid $75 a week, the most he'd ever earned in America. He returned to designing bridges, his dream job, this time for the Columbia Chemical Division in Cleveland.

At work, Mathias felt humiliated by his pretense of being Swiss. "To get a job in America, without which my family would starve, I had to be something other than German. I could not help it. For me it was work or perish." The more he saw Germans scorned as enemies in America, the more he felt like a traitor to himself and the angrier he became.

Finally, he left his job at Columbia for a lower-paying job at Pittsburgh Plate Glass Company. At the new job, he didn't hide his German citizenship. He joined the German Technical Society and began visiting the library at the German consulate in Cleveland to read German technical periodicals. In contrast to its post–World War I financial depression, Germany's economy was now booming. For two years, Mathias had worked in Germany on a hydroelectric power project that channelized the Isar River. Now he idly looked through technical journals and explored the idea of pursuing better-paying jobs in Germany. "I wanted to learn more about a country where my labor was highly in demand and where a man fifty years old was not classified as too old," he told Biddle.

Like many of his German friends in Strongsville, Mathias bore the immigrant's burden. He had one foot on one side of the ocean in Germany and the other in America, which made him an outsider in both places. By nature, identity, and personal history, he was fully German, but in his aspirations and ambition he was fully American. He would live with this dilemma all his life.

After his children were born in America, Eiserloh felt as if he, too, had a stake in America. He paid taxes and invested in his own home, but he stayed connected to his German culture. He ate German food and spoke German, as well as English. On most Tuesday and Thursday nights he drank beer with friends at the Schwarzwald Restaurant in Cleveland. He bought books in German on sale at the embassy in Cleveland. He belonged to two different German clubs—the German Technical Society, a group of engineers and scientists, and the German Nationals Club. "The clubs were purely social," Eiserloh told Biddle.

In a peaceful world, Eiserloh's assimilation into American life would have been smooth. With the outbreak of World War II, his close German ties aroused suspicion. In 1941, agents in Cleveland followed orders and took the next step. They interviewed Eiserloh's former and current employers, his neighbors, acquaintances, and local businessmen in Strongsville.

In addition to Ernie and Helen Hoelscher, Mrs. McGovern, the kind neighbor whom Ingrid had sought out after her mother's altercation with the home invader, was also an informer. When asked whether the Eiserlohs ever had loud parties or strange-looking visitors, Mrs. McGovern said, according to the FBI report, that she noticed "meetings being held at the subjects' home on several occasions. She stated that 20 to 25 people would attend such meetings." When asked about these "meetings" by FBI agents, Eiserloh explained that he often recruited German friends to help work on his house or listen to music on the Victrola and didn't consider such activities disloyal.

While Mrs. McGovern was suspicious of Mathias, she defended Ingrid. "Ingrid is a very nice girl," Mrs. McGovern told FBI agents. "She never talked about Germany or wanted to go there. The trouble on the school bus was started solely by the other children."

One of the troublemakers was Mrs. McGovern's own son, Pat, who when interviewed by the FBI agents accused Ingrid of always "taking Hitler's side." That, according to Pat, was what prompted the taunts on the bus. Ingrid was slightly older than Pat, and she sensed that he wanted to be accepted as a part of the pack but meant her no real harm. Perhaps the boy thought he was doing his civic duty. At any other time, his harassment would have been mild annoyances, but these manufactured charges against Ingrid became part of Mathias's FBI files.

So did her father's anti-Semitic views. As a teenager, Ingrid knew that he shared the extremist view in Germany that Jews, especially Jewish bankers and merchants, were to blame for the country's many economic woes. During the FBI's investigation, Marguerite Dassel, a neighbor who owned a lunch stand in Strongsville, reported that Mathias complained to her about Roosevelt's Jewish advisers, such as the Supreme Court justice Felix Frankfurter. Mathias claimed that "the president's true name is Rosenfeld, not Roosevelt, and he's Jewish," a remark that led Dassel to believe that Eiserloh was not only anti-Semitic but a Nazi spy.

Mathias's German military service hadn't landed him on the FBI's official list of security risks, but during the FBI investigation of 1941 it was another mark against him. It didn't help his case that in 1935 a German official in the Cleveland consulate had taken the time to discover that although Eiserloh had earned the Iron Cross for his service in World War I, he'd never received it. The official came to the Eiserloh home in Strongsville and gave him the medal. Mathias hadn't claimed the medal because he didn't want to be reminded of World War I. His children said the Iron Cross was meaningless to him, but he accepted it. Ensi remembered, "My father hated war. He never picked up the Iron Cross when he lived in Germany and didn't want it. But he felt it rude to reject the representative of the consulate."

On January 14, 1942, only six days after his arrest, Eisleroh was taken from his jail cell in Cleveland and appeared before a local board, administered by Edward Ennis, director of the Alien Enemy Control Unit within the Department of Justice. All over the country, thousands of enemy aliens like Eisleroh were summoned before these boards, made up of citizens. All of the proceedings were in secret, and most lasted less than fifteen minutes. None of those arrested were allowed lawyers. They were not informed of the charges against them and had no opportunity to challenge evidence or confront their accusers. The verdict of the alien hearing boards could not be appealed.

At the hearing, Eislerloh was asked if he'd told his neighbors that he objected to his children taking the oath of allegiance to the American flag in their school. "I merely said that I did not think that children of so young an age could understand what the oath of allegiance would mean," he replied.

Most of the case against him came from a fellow employee at work, who was not present at the hearing, but told FBI agents that Eiserloh was pro-Nazi. The anonymous accuser described Eiserloh as "hotheaded" and said he boasted at work that Germany would win the war. "He said that United States armaments would be obsolete by the time they got to the front and that Germany would have new and better armaments," the source told the agents. Confronted with the charge, Eiserloh said that a "good deal of ill feeling" existed between himself and his accuser. He admitted that he might in anger have made inimical comments about the United States but that he had meant no harm. "I am completely loyal to the United States," he told the board. "My children are citizens of the United States. I only want to make a good and decent life for them."

Eiserloh was not asked about the other accusations made to FBI agents by his neighbors in Strongsville, and he never learned of them. They were a part of his FBI file, but he did not know of their existence and could not refute evidence that was never revealed to him. His brother-in-law John Weiland was present at the hearing and spoke on his behalf. Weiland's own loyalty to the United States was not in question. Weiland had fought with the American

Army of Occupation in Germany during World War I. Weiland said that he'd never heard Mathias make an un-American statement and urged the board to parole him. Initially, the board agreed with Weiland and recommended that Eiserloh be paroled and released on a $1,000 bond under the condition that he not be employed by any company that had anything to do with national defense.

But neither Ennis nor Hoover's FBI gave up. Agents filed two more reports against Eiserloh, one on January 23 and another on January 31. After those reports, the board reconsidered, without Eiserloh present, and recommended his internment. On February 11, 1942, Hoover wrote to Ennis, stating that Eiserloh was "pro-Nazi" and should be interned.

The following day, Biddle issued orders from Washington that made Eiserloh an official enemy alien. His official documents were stamped PRISONER OF WAR. Under a provision modeled on the Alien and Sedition Act of 1798, Roosevelt's three proclamations—Number 2525 on December 7, 1941, and Numbers 2526 and 2527—allowed for the arrest and internment of enemy aliens during war. The proclamations stated, "All natives, citizens, denizens or subjects of [Japan, Germany, and Italy], being of the age of fourteen and upward, who shall be in the United States and not actually naturalized, shall be liable to be apprehended, restrained, secured and removed as alien enemies." Eiserloh was an enemy by virtue of his German citizenship, and the FBI viewed him as a security threat. He was not alone. During the war, Roosevelt interned 31,275 enemy aliens: 10,905 Germans, 16,849 Japanese, 3,278 Italians, 52 Hungarians, 5 Bulgarians, 25 Romanians, and 161 more listed as "others."

On March 4, 1942, Eiserloh was transferred to Camp McCoy, Wisconsin, a sixty-thousand-acre Army base, which had been converted to a prisoner-of-war camp. Johanna had received no word from him for two months and did not know that he had been classified as a prisoner of war. After he arrived at Camp McCoy, she received a copy of a letter Mathias had written to Biddle, asking for a rehearing on his case. "I write this to you on behalf of my wife and three little children for whom I have been the sole support," Mathias told Biddle. "My family has been totally deprived of any means of a livelihood and left alone and isolated. I feel not in the slightest degree guilty of ever having done, or having had any thoughts of doing, anything against the interests or safety of the United States."

Johanna wrote to Ennis herself and asked why her husband was at Camp McCoy and on what charges he was being held. "If you believe in justice and fair play to three American children, such as you may have yourself, you will have your men check our circumstances and my husband's case and send him back where he belongs—to his family and to his job, where they will be glad to have him back and where all of us will be an asset, not a liability, to America," Johanna pleaded.

In response, Ennis explained to Johanna her husband's legal status—prisoner of war—and that the order of internment signed by Biddle would not be reheard. "We realize that the internment of your husband, or any other alien enemy, is a hardship on the entire family," wrote Ennis, "but this is not to be considered as important a feature as the protection of the peace and protection of the United States. If we were to consider these hardships in times such as these, the security of our country would be greatly imperiled."

Ennis justified the arrest and internment, without trial, of internees such as Eiserloh by means of a ruthless but necessary cost-benefit analysis. It was America vs. the Axis powers. Mathias and, by extension, Johanna and his three American-born children were collateral damage. What Ennis did not disclose was that domestic security wasn't the only motivation for the incarceration of foreign-born immigrants from Axis countries. Ennis was also charged with gathering a pool of enemy aliens for the Special War Problems Division to use as leverage in negotiations with Berlin and Tokyo for American prisoners of war. Neither Mathias nor Johanna realized it yet, but they were already hostages in the much larger scheme of prisoner exchange.

By the time Ingrid turned twelve in May 1942, Johanna had sold the house in Strongsville and moved with the children to Cleveland to live with Klara and Frank and their children. They settled in the basement of the two-story house.

Unable to make sense of her husband's arrest, Johanna blamed Mathias. "He must have done something to bring all of this down on us," she told Klara.

Ingrid overheard the conversation and confronted her mother. "How can you doubt him?" Ingrid demanded. "We need to stand by him."

Despite her anger, Johanna did stand by Mathias. She continued writing letters to Biddle and Ennis. "I think my husband should be allowed to take his share of responsibility and help raise the children, get us all back to health," she wrote in one letter. She was indignant with the government for incarcerating her husband and resented her husband for abandoning her with the three children.

Summer turned to fall and winter. Ingrid, Lothar, and Ensi despised living in Aunt Klara's basement. Ingrid felt claustrophobic. Nothing seemed to make sense. One night while the family slept, a fire broke out in the basement. The room filled with smoke. The children's coughing woke Johanna. Ingrid picked up Ensi, then two years old, from her crib and followed Johanna and Lothar upstairs. It was the first vivid memory of Ensi's life. "I remember the fire and then I remember being upstairs, and Uncle Frank picked me up and tossed me in the air, perhaps he was being playful. What I remember most was being afraid. It is my first memory of fear."

While his wife and children struggled with the loss of safety in their own home and the difficulty of life in Klara's house, Mathias also grappled with displacement. That winter of 1943 Mathias was incarcerated at an internment camp near Stringtown, Oklahoma, that was operated by the US Army. When Mathias arrived in a group of 110 Germans, J. T. Carroll, a first lieutenant in the Army and the camp commander, read the list of rules to the prisoners. They would live behind bars in cells with no conversing with the guards. In the stockade, surrounded by barbed wire, the internees were not allowed to congregate in large groups. No one was allowed to speak after 9:00 p.m. If inmates violated the rules, they would be placed in solitary confinement. Under certain circumstances, such as attempts to escape, Carroll told them, "Internees will be shot."

The atmosphere was bleak, and Mathias suffered his first bout of what internees during World War II called "the fence sickness" or, in German, *Gitterkrankheit*. After a time of living behind barbed wire and under heavy guard, many inmates, including Mathias, became depressed. As prisoners of war, they had lost control over the major and minor details of their lives. Camp commanders and guards controlled when they went to sleep, when they woke up, what they did for work, and when they showed their faces for the daily count. Every inmate was regularly graded on his or her behavior. Reports were sent to Ennis at the INS. The report on Mathias at Stringtown gave him favorable ratings on his "general attitude" and his physical condition. Yet he walked around in a daze and was described as "despondent."

During Mathias's internment, Stringtown held about 530 German internees. Most prisoners were like Eiserloh—immigrants who had hoped to become US citizens. In his book *Nazis and Good Neighbors*, the historian Max Paul Friedman wrote that when camp officials refused to allow 531 German internees to salute the Heil Hitler, 15 of that number defied the order. Friedman estimated that about 3 percent of the internees were vocal Nazis, most of them from Latin America. Their German spokesman, Ingo Kalinowsky, was one of the earliest members of the Nazi Party in Costa Rica. In Stringtown, Kalinowsky used his position to hoard Red Cross packages from Germany and distribute them to fellow Nazis.

Friedman reported that eighteen of the internees in Stringtown were German Jews who had fled persecution in Nazi Germany and moved to Latin America, where some were inadvertently seized in the roundup of enemy aliens. Others were arrested because they refused to supply information on suspected Nazis in Latin America to American military officers stationed there. Upon their arrival in Stringtown, the eighteen Jewish refugees were confined to a room in a basement of one of the buildings in camp, apparently in a misguided effort to protect them from Nazi prisoners. The irony of German Jews having to be protected from German Nazis in an American internment camp was not lost on the Jews at Stringtown. A few offered testimony to their experience. Wilhelm Heinemann, arrested in Panama, described the particularly tense atmosphere among Jews in Stringtown: "We were told by a certain rabid element that the Jews would be exterminated." Heinemann said that he and others suffered "extreme mental anguish" that they might be traded for American prisoners of war and sent to death camps in Germany.

Inevitably, the Kafkaesque clash between the Nazis and the Jews had an unsettling effect on other prisoners in the camp, including Mathias. According to his conduct report, Mathias stayed neutral in clashes between different groups. He continued to profess his loyalty to the United States. As months passed, to steady his nerves and pass the time, he made wooden toys for Ingrid, Lothar, and Ensi. He imagined designs for future bridges and drew them in a notebook. He continued to press the government for a rehearing of his case.

On April 8, 1943, Mathias wrote to Ennis again, asking why he had not been granted a rehearing. He did not know that internees had no right to appeal. "If possible," Mathias pleaded, "will you please explain to me the basic facts for my detention so I will be able to defend myself, as I am not aware that I ever in my life have been disloyal to the United States?" This was the riddle that faced the internees. Mathias did not know what his neighbors and coworkers had told the FBI and could not defend himself. It drove him deeper into darkness. "Will you please advise me how I can prove my loyalty to this country? Isn't my hard work enough?"

Ennis answered that there was nothing Mathias could do to prove his loyalty. "It is not the policy of this Department to disclose the evidence by which an alien enemy was interned," replied Ennis on

April 17, 1943. "An individual need not have been guilty of subversive activities to warrant his internment if all the facts appear that he may be potentially dangerous to the internal security of our country during the war period."

Mathias lost his will. He had heard from fellow prisoners that in one camp families of prisoners of war could be reunited in exchange for agreeing to repatriate to Germany. It was a difficult choice. He would be offering not only himself and his wife but also his three American-born children as ransom for American soldiers and civilians in Germany. He would be relinquishing his commitment to making a life for all of them in America. Who knew what the conditions would be inside Germany? The Nazis were likely to view the Eiserloh family as enemy Americans, while the Americans already saw them as German enemies. He worried about Johanna's health and knew he had no way to provide for his family. He questioned his own mental stamina. The fence sickness worsened. "By the law of all humanity and the sake of my family," he asked Ennis, "please have my wife and children sent into a family camp to be interned together with me at the earliest possible date." That camp was located in Crystal City, Texas.

CHAPTER FIVE

A Family Reunion

July 8, 1943

From her hard seat, thirteen-year-old Ingrid Eiserloh stared out the window as the Missouri-Pacific Railroad Company train pulled out of the station in Cleveland, Ohio. It was early morning, just past dawn. As the train snaked slowly along Lake Erie, Ingrid watched the morning sun fall along the water's edge. She wore a cotton pinafore, a white cotton shirt, and a pair of scuffed Mary Jane shoes. Pinned to her collar was a family identification card. She closed her eyes and listened to the rocking of the train. Ingrid had last seen her father, Mathias, eighteen months before. Another two days, she told herself, and then she'd see him again. Only two more days.

She and her mother, Johanna, seven-year-old brother Lothar, and two-year-old sister Ensi, were confined with several other German mothers and their American-born children in a special passenger car bound for Texas, where they would be reunited with their husbands and fathers. In the car the guards, plainclothes agents of the Immigration and Naturalization Service, with long-barreled rifles and handguns on their hips, walked the aisle. They called out the family names of the passengers in the car: Eiserlohs, Gerrigans, Rotterings. One by one, the mothers, including Johanna, acknowledged they were on board.

Lothar's eyes followed the rifles. Ingrid tried to distract him with a game of cards. But Lothar's gaze remained fixed on the guards and their weapons. Finally, Ingrid picked up Ensi in her arms and said to Lothar, "Let's go to the dining car."

During the long months of her husband's internment, Johanna had petitioned the government many times, pleading with officials to tell her when or if Mathias would be released. Her questions went unanswered. She now believed that Mathias would be imprisoned until the end of the war, whenever that would be. Each passing month her children, especially Ingrid, missed their father more.

Finally Johanna asked the Department of Justice to allow the family to be reunited with Mathias in the family camp in Crystal City, what the Justice Department described as "voluntary internment." As an enemy alien, Mathias's official status was "involuntary." Johanna understood that although she and her American-born children would enter the camp in Crystal City of their own free will, they would not be free to leave at will. Once inside the barbed-wire fence, they, too, would be prisoners, living under constant surveillance by armed guards. All of their mail would be censored, and even Lothar's comic books would be inspected for coded messages. They would be subject to daily inspections. Still, Johanna felt she had no other choice, no other way to sustain herself and her children. It was better for the family to be together in a prison camp than separated.

Prior to the trip, Eleanor Neff, a social worker in Cleveland's public relief agency, argued in memorandums to her supervisors that Johanna was not physically or emotionally strong enough to manage the rigors of the trip with the three children. Johanna now weighed less than a hundred pounds and was partially paralyzed on the left side due to the injuries she'd suffered when the intruder broke into her home. The months of living with her children in her sister-in-law's basement had taken their toll.

In a report, Mrs. Neff requested that the INS pay for a female social worker to accompany the Eiserlohs on the trip, noting, "It is our observation that Ensi, her baby, is an active toddler who will require a lot of attention. Lothar, although he is a manly chap, is a normal boy with natural curiosity and probably will demand a lot of attention. Ingrid is a capable girl of thirteen but the responsibility of assisting the mother and caring for these two active children would be too great for her."

On the summer day that Johanna and her children boarded the train, Allied strategy had become more effective. Seven months before, fifty American bombers made the first US strikes against Germany, and in February 1943, the Soviets freed Stalingrad. In the Pacific, the Japanese had lost major sea battles to the Americans. In July 1943, as Johanna and her children made their way to Crystal City, the Germans tried to seize the initiative in the Soviet Union in a major battle near Kursk, but were crushed by Soviets with 75 divisions and 3,600 T-34 tanks. After the loss of the battle of Kursk, which involved more than 2 million men, the Germans could not stop the Red Army's drive to Berlin. On the home front, the shock of Pearl Harbor had been replaced by the relief of the country unified in service to winning the war. The fervor of that cause intensified distrust of German and Japanese immigrants and their American-born children.

From her desk in Cleveland's public relief office, amid the larger setting of the war abroad, Mrs. Neff turned to a logistical problem close at hand, the transport to Crystal City of Johanna and the three children. The dilemma Mrs. Neff faced was of the same sort that Harrison, O'Rourke, the many guards, teachers, doctors, and various other staff who worked at Crystal City from 1942 to 1948 faced: how to serve America's security needs while protecting the humanity of innocent wives, children, and in many cases wrongly accused fathers who would nonetheless be indefinitely incarcerated behind barbed wire. Often, as in this slight matter, protection proved impossible. Mrs. Neff's request that a social worker be allowed to accompany the family was denied. The responsibility for managing Lothar and Ensi fell to Ingrid.

In the dining car, Ingrid, Lothar, and Ensi ate lunch with other German American children and their mothers, all bound for Crystal City. Like Ingrid, everyone else in the dining car wore a family identification card around his or her neck. Under the vigilant eyes of two INS guards, the Eiserloh children ate sandwiches and drank tumblers of milk. Lothar played a game of tiddledywinks with a group of young boys, substituting coasters for chips.

When the siblings returned to the passenger car, Ingrid settled by the window and watched small towns in Ohio and then Kentucky whiz by. The train slowed only when it crossed over wooden trestles. Ingrid was aware that what was happening to her and to her family was unusual. She was on her way to see her father, and the price of reunion was the loss of her own freedom. She paid it gladly.

Ingrid remembered that after war was declared, she wrote two letters in her neat cursive style, letters that she never mailed. One of the letters was to President Roosevelt and the other to Hitler. She asked both men to negotiate their differences so that war could be averted. On the day she wrote them, she slipped both of them into the base of the largest of five trunks built of pressed plywood and forgot about them. Now those trunks carried her family's belongings to Crystal City. Oh, well, she thought to herself, it was too late to send them.

That night, Johanna joined the children in the dining car for dinner. For the first time in many months, it felt as if they were again a family. Even though Mathias wasn't with them, they were traveling to meet him. Ingrid was relieved that her mother looked content, maybe even happy.

On the second day, the train crossed the border into Texas, a word that sounded like heaven to Ingrid. In Texas she would at last see her father. She assumed that she would soon arrive in Crystal City. Instead, the hours passed slowly and the train kept moving. How big could this state be? Texas sprawled over 268,820 square miles and was almost twice as large as Germany or Japan. From her seat, mile after mile flashed by under a vast sky. She tried to picture Crystal City as a kind of true version of the Emerald City as described in *The Wizard of Oz*, magic and shimmering, a place of miraculous reunion. Instead, Crystal City was one of those incomprehensible phrases from the war—*internment camp*, *voluntary internment*, and *family identification card*—that had to be lived through to be understood.

In the peak of summer, Texas was bone-dry and sparse of vegetation. The temperature was over a hundred degrees, thirty degrees warmer than Cleveland when Ingrid had left. The air inside the train was stuffy, and Ingrid's clothes were drenched with sweat and her mouth was dry.

When the train pulled over to a sidetrack to let another train pass, Ingrid received permission from a guard to go to the caboose and get some fresh air. From the caboose, she saw a field filled with striped watermelons. The train stood still in the too-bright light.

"Oh, what a temptation!" she told a guard who stood near her.

"Do you like watermelons?" he asked.

"You can have my arm, but please get me a watermelon."

The guard hopped off the train, picked a watermelon, and brought it back to Ingrid. "Now we are going to feast," he said, taking a pocketknife from his pants pocket. He cut a wedge for her, and she took the piece with her fingers. The guard cut a chunk for himself, and slice by slice they devoured the watermelon. She had often shared this kind of moment with her father. She closed her eyes and remembered details of Mathias's face—his blue eyes, electric to Ingrid, the determined line of his mouth, the lines that creased his forehead. Soon, she told herself, everything would be all right.

As Johanna and the children made their way to Crystal City by rail, Mathias waited behind barbed wire at the nearby Kenedy Alien Detention Center, the all-male camp more than one hundred miles from Crystal City. The camp at Kenedy was at its peak of operation. More than 2,000 aliens, some arrested in the United States and others in Latin America, had passed in and out of its gates: 1,168 German, 705 Japanese, 72 Italians, and 62 men from Romania, Hungary, Bulgaria, Russia, and Sweden.

Turnover at Kenedy was frequent because, like Mathias, many of the internees had agreed before their arrival to repatriate to their country of origin in return for being reunited with their families. Mathias's decision to repatriate was comparable to Johanna's decision to "voluntarily" join him behind bars in Crystal City. Though leery of having himself, his wife, and their three children exchanged for American soldiers and civilians behind enemy lines in Germany, Mathias knew that if he did not agree to repatriate, he would likely not be reunited with his family in Crystal City. He saw no other way to keep his family together.

Johanna had also filed a petition for repatriation, and a letter attached to it provided insight into her perspective: "I am not in favor of Hitler or Nazism. I was a democrat like my father. I consider myself a full-fledged American. I really don't consider myself a German. I have applied for repatriation because I want to get my husband out of camp. I can't go on this way."

Mathias was not the only German prisoner of war in Kenedy eager to reunite with his family in Crystal City. Shortly after he arrived, a group of Germans from Latin America were put on a first-preference list to be transferred to Crystal City. Mathias and eleven other Germans, desperate to join their families, felt a sense of agency, despite the dire circumstances at the Kenedy camp. In a letter to Ennis, director of the Alien Enemy Control Unit of the Department of Justice, they wrote in protest of what they viewed as preferential treatment of the Germans from Latin America: "We beg you instantly to give our cases first and speedy preference and notify us definitely when this misery of our beloved ones will find an end."

Two weeks later, Harrison, the commissioner of the INS, filed an official change-of-status report for Eiserloh with Ennis. As of July 10, 1943, Harrison wrote, Eiserloh's status changed from internment as a prisoner of war at Kenedy to internment at Crystal City.

The reunion took place shortly after 1:00 p.m. on Saturday, July 10, 1943. Mathias and six other German men left the camp in Kenedy before dawn, boarding an olive-green Army bus, accompanied by armed guards, and traveled the sixty miles to San Antonio. Given the small number of mothers and children to be transported to Crystal City, and the difficulty of making transfers from San Antonio directly to Crystal City, O'Rourke arranged for the families to meet first in San Antonio.

Before the train from Cleveland pulled into the station on North Medina Street, west of downtown San Antonio, the INS guards ordered the shades pulled down on the windows in the passenger car that carried Ingrid and her family. San Antonio was a military town with six active Army and Air Force bases. During World War II, American troops stood shoulder to shoulder in the busy train station, a venerable old building with ornate stained-glass windows and a shiny copper-domed roof. A statue of an Indian, also copper, atop the roof was a well-known landmark in the city. O'Rourke's orders were to transport the wives and children as quickly and discreetly as possible. Anti-German sentiment was widespread. In train stations around the country, internees in transit had been heckled.

When the train came to a stop, Ingrid picked up Ensi, and Johanna held Lothar's hand. Johanna climbed down the metal steps of the train one by one into the blazing heat. No shade was in sight. With Ingrid trailing behind, she followed the guards to a large parking lot, where the Army bus was parked.

One by one, seven men, one of them Mathias, stepped off the bus. Ingrid ran to him, arms wide open and feet flying; Lothar was right behind her, followed by Johanna, who carried Ensi. Ingrid thought her father looked strained and tired and he was thinner, but he stood square-shouldered and smiled at her. "He's alive!" Ingrid told her mother. "Gee, he looks good." Johanna and all three children encircled him, and Ingrid cried when her father hugged her.

The wives and children boarded the Army bus with the men. Ingrid noticed a farmers' market on the edge of downtown San Antonio and, beyond it, the city's modest skyline. Mathias looked at Johanna and the children as if he could not believe his eyes. Ensi had been a baby in a crib when he left Strongsville; now she walked on her own two feet. Lothar was much taller, Ingrid looked like a teenager, and Johanna was thinner than he'd ever seen her. At first, conversation was awkward, but as the miles passed, they settled into being together again. Within an hour's time, everyone was talking at once—in English and in German.

In late afternoon the bus finally arrived in Crystal City, and the small town was such a contrast to Cleveland and San Antonio. Ingrid saw a wood-plank sidewalk in front of a hardware store and a small building labeled City Hall. In front of it she saw the iconic statue of Popeye. Men walked the street in cowboy boots and wore ten-gallon cowboy hats. Signs were in English and Spanish: bar and *cantina*, store and *tienda*. To Ingrid, Crystal City didn't seem like a real town at all but a western-movie set.

At the entrance of the camp, inside the barbed-wire fence, an American flag flew. "I remember looking up at the guard towers and seeing the men holding machine guns," Lothar later recalled. "It was all so confusing."

Ingrid saw a group of Germans and their children lined up inside to greet the new arrivals. Three hundred and seventy-five Germans lived in the camp, and 145 Japanese. A full German orchestra, complete with strings, trumpets, trombones, and drums, played Beethoven and Brahms, Ingrid's first time hearing live German music since her father's arrest.

Inside the gate, the bus traveled a few feet on Airport Drive, a paved road, and stopped in front of a community hall. The German School was adjacent to the hall, and on the other side of Airport Drive Ingrid saw warehouses and other buildings. Beyond them stood a row of neat wooden shacks, some surrounded by flowerbeds planted by the internees. She and the others filed slowly down the steps of the bus, sapped by the heat. O'Rourke walked over from a building near the community hall and made a brief speech to welcome the people to the camp. His voice was friendly but firm. He explained that over the next few days they would learn the rules and procedures of the camp. For now, he said, the important thing was to settle in. Unlike regular Border Patrol guards, who wore long-sleeved khaki shirts, pants, ties, and tan-colored Stetson hats, O'Rourke wore a lightweight, tan-colored suit.

"Is he the big cheese?" Ingrid remembered asking her father.

"Yes," Mathias replied. "He's the boss here."

The Eiserloh family was taken to temporary barracks with communal toilets and showers. Clothing—pajamas, socks, underwear, and a change of clothing for the next day—had been provided by workers from the commissary. Ingrid looked out the window of her barracks and saw a general store, a blacksmith, a laundry, and a bakery. Near the fence was a grove of orange trees. Ingrid and all the other children were taken to the camp hospital, where Dr. Symmes F. Oliver, a fifty-year-old career clinician who wore a stiff white coat, explained the hazards of daily life in the camp. Oliver wasn't in the best of health himself, due to bouts of depression and alcoholism. The job as medical director of Crystal City, funded by the Public Health Service, had been a godsend to him. He suggested the children stay indoors during the hottest part of the day, and when they were outside, he warned them to watch for rattlesnakes, scorpions, black widow spiders, tarantulas, and even mountain lions. A few months before, Oliver explained, 131 German nationals had arrived from Costa Rica, 55 of them with whooping cough. He supervised a quarantine of the whole group, and he did not want to repeat the health crisis. Ingrid and the others rolled up their sleeves and took the vaccine shot not only for whooping cough, but also for diphtheria and tetanus.

Later that evening, in the temporary barracks, Ingrid hurried into her new pajamas. All of the Eiserlohs were in the same room—their cots lined up with one another. As Ingrid shone a flashlight on the wall, scorpions scuttled over the beams. In Ohio, she'd never heard of a scorpion, but that night in Crystal City she saw the first of many. She fell asleep on a narrow cot lined up against the wall, content to be under the same roof with her family.

CHAPTER SIX

The Hot Summer of '43

When the Eiserloh family arrived at Crystal City in July 1943, an angry gloom hung over the camp. In the German section where they lived, Germans hostile to the United States had been elected the camp's representatives and had complete control. Only three months before, on April 21—the day after Hitler's birthday—a group of Germans identified by the FBI as loyal to Hitler gathered in the recreation hall and took down the American flag. In its place, they hoisted Germany's red, black, and white flag with the swastika in the center.

A phalanx of American guards on regular patrol, each carrying a rifle, soon arrived. The sight of the Nazi flag, repugnant to them, sparked outrage. With the butts of their rifles, the guards snatched the flag off the wall and tore it to shreds. When pieces of it fell to the floor, the German prisoners glowered and planned revenge. A few days later, a squad of Germans slipped out of their dwellings in the middle of the night and cut down the American flag flying from a pole inside the camp. The culprits were never identified, and thus began a long-running flag war.

"We believe that the flag of the Detaining Power does not belong inside of an enemy alien internment camp," wrote five German nationals in a complaint to camp officials and to the government of Switzerland, the designated protecting power for Germans interned in the United States. Copies of the complaint were also sent to the International Red Cross. In their letter, the German leaders requested that the two American flags in camp—the one in the recreation hall and the other in an open area in the middle of the camp—be removed.

In response, Harrison, who held authority as the commissioner of the INS, compromised. He agreed to remove the American flag in the recreation hall, and the one that flew over the camp was moved mere inches, to a pole outside the fence so that the flag, objectionable to internees, was not flown inside the internment camp. The solution was an indication of other battles to come: with the German leaders in camp, peace was measured in inches. The irony of the situation was that Crystal City had been conceived of as a camp primarily for Japanese enemy aliens and their families, but the first internees were German nationals and German Americans. Their leaders were proving difficult to manage.

The mechanism in place for the day-to-day running of the camp simply did not work on the German side. In line with the Geneva Convention, O'Rourke dealt with complaints from internees through elected spokesmen. He gave internees self-rule based on democratic elections of separate spokesmen for Japanese and German internees.

The Japanese embraced the plan with enthusiasm. They held elections every six months and set up a vast network of elected internee councilmen and assistants. The only undemocratic aspect of the Japanese approach was that neither Japanese women nor their sons were allowed to vote in the elections. The Japanese fathers, issei long humiliated by their incarceration, insisted on exercising control.

The Germans balked at democratic elections. Even compliant prisoners such as Mathias Eiserloh had come of age in Germany during World War I and lived under the tyranny of one *Führer*, or leader, after another. They had no model for self-government. Unlike the Japanese internees, who experienced a protracted history of racial discrimination in America and were more amenable in Crystal City, the Germans had a long tenure as immigrants and by then were the largest ethnic group in America. Behind barbed wire in Crystal City, the Germans became bitter, angry, and vulnerable to misguided leadership.

At the time of the flag incident, the elected spokesman for the Germans, and one of the signers of the complaint, was a tall, commanding figure named Karl Kolb. When the United States had declared war against Germany, Kolb and his family lived in New York City, where he was an executive for Zeiss Ikon, a German camera company. He was arrested almost immediately and interned at Ellis Island. In the summer of 1943, Kolb, his wife, and their seven-year-old daughter were reunited in Crystal City.

Upon arrival, Kolb quickly seized power. After his election as spokesman for the Germans, Kolb demanded that internees not be allowed to talk directly to O'Rourke, insisting that complaints be filed with the council of German internees. As commander of the camp, O'Rourke assigned jobs to both German and Japanese internees, but Kolb wanted that power himself. In an effort to compromise, O'Rourke gave it to him. Kolb took charge of the distribution of jobs and organized strikes among German workers.

During a formal inquiry held in response to the April 1943 flag incident, Kolb played cat and mouse with his interrogators. "Am I being questioned as the spokesman of the German internees or an ordinary internee?" demanded Kolb. "How can I speak as the spokesman when there is an ordinary internee inside that person?" Near the end of the hearing, he was pronounced "uncooperative" and "a capable agitator" and confined to his quarters for a day.

By summer, the tensions in the German section had escalated. Secret distilleries sprang up. Organized bands of agitators roamed the camp, many of them brandishing clubs. When one of the distilleries blew up, the explanation given to O'Rourke by Kolb was that the Germans were making marmalade. Most German immigrants in the camp complied with the rules, but the small group of troublemakers held sway. "It was scary to see grown men walking around that camp with arms raised, giving each other the Heil Hitler salute," recalled Ingrid years later.

In June 1943, Fritz Kuhn, the former leader of the German American Bund, arrived as a prisoner of war in Crystal City. Kuhn was no longer wearing the military uniform of a German army officer, which he had worn seven years before when he paraded with storm troopers before Adolf Hitler, but by now the forty-seven-year-old Kuhn no longer needed a uniform to convey his self-styled importance. He was the most infamous American Nazi in the world.

When Kuhn arrived at Crystal City, the German contingent numbered about 400 people, most of them German-immigrant fathers and mothers, and American-born children. The group also included 230 Germans from Latin America, deported from Bolivia and Peru. The Jacobis, who were German Jews, were one such family from Latin America. Arthur Jacobi, his wife, his two daughters, aged four and fourteen, and his five-year-old son had been transferred to Crystal City from a refugee camp in Algiers, Louisiana. Evelyn Hersey, assistant to Harrison in Philadelphia, handled the delicate arrangements for the Jacobi transfer. The camp in Algiers had a small cluster of Jewish families. Though Jewish by birth, Jacobi had converted to Christianity and was vocal about his religious views, which offended the other Jewish families. He requested a transfer, and the Jacobi family joined the improbable stream of foreigners into Crystal City on April 11, 1943, two months before Kuhn's arrival.

None of the German internees in Crystal City were aware that the success of the Soviet Union's army would help turn the tide of the war. From 1941 to 1944, 95 percent of German casualties were inflicted by the Soviets on the Eastern Front. News was strictly censored. Nor did they know that at the Special War Problems Division negotiations were under way for a prisoner exchange. In return for Americans held by the Third Reich, some of the higher-value internees from Crystal City would voluntarily be repatriated to Germany. Others would go against their will.

To the German government, Kuhn, a well-known figure in Germany with proven organizational ability and propaganda value, was near the top of the list of internees they wanted in trade. Therefore,

Kuhn's arrival at Crystal City added to the complicated political matrix in the German section. In effect, he was a man without a country. Kuhn was born in Munich, Germany, on May 15, 1896. His father was a wealthy businessman in Munich. For the duration of World War I—from 1914 to 1918—Kuhn served on the front lines of the German army as an infantry officer, earning an Iron Cross for his valor.

Despite Kuhn's status as a war hero, his family, according to his FBI file, considered him the black sheep of the family. After the war, he enrolled at the Technical University of Munich to study chemistry. While there, he was caught stealing coats from fellow students. He was arrested, charged, and convicted, subsequently spending four months in jail. After his release, he continued his studies and completed a master's degree in chemical engineering. However, his criminal record made it difficult for him to find employment. His father eventually persuaded a friend who owned a merchandise company in Munich to give Kuhn a job. Within eight weeks, Kuhn had stolen several thousand marks' worth of goods from his employer. His father's friend agreed not to file charges against Kuhn on one condition: he had to leave Germany. In 1924 Kuhn and his wife, Elsa, fled to Mexico, where both of their children were born.

In 1931, the family moved to Dearborn, Michigan, where Kuhn worked as a chemist for the Ford Motor Company. He started at a wage of eighty-seven cents per hour. Three years later, he became a naturalized citizen of the United States. A practical man would have savored the assets of his good American life: a steady job, a wife, and two children. But Kuhn craved notoriety and founded the Michigan chapter of the German American Bund. He attended camp rallies, practiced target shooting, and wore the Bund uniform: a white shirt, black trousers, and a black hat.

He proved to be a better orator than a chemist. Every year that he worked at Ford, his salary went down. The first year he made $1,461.65; by 1936, when Hitler installed him as president of the Bund in America, Kuhn's salary had dropped to only $745.65 a year. "On occasions while working at Ford Motor Company," notes his FBI file, "Kuhn was laid off for a day or two because he was caught practicing speeches in the dark room."

In July 1936 Kuhn and 250 other Bund members in America sailed on the SS *New York* to attend the Summer Olympics in Berlin. Kuhn's celebrity moment occurred when he passed in review in front of Hitler at the Olympics. After the parade, Kuhn presented Hitler with a "Golden Book" signed by several thousand people from the United States and gave the Führer a check for $2,300.

It's difficult to calculate how significant a threat the pro-Hitler Bund in America was to the US war effort. By the time Kuhn was president in 1936, the vast German American population, who'd lived through World War I, did not want another war with the United States. Kuhn boasted that the Bund had two hundred thousand members under his tenure, but the Department of Justice put the number at eighty-five hundred. Other sources suggest that the membership was seventy thousand. This disparity in the numbers suggests that the FBI and the Department of Justice overestimated the Bund's importance.

Nonetheless, Kuhn was cast as the archvillain in a *March of Time* 1938 newsreel titled "Inside Nazi Germany." In the black-and-white film, Kuhn, dressed in a dark suit, stood in front of a swastika flag in the New York office of the Bund at 172 East Eighty-fifth Street. At the screening of the newsreel, Kuhn watched as images of him as the "Number One Nazi" in America unfurled and heard his heavy German accent booed in the theater. Only then did Kuhn realize he'd been tricked by his own vanity. Walter Winchell, the syndicated newspaper and radio commentator, reported that Kuhn left the theater screaming, "I've been ruint. Ruint!"

What the presidency of the Bund did offer Kuhn was a platform for his con games. After Germany and Russia invaded Poland in 1939, the FBI received a tip that Kuhn had hatched a plan to extort $500,000 from Helena Rubinstein, the fabled New York cosmetics manufacturer. According to the FBI's informant, Kuhn's extortion plan was to send Rubinstein, a Jew who was originally from Poland, a threatening letter decorated with a swastika on the envelope. The informant provided a copy of the letter to the FBI, with Kuhn's demand for $500,000 and the threat that if the money was not paid, then Rubinstein's sister, trapped in Poland, would be exterminated by the Nazis.

Hoover ordered FBI agents to interview Rubinstein at her 300 Park Avenue apartment. Rubinstein was sixty-seven years old and a self-made female multimillionaire. Her lawyer was at her side. No, she told the FBI agents, she hadn't received any extortion letters and hadn't paid any money to anyone. As far as she knew, Rubinstein told the agents, her sister was safe.

After the interview, the FBI agents left the Park Avenue penthouse and marked the Rubinstein matter "closed." Even though Rubinstein had not received the letter, she must have been shaken to learn of Kuhn's plan, suddenly brought into her living room.

In February 1939, Kuhn addressed twenty-five thousand people at a Bund rally at Madison Square Garden in New York City. During the speech, he called President Roosevelt "Frank D. Rosenfeld" and fulminated against the New Deal as the "Jew Deal." Enraged protesters rushed the stage and Kuhn had to be carried off by police officers.

Four months later, Thomas E. Dewey, the district attorney in New York, indicted Kuhn on charges of embezzling more than $14,500 from Bund accounts. Dewey's evidence showed that some of the money was used to move Kuhn's mistress from California to New York. The *New York Daily News* reported that Dewey called Kuhn a "common thief." Mayor La Guardia and Commissioner of Investigation William B. Herlands vowed to pursue more charges against Kuhn. When reporters interviewed Kuhn, who was dressed in a vest and a carefully knotted tie, he laughed off his arrest. Never a shrinking violet, he vowed to fight the charges and took malevolent aim at La Guardia, who was half-Jewish, and Herlands: "I'm not running away from the Jew Herlands and that little Red, La Guardia."

Kuhn was convicted of all charges and sentenced to two and

a half to five years. He served forty-three months. When he was released from Dannemora Prison on June 21, 1943, his American citizenship was revoked and the attorney general's office formally declared him a dangerous enemy alien. He was transferred first to Ellis Island and then to Crystal City.

In Crystal City, the flamboyance of Kuhn's strut and the straightness of his six-foot-tall carriage suggested that he was making an effort to ignite the fire of his former bravado. But exhaustion was in his gray eyes, square jaw, and rounded shoulders. In June 1943, Kuhn was reunited in Crystal City with Elsa and his son, Walter Max, a fifteen-year-old with a pallid expression, both of whom had been arrested as enemy aliens. "While Mrs. Kuhn never shared much in the notoriety her husband attained as Bundesfuehrer and uniformed exponent of the Nazi ideals," reported the *New York Times*, "she has admitted membership in the Friends of New Germany, and attendance at various social functions of the Bund, which succeeded the Friends as the outstanding pro-Nazi organization in this country." According to the same newspaper article, Walter was apprehended because he was active in the Bund's youth movement.

One of Elsa's first acts in Crystal City was to ask O'Rourke if he could help her find news of her daughter, Waltraut, who had returned to Germany from America in 1938 and married a German soldier. No one in the family had heard from her since. O'Rourke made note of Elsa's request in his file, but did not follow through. He had no incentive to help her because, since his arrival, Kuhn had acquired a small group of followers.

Within a few weeks of Kuhn's arrival, O'Rourke had a letter of complaint on his desk from Therese Hohenreiner, one of the internees, claiming that Kuhn was in charge of the German internees at Crystal City and had bullied her. She copied the letter to the FBI agent in charge in San Antonio. The agent, R. C. Suran, wrote to O'Rourke and asked if it was true that Kuhn had "maneuvered himself into a position as unofficial spokesman for the other German internees."

By this time, the population of the camp numbered 523 internees—378 Germans and 145 Japanese. The original idea that the camp would be mainly for Japanese had been abandoned. Given the friction among the Germans, there was safety in not buying trouble. Most of the teenagers, including Ingrid, didn't know what to make of Kuhn.

Eberhard E. Fuhr, commonly known as Eb, was seventeen years old when he and his family arrived in Crystal City in July 1943, one month after the Kuhns were reunited there. Eb's experience was typical of that of the other German teenagers in camp. His parents immigrated to the United States with their two sons, Eb and Julius, in the late 1920s. At the time Germany was embroiled in political and economic conflict, and Eb's father decided to leave to escape communism. As German immigrants, legal residents of the United States but not citizens, the Fuhr family settled in Cincinnati. A third son, Gerhard, was born in August 1942. Both of Eb's parents—Carl, a baker, and Anna, a housewife—had been arrested and interned, along with Gerhard, a citizen of the United States. "Had my brother Gerhard not joined my parents, he would have been sent to an orphanage, a fate shared by other internee children," Eb recalled.

After the arrest of his parents, Eb and Julius were left to fend for themselves. Eb, a senior at Woodward High School and a popular football star, supported himself with an early-morning newspaper route. His older brother, Julius, dropped out of college and went to work in a Cincinnati brewery.

"On March twenty-third, 1943, while I was in class, the principal came in and asked me to step out in the hallway," recalled Eb. "I stepped out and two FBI guys grabbed me." He was escorted to his locker and retrieved his football letter sweater. On the street, the FBI agents placed him in handcuffs, and then drove to the brewery where his brother worked. Julius was arrested and handcuffed as well. "I was just seventeen years old. I never returned to school and did not graduate with my class. In fact my picture was expunged from the yearbook," recalled Eb. "I lost many of my personal belongings that day, but also my dignity."

Eb never understood the motive for his or his brother's arrest. Like their parents, the brothers weren't American citizens. Their father, Carl, had not pursued American citizenship because in the struggle to support his family he had neither the time nor the money to go through naturalization. Eb's mother, Anna, expected to inherit property in Germany from her mother and didn't pursue citizenship either. Their older sons followed their lead. But the FBI files show no complaints about the Fuhr brothers prior to the arrest of their parents. After their arrests, a Lutheran minister expressed concern that the boys needed assistance and supervision. Eb has two theories on why they were arrested: the government wanted to use them to expand the pool of potential repatriates in the family camp in Crystal City, and as a signal to other Germans and German Americans in Cincinnati that they, too, were in danger of internment.

The day after their arrest, Eb and Julius were taken in handcuffs to the Civilian Alien Hearing Board in the Federal Building and faced five people—the same people who'd interned their parents seven months before. Eb was asked a question he found ridiculous: "What would you say to your German cousin if he came to you for sanctuary after coming up the Ohio River in his German U-boat?"

"I'd say that a sub couldn't come up the Ohio River," replied Eb. "It only drafts four feet."

After the hearing, the two brothers were taken to the Cincinnati Workhouse, which served as a jail for errant, poor children and adolescents. Guards placed Eb and Julius in small, separate cells. Each cell had a bucket for a toilet. After the doors clanged shut, other prisoners began yelling, "Nazis! Krauts! Huns!" A few days later, they were transferred to a detention center in Chicago, and then taken to Crystal City on a heavily guarded train filled with other German internees. "I was so happy to be reunited with my parents and younger brother," said Eb. "But the conditions there were harsh. The temperature was well over a hundred degrees, and the camp was crawling with insects and scorpions. Our living space was barely tolerable. The fences were high and there were guards every fifty feet with guns. I was at a loss to understand why I was in prison for the crime of being born to German parents."

Kuhn was still in Crystal City when the Fuhr brothers arrived. Eb, like Ingrid, didn't know what to make of him. Perhaps he was a Nazi, as the government said. Perhaps he wasn't. "Anyone could be called a Nazi based on rumors," Eb recalled. "It's impossible to convey the intense terror I felt that spring and the hopelessness." In Crystal City, Eb and his brother Julius played on a soccer team. Kuhn's son, Walter, played soccer as well, on a team with younger players. Eb remembered him as a shy boy who lived in the shadow of his father.

By the summer of 1943, Kuhn had been knocked off his pedestal of power. For all his pomposity, he was little more than a caricature of his former self. After so many years in the limelight—his face a page-one fixture in New York newspapers—the stark reality of exile in Crystal City must have been a shock. The stillness and silence of the desert would constantly have reminded him that the noisy glare of fame was far behind him.

In his office in Philadelphia, Harrison received reports from O'Rourke about the smoldering unrest in the German section left over from the flag controversy of the previous April. By the summer of 1943, internees in America—as well as in Japan and Europe—were considered valuable assets in the prosecution of the war. Harrison understood that the treatment of German and Japanese enemy aliens and their families in Crystal City would directly affect how Americans were treated in Germany and in Japan. Reports from the State Department documented the suffering and malnourishment that Americans suffered in Axis camps. Often the abuse of Americans was meted out in "reprisal" for reports of mistreatment of Axis prisoners in the United States. If news of the flag controversy was taken out of context in Germany, Harrison understood German reprisals against American internees would be inevitable.

A confidential memo went out from Harrison's office to all INS employees: "It is particularly important that officers and employees fully realize that our work is an important part of our national war effort, and that a grave responsibility rests upon each of us because we constantly make the case for reciprocity in securing equally fair and humane treatment of OUR civil and military personnel held in the custody of enemy nations."

To make that case for reciprocity, in Crystal City, Harrison treated the flag controversy with caution. The guards were not punished for losing their tempers and destroying the German flag. The threat of reprisal was too great. Besides, the guards in Crystal City were not professionally trained Border Patrol agents, as it was difficult to attract career Border Patrol agents or other employees to the isolated Crystal City camp. The closest movie theater or shopping center was 120 miles away in San Antonio.

O'Rourke's task was to build and operate a "humane" camp in a desolate part of America with employees who had little or no training for their positions. Most of those he hired—clerks, secretaries, accountants, security guards—were native to Crystal City and the surrounding area. Life in Crystal City, as in all of Texas, was highly segregated. No "Negroes," as the employment manual referred to African Americans, were hired; the few Mexican Americans employed at the camp were maids and stoop laborers. When Mabel B. Ellis, a social worker from New York, visited Crystal City, she filed a report to Harrison that concluded, "Because of the isolated location of Crystal City, the employees of the internment camp have relatively little more freedom than the internees behind the fence."

But at least the employees were not caged. Employees came and went through the front gates. Guards inspected their cars, a mild nuisance that gradually became routine. For internees, such as Ingrid, the reality of internment was the constant presence of the barbed wire. "The confinement was crushing," Ingrid said. Armed guards manned six guard towers, located on each corner of the camp. An internal security force patrolled both Japanese and German sections of the camp. The surveillance was constant. Mostly, Ingrid remembered how unimaginably hot it was that summer. At midday, temperatures regularly reached 115 degrees. She wondered how long she and her family would be there. The phrase that came to her was *for the duration*. Time felt suspended.

Daily life in Crystal City was highly regimented. Every morning the American flag was raised in ceremony, outside the fence. As the camp awakened, sleepy night guards relinquished their posts to daytime guards. Censors fluent in German and Japanese read the incoming mail of internees and cut out portions that related in any way to the war effort. Internees were allowed to write only two letters and one postcard per week, which were censored. Officials kept dossiers on each internee, and a small police force patrolled the camp. At the front gate, vehicles of visitors were searched, both upon entry and exit.

The roll calls seemed endless. Three times a day a whistle blew and all had to run back to their cottages and huts, form lines, show their faces, and stand still for the count in the presence of armed guards. Prisoners met visitors—friends or relatives—in a hut where surveillance officers stood watch. As for escape, everyone knew the penalty was death, and in the camp's history—from December 12, 1942, until February 27, 1948—no one ever risked it.

As a productive distraction, O'Rourke had a large reservoir converted into a swimming pool that would provide irrigation water for the camp farm, as well as for the flowers and gardens that had sprung up in both the Japanese and German quadrants. According to camp records, Italian internee Elmo Zannoi, a civil engineer and one of six Italians in camp, designed the pool. German internee Hans Zerbe surveyed the site.

However, Johanna told her children that Mathias, also a civil engineer, designed the pool. "In fact," recalled Ensi, "she told us the pool was his idea." Mathias must have helped with the design, because he spent much of the summer and fall at work on the pool.

Ingrid, then thirteen, and seven-year-old Lothar positioned themselves near the reservoir at the back of the camp, directly opposite the front gate, and followed the progress of the work from the water's edge.

The first step was to dredge the existing reservoir. Lavender-colored water hyacinths choked the reservoir with their long, spongy stalks. The Germans provided most of the slow, difficult labor, using shovels and wheelbarrows to remove the mud.

One afternoon, Ingrid and Lothar watched as teams of workers brought two fifty-five-gallon drums to the banks. Armed with long-handled sticks with hooks on the ends, the men waded into the muddy water and fished out snakes, many of them deadly water moccasins. The grotesque sight of the fat bodies of the snakes writhing in the air terrified Ingrid. She and Lothar watched rapt as the men dropped the snakes into the large drums. After the job was done, the men took out hunting knives, split the snakes, gathered the skins, and spread them in the hot sun to dry. Later, the men made belts out of these skins.

It took six months to complete the pool, a gleaming, giant oval 250 feet in diameter with a shallow end for young children. After concrete was poured into the space, the pool was filled with clean water, the water dark at the deep end. The internees had created an oasis in the drought-ridden landscape. If Egypt had the Nile, Crystal City had the swimming pool—something concrete, literally and metaphorically, that made life more bearable.

For Ingrid, the swimming pool presented an emotional conflict. The long hours she spent there, watching over Lothar and Ensi, were a glorious respite from the heat. Yet she remembered that Mathias had always planned to build a swimming pool on the top of the homestead in Strongsville. To him, a swimming pool was a symbol of American acceptance and affluence. But the pool he helped build for Crystal City was altogether different: a symbol of internment, as palpable as the flag.

The Eiserlohs lived in C Section, off Eleventh Avenue, near the

German bakery. Every morning they awoke to the smell of freshly made dark German bread. Because of Johanna's fragile medical condition, they were assigned a coveted five-hundred-square-foot bungalow with an inside toilet, a kitchen, and one bedroom, the best living quarters available in camp. Others lived in duplexes, triplexes, and tar-papered Quonset and Victory Huts with communal toilets and showers. All of the quarters had heaters, kerosene ranges, portable ovens, and square-shaped iceboxes.

At only a hundred pounds, Johanna was as thin as a fragile bird. Her limbs were stalky. Sometimes she had dizzy spells. When she took a step, Ingrid watched to see if she would fall. But in the evenings, she pinned her auburn hair to the top of her head, put on an apron, and fixed her attention on the task ahead: preparing the family meal. Before the war, Johanna had been loquacious and efficient. Over the weeks and months in Crystal City, evenings found her in her small kitchen with her husband and children around her, Johanna became that way again. She washed fresh vegetables, baked chicken and roasts in the tiny stove, and poured her children tall glasses of milk. (Every morning teams of internees delivered twenty-five hundred quarts of fresh milk from the cows on the farm to the children in camp. Blocks of ice were delivered daily as well.) This was the pact Johanna had made with the American government: in return for life behind barbed wire, she had the pleasure of her family all gathered at the same table.

Sometimes the Eiserlohs ate at the Café Vaterland, a restaurant and beer garden staffed by internees, many of them professional chefs and bakers. After dinner, Johanna and Mathias would linger at the table with other German couples. When the sun went down and the temperatures cooled, many couples walked with their children around the perimeter of the fence. The sweet smell of oranges and lemons from the camp orchards filled the air. "We felt safe on those walks," recalled Ingrid. "It was the happiest time of the day."

Provisions of the Third Geneva Convention governed the treatment of internees. Every aspect of daily life—the amount of food, allotted living space, payment for work—was prescribed by the convention rules, which were monitored by the International Red Cross. As a result, no one went hungry in Crystal City. Though most internees ate at home with their families, there was a mess hall as well. An average menu for a single day—breakfast: stewed prunes, bran flakes, toast with oleo (a colloquial term for margarine) and syrup, coffee/milk; lunch: beef stew, potatoes, cabbage, bread with oleo and syrup again; and dinner: spaghetti, string beans, cooked carrots, pickled beets, and, again, bread with oleo and syrup. Breakfast was served at 7:30 a.m., lunch at 11:00 a.m., and supper at 6:00 p.m. sharp.

Many of the employees, including the bachelor O'Rourke, ate regularly at the mess hall. The price was right: for $6.67 per month, employees could eat one meal a day. Many of the employees, whose civilian ration cards did not permit them to eat large quantities of meat, sugar, and coffee, complained that internees in the camp enjoyed a better life inside the fence than they had outside it. "Selling these employees on the internment program was an obstacle in itself," wrote O'Rourke, who recorded that he felt "squeezed" between the demands of internees and those of the employees, who believed that "anything received by the internees was too good and too much."

For food, clothing, and other necessities, the internees were issued camp tokens made of pressed paper or plastic and quarter-shaped, like casino chips. Children from six to thirteen, such as Lothar and Ingrid, received $4 in chips a month, two- to five-year-olds such as Ensi received $1.25, and adults received $5.25 a month. Internees were allowed to work only eight hours a day, at ten cents an hour, thus making no more than eighty cents a day.

The camp had two stores, one for the Germans and the other for the Japanese. Each supplied thousands of items, including soap, shoestrings, boxes of buttons, yards of gingham, candy, soft drinks, peanut butter, spaghetti sauce, beer for the Germans, and sake for the Japanese. Mathias was never out of cigarettes, with the German store carrying three popular American brands: Lucky Strike,

Philip Morris, and Chesterfield. From morning till night, internees piled goods into handmade wooden carts and took them home. Both stores were well managed, and by the end of 1943, O'Rourke reported the combined gross sales of the stores was an impressive $200,000.

The heavy summer dragged on. At twilight, an immense chorus of cawing crows and shrill cicadas filled the air. Wild cats fed on baby birds that fell from nests. One day Lothar saw a newborn crow fall from its nest and ran to save it from the cats. He built a cage for the crow out of an orange crate and fed it droplets of milk. To further protect the bird, Mathias constructed a closed-in porch for the barrack. After that, Ingrid, Lothar, and the baby bird slept on the porch.

The struggle to protect the baby crow reflected the psychological impact of internment. Mangione, the writer who worked for the INS, often received letters from internees. In one letter, an internee described her efforts to save and rescue a bird. "No living thing should be locked up," said the letter writer. "When I am free, I want to live in a house without locks, even without doors. It will be a house made up of windows and the view must not be obstructed by anything, not even mountains."

In August, Johanna and Mathias had a scare. The driver of a sprinkler truck pulled up in front of their house to water a section of the road. Looking out of his rearview mirror to back up the truck, the driver saw a small group of young children running behind his vehicle to stand under the sprinkler, as if enjoying a waterfall. The driver yelled at the children to move, but two-year-old Ensi, her blond hair bleached white by the sun, among them, did not hear the warning. The driver backed up and Ensi fell to the ground. When the driver stopped the truck, he heard Ensi crying and found her curled underneath the truck, hands over her tiny ears. Fortunately, the wheels had missed her. The driver rushed her to the camp hospital, where she was treated and released.

CHAPTER SEVEN

"Be Patient"

One of Earl Harrison's good intentions was to recognize the INS's obligation to offer an American education to the children confined in the Crystal City camp, the majority of whom had been born in America. Three types of schools were established in the internment camp: the American School, called the Federal School, the Japanese School, and the German School. Each provided an elementary, junior high, and high school education. The assumption was that most students would attend the Federal School, which offered an American-style education and was fully accredited by the Texas State Board of Education. State-certified teachers were hired for the Federal School, and classes were taught in English. In the Japanese and German schools, internees taught students in their native languages. The German leaders who had instigated the flag controversy also pressed German parents to register their children in the German School. Most parents complied.

All through the summer of 1943, Mathias and Johanna, Ingrid's parents, had debated the issue. Johanna preferred that Ingrid and Lothar be enrolled in the Federal School for an American education. After all, they were born in America, as was their younger sister, Ensi. But Mathias pressed for the German School. In return for having their family reunited in Crystal City, Mathias and Johanna had agreed to repatriate to Germany. Neither Ingrid nor Lothar was fluent in German, and Lothar could barely speak it at all. As a practical matter, they both needed to learn the language and the culture of Germany. Mathias had the strongest argument, but now Johanna was reluctant to repatriate, even though she had agreed to it and signed the repatriation document.

The conflict between Mathias and Johanna was indicative of what happened in Crystal City during the summer of 1943 and well into 1944. Some Germans and Japanese would remain in the camp and adapt to the tiny civilization, run by O'Rourke, while others would either be shipped off against their will or, like the Eiserlohs, be readied for voluntary repatriation in exchange for American soldiers and civilians in Europe and Japan. One practical function of the German and Japanese schools was to prepare the children of enemy aliens as trade bait.

Mathias, like other Germans, feared that if he placed his children in the American School, there would be reprisals from the German leaders in camp. For the duration of the camp's operations, fewer than twenty-four German parents enrolled their children in the Federal School. Kazuko Shimahara, a young Japanese American internee, remembered a German girl who was briefly in Kazuko's class at Federal Elementary School. The German American schoolmate confided to Kazuko how difficult it was for her to come to school because her German neighbors shunned her and her family.

Mathias prevailed, and on September 7, 1943, when the German School opened in a four-room facility, Lothar reported for fourth grade and Ingrid for seventh. Both struggled with the language. In addition, the school in Crystal City was structured on the German model, stricter and more rigid than an American-style education. Both Lothar and Ingrid took classes in German, arithmetic, botany, and geography. There were no classes in American literature and no music lessons—nothing to satisfy Ingrid's creative appetites. The teachers, German internees who were mostly uneducated, working-class men, controlled the curriculum. For instance, one of Ingrid's language teachers was an electrician. The man who taught her mathematics was a farmer.

At home in Strongsville, Ingrid had been aware of her German heritage. She enjoyed the oompah-pah bands at the community beer garden, German food, and German operas. But she didn't identify herself as a German because she was born in the United States. In the German School, she felt pressured to think, write, and speak in German.

The reality of day-to-day life behind the fence was ineluctable, as sure as night follows day: nothing about it was normal. The political considerations that the Eiserlohs and other families had to take into account in their choice of schools highlighted the continuing tensions on the German side of camp. All that autumn of 1943, conflicts continued.

By October, the tedium of Crystal City was such that Kuhn decided to pass himself off as an informer to the FBI. The Department of Justice was still investigating the Bund, and one of the investigators in Philadelphia wanted Kuhn as a witness. Kuhn agreed.

On October 10, Kuhn left camp under heavy guard and was driven to the Gunter Hotel, an eight-story luxury hotel in downtown San Antonio founded in the 1800s by two wealthy German immigrants. A deputy US marshal and an FBI agent from San Antonio were under orders to entertain Kuhn and "create a friendly frame of mind" for his upcoming testimony in Philadelphia. They took him to dinner and to a rodeo, then went back to the hotel to question Kuhn.

During the interview, Kuhn drank whiskey and regaled them with stories. He described one night in Los Angeles when he addressed a crowd of forty thousand. He grew wistful when he remembered that after his speech, most of the crowd stood and gave the Heil Hitler. He told them that Hitler's government sent the Bund $1 million a year for their activities. It was an improbable claim—the FBI had no evidence that Germany funded the Bund. In fact, it was the other way around: the Bund sent small amounts of money to Germany.

Soon the wires were whistling between San Antonio and FBI headquarters in Washington. "Can this be true?" scrawled one of the agents in Washington at the bottom of the report filed in San Antonio. "If it was in fact Kuhn send memo to A.G. at once." The FBI agent on the ground and the deputy US marshal convinced their superiors that Kuhn's wild claim had to be a "joke."

But Kuhn was not finished toying with the FBI. He next told investigators that, on his orders as president of the Bund, monthly reports were submitted about membership and finances to national headquarters in New York. Kuhn claimed that the reports were not destroyed. On October 18, 1943, Hoover himself sent out an urgent wire from Washington to agents in New York. "Department of Justice anxious to procure copies of these reports if possible," wrote Hoover. "Desire these inquires to be conducted immediately." The goose chase was on. Nothing substantial was turned up, and Kuhn returned to Crystal City.

By December, Heinrich Johann Hasenburger, considered a troublemaker by O'Rourke, had followed Kolb as the official spokesman for the camp's German population, despite Hasenburger's not having been duly elected. A few brave German and German American internees tried to contest his appointment. According to their count, Hasenburger received 149 votes out of 631 cast—a clear indication that the majority of Germans in camp did not want Hasenburger as spokesman. In the January 15, 1944, issue of *Das Lager*, a mimeographed newsletter published by the Germans, Hasenburger demanded a referendum on his leadership. A recount of the election was not held, but Hasenburger assumed the position. One female internee wrote a feverish letter to Washington about Hasenburger's techniques, calling him an "Imitation Dictator." She appears to have been right. Hasenburger kept his position and set out to punish his enemies. Families that opposed his election were, on Hasenburger's orders, "excluded from the community." They could not purchase food at the German store or the mess hall, or frequent the barber and beauty shops, or participate in community activities. One entire family whose father refused an order from Hasenburger was deprived of food for four days. When O'Rourke discovered it, the family was admitted to the camp hospital, which offered protection from Hasenburger.

That fall, Harrison set out his expectations for the kind of conflicts that O'Rourke confronted with Hasenburger and other Germans. Under the heading "Be Patient" in the manual of conduct for INS employees, Harrison wrote, "It is often difficult to be patient and exercise an unruffled self-restraint in the face of scathing verbal criticism, or when threatened with physical violence, but it always enlists sympathetic support and pays dividends. No matter how exasperated the circumstances become, officers must bear in mind they are representatives of our government and must conduct themselves in a worthy manner. To become impatient, sarcastic, hostile or personal in remarks is an admission of weakness and defeat and, needless to say, should never occur."

In February 1944, Washington and Berlin completed negotiations for a prisoner exchange. As part of the deal, 634 Germans and German Americans interned in Crystal City would be repatriated to Germany on the MS *Gripsholm*. To O'Rourke's great relief, Hasenburger's name was among the 634. The problematic German spokesman's loyalty to Germany was such that he volunteered himself and his family for the first repatriation from Crystal City. Kuhn was number 68 on a list of 131 German nationals requested by the German government. However, the Military Intelligence Service, one of four US security agencies that had to clear the list, scratched Kuhn's name. His probable value to the Germans was too great for the MIS to risk. Kuhn's wife, Elsa, and his son, Walter, were on the approved list for the first repatriation. When it came time for them to leave Crystal City, Elsa and Walter gathered at the front entrance with the crowd of repatriates, including the Hasenburger family. A band played and the remaining internees marched around in ceremonial fashion. Slowly, the repatriates, carrying their luggage and footlockers, boarded buses that would take them to a waiting train. The February 19 issue of *Das Lager* reported the departure of the Germans and described the atmosphere within the German section as that of a "ghost town."

Shortly after the last bus pulled out of camp, O'Rourke segregated Kuhn from the remaining Germans and German Americans in a heavily guarded detention center inside the internment camp—in effect, a jail. Months later, Kuhn was transferred to Fort Stanton in New Mexico, a high-security prison for problem internees. According to Eb Fuhr, who remained in Crystal City, Kuhn carried the aura of being the man who knew too much about America to trade to the Germans. For a little while more, Kuhn stayed in America, but he was no longer a factor in Crystal City.

With two of O'Rourke's most difficult German internees gone from Crystal City, he wasted no time in taking decisive action against a third: Karl Kolb, the first German spokesman. Three months after the departure of the repatriates, O'Rourke wrote a letter to Kolb: "It is the honest opinion of this office that for the welfare of the entire German group, you should be removed from this camp." Shortly thereafter, Kolb, his wife, and his daughter were transferred to an internment camp in Algiers, Louisiana. In a telegram to INS headquarters in Philadelphia, Kolb protested his transfer as "unacceptable" because of the "racially mixed couples," a reference to the German Jews, in Algiers. His telegram was ignored, and he and his family waited in Algiers to be repatriated to Germany.

Even after three major agitators had left the Crystal City camp, O'Rourke struggled to maintain order in the German section. Most of the disputes were trivial. A few German internees were caught cheating on their hourly wage. The Japanese complained that German children raced through their carefully tended gardens. The May 6, 1944, issue of *Das Lager* pleaded for parents to control their children. "Children have thrown balls and pieces of wood into the movie operator's cabin while playing in the big hall of the auditorium," wrote the editor. "Instruct your children at once to cease this careless or even mischievous habit."

Unfortunately, even the pettiest of these disagreements could escalate into violence. For instance, in August 1944, George Kreuzner accused his anti-Nazi neighbor Anna Vogl of eavesdropping at the window of his bungalow. Mrs. Vogl told him that she was looking for her cat. Kreuzner threatened her and Mrs. Vogl immediately filed a report with Larry R. Elwood, assistant chief internal security officer of the camp. At the beginning of the interview, Officer Elwood asked Mrs. Vogl to tell him in her words exactly what had happened when Kreuzner arrived at her house.

"He told me, 'Mrs. Vogl,' he said, 'if I catch you once more listening at my window, then I am going to throw hydrochlorine acid in your eyes.'"

"What has your observation been of Mr. Kreuzner's general activities in the camp?" asked Elwood.

"I just know that he is a drinker," said Mrs. Vogl. "Everybody knows that."

Almost every day brought some kind of flare-up. Mathias once went to the German camp store a little before noon and picked up a ration of meat that he thought was too fatty and not fresh. On the way home, he encountered one of the German leaders, and the two got into an argument. In frustration, Mathias threw the package of meat into the street and stalked off. The spokesman reported him to security officers, who stored the meat in the butcher shop as evidence. Mathias was called in for questioning and asked to explain himself. He had no explanation, other than that the confinement and long hours of boredom in the camp had left him jumpy.

Even as O'Rourke had to contain and parry the aggressive behavior of the first three German spokesman as well as cranks such as Kreuzner, he also listened and attended to the seemingly minute concerns of quieter inmates, whose misery or relative contentedness was nonetheless important to him.

On most mornings, O'Rourke, divorced and estranged from his wife, awoke in his small house adjacent to the internment camp with a hangover and a full day's work ahead of him. At night, he cruised the streets of Crystal City in his 1942 Studebaker sedan and took his comfort in cantinas—the small, smoky bars common in South Texas.

Only forty-nine years old, O'Rourke had been a Border Patrol agent for twenty-two years. His job as officer in charge of Crystal City paid a good salary of $5,500, the equivalent of roughly $70,000 today. He was responsible for approximately 3,000 internees and oversaw 160 employees assigned to key divisions: Administrative Service, Surveillance, Internal Security, Internal Relations, Maintenance, Construction and Repair, Education, and Medical. The responsibilities of the job made him more deliberate in his speech and actions than he had been in his younger years. Since his arrival in Crystal City, he had become increasingly exacting in his decisions, even the most casual ones. Many men would have become embittered by the job, but O'Rourke found that it suited him.

Most of O'Rourke's concerns were for the overall functioning of the camp, but as with the problems of Kolb, Hasenburger, and Kuhn, some centered on explicitly German or Japanese issues. O'Rourke would not forget the day that the Reverend Ryuchi Fujii, a Buddhist priest from Clovis, California, who was the elected spokesman for the Japanese in camp, brought up the subject of tofu. O'Rourke liked Fujii, a calm, reasonable man who had been elected several times by the Japanese group as their spokesman. A sharp contrast to the German spokesmen, Fujii was not uncooperative or difficult. His strategy seemed to be to ask for many more things than he truly expected to receive, but on the subject of tofu, Fujii was unbendable.

Upon the arrival of the first Japanese in camp, O'Rourke had ordered that the camp grocery store include items consistent with both the Japanese and the German diets. By the summer of 1943, twenty-two German and thirty-six Japanese clerical workers staffed the warehouse, meat market, and grocery store. Most days, the German and the Japanese workers cooperated with one another. However, a blowup occurred one day when the Japanese butchers, who were cutting fish, saved the meatiest portions for Japanese customers and distributed the tails to Germans. In retaliation, the Germans complained about the vast amount of space occupied in the warehouse by Japanese food: miso paste, soy sauce, rice, noodles, seaweed, and dried shrimp.

No matter how much tofu was on the shelves, there was never enough for the Japanese housewives. Fujii's complaint to O'Rourke was twofold: the quality of the store-bought tofu was inferior, and the quantity was insufficient. At first, Fujii suggested to O'Rourke that the store stock enough tofu for each Japanese household to have it, in lieu of leafy vegetables, once a week. O'Rourke agreed, but the weekly share of tofu only increased the demand for more. "If only you would allow us to produce our own tofu," Fujii told O'Rourke, "it would take the place of all other demands."

O'Rourke assumed a bemused and thoughtful approach to the request. In his research, O'Rourke learned that tofu is soft, made from soy milk treated with *nigari*. *Nigari* is related to the Japanese word for "bitter," *nigai*. Bitterness gives tofu its particular flavor. In Japan, *nigari* is created by evaporating seawater. In the absence of seawater in Crystal City, Fujii explained that the soy milk could be treated with calcium chloride to achieve the desired level of bitterness.

O'Rourke assigned one of the Victory Huts in the Japanese section of camp as an experimental laboratory for the making of tofu. Crowds of Japanese women filled the space, which they cheerfully christened the Tofu Factory.

A problem immediately surfaced that threatened to fell the venture. Bags of soybeans were carried into the hut in preparation for the making of soy milk. The beans were covered in water, then had to be ground to a mushy consistency. In Japan, soy grinders are efficient, as ubiquitous in households as stoves and sinks. But most of the Japanese housewives had left behind their soy grinders—along with most of their other possessions—when they were interned. Now, with the war on, soy grinders could not be requisitioned from the enemy.

As O'Rourke pondered the problem, one day he went into town to a local Mexican restaurant that he frequented. While having lunch, he saw a woman with a stone pestle in her hand grinding lime-treated corn in a chiseled-stone bowl called a *molino*. The ground corn, called *masa*, was used for making tortillas. Perhaps, O'Rourke thought, *molinos* could also be used to make tofu.

Back at the Tofu Factory, the women, pestles in hand, experimented with grinding the soybeans in the stone bowls. Much to everyone's delight, the *molinos* worked, and the rest of the process went smoothly. Once ground, the beans were cooked in steam kettles, then placed in cloth bags and strained to remove any solids. Calcium chloride was added. The liquid mass was poured into wooden forms, allowed to set until solidified, and then cut into one-pound squares of tofu. Each day, long lines of Japanese woman formed outside the Tofu Factory to purchase it with the camp token money.

With the tofu problem solved, Fujii met with O'Rourke and complained that German internees had better housing and more pleasant facilities for schools than the Japanese. O'Rourke was ready with his reply: "We gave you tofu. You said it would take the place of everything." The two men shared a laugh.

Unfortunately, other problems beyond tofu in the Japanese section would not be so easily smoothed over.

CHAPTER EIGHT

To Be or Not to Be an American

While fifteen-year-old Sumi Utsushigawa stood with her mother, Nobu, on the pier in Jersey City, New Jersey, on September 2, 1943, members of the crew of the MS *Gripsholm* scurried like ants to load supplies. The enormous sign hanging from the side of the Swedish liner read DIPLOMAT. The pier was crowded with more than a thousand Japanese and Japanese Americans, all in line to board. Sumi and Nobu were near the back of the line and strained to take in the confusion.

Three days before, Sumi and her mother had been in the hot, dry desert, behind the barbed-wire fence of Wyoming's Heart Mountain Relocation Camp. On the train trip from Heart Mountain, Nobu had explained that Sumi's father, Tokiji, an enemy alien incarcerated at the Santa Fe Internment Camp, had signed an agreement to voluntarily repatriate to Japan. Nobu made it clear that she and Sumi would return with him. When war broke out, Sumi's two older sisters, Yoshiko and Haruko, were in Sendai, Japan, visiting their grandparents; they were still there. Tokiji was sixty-six years old, ill with kidney disease, and had suffered as a prisoner in American internment camps for the past eighteen months. In Japan, he would at least be free from prison and accepted by his own kin. The family would be reunited. Other than her two sisters, Sumi had no solid ties to Japan. She knew her own mind but understood she had no

121

choice. American or not, she could not defy her Japanese father. She had nowhere to go except with her parents.

"Shikata ga nai," Nobu told her, a phrase Sumi had heard her mother repeat often. It meant "Grit your teeth and bear it."

At the New Jersey harbor, the air was cool and the sky was gray. Tokiji was nowhere in sight. Sumi and Nobu waited as families in front of them filed onto the *Gripsholm*. They were there because the Special War Problems Division had at long last successfully negotiated with the Japanese government for an exchange of approximately 1,330 Japanese civilians for the same number of American diplomats, missionaries, journalists, and businessmen held prisoner by Japan. Soon, the *Gripsholm*, chartered by the US government as an International Red Cross exchange ship, would slip out of the harbor. It would travel for six weeks on an unsecured sea route across the Pacific Ocean, where American surface ships and submarines actively trolled to sink Japanese vessels, until it arrived in the port of Mormugao in the Portuguese colony of Goa, on the west coast of India. Mormugao was a neutral location, selected in advance by diplomats from both the United States and Japan. There, a Japanese ship, the *Teia Maru*, would arrive from Tokyo, carrying 1,330 American citizens. An exchange would take place. Reciprocity was key. For every American who disembarked from the *Teia Maru*— and took their first steps into freedom—a Japanese repatriate had to transfer from the *Gripsholm* and pass to Japanese authority. Sumi, Nobu, and Tokiji were to be exchanged.

This was the second such exchange between the United States and Japan. The first exchange of prisoners, composed primarily of government officials from both countries, occurred in June 1942, six months after Pearl Harbor. One month prior to that exchange, the Japanese were still on the offensive. They had taken the Philippines, Malaya, Singapore, and the Dutch East Indies and were planning to strengthen their hold on the Solomon Islands and take New Guinea, cutting Australia off from the United States. However, between June 4 and 7, as the negotiations were in progress, the US

Navy secured a decisive victory against the Imperial Navy at the Battle of Midway. The battle helped turn the tide of war against Japan.

During the first exchange, 268 American government officials and 2,500 US civilians trapped in Japan were returned to the United States. Joseph Grew, the American ambassador to Japan, who had been confined to the American embassy grounds in Tokyo since December 8, 1941, was among those on board the *Asama Maru*, which left Yokohama harbor early on June 25. Grew described his emotions in a diary passage: "And then came the greatest of all moments. I awoke at 1 a.m. on June 25th, seeing that something was happening. I looked out of the porthole and saw a piece of wood slowly moving past in the water. We were at last underway, slowly accelerating until the ship was finally speeding at full steam away from Yokohama, away from Japan, pointing homeward. Ah, what a moment that was, even though we had 18,000 miles to cover and seventy days in all before we should pass the Statue of Liberty in New York Harbor."

As Grew sailed away from Japan, his counterpart, Admiral Kichisaburo Nomura, the Japanese ambassador to the United States, left the port of New York on the *Gripsholm* along with other Japanese officials and civilians. The actual exchange took place on July 23, 1942, in Port Marques, Portuguese East Africa. The Japanese repatriates disembarked from the ship, passed in a line on one side of the dock, and transferred to the *Asama Maru*. The weary Americans, including Grew, filed off the *Asama Maru*, formed a second line, and walked onto the stern of the *Gripsholm*, where they feasted at a buffet and toasted with champagne.

Given the success of the first exchange, the Special War Problems Division identified 7,050 more American civilians still inside enemy lines in Japan, many living in prisoner-of-war camps, and pressed Japanese officials for additional exchanges. The goal was to rescue all Americans from both Japan and Germany. However, negotiations for the second exchange with Japan stalled as each side struggled with the complicated task of compiling passenger lists.

The work was tedious and complex, fraught with conflicting

points of view. On the American side, State Department officials refused to release Japanese internees who they believed were security risks that might help Japan's war effort. The Japanese government, on the other hand, insisted that it must have the complete authority to choose which Japanese nationals would be returned to Japan as well as the authority to exclude others. During the first round of negotiations, the Americans altered their list to include 580 people explicitly designated by the Japanese. However, 900 others were on the American list that the Japanese had not named. The majority of the 900 were Japanese nationals imprisoned in American internment camps, such as Tokiji, Nobu, and Sumi.

Negotiations stalled. Between the summer and fall of 1942, lists went back and forth between Washington and Tokyo. In December 1942, the issue landed on Roosevelt's desk. The president was faced with the choice of whether to return to Japan people identified by the FBI and military as dangerous to the American war effort. If he did so, American citizens held in Japan would come home. If he didn't, they might be held in Japan for the duration of the war. Heavy on Roosevelt's mind was the high death rate of American soldiers in Japanese prisoner-of-war camps.

In February 1943, Roosevelt instructed the State Department to agree to return as few Japanese security risks as possible in return for the greatest number of Americans. A plan was developed for at least three more trades to return 4,500 Americans from Japan and equal numbers of Japanese from America. But in May 1943, Tokyo refused Roosevelt's offer for additional exchanges and presented an ultimatum: take the Japanese list for a second exchange, or the Japanese would suspend all future exchanges.

After the successful Battle of Midway in June 1942, Roosevelt could afford to reverse his policy. He decided it was more important to bring Americans back home to the United States and instructed the State Department to accept Japan's demands.

Within the State Department and the Japanese Foreign Ministry, the human chess game continued. In addition to the Japanese from the United States designated by the Japanese government, ten Japanese merchants from Peru and Bolivia were identified and put on the list, as well as seventy-five Japanese diplomats from Chile, twenty-five from Mexico, and sixty from Canada. The State Department asked for the return of twenty-five US officials in the Philippines and eight hundred and fifty Americans from occupied China.

In September 1943, as Sumi and Nobu waited on the dock in the New Jersey harbor to board the *Gripsholm*, they were oblivious of their small place in the larger context of these world events. Negotiations continued right up until the moment the ship was allowed to sail. In the end, 1,437 Japanese were assembled and ready to board, with only 1,330 slots for exchange. Ninety-seven individuals would be cut from the list.

To their surprise, Sumi and Nobu were pulled from the line by military guards with machine guns. Sumi had no idea what was happening. She had assumed her father was already on board the ship. Now she and her mother were directed toward a group of several dozen Japanese women and children who had also been removed from the line. By then, it was dark. With machine guns aimed at her back, Sumi put one shaky foot in front of the other.

The guards led Sumi and the others to a Coast Guard cutter, which crossed the bay to Ellis Island. They were taken upstairs to a cavernous room. Row after row of Japanese internees slept on Army cots. Sumi and Nobu settled on two side-by-side cots with thin, sheetless, filthy mattresses. Sumi lay awake and listened to the snores, moans, and cries that filled the space.

The next morning, Sumi and Nobu went upstairs to a mess hall, where Sumi ate a bowl of cold cereal with no milk or sugar. By then, she was accustomed to food that did not agree with her preferred Japanese diet. In Heart Mountain, she had stood in long lines and been served mutton stew, which upset her stomach. By comparison, the cold cereal that morning wasn't so bad. After a while, a group of Japanese men, including Tokiji, was escorted into the mess hall. Across the room, Sumi saw her father for the first time in eighteen months and realized he was not on the *Gripsholm*. She and her parents were among the ninety-seven individuals cut from the exchange list at the last moment. Tokiji looked older and much thinner. He and Nobu greeted each other formally, without embracing, as was the custom of traditional issei fathers and mothers.

"Hello, Mama," Tokiji said with a small bow. Then he turned to Sumi, looking her over carefully. "You grew up. You're big now."

Sumi smiled with relief that she and her parents were not on the ship sailing to Japan. It was her first lucky break since the war began.

Not far away, Yae Kanogawa, a seventeen-year-old born in Seattle, Washington, saw her father for the first time since his arrest on the night of December 7, 1941. Like Sumi, Yae was overjoyed about her deliverance from forced repatriation to Japan. Before the events of Pearl Harbor, Yae's father owned a small grocery on Washington Street in Seattle. Since then, he had been imprisoned in internment camps at Missoula, Montana, and Santa Fe and Lordsburg, New Mexico. Meanwhile, Yae, her mother, and three brothers were interned in Minidoka, Idaho. "I was so happy to see him," Yae recalled. "The last time he saw me, I was too young to wear lipstick. But that day in Ellis Island, I had on lipstick, and when I hugged him, I smeared lipstick on his face."

Later that day, Sumi's family, Yae's family, and two others on Ellis Island were told by guards that they would be transferred to Crystal City to await another exchange. Since the fathers were prisoners of war and had agreed to repatriate, they could not return to male-only relocation camps. The camp in Crystal City was the one that housed familes, the only available next step.

They stayed four days and three nights on Ellis Island. In the toilsome daily routine they were awakened at 5:30 a.m. for no reason that Sumi could comprehend, because there was nothing to do all day. Breakfast was at 7:30, lunch at 11:30, and dinner at 4:30 p.m. Most of the day, they were confined to the cavernous room with little to occupy their time, and at night they slept there on the uncomfortable cots.

The first Japanese prisoners seized by Americans in battle were housed at Ellis Island. Sumi and Yae noticed that the prisoners kept their heads down and did not make eye contact. Yae wanted to ask if they'd been captured, but her father told her not to talk to them. It was considered a disgrace for Japanese to be captured; their deepest shame was in not committing suicide.

In wartime, train travel was difficult. O'Rourke traveled to New York to expedite the arrangements for the twenty-one Japanese waiting on Ellis Island to go to Crystal City. On September 5, O'Rourke met the group at Grand Central Station, which was crowded with soldiers and civilians. Both Yae and Sumi felt swallowed up in the large space. Their march to the train was carefully choreographed; military guards, one in front of the group and one behind, escorted them to a private car. Some of the onlookers in the station stared angrily at the Japanese; others seemed curious. Both Yae and Sumi remembered the tension in the air and how afraid they felt. It seemed like an eternity before the odd parade of twenty-one passengers filed safely into a single car on the train.

As the train left the station, the shades were pulled down. Sumi settled in a seat beside her mother. Yae sat with her brothers Sei, who was one year older, and Shoji, three years younger. Parts of the train were air-conditioned, including O'Rourke's Pullman car and the dining room. However, the passenger car for the prisoners of war and their families had no air-conditioning and was dark and broiling.

Sumi thought about all that had happened since her father's arrest. On May 9, 1942, under the provisions of Executive Order 9068, signed by Roosevelt, she and Nobu had been sent to Ponoma Assembly Camp, located on a fairground in Los Angeles. On August 25, they were put on a train to Wyoming, where they entered Heart Mountain Relocation Camp, a 740-acre camp with a high, barbed-wire fence and nine guard towers.

In Heart Mountain, Sumi and Nobu lived in black-tar-papered barracks in Block 14 with other Japanese women and children. In the center of the dormitory space was a round-bellied stove fueled by coal. A city kid from Los Angeles, Sumi did not know how to start a fire. When the weather turned cold, she stacked pieces of coal in the stove, struck a match, and waited for the fire to ignite. But the coal did not catch, and after several failed attempts, Sumi lined the bottom of the stove with newspaper and kindling and lit the fire. Soon, the dormitory was warm.

Behind the barracks stretched a laundry line. Nobu washed their clothes on washboards in a central laundry room. Sumi hung the clothes on the line to dry. In the winter, when temperatures dropped to twenty-eight degrees, the sheets and their clothes froze stiff on the line. When Sumi brought them inside to fold, the sheets cracked and ripped. In Heart Mountain, the joke among the teenagers was that even their goose pimples had goose pimples.

Both Sumi and Nobu struggled with the lack of privacy in communal showers. Rather than expose herself, Sumi showered in a bathing suit, and Nobu didn't shower at all. She wiped herself clean with a washcloth at a sink.

Food was a problem for Nobu, as well, and she didn't eat much in Heart Mountain. The goulash served in the mess hall made her ill. With the unfamiliar food and her depression, Nobu dropped more than twenty pounds. Sumi, worried about her mother's health, gathered dandelion greens around the fence line. From them, Nobu made *tsukemono*—Japanese pickles.

In Heart Mountain, Sumi suffered her own bout of fence sickness, triggered by her anger. None of what had happened made sense to her. If Japanese from the West Coast were interned because they were potential spies and saboteurs, why were they any less dangerous in isolated Wyoming? Inside the gate, Heart Mountain was a strange, new world. Sumi was given a test to determine where she would be placed in the camp school. In Los Angeles, she had completed the seventh grade. Sumi was so angry about her internment that she failed the test in Heart Mountain on purpose, but the officials there placed her in ninth grade anyway. "I got promoted for failing the test," recalled Sumi. "I never went through the eighth grade at all." Sumi wanted nothing to do with school, but her mother insisted.

In Heart Mountain, Sumi invented a tough, tomboy persona as an outlet for her indignation. Instead of skirts and dresses, she wore jeans and baggy shirts. She refused to talk in class and allowed her grades to drop. In time, she earned the ire of a gym teacher, a woman who insisted that Sumi keep her hands out of her jeans pockets while doing drills, even on the coldest of days. The teacher thought Sumi's pocketing of her hands was a gesture of defiance. That winter in Heart Mountain, the teacher made Sumi run laps around the track without gloves, with her hands out of her pockets. Sumi would not be broken and never shed a tear. She ran the drills in the snow with freezing hands. Her satisfaction was in not caring what the teacher did to her.

When she returned to the barracks with frostbite, Nobu sat Sumi down and explained that she was only hurting herself. Beneath the anger, Nobu told her daughter, was the pain of leaving Los Angeles, the loss of her father, and the humiliation of internment. She reminded Sumi of the Japanese custom of *gaman*. Nobu spoke the ancient word as a charge to her daughter: to have *gaman* was to endure the unbearable with dignity and forbearance. It was the Japanese way of managing hardship. Usually, *gaman* required some specific pursuit—the practice of Buddhist meditation, as Nobu did, the art of calligraphy, the performance of the tea ceremony, or martial arts, such as judo or kendo. Tokiji's pursuit was photography. In other camps, Japanese men carved birds out of wooden crate ends and made lovely lapel pins out of castor beans. The point, Nobu told Sumi, was to find some disciplined way to endure suffering without losing one's sense of identity, dignity, and purpose. "We have to have *gaman*!"

Even though her family was Zen Buddhist, Sumi did not practice meditation. The traditional Japanese customs were part of her life, but they did not feel as if they belonged to her. She was a part of the nisei, second-generation Japanese Americans. They lived between two worlds—Japan and America—and during the internment many, like Sumi, felt betrayed by their government and uncertain of their American identity. Sumi could not imagine what her own *gaman* might look like, but she decided to befriend others her age who shared her predicament.

"I promised Mama that if I got a chance to go to another place— even if it was another camp—instead of being the toughest, most unfriendly girl in camp," said Sumi, "I'd become the friendliest."

On the train to Crystal City, Sumi surveyed the faces of the teenagers on board. In particular, she noticed Yae and her two younger brothers, fourteen-year-old Shoji and thirteen-year-old Reo. One afternoon, Sumi watched Yae and her brothers playing cards on a wooden box they'd found somewhere on board.

No one on the car had any suitcases. Their luggage had previously been stowed on the *Gripsholm*, now steaming its way to India. Everyone had only the clothes on his or her back. They were segregated from the other passengers, and at mealtimes, guards escorted them to the dining car and kept them under surveillance while they ate. "I felt like a refugee," Sumi said. She slept in her seat, next to her mother, as the train made its way south. Yae dozed nestled close to her father.

Somewhere in Mississippi, the train stopped, and O'Rourke left. Both Sumi and Yae remembered that when he returned, he was laden with sacks of ice cream bars. He walked through the train car and distributed the ice cream to the children and teenagers on board. The teenagers unwrapped the cold bars and quickly ate them. Yoji J. Matshushima, another teenager on the train, later wrote about the trip: "It seemed like a lifetime from the time we left New York to Texas. I remember the flooding along the Mississippi River and the corn growing along the track. Mr. O'Rourke bought the kids ice cream on a stop because it was so hot. He felt sorry for us kids. I remember washing out clothes because we had no change. The train was so hot. We would open the windows, but the smoke from the engine would come into the car, so we had to keep them closed."

The train trip took several days. For much of the way, the shades remained down. The guards told the English-speaking children that it was for their own protection. On previous trips, trains carrying prisoners of war had been pelted with rocks.

When the train stopped at a small station in Texas, Yae's younger brothers left the train to use the restroom in the station house. Two white men barred them from the first bathroom they tried, pointing to the WHITES ONLY sign over the door. In Seattle, where they were born, Jim Crow laws did not exist. They did know that in the American South, schools, swimming pools, water fountains, buses, and trains were segregated by race. The men directed them to the "Negro" bathroom. As Japanese, they didn't understand where they fit into the racial equation, but they did as instructed. "It was strange. I figured a bathroom was a bathroom and a water faucet a water faucet, but that day in Texas, I learned differently," Shoji said.

On September 7, the travelers arrived at the small railway station in Crystal City. On the short drive to the camp, Sumi saw the statue of Popeye on Main Street. She remembered the lyrics to the Popeye song from the cartoons: "I'm Popeye the Sailor Man. . . ." How odd, she thought, a town that raised a statue to Popeye.

Once the new arrivals were safely inside the fence, officers from the surveillance division examined what few papers and personal effects each person carried. O'Rourke explained the rules of roll: Every day at 5:30 p.m., roll call would be taken in the Japanese area of the camp. Three blasts on the air horn in the center of camp would signify the beginning of the count. All of the internees, including children, were instructed to stand in front of their residences and show their faces. When the daily count was finished, the air horn would sound twice.

Finally, the families of Sumi and Yae were escorted to their assigned quarters. As they walked to the northeast quadrant of the camp, they were surprised to see so many Germans. While no physical barriers separated the German and Japanese sections, each group generally kept to its own area.

That first night, Sumi and her family were taken by truck down Airport Drive to what was known as the T section. The housing here was much different from Heart Mountain, where Sumi had stayed in a crowded dormitory. The *T* section stood for "triplex"—720 feet of floor space divided into three small apartments. Each had a kitchen with running water and a toilet, with a community shower. The prospect of living with only two other families brightened Sumi's outlook. Nobu would be able to shop for food in the Japanese store, pay for it with camp money—which Sumi called "funny money"—and prepare all of their meals. Even though they still lived behind a fence, without liberty, an important part of their family structure was restored: eating together.

On the first morning after arriving in Crystal City, Sumi looked outside and saw the strange sight of mounted guards on horseback, something that did not exist in Heart Mountain or other camps. Then she saw a Japanese woman pulling a creaking wooden cart, which stopped at the bungalow and delivered bottled milk. A little while later, two men in a truck delivered ice for the cooler. At breakfast, her mother and father were seated together, no longer worried about each other's whereabouts. "The countryside was bleak and the weather was hot and humid," recalled Sumi, "but that first morning in Crystal City, we were together again. I was happy."

On the morning of September 20, 1943, Sumi left her triplex, numbered T-37-B, located near the citrus orchard on the southernmost edge of the camp. She walked a short distance to the Federal High School, also known as the American School, where she would start ninth grade.

Everything about this first day of school felt different. The student body at Sumi's new school numbered about 150, a group made up mostly of Japanese Americans from the continental United States. Here, unlike on any first day of school in Los Angeles, Sumi knew none of her classmates. All of the students were strangers to each other, every student in the room a transfer from some other camp.

It often took months for new students' transcripts to arrive from different camps. The wait did not stall the steady pace of the school year. A Hawaiian girl who was a senior that year received her transcript just one week before graduation. Every student, including Sumi, was placed in a grade on the strength of his or her word. As a measure of how honest the Japanese American students were despite the humiliation of internment, camp records show that once transcripts finally arrived, less than 1 percent of students were demoted for misrepresentation.

As the students in Sumi's class filed into the prefabricated building that housed the Federal High School, all were headed into the unknown with no choice but to quietly take their hard seats in the used school desks. The first class was English. Sumi stared at the tall, willowy woman with the soft brown hair who stood in front of the blackboard. The woman had a straight spine and a confident air, as if she was used to getting her way. In clear, graceful cursive, she wrote her name in chalk on the blackboard: Miss Goldsmith.

By the time she stood before Sumi's class, Kathryn Goldsmith, a graduate of North Texas Teachers College in Denton, Texas, had been a classroom teacher for twelve years. On the first day of class, Miss Goldsmith read several long assignments aloud. Like all of the other students, Sumi understood English, but Miss Goldsmith's thick Texas drawl was unfamiliar. Her rolled *r*'s and dropped *g*'s were confusing. A phrase like *taking a bath* on the printed page sounded like *takin' a bath* in Miss Goldsmith's mouth. *Fixing* was chopped to *fixin'*. She said *y'all* instead of *you guys*. The cadence and rhythm of Miss Goldsmith's voice struck Sumi as comical. "Her Texas accent sounded so funny," recalled Sumi, "the whole class laughed."

Miss Goldsmith's English class was Sumi's favorite: "She was strict, but she was fair and went out of her way to make us feel like normal kids in a normal school." To capture their interest, she

133

directed the students in plays—*Snow White and the Seven Dwarfs*, *The Night Owl*, and *The Wizard of Oz*.

R. C. (Robert Clyde) Tate, a former high school principal in Crystal City and the supervisor of education at the internment camp, had recruited Miss Goldsmith. A native Texan, Tate had a storied record as a football and baseball coach in a number of rural South Texas schools. Even in midlife he was built like a quarterback, with strong, blocky shoulders and long, springy legs. A Christian man, Tate read his Bible through wire-rimmed glasses. He was early to rise and late to rest. His players called Tate by his nickname: Old Warhorse. As supervisor of education at an internment camp, Tate had a multifaceted job, overseeing both the German and the Japanese schools, which had their own internee-elected school boards and hired their own teachers from within the ranks of internees. But the structures of the Federal High School and Federal Elementary School were different. None of the teachers or administrators in those schools answered to the parents or to a school board. From his office in Philadelphia, Harrison held ultimate responsibility for the American schools. In the camp records, O'Rourke was listed as "president" of the school board and Tate as "superintendent."

Tate's most challenging job was recruiting teachers, given the nationwide teacher shortage during World War II. He had to find public-school teachers, most of whom had relatives fighting on the fronts in Europe and Asia, who were willing to educate the children of prisoners of war in sweltering South Texas. Unlike other school districts, Tate could not offer potential internment-camp teachers firm contracts. As employees of the INS, teachers might be transferred with little notice.

Indeed, Old Warhorse was worried about job security himself. Tate had three boys. One was in junior high, and the other two attended Crystal City High School, where they were mainstays on the football team. "The job uncertainty was a concern," he said in an oral history. "Who knew when I might be transferred from Texas to the Canadian border. The INS network was large. My job was uncertain."

What did help, however, was that the INS was willing to pay higher salaries than other Texas schools. In 1942–43, the average yearly pay for a teacher with a four-year degree at an accredited school was $877.50. The INS offered internment-camp teachers in Crystal City more than twice that. The higher wages attracted good teachers, such as Miss Goldsmith. Tate was paid $3,200 a year, equivalent to approximately $45,000 today, a salary sufficient to make the risk of transfer worth his while.

Over time, Sumi and the others settled into a familiar pattern. School began at 8:00 a.m., Monday through Friday and Saturday mornings. The Federal School required two years of math for graduation. As ninth-graders, Sumi and the others studied algebra. Later, Sumi took plane geometry. Basic science was taught, but physics and chemistry were not offered. As superintendent, O'Rourke had decided that a fully equipped chemistry laboratory in an internment camp was too great a security risk. He didn't want to take the chance of malcontents blowing up the lab. That first year, Tate offered home economics for girls and agricultural training for boys, but few signed up. When Tate learned that the issei Japanese fathers suspected he was attempting to make domestic laborers out of their daughters and farm laborers out of their sons, the vocational classes were canceled. This decision was another example of caution against inciting complaints from Japanese fathers that might result in reprisals against Americans held in Japan.

Unlike in the German section, where many of the fathers were laborers and craftsmen, the fathers in the Japanese section were, as Tate described it, "the cream of the crop"—Buddhist priests, wealthy businessmen, accomplished farmers, and well-educated teachers. The majority of their children were straight-A students. Sumi struggled to keep up with the others; she was happy with Bs.

The parents of the Japanese American students pushed them to study, to follow the rules of the school, and to show respect for the

American teachers. Like Sumi, most strived to be accepted as Americans and to be normal. "Yet the attitude of most of the people in town was that all Japanese were damn Japs," recalled Tate in his oral history. "And they ought to all be hung." The aftermath of Pearl Harbor still hung thick in the air.

Some Japanese American students approached their internment with a kind of gallows humor. For instance, Tai Uyeshima, who was from Los Angeles, like Sumi, and who played football for Tate at the camp high school, often gathered his buddies in the evening for "razzle-dazzle" football drills, more commonly known as "out of sight" plays. When they were tired from exercise, Tai and the other players serenaded the guards in their towers along the barbed-wire fencing. Night after night, they crooned many choruses of one of the top tunes on the hit parade, "Don't Fence Me In." That song became the most popular tune in camp.

Sumi spoke and heard from her classmates American slang, the words of marginalized Japanese Americans striving to be more American than Japanese. The September 1943 issue of *Jiho*, the English-language version of the school newspaper, printed expressions commonly heard in school. Sid Okazaki's favorite expression was "No! It can't be!" Rose Taniguchi's signature was "Watcha know." Hollywood Sawamura greeted everyone with "Check, check." And then there was "Lover" Yasuda, whose signature phrase was "Hello, sweetheart."

Every day at 4:00 p.m., Sumi left the Federal High School and studied Japanese at the Japanese School, where the atmosphere was old-world Japan. Her instructor—*sensei* in Japanese—was the Reverend Kenko Yamashita, a Buddhist priest from Hawaii. The short walk between the two schools represented the mammoth divide between two worlds. The full-time students enrolled at the Japanese School were mostly from Hawaii, Peru, or other Latin American countries. The structure of the Japanese School was rigid; no small talk about sweethearts or American movies was allowed. After morning calisthenics, students were required to stand at attention alongside their desks. When the teacher entered the room, they bowed deeply. All of the full-time students took *sushin*, a class on ethics that emphasized respect for elders, especially fathers and teachers.

From time to time in class, Sensei Yamashita reminded Sumi and the other Americanized nisei, who were born and educated in the United States, that they lacked the traditional Japanese virtues of honor, sacrifice, and courage. *Wagamma no tairiku no nisei*, he called them, which meant "spoiled American nisei."

Like the other nisei in camp, Sumi was torn between the opposing stereotypes of her generation, American-born children of Japanese parents: Were they 100 percent loyal to America, or were they a racially marginalized minority with questionable commitment to the United States? Though framed as a black-and-white choice, the issue of loyalty was less certain, more a riddle than a given. As with other nisei in the camp, Sumi's answer to this conundrum had to be found in personal circumstances far beyond her control, as much rooted in Japan as in the United States. On November 11, 1943, Tokiji sent a message through the Red Cross to his daughters in Japan: "All reunited in good health. Will repatriate. Wait and be good. Be obedient to Uncle and Aunt. Take good care of Grandmother until we join. Regards to relatives."

Sumi's fate was decided. In his petition requesting repatriation, Tokiji made plain his reasons. He described the "mental shock and disappointment" of years of harsh internment in all-male camps. "I am sixty-seven years old and I have no other desire than to be repatriated to Japan to spent the rest of my life in my father-land," he wrote. Sumi's desire to stay in America counted for nothing. Nobu realized that her husband needed plenty of space and time to heal from the effects of internment. The only way for Tokiji to become sound in mind and body was to leave America and return to Japan. Nobu supported his decision.

In Crystal City, Sumi felt bewildered and alienated. As part of the Texas curriculum, Sumi and the other students had social studies, which included lessons in citizenship. It was baffling to read the freedoms enumerated in the Bill of Rights—the freedom of religion, of speech, of the right to assemble, of protection against unwarranted searches and seizures—from inside the confines of what the Japanese called the Crystal City Concentration Camp. Everything about her life seemed a contradiction of the promises of citizenship. "None of it added up," said Sumi. "I thought of it as another lesson in *gaman*. Nothing to do but persevere." Many people, maybe even most people, would have become embittered by Sumi's circumstances, but she made it a point not to struggle unnecessarily with unresolvable dilemmas.

CHAPTER NINE

Yes-Yes, No-No

After Pearl Harbor, Japanese Americans serving in the US military were reclassified as 4C—enemy aliens—and many were discharged. Their weapons were taken from them, and they were imprisoned in internment camps, as were their disgraced issei parents. Then, on February 1, 1943, Roosevelt lifted the military ban on Japanese Americans and approved the formation of the 442nd all-nisei combat team. "No loyal citizen should be denied the democratic right to exercise the responsibilities of his citizenship, regardless of ancestry," Roosevelt said.

The key word in Roosevelt's statement was *loyal.* Only nisei were eligible for military service. After Roosevelt's decision, the War Relocation Authority (WRA) distributed loyalty questionnaires to every internee over the age of seventeen in all of the camps, issei and nisei alike. The tests were mandatory, and the purpose was twofold: to identify dedicated nisei for military service and to determine the loyalty of both issei and nisei. The list of questions was long, but the ultimate test of allegiance came down to yes-or-no answers to the final two questions, 27 and 28.

Question 27, distributed to nisei men, read, "Are you willing to serve in the armed forces of the United States on combat duty wherever ordered?" For women and all issei internees, question 27 was slightly different: "If the opportunity presents itself and you are found qualified, would you be willing to volunteer for the Army Nurse Corps or the WAAC?"

Question 28, worded the same for all respondents, read, "Will you swear unqualified allegiance to the United States of America and faithfully defend the United States from any or all attack by foreign or domestic forces, and forswear any form of allegiance to the Japanese Emperor, any foreign government, power or organization?" Japanese nationals were asked to give up allegiance to the country of their birth and swear allegiance to a country—the United States—that had imprisoned them. Some wondered if they would be without a country if they answered yes, since Japanese were not allowed to be naturalized citizens of the United States.

If respondents answered those two questions yes-yes, it was considered proof of their loyalty to the United States. If they answered no-no, they were considered disloyal. Prior to the mandatory tests, the two reasons given for the mass incarceration of the Japanese were that military advisers believed they posed a security threat, and Roosevelt needed a pool of internees to trade for Americans in Asia. With the implementation of the tests, the government added a third: recruitment of Japanese American soldiers to join the fight in Europe and Asia. For issei parents, the prospect of their American-born children fighting for America against Japan represented a crucible. Nisei wrestled with their allegiance to the country of their birth and their duty to their parents. Despite the conflict, more than 75 percent of nisei answered yes to both questions and were forever branded "yes-yes boys." Many joined the 442nd Regimental Combat Team, the all-Japanese unit whose slogan was "Go for broke." Those in the less than one-quarter that answered the questions no were equally branded "no-no boys." Inside the camps, the loyalty tests became the most acrimonious chapter of the Japanese internment.

In the winter and spring of 1943, as military recruiters poured into Crystal City and other camps to register nisei men for the 442nd, internees were indignant and defiant. In every bungalow, parents of drafted nisei viewed the recruitment as a conspiracy to deprive them of their children. Mary Tsukamoto, a nisei teenager, wrote, "People walked the roads, tears streaming down their troubled faces, silent and suffering. The little apartments were not big enough for the tremendous battle waged in practically every room." On the walls of camp barracks, anonymous poems appeared. One poem read:

> *The cream of the crop—*
> *Nisei soldiers—raised*
> *By wrinkles on the parents' brow.*

In Crystal City, the battle between father and son and of brother against brother was particularly evident in the quarters of the Uno family of Los Angeles. George Uno, a native of Sendai, Japan, was nineteen years old when he immigrated to the United States in 1905. In 1912, he married Riki Kita, and they had ten children.

When war broke out, their eldest son, also named George but known as Buddy, was working for the Japanese army in Shanghai as a liaison between the army and foreign correspondents. Like the other Uno children, Buddy was born in the United States and had a typical nisei upbringing. He went to junior high in the Boyle Heights section of Los Angeles, not far from where Sumi grew up in Little Tokyo. He loved Hollywood movies. At the age of nine he saw his first film, *Three Jumps Ahead*, starring Tom Mix and his horse, Tony. As a senior at Compton High School, a primarily white school, Buddy worked for *Rafu Shimpo*, the Japanese newspaper of Los Angeles. His column, "A Nisei Melodrama," which offered opinions on social and cultural matters, was published in Los Angeles, San Francisco, and Seattle.

As a child, Buddy felt marginalized by racism. At twelve, when the Uno family lived in Utah, he was rejected as a member of the Boy Scouts because of his race. In the 1930s in Utah, Japanese Americans were denied access to public swimming pools and sat in the balconies with African Americans in movie theaters.

Over time, Buddy grew curious about his Japanese heritage and in 1939 moved to Shanghai. When the war between Japan and the

United States began, Buddy was an employee of the Japanese Army Press Bureau and was named editor of the government-controlled *Shanghai Evening Post and Mercury.* He wore an army uniform and brandished a military sword. One lieutenant colonel in the Japanese army described Uno as a "Yankeefied Japanese officer." After the attack on Pearl Harbor, Buddy wrote an editorial that proclaimed, "The year 1942 will be remembered as a year of emancipation for the peoples of East Asia, for during the brief twelve months, through the consistent victories of the Imperial Nipponese Armed Forces, millions have been released from the shackles of Anglo-American imperialism."

The Japanese army transferred Buddy to Bunka Camp in Tokyo, where American prisoners of war were held. At the camp, he attempted to coerce POWs into writing anti-American radio scripts for broadcast. Many POWs testified that Uno was abusive. George H. Henshaw, an American POW, wrote of Uno in his diary, "He threatened us with everything from a firing squad to the tortures of a Gestapo dungeon if anyone ever dared to question an order from this camp again."

Given Buddy's activities in Japan, the FBI of course profiled his father in Los Angeles. Agents made several trips to his home after the attack on Pearl Harbor. Kay Uno, the youngest of the ten children, remembered the moment on December 7, 1941, when she learned about Pearl Harbor. She was nine years old and on her way to Sunday-morning service at the Church of Christ, where the Uno family regularly worshipped. "We were in the car, going to church, and the radio was on and said that the war had started," Kay wrote in an essay published in *A Fence Away from Freedom.* Her father turned the car around and went back home. Her brothers wanted to go outside to find out more about what was happening in Hawaii from their friends, but Riki, their mother, ordered them to stay inside: "You boys, you cannot go anywhere."

Kay's brothers shared a love of model airplanes, which hung from their bedroom window and over a table where they worked. George had sent the plans for one of these models to Buddy, the oldest brother, in Japan. On February 1, 1942, when agents came to the house to arrest George, they removed all the model planes from the house and told George he was considered a spy because he sent airplane plans to Buddy in Japan. An innocent gift to Buddy was now evidence of George's disloyalty.

Shortly after George's arrest, Riki and the children relocated to the Santa Anita racetrack, not far from Los Angeles. As Kay remembered, they stayed in a tar-paper barrack on the parking lot, the scent of manure from the horse stalls wafting through the tar paper. Later, while the children moved to Camp Amache in Colorado, George, classified as a dangerous enemy alien, shuttled through a succession of camps: Missoula, Fort Lincoln, Lordsburg, and Santa Fe.

In Camp Amache, one of his sons, Ernest, known as Ernie in the family, turned eighteen and answered yes-yes to the loyalty questionnaire. With his voluntary application for the 442nd already signed, Ernie traveled to the Santa Fe Internment Camp to seek his father's blessing. American surveillance officers at the Santa Fe camp monitored the painful meeting of father and son. George listened as his son explained his decision to join the US Army. After a prolonged silence, George told his son he disagreed with his decision. The battle was joined between father and son.

As a Japanese man, George Uno was trained to believe that a soldier goes to war with the idea that he will never return. "You should go and be prepared to die," Uno told his son. When Ernie was shipped out with the 442nd to fight in Italy, he left believing that his father wanted him to die. Many years later, George explained that he only wanted Ernie to recognize that if he joined the military, he should be prepared for death.

For Ernie the decision to become a US soldier wasn't easy. He felt particularly let down by President Roosevelt. One year after Roosevelt had signed Executive Order 9066, leading to the incarceration of 120,000 Japanese and Japanese Americans, Roosevelt urged the formation of the 442nd. Ernie understood what was on the line for him and other Japanese Americans. The issue was whether Japanese Americans would fight and, if necessary, die for America. The paradox was that Roosevelt asked loyalty of a disenfranchised group of people—people like Ernie, who'd been stripped of their rights as Americans. Ernie decided to pay the price of Roosevelt's loyalty test. It was personal. He felt it was his duty to fight for America to counterbalance the actions of Buddy, his brother who fought on the side of Japan.

Two other Uno brothers, Stanley and Howard, also answered yes-yes to the loyalty questions. They were among the earliest nisei volunteers in the Military Intelligence Service, two of more than six thousand Japanese Americans performing secret operations in the Pacific. Like the other volunteers, Stanley and Howard translated and deciphered enemy codes. The men in this service were known as Yankee samurai. World War II historians have credited the work of the MIS in the Pacific with shortening the war by approximately two years.

As Ernie felt the need to atone for Buddy's loyalty to Japan, so did Howard and Stanley. In a letter to his younger brother Robert, Stanley urged him to join the US Army and fight for the country of his birth rather than side with Japan and his disloyal brother. "I tell you that I love this country, above any and all things which may be on this conflicted world," Stanley told Robert. "I am unashamed of my love. On the contrary, I am proud."

As in the American Civil War, when brothers from the North fought against brothers from the South, so it was with the Uno brothers. Stanley expressed his fury with Buddy for fighting alongside the Japanese. He vowed that, if given the chance, he would destroy Buddy. "We infantrymen live by the ghastly phrase of 'kill or be killed,'" Stanley wrote. "To uphold the American principles by which I live, I will fight even Buddy."

When Stanley wrote the letter, Robert was a teenager interned in Crystal City with his father, his mother, his sister Kay, and his brother Edison. Edison was two years younger than Sumi, and a nisei leader in camp. Easygoing and good-looking, Edison was elected class president every year he was in school. Even in the face of arbitrary internment, Edison urged his peers to value their American citizenship and to stand against what he labeled their "too Japanese-y" issei fathers.

From behind barbed wire in Crystal City as a teenager, Edison made speeches, urging young Japanese Americans to not give up on their country. "This internment is against our constitutional rights. We're American citizens, and as American citizens we should not have been put into camps," Edison told his fellow students. "If you were in Los Angeles, and you were taken into prison, and they found out that you were not supposed to be in prison, they would let you go and give you a letter of pardon. We need that pardon."

With those words, Edison became the first Japanese American from inside an internment camp to ask for official redress. Edison believed that the way to prove his loyalty as an American was to claim his right—and the rights of other Japanese Americans—to challenge the internment of the Japanese and their children on the basis of race as un-American and unconstitutional.

The family of Alan Taniguchi faced similar disagreements. In the early 1920s, Alan's father, Isamu, an immigrant from Japan, worked as a farmer on the San Joaquin Delta near Stockton, California. In those days, the delta farms were remote and inaccessible by automobile. The only access to the four-hundred-acre farm where Isamu grew tomatoes, melons, cauliflower, and other vegetables was by pack boats that plied the San Joaquin and Sacramento Rivers. In 1922, Sadayo, Isamu's wife, pregnant with her first son, moved to a boardinghouse in Stockton owned by Isamu's parents. Alan was born there, but his given name was not Alan. Sadayo named her son Yamato, an ancient name for the spirit or soul of Japan. A second son, Izumi, was born in 1926.

Isamu had a keen mind, a strong back, and skillful hands. As a boy in Japan, he was schooled in the art and philosophy of horti-culture. As a result, his farming business in the United States prospered. The family moved to Brentwood, halfway between Stockton and Oakland. Isamu and five other Japanese farmers started the Brentwood Produce Association, which built its own packing plant to process and ship produce directly to markets. In 1932, Isamu cross-pollinated two varieties of tomatoes, which were shipped by the Brentwood co-op to the East Coast market at favorable prices. While many Americans suffered during the Depression, the Taniguchi family prospered. Isamu's success was the realization of a long-held dream.

After Pearl Harbor, the lives of the Taniguchis followed the predictable pattern. Around noon on March 7, 1942, all four members of the family, plus a farmer who was boarding with them, were gathered at the table for lunch at their Brentwood home. Two FBI agents arrived at the door. Isamu was not surprised. All of his other partners in the co-op had been arrested. Isamu's suitcase was already packed. One of the agents was older, calm, and experienced. The other was young, with red hair and a spring-loaded temper.

The young agent pointed to the table, spread with a typical Japanese lunch of fish, rice, and assorted vegetables, and blurted, "This is why you'll never be Americans. You are Japs and have to have Jap food."

Isamu sat silent and still. His family followed his lead. But the boarder, a Japanese American, could not contain his anger. "You're no different," he shot back. "With your red hair and temper, you must be Irish. You eat your potatoes, cabbage, and corned beef. Does that make you less of an American?"

The older agent sent the other outside and finished the search himself. By then, Isamu and Alan had already turned all contraband items—shortwave radios, cameras, rifles, and swords—to the constable's office. The agent found nothing. Wordlessly, Isamu picked up his suitcase and was taken to the county jail in Stockton. Alan, then nineteen and a freshman at the University of California at Berkeley, dropped out of school and came home to take his father's place.

Isamu was granted the usual hearings, and the charges against him were unsurprising. On the farm, Isamu had an incinerator that he pulled behind a tractor to burn brush. In the hearing, Isamu was accused of sending smoke signals to the Japanese with the burning brush. In addition, FBI agents suspected Isamu of arranging six-foot-by-twenty-five-foot muslin sheets, used for protecting tomato beds from frost, in arrow shapes that were supposedly pointed toward military installations. He denied all charges.

Nonetheless, Isamu was classified a dangerous enemy alien, and the family was separated. After his arrest, he was taken to the Silver Avenue Detention Center in San Francisco, then to the Santa Fe Internment Camp, and subsequently transferred to the internment camp in Lordsburg, New Mexico. While Isamu was incarcerated in Lordsburg, on July 27, 1942, 145 issei prisoners arrived at the train station near the camp. Armed guards instructed the prisoners to walk the two miles to the entrance of the camp. Shiro Kobata, fifty-eight, had suffered from tuberculosis, and Hirota Isomura, fifty-nine, had a spinal injury that slowed his walk. Both men fell behind on the march to the camp. A guard, armed with a twelve-gauge shotgun, believed they were attempting to escape and ordered them to halt. When they kept moving, the guard took aim and killed them both.

The incident intensified Isamu's sense of disillusionment. Always quiet, Isamu grew insular, and that summer he decided to request repatriation to Japan for himself, his wife, and his American-born sons.

By then, Sadayo, Alan, and Izumi were interned in the Gila River Relocation Camp in the desert of Arizona, where temperatures rose to 125 degrees in the summer and dropped to 30 degrees in the winter. Sadayo and her sons lived in a crowded barrack with communal toilets. The rules of the camp required all of the thirteen thousand internees to be in their barracks by nine with lights out by ten. Guards in sentry towers had orders to shoot anyone who approached within twenty feet of the fence.

Izumi, Alan's younger brother, worked as a timekeeper for the

Block 66 mess hall, tracking the hours of the people who worked there. Mealtimes at Gila River were busy and chaotic, as thousands of people filed into the mess hall to eat food prepared by untrained cooks. Izumi and Alan referred to the food as "slop suey." Worse than the quality of food was the loss of traditional Japanese family meals. Instead of gathering around a family table, they were crowded in a mess hall with thousands of others. Conversation was impossible, table manners forgotten.

On April 23, 1943, Izumi was in the mess hall when Eleanor Roosevelt arrived for a camp inspection, accompanied by Dillon Myer, national director of the War Relocation Authority. Eleanor was on a mission from FDR. Earlier that month, Roosevelt had received a letter from Interior Secretary Harold Ickes, who reported that morale among Japanese American internees had dangerously declined. While internees had "first accepted with philosophical understanding the decision of their government," Ickes told Roosevelt that these imprisoned Americans, charged with no crimes, were now bitter. "I do not think that we can disregard the unnecessary creation of a hostile group right in our own territory."

As Eleanor toured the camp, hundreds of Japanese American teenagers, including Izumi, surrounded her. She told them that she was proud of their resourcefulness. In the challenging desert terrain, internees raised livestock and produced enough vegetables to feed the entire camp. On-site was a camouflage-net factory, where nineteen-year-old Alan worked, that manufactured enough nets for the US Army. "Everything is spotlessly clean," Eleanor later wrote in her report. "The people work on their whitewashed barracks constantly, and you can see the results of their labors."

The first lady experienced the unrelenting dust storms in Gila River that turned everyone's hair white and eyes red. "It chokes you and brings about irritations of the nose and throat," she wrote. With Myer at her side, Eleanor toured every facility essential to the camp's life: the wards in the hospital, the barracks that had been set aside for nursery and elementary schools, a high school, a library. She noted that the tiny living quarters were decorated with paper flowers, poems, and paintings.

Eleanor witnessed as well evidence of the declining morale of the internees. In Gila River, as in other camps, the loyalty test had sparked outrage. In her report to FDR, she argued that it was time to disband the camps and allow the Japanese to return to their homes. "To undo mistakes is always harder than to create them originally, but we seldom have foresight," Eleanor told her husband. "Therefore, we have no choice but to try to correct our past mistakes."

In March 1943, one month after his visit to Gila River, Myer publicly called for an end to the relocation camps. He reported that they were too expensive to build and maintain and said that in his opinion the Japanese Americans, as a group, no longer constituted a military threat. "After many months of operating relocation centers, the War Relocation Authority is convinced that they are undesirable institutions and should be removed from the American scene as soon as possible," wrote Myer. "Life in a relocation center is an unnatural and un-American sort of life. Keep in mind that the evacuees were charged with nothing except having Japanese ancestors; yet the very fact of their confinement in relocation centers fosters suspicion of their loyalties and adds to their discouragement."

While Roosevelt agreed with Eleanor and Myer that the incarceration should end as soon as possible, his military advisers warned that subversive activities among Japanese and Japanese Americans were still a danger to the war effort. Roosevelt again sided with the military advisers. The internment dragged on.

While in Gila River, Alan and Izumi Taniguchi received permission to visit their father in the Lordsburg camp in New Mexico. During the face-to-face meeting, Isamu demanded that both of them refuse to volunteer for the American military. Alan was nineteen, and Izumi was sixteen—one year away from eligibility for the draft. Even though both sons were born in America, had pledged allegiance to the flag, and had sung the national anthem, Isamu now demanded they put their loyalty aside and consider themselves as young men without a country. Izumi bitterly refused. He told his father that he'd never even been to Japan and that his loyalty was to the United States. To prove his allegiance, Izumi vowed to join the US military as soon as he turned seventeen. Alan was more measured, but equally firm: he told his father that he would do whatever was necessary to stay in the United States, his homeland.

When Alan returned to Gila River, he confronted the infamous two questions: number 27, concerning his willingness to fight for America; and number 28, about forswearing allegiance to Japan. Alan wanted to answer yes-yes, but he could not bring himself to officially defy his father. He told authorities that, until his constitutional rights were restored and his family was released from internment, he would not answer the questionnaire at all. Officially, that made Alan a no-no, which meant that he was likely to be sent to Tule Lake camp in California, where internees considered "disloyal" were segregated and lived in punitive conditions. To avoid transfer, Alan formally asked the Religious Society of Friends, known as the Quakers, who had important contacts with the INS, to petition for his parole from Gila River so that he could resume his education. The Quakers were the only group in America that consistently opposed internment and offered protection for internees. They agreed to plead Alan's case.

In the spring of 1943, shortly after Eleanor's visit to Gila River, Isamu asked for a transfer to the Crystal City Internment Camp, where he was reunited with his wife and younger son. Alan, who was no longer a minor, refused to go to Crystal City, but Izumi had no choice. When his mother and brother left Arizona in May 1943 for Crystal City, Alan stayed behind in Gila River. A few months later, the Quakers negotiated Alan's release. He moved to Detroit, where he lived with relatives and continued his education at the Detroit Institute of Technology.

In Crystal City, Isamu filed repatriation requests for himself, his wife, and Izumi. Alan traveled to Crystal City and told O'Rourke that his father was determined to return to Japan and explained he was there to prevent his younger brother's repatriation. By policy, visiting relatives of Crystal City internees met with their families only in the Visitor Center, where security officers monitored conversations. However, O'Rourke granted permission for Alan to stay with his parents in their bungalow during his visit, a privilege that O'Rourke did not ordinarily grant.

After Alan entered the camp, issei leaders summoned him to a meeting, where they accused him of disrespect for his father and betrayal of his Japanese ancestors. "Traitor," they shouted. Alan was pushed to the ground and beaten. Undeterred, Alan picked himself up and told the issei leaders that there was no place for him or for his brother in Japan. They were American-born, they had their own lives to lead, and they would stay in America.

After the meeting, Isamu relented. He could not go against both of his sons. He withdrew his application for repatriation and gave Izumi permission to live in Detroit with Alan. As soon as Izumi was eligible, he volunteered for the US Army and joined the all-Japanese branch of the Military Intelligence Service.

Isamu and Sadayo stayed in Crystal City. Isamu worked as supervisor of the carpentry shop. He built tables and chairs, repaired walls, and constructed new buildings. In his leisure time, he devoted himself to the planting of gardens. Over time, he decided that the wishes of his American-born sons were paramount. "I want one thing only," he told his sons in letters. "Peace."

Near the end of 1943, as the Unos, the Taniguchis, and others struggled to reconcile their choices, news of the camp in Crystal City took center stage at a meeting in New York. In a speech on November 11, 1943, at the Waldorf-Astoria in New York, Attorney General Francis Biddle described a scene in faraway Crystal City that illustrated the high cost many Japanese Americans had paid to prove their loyalty. The speech was given to the Jewish Theological Seminary of America, and that day, the dining hall of the famed hotel was filled with rabbis. Biddle told his audience about a Japanese husband and wife interned in Crystal City who were among

169 Japanese repatriated in August 1943 to Japan from that camp. Both of the couple's sons were being released from the internment camp because they had volunteered for the 442nd.

"The morning the repatriates were scheduled to leave, the two Japanese boys returned to the camp to say good-bye to their parents," said Biddle. "Just at sunrise, as the American flag was being raised, and as the entire population of the camp gathered around the flagpole for a farewell ceremony, the two young Japanese Americans stepped forward, saluted the flag, and sang 'God Bless America.' Then they left to join the American Army."

By the time Biddle made that speech, more than five thousand Japanese Americans had joined the 442nd, and many were fighting side by side with other Americans on the Italian front. "Is anything more needed to entitle the loyal Japanese Americans to recognition?" Biddle asked. As attorney general, Biddle had not supported the mass evacuation of the Japanese from the West Coast, but he had implemented their removal—and the removal of their American-born children—on orders from President Roosevelt. Now Biddle expressed regret. On that day, the conflict over loyalty between sons and fathers, played out in Crystal City, was finally understood at the highest level of government.

CHAPTER TEN

A Test of Faith

January 26, 1944

All he could see was the narrow path ahead between two rows of American soldiers, who stood six feet apart and carried rifles with fixed bayonets. It was early morning and snowing at the train station in Santa Fe. The icy air straightened the Reverend Yoshiaki Fukuda's already rigid posture. At forty-six and standing five feet ten inches, Fukuda was the tallest of the twenty-three Japanese enemy aliens gathered at the train station. All were considered treacherous by the American government.

The Japanese men boarded a specially chartered Missouri Pacific train that would take them directly to the small depot in Crystal City. Gas lamps hung from the old train's walls, and a coal-burning boiler fueled its motion.

In his seat, Fukuda took a black leather notebook from the pocket of his shirt, and in the dim light of the car he jotted down his thoughts. "I came to this country through divine will, and therefore I feel I must do my utmost to stay here," he wrote in bold cursive. His mission in life was to spread the Konko faith, a Shinto sect little known outside of Japan, in America. He was a missionary—not a politician, but a preacher who did not quietly accept the internment of Japanese and Japanese Americans. He wrote strongly worded letters to American officials in which he detailed abuse of Japanese

internees and called for an end to the mass internment. His outspo-
kenness had made him dangerously influential.

In the two years since his arrest by the FBI on December 7, 1941,
Fukuda had been imprisoned in two other internment camps. In
the first camp, in Missoula, Montana, in the middle of the Northern Rockies, he'd cleaned Army stables and constructed roads and
airfields in temperatures as low as fifteen degrees below zero. At the
second camp, in Lordsburg, New Mexico, situated on a plain just
north of the Mexican border, he did more of the same in temperatures as high as 120 degrees. One day in Lordsburg, Fukuda was
building a road during the hottest part of the day. The Japanese crew
leader asked the officer in charge if the men could rest. In response, a
watchtower guard shouted at the men to keep working and barked,
"Japs, we'll kill you."

Fukuda had good reason to believe the threat was real. Like
Isamu Taniguchi, Fukuda had been in Lordsburg when Kobata and
Isomura, two elderly Japanese internees, were shot and killed. Fukuda's recollection of that day was more detailed than Taniguchi's. In
his memoir, *My Six Years of Internment*, published in 1957, Fukuda
described the other guards' response to the killings: later that day,
they praised the shooter of the two issei internees for "avenging the
treacherous attack on Pearl Harbor." Fukuda said that the other
internees in Lordsburg were forced to dig the graves of the two dead
men. "The grave diggers found that the ground was very hard, and
requested a rest period. The guard refused their request and told
them, 'These graves are going to be used to bury Japanese. Keep
digging. If you don't, I'll make you dig two or three more graves.'"

Like many enemy aliens, Fukuda was well read in the Geneva
Convention, the agreement signed by many countries, including
Japan, that mandated and defined humane treatment of prisoners of war. Fukuda's copy was dog-eared. After the deaths of the
two internees in Lordsburg, Fukuda petitioned the Spanish consul
and the US Department of Justice and documented other stories of
physical abuse. One such story noted, "The Issei never *monku-ed*

(complained) . . . very few talked about the abuse they received from the guards. . . . I was kicked, hit, and was sobbing. . . . What did they want? I was just a farmer. What could I have done to be arrested and taken away?"

Fukuda's petitions for redress piled high in the Spanish consul's office. To camp authorities, Fukuda was a troublemaker, but to many of the internees, he was a prophet. A strong man, long trained in the art of judo, Fukuda had thick forearms and an ample chest. His black hair was closely cropped, as was his thin mustache. In Lordsburg, the desert sun had aged his face. The rules in the Lordsburg camp were the same as in Missoula: no books in Japanese; all mail censored; no display of emperor-worshipping Shintoism allowed.

In Missoula and Lordsburg, Fukuda, who had a magisterial voice, conducted Konko worship services every morning at 5:30 a.m. and made speeches on Sundays, Thursdays, and Fridays. Life behind barbed wire was a test of his faith. "Even fish will lose their vitality if they are taken from the seas or rivers and placed in a tank or pond," Fukuda wrote. "Likewise, internees suffer from the bleak life that they live. They become irritable and quarrel over trivial matters. They become sleepless, worrying about the plight of their families."

In each of the camps he was assigned, Fukuda used his internment to practice long hours of meditation, to improve his skills in judo, kendo, and Japanese calligraphy, and to strengthen his personal will. When internees in Lordsburg argued over who would do demeaning work, Fukuda volunteered to do the most unpleasant tasks. He cleaned communal toilets, disposed of garbage, and worked in the kitchen. More often than not, others followed his example. The black notebook went everywhere with Fukuda. He frequently reminded himself of one of the central Konko teachings: "Misfortune is a blessing in disguise."

Already, Fukuda had begun to see some of his experiences of internment as a blessing. In camp, he met Japanese leaders—ministers, businessmen, and teachers—from all over the United States and Latin America. He learned how to negotiate with American camp officials.

When the war ended, Fukuda believed these contacts and skills would help him fulfill the central mission of his life: to propagate the Konko faith in America.

Outside the window, the train snaked its way across the great Southwest from Santa Fe, crossing into Texas sometime during the night. Fukuda pulled back the shade and looked into the vast Texas night. Fukuda was genuinely happy for the first time in many months, since the train was bound for the Crystal City Internment Camp. After fourteen months of separation, he would finally be reunited with his wife, Shinko, and their seven children, all born in America.

At 1:30 a.m. on January 27, 1944, the train came to a stop at the small depot in Crystal City, and the soldiers escorted Fukuda and the others off the train. It hardly felt like winter at all, and above them was the primeval sight of a thousand stars. Fukuda climbed onto the bus with the others, and the bus drove slowly past the town and approached the front of the camp.

Inside the gates, news of the men's arrival had preceded them. In the cluster of Japanese women who were there to greet them, Fukuda saw Shinko, who had arrived with their children almost twelve hours before on a bus from San Antonio. A Boy Scout band, made up of Japanese boys dressed in crisp uniforms, played. Like other issei, Fukuda guarded his emotions, repressing them to a hairbreadth—even on a day as momentous as this one. Instead of rushing to embrace, as Americans might have, the women lined up at some distance from the men. The long-separated wives and husbands then bowed to each other.

O'Rourke approached Fukuda and extended his hand, an uncharacteristic formality to his casual, cheerful deportment. In his hand O'Rourke held a piece of paper, which he presented to Fukuda. The memorandum from the Department of Justice forbade Fukuda from making any public statements in camp or assuming any leadership role. He was profiled as among the most dangerous of Japanese enemy aliens.

Fukuda did not protest; instead, he nodded and told O'Rourke that he understood. The minister was not surprised; he knew that O'Rourke had read his FBI file and knew every aspect of his history.

Fukuda was born in 1898 in a mountain village in the Nara prefecture of Japan. In 1918, Fukuda was conscripted into the Japanese army and served five months as a second lieutenant. Afterward, he attended an elite junior college; in 1925, he enrolled in the Imperial University of Tokyo, where he studied sociology and law. While at the university, he suffered a relapse of tuberculosis, which he had contracted as a younger man. In desperation, he sought the help of a Konko minister, who prayed with Fukuda. The symptoms went away, and Fukuda converted to the Konko faith, which had broken from many of the teachings of Shinto, the official religion of the Japanese state.

In 1927, after graduation from the Imperial University, Fukuda entered a spartan style of religious training at a Konko seminary in Tokyo. Every morning at three, he awoke and took cold showers for spiritual purification. At 3:45 a.m., he went to the worship hall for silent prayer. A worship service was held at 4:00 a.m., followed by breakfast. At 5:20 a.m., Fukuda and the other religious trainees cleaned wooden floors on their knees. They fasted regularly.

At the end of his rigid training, Fukuda was ordained a minister at the headquarters of the Konko faith in Tokyo in 1928. In an arranged marriage in April of the following year, Fukuda married the daughter of the ruling leader of the Konko faith. The marriage was fortunate in more than bloodline: Shinko, his wife, had trained as a Konko minister, as well. Fukuda pressed his superiors to send them both to America to start Konko churches.

Three years after he began training, Fukuda finally received permission to become an American Konko missionary. On October 17, 1930, Fukuda and his wife boarded the cargo ship *Hawaii Maru* at the port of Yokohama. In photographs taken that day, Shinko wore an American-style dress and hat, not the traditional wear of Japanese women. Fukuda wore a crisp silk suit, not the faded-black *haori* jacket and torn *hakama* pants he typically wore in his day-to-day duties as a minister. "Banzai, Reverend Fukuda!" roared the crowd that had gathered to send them off.

Only five months later, the Fukudas had started a Konko church on Bush Street in the heart of Japantown in San Francisco and had attracted two hundred members. With the onset of the Depression, many Japanese workers in San Francisco worked at menial jobs as gardeners, restaurant workers, and salesclerks at curio shops. Young nisei worked as "schoolboys" or "schoolgirls"—domestic servants— in Caucasian households. "We grew up during the Depression, and it was hard times," said Nobusuke Fukuda, the second-born son of the Fukudas. "Our church took care of the neighborhood. My mother cooked for everyone and never sent anyone away hungry. My father treated all the church members as though they were family. He found them jobs, loaned them money, married and buried them."

Fukuda kept the same severe schedule on Bush Street in San Francisco as he had during his religious training in Japan—the cold showers, fasting, and meditation. Before dawn, he silently swept the streets in front of the Konko mission as an act of prayer. After a reporter from the *San Francisco Chronicle* mentioned Fukuda's predawn sweeping, crowds showed up to watch the ritual, and the Konko minister became mildly famous.

On December 7, 1941, Fukuda, Shinko, and their younger children were in San Jose, where Fukuda led a worship service at a new Konko mission. His three older sons—nine-year-old Michi-suke, eight-year-old Nobusuke, and seven-year-old Saburo—were at home on Bush Street in San Francisco.

Two FBI agents knocked at the door on Bush Street. Michi-suke, the eldest son, also known as Mitch, answered the door. The men ordered the boy to get his father. "He's in San Jose," answered Michisuke. "At church."

On Monday, December 8, 1941, the *San Francisco Call-Bulletin* put out a "blue streak edition" with the banner headline

U.S. DECLARES WAR! A text of Roosevelt's war message appeared on the front page. On page two, under the headline "F.B.I. Rounding Up Japanese Aliens in the Bay Area," was the story of the arrest of Fukuda, who was identified as a "Japanese preacher," and thirty others who were among the first group to be picked up in the roundup. In addition to a full sweep of Japantown, the story noted, all cars and trucks driven by Japanese on streets or bridges, including the Golden Gate Bridge, were stopped and searched for explosives. Nationwide, the number of Japanese men arrested on December 7 was 736.

In Fukuda's heavily redacted FBI file, agents described his arrest in San Jose and noted, "The subject is a minister in the Konkokyo Federation of North America, Japanese churches composed of the doctrine of Shintoism, which is a strongly nationalistic doctrine." He was booked at the Santa Clara County Jail and later transferred with other issei men to a jail at an immigration station in San Francisco.

Fukuda and the others were held in San Francisco for ten days. During that time, the FBI interrogated many members of his church, including his wife. In addition to caring for her six children, Shinko took charge of the vital functions of the Konko mission. She conducted prayer services and comforted the families in the congregation, who wondered when they would be forced to evacuate from their own homes.

Her title at the Konko Church was second head minister, Fukuda being head minister. In the days after his arrest, the streets in front of the church were not swept. Shinko cooked great quantities of rice and spaghetti. Almost twenty people, members of the church whose fathers and husbands had also been arrested, moved in with Shinko and her children. They had no other place to live. Finally, in the midst of raising her children, carrying out her ministerial duties, and sheltering the homeless parishioners, Shinko discovered she was pregnant with her seventh child. Without her husband, she told her friends, "I am just like a monkey who has fallen out of a tree."

At his hearing on February 2, 1942, before a three-man panel,

Fukuda was surprised at how much information the FBI had gathered on his activities and how long he had been under surveillance. The case against him centered on eight activities. His connections to officers of the Japanese Foreign Service, many of whom were classmates from Tokyo, were carefully documented. Members of the Japanese army and navy had stayed with the Fukuda family as guests on Bush Street. He had recently met with Fritz Wiedemann, consul general of Germany, in San Francisco. Fukuda described this as an innocent meeting, during which he asked Wiedemann, based on his experience with Germans in America, how the Japanese in the United States might expect to be treated in the event of war. The FBI agents also knew that Fukuda was a reserve officer in the Japanese army and a member of the Japanese Veterans Society of California. On several occasions, he had held receptions for Japanese navy officers when they visited San Francisco. Moreover, he sent care packages to Japanese soldiers, and on a previous visit to China, Fukuda had visited Japanese soldiers.

Fukuda argued that all of what he had done was a courtesy to his fellow countrymen on their visits to the United States and to facilitate the growth of the Konko Church in San Francisco. Like the others who were arrested that day, Fukuda was incarcerated without charges. He had no lawyer, but offered his own defense, arguing that none of the accusations against him could be classified as acts of espionage, crimes, or subversive activities. He was a citizen of Japan, but he was also a legal resident of the United States. He insisted that he was no danger to the United States, only a missionary.

At home on Bush Street, Shinko, also a legal resident of the United States, maintained her husband's innocence. Later, however, she confided to him that a part of her wondered if he was in fact a spy. If so, she knew that he would never reveal his identity, not even to her. As a traditional Japanese man of his era, he would rather die.

The Konko religion has an equivalent to the Judeo-Christian Bible's story of Job, the Hebrew poem written at the beginning of the fourth century BC that confronts the universal question "Why do good people suffer?" The founder of the Konko faith, Bunjiro Kawate, a farmer, endured his own version of the Job story. Job lost seven sons and three daughters and was visited by plagues and boils. As a young man, the Konko founder lost five members of his family, and in his forties he suffered a serious illness. In the face of such losses, both Job and the Konko founder were first silenced by grief, but then spurred to seek spiritual answers from God to major questions about life and death. For Shinko and Yoshiaki Fukuda, internment was a Job-like experience.

In March 1942, the fourth month of the war, notices for Evacuation Order No. 19 appeared all over Japantown in San Francisco. Shinko knew that she and the children would be forced to evacuate their home. She made lists of what she could take: one suitcase per person, cups and bowls. On the day they left their house, the sky was sunny and clear, and a cool wind blew off the bay. The streets were noisy and crowded with American soldiers and hundreds of Japanese evacuees and their American-born children. Buses squeezed into Japantown to pick up evacuees. Shinko had her family's government-issued number pinned to her dark coat, and she hung white tags with the same identification number around the neck of each of her children.

A tall, lean white woman dressed in trousers approached, her gait marred by a limp, her right leg partially paralyzed from polio. She raised a boxy camera and motioned to Shinko and her children to stand still. The camera clicked. In the photos, Shinko's dark hair is pulled back into a hard bun, revealing a magnificently open and decent face ravaged by worry. She was thirty-six years old and pregnant with her seventh child. In her arms, she cradles one of her young sons. Five-year-old Makiko, her only daughter, wears a short dress covered by a sturdy wool coat. Standing beside Makiko is an American soldier, gesturing for the family to board a bus. With one hand, Makiko tugs at her mother's coat; with the other, she holds a doll.

Shinko and her children were taken by bus to the Tanforan racetrack, located on the outskirts of San Francisco. Tanforan was one of the sixteen assembly centers established by the Army. All summer, Shinko, her children, and two other members of their church lived behind the racetrack in a stall in a stable that was ten by twenty feet. At night, they slept on mattresses stuffed with straw. Twice a day a siren blew, and they stood in front of their stall for a head count; three times a day they lined up at the mess hall.

Shinko stayed behind on her mattress in the horse stall, too weak to stand in line. The walls were whitewashed, but on warm days, when the flies were bad, the smell of horses rose up from the floors. On June 6, 1942, she went into labor and was taken to a hospital in nearby San Bruno, where she gave birth to a son that she named Koichi. As she recovered from childbirth, one of the families from the Konko Church in San Francisco volunteered to take care of the newborn Koichi. The older boys took care of Makiko and the younger sons. Much of the time, Shinko was alone in that stall.

On the day following Koichi's birth, June 7, General John DeWitt, the Army general who'd convinced Roosevelt to evacuate all Japanese and Japanese Americans from the West Coast, announced that the removal of all 120,000 of them was complete.

Four months later, Shinko and all of her children left the assembly center at Tanforan and were sent to the Topaz internment camp in the highlands of Delta, Utah. The train trip to Topaz took more than a week and was hard on Shinko. By the time she arrived at camp, she had to be hospitalized. A Japanese doctor in the camp diagnosed her with rheumatic heart disease.

By February 1943, her condition was critical. The Japanese doctor, Ben Kondo, thought she was near death and asked the camp officer in charge at Topaz if Fukuda could visit her. The officer declined the request. Incarcerated enemy aliens, especially those as notorious as Fukuda, were not allowed to visit their families. The doctor went on strike for one week in opposition to the decision. He refused to see patients in the hospital until Fukuda was allowed to see his wife.

In a rare move, Fukuda was given temporary leave to visit his family in Topaz. Over time, Shinko's health improved, and in Topaz, Fukuda first saw Koichi, his newborn son. Fukuda was preoccupied with internment issues, and the Fukuda children knew that their father's ministry was his first priority. "I was the youngest," said Koichi many years later, when he was a grown man living in San Francisco. "I knew I had to obey my father. He was so busy with the church and the community. I was really raised by my two older brothers—Mitch and Nob. It took me a long time to understand him."

During Fukuda's stay at Topaz, he held worship services that drew large crowds. In a political meeting with fifty other issei men, he announced his plan to request that he and his family be transferred to the Crystal City Internment Camp. "Crystal City is the showcase for President Roosevelt," he told his peers. The food, shelter, and schools would be better than in any other camp. It was imperative, Fukuda said, that separated Japanese families reunite.

Several men, including one powerful minister in camp, disagreed with Fukuda. The opponents argued that volunteering to transfer to Crystal City would prolong their children's imprisonment, and they feared that their sons would face increased pressure to join the American military in Crystal City. Fukuda replied that Japanese men, such as himself, should remain loyal to Japan, but nisei children, born in America, should be loyal to the United States. It was a provocative statement: most of the issei loyal to Japan wanted their children to be devoted to the home of their forefathers.

Internment camps were sieves of gossip. That night, an informer noted Fukuda's declaration of loyalty to Japan in a secret memorandum, which quickly made its way to the authorities in Topaz. By morning, Fukuda learned that he would be expelled from Topaz because of his statement, and as soon as he received the news, he went to his barrack to warn Shinko.

Two days later, Fukuda was on his knees, digging a small garden in front of the family bungalow, when a guard approached him and escorted him out of Topaz. His wife and seven children did not see him again until January 26, 1944, when they greeted each other just inside the gate of Crystal City Internment Camp.

In Crystal City, the Fukuda family settled in a five-hundred-square-foot bungalow, number 26 in the T section, not far from the swimming pool. The children slept on Army cots. The two older boys, Mitch and Nob, alternately carried their younger brother Koichi on their backs. All of the Fukuda children went to the Japanese School. Shinko prepared family meals in the small kitchen. They had their own bathroom. Once the stress of the journey was relieved, Shinko's health improved. Other members of the Konko Church in San Francisco were in camp, and she enjoyed seeing old friends.

The camp's population was now at its peak at roughly four thousand, two-thirds of the internees Japanese or Japanese Americans. Fukuda held Konko services for believers. He also became involved in the community outside of the Konko ministry, teaching judo at the Japanese School and working with the Boy Scouts. On movie nights—Wednesdays and Saturdays—he sometimes ran the 16 mm projector in Harrison Hall. The film program that year included *Chip off the Old Block*, with Donald O'Connor and Ann Blyth; *Tender Comrade*, with Ginger Rogers and Robert Ryan; and *Bowery to Broadway*, with Turhan Bey and Susanna Foster.

Fukuda worried that he and his family would be forced to repatriate to Japan. If he was sent back to Japan, he would regard himself as a failure as a Konko missionary. Moreover, he knew his children's future was in America, not in Japan. To O'Rourke, the Japanese men in camp fell into two distinct groups: those who were eager to repatriate because they were loyal to Japan, and those with a pro-American stance who wanted to stay in the United States. Fukuda did not fall into either of those groups; rather, he walked a thin line as he stayed loyal to his homeland without being disloyal to America.

Despite the order to stay out of politics, Fukuda could not stay silent for long. On February 7, 1944, less than two weeks after his arrival, he wrote a petition to Willard Kelly, assistant commissioner of the INS in Philadelphia, on behalf of 250 internees in Santa Fe that he'd left behind who had requested transfers to Crystal City: "As you know, they are very uneasy and irritated because your government announced the family reunion program more than one year ago, but the programs were changed often, and thus they are still separated from their loving families." Some, Fukuda added, were organizing "propaganda activities" to ask the Japanese government to punish American prisoners in Japanese camps in retaliation for the denied transfers to Crystal City. This was the threat of negative reciprocity that Harrison and Kelly had labored to avoid.

"You may think such action is very foolish, but I would like to ask your deep understanding and warm sympathy about the fact that most of the psychology of the internees is becoming unordinary," continued Fukuda. "I sincerely felt this fact during my internment life of family separation at Santa Fe and heartily sympathized with them." He told Kelly that foreigners such as himself could not understand Japanese. "Outwardly, the internees might have appeared patient. Yet, when they pass the limit of patience and decide to do something, they will execute it surely and bravely. They will give up their own lives—individually or in mass—to save the interests of their friends."

On February 14, Kelly sent Fukuda's letter to Harrison and to the Special War Problems Division, which decided who would be repatriated and who would not. He attached a private memo in which Kelly explained that Fukuda "has shown himself in a number of ways to be a trouble-maker. He was, without doubt, one of the leaders, if not the leader, of the element in Santa Fe which recently delivered several threatening ultimatums."

Fukuda had good reason to fear involuntary repatriation, and Kelly's anger was understandable. The brutality of Japanese soldiers toward Americans in POW camps was well known. On January 1, 1944, Japanese soldiers occupying the Andaman Islands in the Indian Ocean theater killed forty-four Indian civilians who were suspected spies. In what later became known as the Homfreyganj Massacre, the civilians were shot dead at point-blank range. Moreover, the treatment of American civilians in Japanese internment camps was far worse than the treatment of Japanese in American internment camps. A report from the Red Cross compared the amounts of food furnished to Americans in one Japanese camp, the Kanagawa Civil Internment Camp, with the average food allowance in US camps. In Kanagawa, American internees received no eggs, milk, margarine, cheese, sweets, or coffee. Fish was allowed when available, and internees picked their own fruit in season. Meat was rare. The total daily food allowance was listed as 3.549 pounds per person in Kanagawa, in contrast to the US allowance of 5.298.

Angered by Fukuda's complaint, Kelly's response was direct. He assured Fukuda that "appropriate steps" were being taken in Santa Fe to reunite internees with their families in Crystal City. Then he reiterated O'Rourke's warning that Fukuda was not allowed to act as a spokesman for Japanese in Crystal City. "Your attention is invited to Article 43 of the Geneva Convention, which provides that prisoners of war (internees) shall be allowed to appoint agents to represent them directly with the military authorities and protecting powers, but that such appointment shall be subject to the approval of the military authority, or, in this case, the Immigration and Naturalization Service," wrote Kelly. "You are advised that should you be appointed to represent any group of internees, such appointment would not be approved by this Service."

In Crystal City, Fukuda temporarily suspended the writing of petitions, concentrated on his ministry, and spent more time with his seven children than in any other period of his life. That summer, he took his children to the pool and taught them to swim and ate most meals with his family.

On the morning of November 14, 1944, Shinko noticed that the face of her fourth son, Yoshiro, was swollen. Yoshiro was eight years old and only the day before had participated in a sumo match at the Japanese School. That morning, he was sluggish and complained of pain. His parents took Yoshiro to the camp hospital, where a female Japanese doctor examined him.

After a variety of tests were run, the doctor told the Fukudas that Yoshiro suffered from kidney disease and that his condition was grave. He was immediately admitted to the hospital and placed in the pediatrics section in a bed that was too small for him. He cried out for his parents.

Yoshiro's illness forced Fukuda and his wife—separately and as a couple—to come to new understandings of their faith. On the walk home from the hospital, Fukuda told his wife that he felt guilty for causing Yoshiro's internment. He realized for the first time how much he loved his children and how often he had neglected them. Though it was still hot in November, Shinko had been told that Yoshiro would not be allowed to drink much water in the hospital, as it might aggravate the swelling. That night, she refused to drink water as well.

Official visiting hours at the hospital were limited to 7:30 to 8:30 p.m. daily, and no more than two visitors at a time were permitted. The next day when the Fukudas went to visit Yoshiro, he complained that he had not slept and did not want to be alone. O'Rourke intervened, and the Fukudas were allowed to visit Yoshiro twice a day.

Weeks passed. The Fukudas debated how to get Yoshiro better medical care. His doctor was married to a Japanese surgeon, who also worked at the camp hospital and helped to take care of Yoshiro. The surgeon was a friend of Fukuda's; they had both attended the Imperial University of Tokyo. Fukuda did not want to offend his physician friend and his wife, but he knew that neither of them was an expert on kidney disease. Fukuda knew the importance of saving face in Japanese culture and did not want to show disrespect to his friend the surgeon, but he considered requesting that Yoshiro be taken outside the camp, to San Antonio, to be treated by a kidney specialist. Shinko urged against it; she didn't want to be separated from her son. Besides, O'Rourke had been kind to them, and she did not want to run the risk of offending him.

Fukuda put his heart even more strongly into his faith. In the Konko religion, the word for god is *kami*, which is generally defined as a divine parent. Fukuda built a special altar in his barrack, and three times a day he prayed on his knees for Tenchi Kane No Kami, the principal deity of Konko, to cure his son. As a minister, he'd performed "mediation," a mystical healing ceremony, on people with all kinds of maladies and diseases. Now, he realized, he had never fully understood how helpless parents felt when their children were seriously ill.

Within a few days, Yoshiro was moved out of the pediatrics ward and into a room in the tuberculosis ward, which was crowded with patients. Yoshiro complained that he was frightened of catching tuberculosis and did not want to stay in the ward. Fukuda requested that Yoshiro be transferred to the adult ward, and his request was granted. Slowly, Yoshiro's condition began to improve.

Near the end of December, around Christmastime, Yoshiro was discharged and returned to the family bungalow. Mitch and Nob gave him sips of orange juice. Every night, Fukuda bowed humbly before the altar that he'd made. Of all the children, Yoshiro looked the most like his father and was smart and excelled in judo. Even at the age of eight, he understood his father's expectations of him, and often, as he lay on his Army cot, he said, "I want to be a minister like my father." As the year drew to a close, the Fukuda family huddled in their crowded bungalow, each with their own sorrow. Yoshino's illness remained grave.

CHAPTER ELEVEN

The Birds Are Crying

In any other high school in America, it would have been a simple event. Yet in May 1944, when a group of graduating juniors and seniors at the Federal High School in Crystal City approached O'Rourke about the possibility of having a prom, the request triggered an international incident.

Ken Dyo, a Japanese American senior with straight As, made the request, and O'Rourke immediately said yes. It was the end of the first full school year in camp and the first opportunity to have a prom—a time-honored American custom. O'Rourke generally seized every opportunity to give the American-born students in Crystal City as much of a normal life as was possible in an internment camp. Most of them were good kids. All were innocent. It was their fathers, and in a few cases their mothers, who were prisoners of war.

O'Rourke was particularly fond of Ken Dyo and his younger brother, Sei. Ken's father, Tsutomu, spoke Spanish and served as a cooperative liaison between O'Rourke and members of the Spanish consul's office, which served as the neutral power on behalf of interned Japanese. Back home in Santa Barbara, California, before their internment, the Dyo brothers were Boy Scouts and had participated in victory drives to help the American war effort. Now, Sei was the only boy in Crystal City at work on his Eagle Scout rank, the most prestigious award in scouting. He accumulated his badges in secret under the supervision of Tate, the principal of the American high school. Otherwise, the pro-Japanese leaders in camp would have made life difficult for Sei as well as for O'Rourke. The Japanese had their own scouting program in camp, led by former Japanese military officers, who conducted marching drills and emphasized loyalty to Japan.

That summer, as Axis powers suffered catastrophic defeats and it became clear that Germany and Japan were not a match for Allied forces, the American-born children in Crystal City lived isolated, emotionally tangled lives. Every internee, whether pro-American or loyal to Germany or Japan, fought his or her own private war. O'Rourke knew that the future lives of all the children, particularly the students in the Federal High School, the majority of whom were Japanese American, would be affected by decisions that he made as officer in charge. On the issue of the prom, he decided to side with the students, not their parents.

By social custom, Ken Dyo was expected to ask formal permission of his Japanese elders, the issei leaders, to hold the prom. However, he also knew they would oppose it. Instead, he went directly to Ryuchi Fujii, the elected Japanese spokesman in camp, and asked him to publicly endorse the prom. Fujii, a Buddhist priest, turned him down. Like the other elders, Fujii viewed the prom as an insult to Japanese parents, an effort by O'Rourke to Americanize their children and he advised Dyo to withdraw his request to O'Rourke.

The battle over the dance was joined. Fujii called a meeting of all the members of the Japanese council, and they voted 322–20 against the prom. In a letter to O'Rourke, Fujii listed the reasons why leaders opposed the dance: "All Japanese leaders have disapproved of having any dance party in this camp because it may have a bad influence on all children." He cited the war itself, saying it was "offensive" to hold a dance "at this time when other people are suffering in a life and death struggle."

O'Rourke's answer was swift: the prom would go on. He told Fujii that he would not allow the Japanese council to call off an event at the Federal High School, which was operated by the US government and attended by mostly American citizens. Many of the issei men opposed to the prom did not even have children enrolled in the school; their children went to the Japanese School. For O'Rourke, the line was clear. He would not allow the issei leaders to impose their cultural standards on American-born teenagers.

Fujii refused to give up the fight and sent a formal letter of complaint to Harrison and copied the Spanish consul: "According to time-honored Japanese customs, social dance has been condemned morally and religiously and is prohibited by law. A dancing girl is despised as much as any prostitute. Any girl of a well-to-do family never attends a social dance." If the dance was held, Fujii warned, teachers at the Japanese School would resign in protest.

In every bungalow and Victory Hut in the Japanese section of camp, the issue of the dance was debated. In many of the other Japanese relocation camps, such as Manzanar and Tule Lake, where anti-American feelings ran high, strikes and demonstrations had broken out over such issues as the mandatory loyalty oaths and harsh treatment by guards. In Crystal City, what seemed like a minor event—a junior-senior prom—turned children against parents, students against teachers, and the Japanese leaders against O'Rourke.

At school, the prom was all anyone talked about, but Sumi did not bring up the subject at home. Since their arrival in Crystal City, Tokiji had become more temperamental—a symptom of fence sickness. Once, Sumi visited a girlfriend in a different bungalow and was supposed to be back by 8:00 p.m., but arrived home an hour late. Her father slammed the door in her face and screamed at her. "There was no way I would ever have asked him if I could go to the prom," recalled Sumi. "If my father saw me talking to a guy, he would have been furious. I knew he would never let me go to a dance."

Sumi's friend Yae Kanogawa, whom she'd met on the train from Ellis Island to Crystal City, loved to dance and wanted to go to the prom, and was encouraged to go by her father, Sho, who worked as a cook in Crystal City. Sho received a circular, signed by Japanese leaders in camp, warning against allowing students to attend the prom. Yae was a student at the Japanese School, and her teacher pressured her father to keep his daughter home. "Only prostitutes dance in Japan," said the teacher.

However, Sho was a *michiro*, a trained Japanese dancer, and he saw no harm in the prom. Indeed, he encouraged Yae to go to the dance with her brother Shoji. "He told me I had to go," recalled Yae. "He thought everyone should learn to dance." Meanwhile, Japanese block managers went door-to-door among the Japanese bungalows, asking that parents not allow their children to attend the dance. Ultimatums flew back and forth.

Nevertheless, on May 26, 1944, a Friday night, thirty brave Japanese American and fourteen German American teenagers gathered in Harrison Hall for the dance. The hall was festooned with balloons, and the walls were lined with tables laden with punch bowls and platters of cookies. O'Rourke, Tate, and several teachers in the American School attended as chaperones. They kept their eyes on the windows and the doors.

It was summer, and school was almost over for the year. The pool had been open for a month, and days slipped away under the burning desert sun. That night, the guards were especially attentive at their tower posts, and after dusk, the air grew cooler. Soon, the music of Bing Crosby and the Andrews Sisters, Judy Garland, and Harry James floated through the breeze.

Inside the hall, many of the boys stood with their hands shoved in their pockets. In time, the smooth-chinned young men summoned the courage to approach the girls, equally shy in their cotton dresses. Some couples awkwardly stepped on each other's toes, while others glided easily to the music. Yae took to the dance floor early and urged her friends to join the fun. The sound of their feet—*thump, thump, thump*—echoed from the wooden floors in the first dance that many of them had attended since the war began. To Yae, the dance felt like the most natural, necessary thing in the world.

Halfway through the party, O'Rourke announced an intermission. The music stopped, and the teenagers were served refreshments. While they drank punch and ate cookies, several of the teachers from the Japanese School crashed the hall and ordered all the Japanese children to leave the prom.

Yae's teacher confronted her and said that, because of her attendance at the dance, he was forced by his principal to quit his job at the Japanese School. He said her lack of morals indicated his failure as a teacher and called her a "harlot, a dancing harlot." Like many of the Japanese Americans in camp, Yae felt scapegoated by her government for forcing her to evacuate her home and navigate existence behind barbed wire simply because of her Japanese heritage. Now she felt blamed by her Japanese teacher and forced to bear his burdens, as well.

After the teachers' outburst, no one at the prom felt like dancing. Yae and her friends sulked home. The leaders had succeeded in breaking up the prom.

The following day, Yae sent a letter to a friend outside the camp. Before it was mailed, a censor read it and sent a copy to O'Rourke. In her letter, she used American vernacular and wrote, "Gee, the atmosphere around here between teacher and student, issei and nisei, is really sharp and annoying." She commented on how the Japanese leaders had forbidden students to go to the event: "Isn't that positively outrageous? And it was against the H.S. [high school], which was real earnest about giving the students a decent time, 'specially at graduation, and that's some memory one cherishes. I went too, but after intermission, the fireworks began. The Japanese School sent spies to see which students from the tip school went—one of them saw me, and now I'm in a position where I have to quit school. Honestly! It's inhuman. When you get in a place like this, you honestly wonder if these Japzip in here are really human! I pity the Caucasians who have to work with them."

Yae was more Americanized than the Japanese leaders in camp could have understood. She blamed the Japanese leaders—the "Japzip," as she referred to them—for the bitter atmosphere, not O'Rourke and the teachers in the American School.

She was not alone. Another student, Sachi Sasaki, was not allowed to go to the dance. In a letter forwarded to O'Rourke by censors, Sachi wrote that she loved to dance and said, "Of course my pop thought it was better if I didn't go, so I had to stay home and suck my finger. I was so mad that I bawled for the first time in ages. I'm telling you, I never saw so many narrow-minded, ignorant Japs in my life. Pardon my language. The American teachers are our true friends."

Maruko Okazaki, another student, wrote of the prom controversy to a friend outside the camp: "The atmosphere here hasn't been any too good. Last night, they had the Prom (I didn't go) and bang! Trouble after trouble has come up already. It's too disgusting. We know there's a war on—they keep reminding us that we shouldn't go out and enjoy ourselves when soldiers are fighting with all they've got, and we realize that, too—but it's just a dance a year. I don't think that's hurt anyone."

The prom became a standoff between O'Rourke and the Japanese leaders, and the teenagers were caught in the middle. The issei leaders kept the prom from being successful by intimidating the parents of most of the Japanese American students and disrupting the event. As Fujii threatened, Japanese teachers staged a strike at the Japanese School, closing it for several days after the prom. But O'Rourke won the cultural battle. If the dispute over the prom proved anything, it was that the students in the American high school were primarily Americans. Many stayed home from the prom out of respect for their parents, not out of loyalty to Japan.

Yae, in one of her letters the morning after the disastrous prom, felt sorry for O'Rourke: "You know Mr. O'Rourke waza-waza sponsored the prom himself so the grads could enjoy themselves for one nite. I feel perfectly horrible. My eyes are all swollen from last night. Gee, more trouble!" In the margin of the letter, the censor who reviewed the letter translated the phrase *waza-waza* as "specifically."

From the safety of their desks in the Internal Security Division, the censors monitored the travails and dramas of camp life. The mail instructions from O'Rourke were complex. Internees were allowed to send only two letters and one postal card (on approved stationery) per week. Domestic letters could not exceed thirty-five lines; international letters couldn't exceed twenty-four. Letters had to be legible, and any extremely small written script was cause for rejection. Telegrams were relayed to Western Union with the words *internee telegram* in the body of the messages.

In May 1944, a married Japanese woman began writing love letters to a Japanese American writer and artist in Denver. Before the war, they had shared interests in music, poetry, and art, eventually falling in love. To evade the censors, the woman wrote her feelings in minuscule letters hidden underneath the stamps of the letters. Despite her efforts, the censors found her out.

In one chatty dispatch on approved stationery, the woman described mundane details of her daily life in camp: "The climate here is bad. Both children have taken cold. I feel badly, too, and am in bed. I am not able to play music, either, and have really become thin recently." But underneath the stamp was this message: "Beginning today, I am going to try the tactics of fasting. I am weeping as I look at the clear, bright moon. The birds are crying, too. My home is just like hell. I shall not write for four or five days. If you become angry and do not care about me, I shall die. I hate everything, and am beating my pillow in anger." The censors discovered the message, and charged with "violation of censorship," the woman lost her mailing privileges for thirty days.

Eventually, she wrote again to her lover and told him that she needed to end their relationship. She was older than he was, trapped in marriage, and behind barbed wire in Crystal City. Her suitor wrote back, "If you cannot come out, I cannot go on living. I shall not let anyone know where or how I shall die. I do not need any other woman but you. I do not like young women. I do not want any other person to call my wife except you. Whether I walk, stand, or sit, I am thinking of nothing but you. Please come as soon as you can."

While O'Rourke managed quarrels and monitored mail in Crystal City, Harrison waged larger, tougher battles in Washington. By 1944, Harrison had been INS commissioner for two years and had reorganized the service following its transfer from the Department of Labor to the Department of Justice. In addition to running Crystal City and other internment camps, Harrison dealt with Congress on refugee matters. Although the country was still anti-immigrant and isolationist, Harrison urged Congress to lower racial barriers to allow more Jews from Europe to immigrate to the United States. In a report to Biddle, the attorney general, Harrison confided that "practically the only disappointing experience" of his job was the lamentably slow progress to reform discriminatory exclusion laws that kept European Jews from finding refuge in the United States. As early as 1939, Harrison and his wife, Carol, had sheltered Jewish families in their home in Rose Valley. "My mother always took people in," remembered Bart Harrison, his son. "Our house was the house of last resort."

When in 1943 Congress repealed the Chinese Exclusion Act, passed in 1882 to keep Chinese from immigrating to America, Harrison told the *Washington Post* that the repeal was a "commendable one," but pressed Congress to go further: "The old theory of inferior peoples should be declared as something no longer worthy of America." Harrison also pressed for bills to lift barriers that had been designed to keep Filipinos, East Indians, and other Eastern peoples, including Jews, out of the United States.

The debate over immigration was grounded in the realities of World War II. The Chinese Exclusion Act was repealed because China was America's ally. Harrison's argument was that existing immigration laws against Europeans were comparable to the racial laws of Nazi Germany. "The only other country in the world that observes such racial discrimination in matters relating to immigrants is Nazi Germany, and we will agree that that is not very desirable company," he told Biddle and the press.

Congress refused to act on the additional bills. On July 20, 1944,

Harrison resigned in protest. In a story in the *New York Times*, Roosevelt praised Harrison for his reform of the Immigration and Naturalization Service, "notwithstanding the wartime additions to the work of the service, such as the civilian internment program." The *Washington Post* said in an editorial on July 24, "Hats off today to Harrison, who resigned that position in protest of our immigration laws, which he compares to the racial laws of Nazi Germany."

The "Jewish question" was now impossible for Roosevelt to ignore. At the beginning of the war, Roosevelt concluded that America could save the Jews of Europe by quickly defeating Hitler and his troops. But he worried about anti-Semitism in America and finally took on the issue directly. In speeches during 1943, Roosevelt said that any American who condoned anti-Semitism was "playing Hitler's game." However, immigration restrictions stayed in place.

Biddle named Ugo Carusi, an Italian American who served as Biddle's assistant, to succeed Harrison. In Crystal City, O'Rourke sent out notices to the camp about Harrison's resignation. A Japanese internee, Tsurukichi Toriu, drew a portrait of Harrison based on a photograph, and O'Rourke sent it to Harrison. In an accompanying note Toriu told Harrison that while indefinite internment was difficult to accept, he wanted Harrison to accept the gift as a symbol of "enduring friendship" from the Japanese internees in Crystal City, who appreciated his "noble, indefatigable spirit." The gesture indicates that at least some of the internees understood that their treatment could have been far worse.

Those behind the barbed wire at Crystal City had few ways to escape the furnace-like heat. In the middle of the day, temperatures climbed to 120 degrees Fahrenheit. The living quarters all had thin roofs and walls, built without insulation. When children touched the metal parts of their beds, their hands were scorched. When men went into the orchards and family gardens to water, dust flew up from the ground. At night, parents hosed down the roofs of barracks and washed the floors with water.

In August 1944 the hospital reported eight births. However, statistics also show five cases of "threatened abortions" and many other maladies that summer. A forty-seven-year-old Japanese man died of tuberculosis. A German woman stated that her severely depressed husband had lost his mind and needed shock therapy. Nothing could be done for him. On average, the hospital treated sixty patients a day for malaise.

One place alone offered relief from the heat: the swimming pool. The size of a football field, it was large enough on the deep end for three diving platforms. The pool was a refuge, a place where fear, boredom, and anger were washed away. The water shimmered; people were energized. When birds flew over the heads of the swimmers, some thought of it as a kind of blessing. The Germans, Japanese, Italians, and Latin Americans from many different countries all spoke in their own languages. The Germans and the Japanese had separate bathhouses. Like the image from a crystal, the pool reflected many histories and perspectives.

All that changed on the afternoon of August 15, 1944. Ty Nakamura, a student at the American School, was a lifeguard that day. Two Japanese Peruvian girls, thirteen-year-old Sachiko Taname and eleven-year-old Aiko Oykawa, played in the shallow end of the pool. The girls were best friends and lived with their families in a triplex near where Ty lived with his family. Often, Ty heard them singing Glenn Miller's "Chattanooga Choo Choo" in the showers. The song told the story of a famous train and the last line was "Won't you choo-choo me home?" The girls loved the song.

Aiko and Sachiko strayed into the deep end. A safety cable and ropes divided the shallow and deep ends. Before the two girls reached the cable, they slipped on a deep shelf and plunged under the water in the murky floor of the pool.

Alice Nishimoto, another Japanese Peruvian girl, was in the pool that day with four of her friends. Like Aiko and Sachiko, they, too, inched their way from the shallow to the deep end of the pool, but they held on to the cable. While in the deep end, gripping the ropes,

Alice and her friends watched lifeguards bring the lifeless bodies of the two drowned girls up from the bottom of the pool and carry them out of the water.

Others saw it as well. "I was swimming with my friends," Bessie Masuda recalled in an oral history. "We actually saw the girls drowning at the deep end of the pool. We all grabbed hands and we tried to reach them and to save them, but the floor beneath us was too slippery. It was so sad that we couldn't help them."

Frantically, Ty and other lifeguards searched for the girls in the dark waters. Soon, they found them and rushed their bodies to the shore. Dr. Martin, the medical officer, and O'Rourke huddled over the girls. Both applied artificial respiration in an attempt to revive them, to no avail.

A group of teenagers formed a circle around the men and the girls. Suddenly, someone shouted from the circle, "Hot rice! Get hot rice!"

Soon, Japanese women from all over the camp brought pot after pot of hot rice, which was poured on the bodies of the girls in an effort to keep them warm. Toni Takeuchi, one of Sumi's closest friends, remembers her mother making many pots of hot rice in her small kitchen. Toni's mother didn't yet know that Dr. Martin had already pronounced Aiko and Sachiko dead, the official cause of death on his report being "drowning by submersion." Toni's sister worked as a nurse in the hospital, and when the bodies of the girls were brought in, they were wrapped in soggy blankets covered with rice, which left a sticky trail on the floor.

That night, one of the mothers of the girls attempted suicide. The other mother could not be consoled and was put on a suicide watch.

A few days later, a large Buddhist funeral was held for both of the girls. By then, more than forty Buddhist priests were in camp. The priests, dressed in flowing robes, led the chants and solemn rites of the ceremony. Virtually all of the more than six hundred Japanese Peruvians in camp attended the funeral. Never before had there been such an elaborate funeral in Crystal City. Many said how sad it was that the young girls, civilians who were guilty of no crime against the United States, had died behind barbed wire. The funeral offered no consolation to the parents of the girls, for their resting place was an internment camp, far from their home country of Peru.

Witnesses at the pool on the day the girls died reported that O'Rourke wept over their bodies. Given the quarrelsome atmosphere in the camp, the resignation of Harrison, and the deaths of the girls, it had been a difficult summer.

PART THREE

THE EQUATION
OF EXCHANGE

CHAPTER TWELVE

Trade Bait

January 2, 1945

As good-bye ceremonies went, this one was the most complicated of Ingrid Eiserloh's young life. On this cold winter day in Crystal City, the trees beyond the fence line were bare. Early in the morning, Ingrid gathered in the dining hall at the internment camp with 428 others—German nationals, American-born children like herself, and a large contingent of German families from Latin America. Ingrid ate a hearty serving of eggs, fried sausage, and warm tortillas. It was her last meal in Crystal City.

After breakfast, the group walked outside and convened in front of a stage, where O'Rourke stood at the podium. He publicly recognized the German men who had built roads, cabins, and other buildings in the camp and singled out Mathias for his work on the swimming pool. Ingrid, just four months shy of her fifteenth birthday, stood proud and straight next to her father. She remembered the hot summer days in camp when she slid into the swimming pool and took high dives into the deep end.

Eighteen months before, she had been sent to Crystal City against her will. The confinement had been agonizing, yet the Eiserloh family had been reunited and found a measure of safety and security. "We were back together again there," recalled Ingrid many years later. "Some of the worry was taken off my parents. We had food and clothes. We were with other people who shared our isolation and the stigma of internment."

Near the end of the ceremony, German American children who attended the American School sang "God Bless America." The rest of the German population, a few with arms outstretched in the Nazi salute, then sang the German national anthem, "Deutschlandlied." The singing of both patriotic anthems would have been irrational and completely out of place in most settings. But on this day in Crystal City, the singing of both was necessary and expressed the conflicted emotions and allegiances of the 429 internees who were preparing to leave the camp.

Ingrid glanced at her white lapel tag, which branded her with a new government identity—no longer was she a "voluntary internee" at Crystal City, even though, from Ingrid's perspective, there had never been anything voluntary about her internment. Now she was an official "repatriate"—an equally ironic label for an American teenager bound for war-torn Germany with her family. Technically, the word *repatriate* means "to restore or return to the country of birth, citizenship, or origin." But Ingrid, Lothar, Ensi, and the other American-born "repatriates" in the group that day were citizens of the United States. Yet, according to their government, if the German parents were repatriates, so were their children. In an Orwellian use of rhetoric, the word *repatriate* was designed to reassign the official status of American children of selected ethnicities, when in fact the term forced American-born children to become displaced persons. They were, in effect, without a country.

For months before this day of departure, O'Rourke had worked with the State Department and the Immigration Service to prepare to transport the 429 internees from Crystal City to the port of New York, where they would board the Swedish liner MS *Gripsholm*, sail to Europe, and be traded for American prisoners of war and civilians. Potential lists of internees who would be repatriated to Germany flew back and forth between Washington and Berlin.

Meanwhile, the Germans waged a two-front strategy for survival. Allied forces had advanced quickly from Paris to the Rhine. As Ingrid and the others prepared to leave Crystal City, the Battle of the Bulge was under way. Hitler was within weeks of firmly ensconcing himself in his bunker in Berlin with Eva Braun.

The January 1945 exchange was the sixth and last of the transatlantic exchanges. By then, 2,361 Americans, caught behind enemy lines in Europe, had been returned from Germany and Italy in exchange for 4,500 German nationals and 124 Italians who had previously been interned in US camps. During the negotiations between Berlin and Washington about this final exchange, Berlin insisted that the United States deliver many German citizens seized in Latin America and interned in camps in the United States, including Crystal City. The Germans pressed for a one-for-one exchange: for every American prisoner of war or civilian freed by Germany, they wanted one German. In the tedious process every name on the two lists was scrutinized by multiple government agencies. Negotiations dragged.

Even on the morning that the group of repatriates from Crystal City prepared to leave camp, the final exchange list was incomplete. Nonetheless, William Mangels, a special FBI agent from New York, arrived in Crystal City on the evening of December 28 to clear those who had been identified for departure.

Ingrid and her family and most of the others had been on lockdown inside the camp for about two weeks. The repatriates were separated from other internees and not allowed to have contact with anyone other than their families, for fear some might attempt to smuggle money, maps, or codes into Germany. "All repatriates were kept incommunicado after final customs examination and body frisk," wrote Mangels in his report to Washington. "At no time were they able to pass or receive any verbal or written communications." All who were leaving the camp were searched for concealed contraband items, and repatriates designated as high security risks were strip-searched.

The State Department issued a list of what the repatriates could take with them from Crystal City. The list included German clothes, passports, American birth certificates, baby carriages, and personal items such as family photos. The list of what could not be taken was much longer and included electrical appliances, radios, binoculars, garden tools, and sketches. Apparently, the State Department viewed these items as potentially helpful to the war effort in Germany.

Customs agents methodically examined everyone's baggage. The Eiserloh family had five handmade wooden sea trunks, each four by four feet wide and three feet tall. Like many other repatriates, the Eiserlohs had spent all the family's accumulated quarter-shaped tokens at the camp store on items that would be scarce in Germany. Johanna purchased heavy coats and sturdy shoes for every member of the family and many cartons of cigarettes for Mathias. On December 29, their luggage, with that of all the others bound for Germany, was loaded onto six baggage cars attached to two Pullman trains at the small station in nearby Uvalde.

Johanna was nine months pregnant with her fourth child and torn about their repatriation. If Johanna gave birth before the day of departure, she planned to stay in Crystal City with all of the children. Yet Mathias was adamant: he would return to Germany, even if he had to go alone. Ingrid would lose her father for a second time. She didn't think she could stand that. Night after night, she listened to her parents argue.

Johanna had married Mathias because he wanted to make a new life for them in America, and now that life was finished. With three children and one on the way, she needed her husband's support and protection, which now depended on whether she carried through with her previous decision to repatriate. All of this was complicated by her pregnancy. She had not even wanted another child, but after their reunion in Crystal City, Mathias had insisted.

Finally, the day of reckoning—January 2—arrived. On that morning, Dr. Robert Martin, a physician at the camp, signed a medical release certifying that Johanna was fit to travel by train to New York and by boat to Germany. Johanna never announced her decision, but boarded the bus for Uvalde with her family and the large contingent from the camp.

Before exiting the gates of the camp, Mathias and Johanna, like the other adult internees, signed an oath promising never to disclose details of their internment or the upcoming exchange. Mathias, like all adult German repatriates, signed a second oath not to perform military service in Germany. For the rest of their lives, Mathias and Johanna kept silent partly because they feared US government reprisals and partly out of shame for their internment. "Goddamn war," Mathias said as he left Crystal City. Over the years, that phrase became his standard explanation for what had happened to his family.

All day and well into the night, FBI agents supervised the departure of the contingent from Crystal City. The passengers were loaded onto two separate trains at the station in Uvalde. The first train left Uvalde at 11:00 p.m., accompanied by three FBI agents, one doctor, and twenty-two border patrolmen. The second, with the same number of personnel, left at 11:15 p.m. Ingrid and Lothar remembered that the weather was cold—unusual for Texas—and both were sleepy and tired when they finally boarded the train. "It was literally the dead of night," Lothar said. "We stumbled on board. I wasn't sure what was happening."

Their family was assigned to a Pullman car, a compartment designed for two persons to sleep on the lower level and one on the upper berth. Lothar and Mathias crowded into the upper berth; Johanna and the two girls took the lower level.

Security was tight. Armed Border Patrol agents, stationed at the ends of each car for the duration of the trip, explained that the passengers were to remain in their separate cars. No communication between passengers in separate cars was allowed, and as a general rule, the shades were kept pulled down. The internees were not allowed newspapers.

The train barreled down the tracks. Beside Ingrid in the cramped car, Johanna moaned and groaned, her cries in painful harmony with the movement of the train. The space felt closed, and the air was stagnant. Ingrid gripped her mother's hand as if to say, *Get a hold of yourself.*

By morning, Johanna was in hard labor, and Mathias asked one of the guards to bring the doctor. After Dr. Martin and a nurse arrived, Mathias and the three children walked to the dining car and ate breakfast. As the train traveled toward New Orleans, Johanna's family paced the hallway. Mathias's fingers, stained by tobacco, reached for one cigarette after another, and the hallway filled with smoke.

A half hour or so before the train crossed over the Mississippi River, the guards allowed the dark shades to be raised. Morning light flooded the passenger car. From the hallway, Ensi, Ingrid, and Lothar pressed their faces against the glass and watched the immense river pass by while their mother labored on.

Finally, Dr. Martin and the nurse emerged from the car and announced that Johanna had given birth to a boy. Mathias named his second son Guenther. According to Ingrid, Dr. Martin tried to convince Mathias to have Guenther placed for adoption. "Don't take this infant into a war zone," Martin said. "He might not survive." He offered to arrange the adoption himself.

"I understand the risk," Mathias said, "but I have to keep my family together."

In fact, Mathias did not understand the risk. None of the repatriates on board the train understood their desperate part in the context of the war. In Crystal City, war news was censored, and rumors among the internees were rampant. Most German fathers who left camp did not realize that Germany was losing the war. Indeed, most believed, without evidence, that Germany would prevail. While Mathias did not know what he would find in Germany, he followed the fantasy that he would find work there and live as a free man with his family. It would be better, he was sure, than life behind the barbed-wire fence. Mathias did not understand that Guenther, only hours old, would become one more name on Washington's side of the exchange list, an infant pawn.

In his written report, Dr. Martin described details of the birth but made no mention of his offer to place Guenther for adoption. "The birth of the child en route was anticipated, and sterile obstetrical packs and instruments were taken along by the doctor and the nurse accompanying the train for use in this case," the doctor wrote. After the delivery, the doctor signed Guenther's birth certificate and listed New Orleans as his place of birth.

Two days later, the Eiserlohs' train arrived at Pier F, Jersey City. From the pier, Ingrid got her first look at the *Gripsholm*, a large Swedish ocean liner, 573 feet long with a 74-foot beam. The white ship was brightly lit and garlanded with Swedish flags. In addition to the 429 internees from Crystal City, the pier was crowded with 47 repatriates from Fort Stanton Internment Camp in New Mexico, 208 from Fort Lincoln in North Dakota, and 114 from Seagoville in Texas.

The trains arrived in Jersey City every thirty to sixty minutes. For the American authorities, logistics were a nightmare. Each person's baggage and documentation was carefully processed for embarkation, taking more than a day.

Shortly before midnight on January 7, all of the repatriates— a total of 183 German prisoners of war and 856 civilians, including Ingrid and her family, were on board the ship. Once the repatriates crossed the gangplank, they were in the hands of Swedish authorities. On board, it was utter chaos as members of the crew scurried on deck like busy ants, baggage was stowed, and passengers, who wore tags on their coats, struggled to find quarters.

The whistle blew, and the ship left the pier. Twenty-two years before, Mathias and Johanna had arrived in New York to start their lives in America. From the deck of the ship, Mathias saw a silhouette of the Statue of Liberty, which was not brightly illuminated because of the World War II blackout. When he was a young immigrant years before, the statue had been a symbol of promise. That seemed a long time ago. Now he and his family were leaving the United States, sent by their adopted country across the Atlantic—into war.

Johanna and Guenther were taken below to sick bay, on the third level of the ship. Ensi went with her mother and was supervised by nurses. All the life seemed drained from Johanna's face, and she was too frail to produce breast milk. When she attempted to feed Guenther, her breasts were dry and her nipples bloody. Nurses fed the newborn bottles of milk, and Johanna sipped black tea. Even at four years old, Ensi understood that her mother did not want to return to Germany. "All I remember is her fear and helplessness," Ensi recalled. "She was in sick bay for the entire voyage. What I remember most about the trip was how lost I felt." Ingrid was assigned to a bunk on the same level, but not in sick bay, and was grateful that she was separated from her mother and younger siblings. Mathias and Lothar had separate quarters in a dormitory-type facility on the first level.

During the first few days, the sea was rough, and most of the passengers were seasick, but Ingrid stayed well. On the train trip, she'd taken a half teaspoon of baking soda each day, and the remedy worked. She roamed the ship and shadowed her father as he kept a watchful eye on the family's belongings. Some of the passengers were terrified that German U-boats might attack the crowded ocean liner. "Wouldn't that beat all?" Mathias told his daughter.

He sought out and had conversations with German soldiers on board who were going back into the war. Many were young and had lost arms and legs in battle, and Ingrid stared at the absence of limbs and didn't know how to react. After all, these were not her countrymen but German prisoners of war. She was an American, yet they were all on the same boat, bound for Germany. Nothing was simple.

Ingrid asked her father to resume the dancing lessons that he'd started when they lived in Strongsville, Ohio. Before his arrest, Mathias had taught young Ingrid the waltz. The dance lessons had stopped after Pearl Harbor, when the Eiserlohs, like other German nationals, surrendered their radios as contraband. Now, on board the *Gripsholm*, Mathias attempted to teach Ingrid the basics of the American swing dance, but his footwork was clumsy. One of the German

POWs cut in on father and daughter and offered to help Ingrid master the basic steps. The two of them, fourteen-year-old Ingrid and a young German POW, swirled in circles on deck to the sounds of Duke Ellington and the Andrews Sisters.

Meanwhile, Lothar had the run of the ship, which was a luxury liner, not a standard troop ship. The ship had a sports deck on top with a swimming pool, a cinema for movies, and a dining hall. Many of his friends from Crystal City were on board. The food was plentiful: beef, potatoes, vegetables, fruit, and simple desserts. Many of the crew and the Swedish guards on the *Gripsholm* knew that food was scarce in Germany. Knowing what faced these children, they encouraged them to eat their fill.

As the ship followed the currents toward Europe, a school of dolphins appeared on either side of it. Ensi came up top from sick bay to see them and cried, "Flying fish! Flying fish!" As if arranged by a Hollywood casting company, the dolphins continued with the ship, romping in its wake. Both sides of the ship were lined with children. The air was sweet and the ocean smooth. For Ingrid, Lothar, and Ensi, the few days of watching the dolphins as the *Gripsholm* plowed across the Atlantic and into the Mediterranean were the happiest since the outbreak of the war.

On January 18, sixteen days after the Eiserlohs left Crystal City, the ship sailed east past Gibraltar. To the left was Spain and to the right North Africa. Morning sun glistened on the water as the *Gripsholm* passed through the narrow strait. Ingrid stood on deck, on the other side of the Atlantic from her homeland, and stared at the steep face of the strongly fortified Rock of Gibraltar.

Three days later, on January 21, the ship sailed into the formidable port of Marseille, a strategic asset for both the Allies and the Axis. The Nazis had occupied Marseille in November 1942 and afterward destroyed thousands of buildings in the historic center of the city, and thousands of resident Jews were sent to death camps. Two years later, now under the control of the Victorious Allies, the city was a pile of ruins. As the *Gripsholm* entered the harbor, the ship was caught in a net of leftover German mines. Lothar was on deck when the ship struck the first mine and took on water; then the ship hit another mine. A whistle blew; life jackets were issued; lifeboats were lowered. People panicked. Lothar hurriedly put on his life jacket and positioned himself near one of the lifeboats. "If the ship went down," recalled Lothar, "I wanted to be on the first lifeboat."

Ingrid stayed close to her father, and Johanna, Ensi, and Guenther were brought on deck to prepare for evacuation. Divers were sent into the water to sweep the mines and clear the harbor. For hours, the ship was at a standstill. Finally, the mines were cleared, and the ship proceeded to the dock in Marseille, its human cargo intact.

Once inside France, the repatriates entered into the charge of the American military police (MP). Under the guard of the MP, one by one the 183 German soldiers and 856 civilians were loaded onto waiting French trains at the harbor. The German POWs boarded a train bound for Kreuzlingen, a small Swiss town located near the German border on Lake Constance. This was the agreed-upon exchange point.

The first of the civilian trains, with 540 on board, left Marseille in the early evening on January 21. The second, with 316, left at midnight. There was nothing to eat on board the train. Fortunately, before Ingrid left the ship she stopped at the mess hall and picked up cartons of cigarettes for her father and oranges and chocolates for the rest of the family. Johanna had brought a small supply of powdered milk for Guenther.

One of Lothar's closest friends from Crystal City, Ruth Becker, later recalled a similar experience during an interview with the historian Stephen Fox about the arrival in Marseille and the subsequent train trip to Switzerland. "We were coming up from Marseille on my sister's birthday. The French didn't feed us anything. I don't know what the length of time was, but it was enough to get very hungry. Mother had an orange that she must have taken from the boat, and that became my sister's birthday present."

Armed American MPs stood watch in each of the passenger cars. Some shared their packaged K rations with the younger children, while warning their parents that Allied air attacks had intensified and Germany would soon be defeated. By then, Allies had crossed the Siegfried Line, a 350-mile German defense system of bunkers, tunnels, and tank traps that ran along the western border of Germany and all the way to the border with Switzerland. Portions of the Siegfried Line were defended to the death.

"You're making a big mistake," one soldier told Mathias.

Once the train stopped in Geneva, the repatriates were delivered to the control of Swiss guards, dressed in green-gray uniforms, who were not pleased to receive the onslaught of repatriates from America in their country. When the train doors opened, Ingrid remembered hearing the barks of the Swiss authorities: *"Raus!"* It meant "Out!"

The passengers felt the blast of icy wind. Most were layered in shirts, sweaters, and coats from the camp store in Crystal City, but all were unprepared for the transfer from South Texas in January into the worst recorded winter in Europe in a hundred years. Snow covered every surface. Some of the Latin American children had never seen snow and were frightened of it. After the mild winters and blistering summer heat in Crystal City, even the Eiserlohs, who were accustomed to snow, were paralyzed. Ingrid wrapped herself in a woolen coat and stood immobilized at the station. She watched as Johanna bundled Guenther in a blanket and tucked him inside her heavy coat; Ingrid overheard her mother ask Mathias how, in such cold weather, they would keep the younger than one-month-old infant alive.

After several days in Switzerland, the Eiserlohs and other repatriates from Crystal City took a train to Swiss-controlled Kreuzlingen. Meanwhile, the American prisoners who were held by the Germans traveled to Switzerland by train from nearby Konstanz, Germany. The trains parked side by side at the station in Kreuzlingen. Over the course of two days, Swiss officials boarded both trains and were in charge of the exchanges. The train from Konstanz brought 565 American POWs, many of them badly wounded, and other civilians in Germany. The train from Switzerland brought the group from Crystal City. The one-for-one exchange negotiated by Berlin and Washington was completed.

Bert Shepard, a young American pilot, was one of the prisoners of war exchanged that day by the Nazis. Shepard was from Hesperia, California. In May 1944, while on his thirty-fourth mission as a P-38 pilot, Shepard's plane was downed by antiaircraft fire on his way to Berlin. Flak came up straight through the floor of the cockpit, and Shepard's right foot was shot off. His plane crashed near Berlin, and he was taken prisoner by German troops. Ten days later, at a hospital in Ludwigslust he awoke to find that his infected leg had been amputated and that he was a prisoner of the Germans.

Shepard and other disabled POWs were moved to a hospital in Annaberg, a town south of Berlin. There they learned they were scheduled for exchange. Night after night, they rose from their beds, walked to a schedule pinned on a bulletin board, and struck matches to see if their names were still on the list.

"That list," said Shepard, "was a magical thing."

At the station in Kreuzlingen, Shepard was the last American POW off the train on the second day of the exchange. He saw the trains that carried German POWs and internees from Crystal City. "We got on their train," remembered Shepard, "and they got on ours."

The exchange was anticlimactic for the Eiserloh children. They were too young to be aware that they were headed into war, while others, including Shepard, were headed to freedom. Lothar and Ensi do not remember the side-by-side trains that Shepard described. But Ingrid recalls an incident that occurred shortly after their train arrived at the station.

Mathias needed a cigarette, so Ingrid got off the train with him to stretch her legs while he had his smoke. While they stood on the platform, two soldiers in American uniforms walked toward them, each carrying a ration of bread. The soldiers got a whiff of Mathias's cigarette and stopped to talk.

"Do you smoke?" Mathias asked.

"Yes," said the soldiers.

Mathias pointed at the bread and held up two packs of cigarettes. "Trade you?"

The soldiers said yes, and Mathias traded the luxury of his cigarettes for food and began to understand the difficult future that he and his family would have in Germany.

After this encounter with the two American soldiers, Ingrid and her family, each of them carrying one suitcase, left the train station on foot and crossed the border into Germany. There was no official welcome by German authorities. Their destination was Johanna's hometown of Idstein, about 180 miles north across Germany. While Europe had all but fallen from Hitler's grasp, Germany continued to wage a last, desperate war on two fronts—east and west.

From the station in Kreuzlingen, the Eiserlohs took a four-hour train trip to Bergenz, a port located at the far eastern end of Lake Constance. Bergenz was the capital of an Austrian province annexed by Germany in 1938 and now part of the Third Reich. In Bergenz the Eiserlohs were processed by German authorities. All of the baggage from the *Gripsholm*, including their sea trunks, was placed in storage in a warehouse in Bergenz. Each carried only one small suitcase.

They stayed in Bergenz four days. A woman named Lulu Von Ramien, who worked as a nurse for the Red Cross, befriended Johanna. The Eiserloh family stayed with her in a castle where Von Ramien worked. Other repatriates, such as Ruth Becker, remembered staying in small, unheated houses in Bergenz. "I froze the entire week," recalled Becker. "I was hungry as well. There was so little food." Conditions where Ingrid and her family stayed were much better. Von Ramien helped Johanna find warm clothes for the family and served them hot soup and black bread, and Guenther had plenty of milk. She gave Ensi a doll carriage, and she placed her brother in the carriage and wheeled him around the large rooms of the castle. A man who lived nearby gave Lothar his German stamp collection.

On the fifth day, the Eiserlohs left the castle and made their way to the train station in Bergenz. As they neared the station, Ingrid and Lothar heard the sound of air-raid sirens. "Run," Mathias said. "Run."

The whole family—Mathias, Ingrid, Lothar, Ensi, and Johanna, carrying Guenther—hurried into a shelter and stayed there until the all-clear sounded. Then, wrapped in warm coats, they kept walking north, into war.

CHAPTER THIRTEEN

The False Passports

On the morning of January 20, 1945, while Ingrid was still at sea on the MS *Gripsholm*, a fourteen-year-old girl, Irene Hasenberg, slept on a narrow wooden shelf in a barrack with three hundred Jews at Bergen-Belsen concentration camp. Irene weighed only seventy-three pounds and was infested with lice. For Irene the worst moment of the day was waking up and wondering if her mother or father was dead. On this day, her father, John, a human skeleton dressed in rags, had already gone to work. In the barrack, Irene and her brother, Werner, wakened her mother, Gertrude, who was so undernourished she had not been out of bed for months, and helped her get dressed.

For the past eleven months, Irene and her family had survived in Bergen-Belsen for only one reason. As "exchange Jews" they were more valuable to the Nazis alive than dead. That morning word came back to the barrack that an exchange transport was imminent. The Germans were expected to deliver 856 Americans for an equal number of Germans.

Now, late in the war, the Allies had won the Battle of the Bulge, and Germany was on its heels. Russian troops had crossed into Germany and at that moment were fifty miles from Berlin. Auschwitz would be liberated by Russian troops seven days later, on January 27. Bergen-Belsen, however, was still crowded with Jews from around the world. Few American citizens were left in Germany, not enough for Germany to make its 856 quota for the trade. On this morning a *Kapo*, a Jewish prisoner who acted as a trustee, walked into Irene's barrack and announced that anyone who had any kind of passport other than German might make it out of Bergen-Belsen in the next few days. The Hasenbergs did not have American passports, but they did have falsified passports from Ecuador. As a result, their names were hastily added to the list for this last exchange of the war.

In the massive disruption of World War II neither Irene nor Ingrid knew that each was part of the one-to-one exchange. Though they had no idea of each other's existence, Ingrid and Irene nonetheless shared other things in common: each had lost her home, school, and friends. They were roughly the same age and looked alike, having blue eyes and being naturally thin as reeds. Irene's hair was light brown, Ingrid's brassy red. The exchange was intended as Germans for Americans, but these two teenagers were exceptions: a German Jew in Bergen-Belsen traded for an American in Crystal City. For Irene, the right passport made the difference between life and death, and she would later call it the first miracle of her survival. As for Ingrid, her American birth certificate spared her nothing.

As a victim of the German Holocaust, Irene's experience was much worse that Ingrid's internment in Crystal City. However, their exchange was both rooted in internment. Like Crystal City, which housed numerous nationalities and existed in part for exchange, Bergen-Belsen was started in 1943 specifically as an "exchange camp," a place where Jewish prisoners were held for exchange for Germans in other countries or for cash. When Ingrid left Crystal City, she left a camp of slightly more than four thousand, with Japanese outnumbering Germans. When Irene arrived at Bergen-Belsen in February 1944, the camp housed fifteen thousand Jews—from Romania, Yugoslavia, Hungary, France, North Africa, Albania, and other countries—all living behind high barbed-wire fences with SS guards in watchtowers training their weapons on the prisoners. As Irene remembered it, the Dutch Jews were congregated in an area called the Star Camp, while Irene and her family lived in a section designated for exchange Jews.

When Irene's family arrived at Bergen-Belsen, the Hasenbergs were herded into their barrack by SS guards with German shepherds straining at their tight leashes and barking. "Remember, dogs that bark don't bite," Gertrude told Irene, in an effort to calm her daughter's fear. But the bark of the large dogs was vicious, and Irene was not comforted.

Unlike the relaxed daily count at Crystal City, Irene took her place for the first daily *Appell*—German for "roll call"—at 4:00 a.m. A second roll call occurred at night. Prisoners were made to line up in rows in the bitter cold, and they were counted and recounted. The Nazis were obsessed with documentation, getting the count right. Once Irene stood for nine hours in snow without shoes for the daily count. She was issued a single thin blanket, a wooden bowl, and a spoon. Each day Irene was given one bowl of thin turnip soup and a two-inch piece of hard, dark bread. She ate huddled with her family in their bunk in the barrack. Even the air tasted like sawdust. Gray clumps of individuals with yellow stars pinned to their clothes wandered the camp, chronically exhausted from lack of food.

Eleven months after Irene had arrived at the camp, the situation had worsened. In the first few months of 1944, thousands more Jews, many forced to march from Auschwitz and other concentration camps, were brought to Bergen-Belsen. The camp was too crowded, and food and water were scarce. Many died of starvation, and in late 1944, a typhoid epidemic broke out in the camp and killed more prisoners. SS Captain Josef Kramer, the commandant of Bergen-Belsen, gave standing orders to SS units to shoot prisoners with typhoid for the fun of it. He was known as the Butcher of Bergen-Belsen.

Conditions deteriorated by the day. In time, administration of the camp was turned over to the *Kapos*, who were often harder on the prisoners than the SS guards. Many carried rubber hoses, and

Irene witnessed people beaten for not walking fast enough to work or for no reason at all. The bodies of the people in camp told their stories: loose teeth, shaky hands, missing eyes, arms, and legs.

A *Kapo* entered the barrack on January 20 and told the Hasenbergs about the exchange. To leave camp, the transports—those people on the list—had to be screened by a *Stabsarzt*, a medical officer. If a prisoner could walk into the hospital, the medical officer would give clearance for transport. Irene and her brother, Werner, who was two years older, coaxed Gertrude from her bed and explained to her that to leave camp she had to appear before the Nazi doctor. Gertrude was confused but agreed to see the doctor. Her children helped her walk, but once outside the barrack, she collapsed. Irene and Werner carried her back to the barrack, then the two of them went to see the doctor. He looked them over and absentmindedly checked them off the list.

Hours later, John returned home to the barrack from his slave work of digging trenches. "He was in very bad condition by then— terribly emaciated and undernourished," Irene recalled. That day John had been severely beaten by a *Kapo*. His body was bruised and he was delirious, and neither Irene nor Werner could understand what their father tried to tell them. For so long, John had lived with the firm belief that he and his family would survive, that a reprieve was on its way. The work was hard on him, but he did not talk about it. The only task he concentrated on, day by day, was keeping himself and his family alive. He knew the Nazis' goal: extermination. The only dignity he had left was in his ability to resist.

On this day, salvation was at hand. Werner explained that John had to get clearance from the medical officer. John agreed to go, and while Werner stayed with Gertrude, Irene accompanied her father, steadying him as he slowly made his way to the office.

"What's your name?" asked the officer.

John stared at him in silence.

The officer looked at the list, ran his index finger down the page. "Are you John Hasenberg?"

John nodded yes.

"Well, your children have been here already." The officer looked at Irene and mistook her for Gertrude. Mother and daughter weighed about the same and were the same height. Irene's bony face and hollowed blue eyes—all symptoms of starvation—disguised her youth. By sheer luck, her mother was now on the list as well.

"Be ready tomorrow morning," said the officer.

John and Irene walked back to the barrack and told Gertrude that they had all made the list. Gertrude was barely responsive. They grappled with the next problem: If Gertrude couldn't walk to the doctor, how could she get to the train? John told his wife that the time was now. If they were going to get out of Bergen-Belsen, she had to summon the energy to leave. She looked at her children's faces and nodded, telling her husband she would do what she had to do to save Irene and Werner.

The next morning, with the help of her family, Gertrude hobbled to the bathhouse. A female SS guard ordered Irene and her mother to remove their clothes, and they took showers to supposedly rid their bodies of lice. These miserable little things crawled all over their bodies—were in every nook and cranny. She showered, but Irene knew there was no real way to get rid of the lice.

While they were seated naked on a bench, the guard pointed to Gertrude, who was half-conscious. "This woman looks as if she's dying. I don't think you are fit to go."

"Oh," said Gertrude. "It's just my stomach. I think . . . um . . . I must have eaten something that disagreed with me."

Irene hurried to help her mother get dressed. When Irene put on her clothes, the incubated lice eggs hatched. When they left the bathhouse, she and her mother had more lice on them than when they arrived. For a small moment, Irene savored the defeat of the infamous Nazi efficiency: it was no match for the tenacity of lice.

Before Irene left Bergen-Belsen, Hanneli Goslar, one of her friends, asked Irene to walk with her to the Dutch section of camp. They took some clothes and threw them over the fence to a bald girl

with sunken, dark eyes and a dark stubble of hair on her head—
Anne Frank.

Both Hanneli and Irene knew the Frank family from the neighborhood they previously shared in Amsterdam. Hanneli was a closer
friend of Anne's than Irene. Anne, eighteen months older than
Irene, was two grades ahead of her, and Irene remembered Anne as
the smart, popular girl in school, the one with charisma and style.

Irene no longer recognized Anne. The bright girl in Amsterdam
with the shiny black hair and beaming grin was gone. This Anne
wore no clothes except a blanket wrapped around her shivering
body, which bore all the signs of starvation: the bony frame, the
muscle atrophy, the feet swollen with edema. Anne spoke calmly
but told them her sister, Margot, had typhus and was too ill to leave
her bed; Anne, too, had the fever. She thanked them for the clothes.

Later, through the barbed wire, Anne told Hanneli that she
believed her father, Otto, and her mother, Edith, were both dead.
She said that she didn't have the strength to live anymore. Another
of Frank's friends, Lise Kostler, visited her later and in the 1995
documentary *Anne Frank Remembered* said, "After her sister died,
she was just without hope. But she didn't know [that her father was
alive] and so she really had nothing to live for."

Irene's hands and face felt cold that day at the fence. Clouds blot-
ted the sun, and the sight of Anne, a frail shadow of her former self,
brought the past into sharp relief. They both were born in Germany
(Anne in Frankfurt and Irene in Berlin), and before the war, Irene's
father was a partner in a business that her grandfather had founded
in Berlin. The Hasenbergs, enjoying a comfortable, protected life,
ate meals together as a family, walked in the parks, and went to con-
certs. By 1936, with the Nazi persecution in full force, Jews could
not attend public schools, go to the movies, or live in certain sections of Berlin. Synagogues were destroyed and Jewish businesses
seized.

Irene's father looked for ways to get out of Germany. He was
offered a job with the American Express Company in Amsterdam

and took it. The Hasenberg family became one of three hundred thousand Jewish families that left Germany between 1933 and 1939. In the beginning, the move was difficult for Irene. She did not speak Dutch on arrival, but soon became fluent and settled in at school. The family went to temple on Saturdays, and Werner was bar mitzvahed in Amsterdam.

When the Germans occupied Amsterdam after the invasion of the Netherlands on May 10, 1940, the flow of mail between Amsterdam and Berlin stopped. John lost his job at American Express because the Nazis would no longer allow the company to employ Jews. It was a particularly sad day for Irene when she had to turn in her bicycle. Oddly, she never minded wearing the yellow star on her coat. In the beginning, Irene found her Dutch friends supportive. She felt proud to be a Jew, and the star was a symbol of her Jewishness. Initially, the practical difficulty was the Nazi requirement that she have it on at all times. In the winter, she pinned it to her coat, but when she took it off, she was starless. Finally she solved that problem by wearing the star stitched onto a vest over her clothes, but the risk was constant. She witnessed Jews stopped on the streets who had their stars ripped off their clothes by police and were then punished for not wearing them.

Irene's father weighed the risks of going into hiding, along with Anne Frank's family and the other twenty-five thousand Jewish families in Amsterdam. But John and Gertrude were ambivalent. It was hard to find people willing to hide Jewish families, and no amount of money could secure trust. Once families went into hiding, they could not buy food with coupons, but had to depend on the expensive and unreliable black market. Irene remembers her parents debating the issue. Aside from the fear of betrayal and the lack of food, both of her parents knew the penalty for defying the Nazis. If they were caught, as one-third of those families in hiding were, they would be shot on the spot or deported and killed in Germany. In the end, John and Gertrude decided to wait out the situation.

One day John met a businessman, a friend of his, on the street in Amsterdam. He told John that he'd recently secured false South American passports for his family from a broker in Sweden. He gave John his contact and explained how to go about the secret transaction. No money was involved; the man wanted to help save the Hasenberg family. John immediately had passport photographs taken of himself and the rest of his family and sent a letter to the broker as if the two were old family friends, saying, "We haven't been able to write you for a long time. You probably wonder what the kids look like. I'm enclosing the pictures." Months passed and the passports did not arrive.

After February 22, 1941, when Germans arrested hundreds of Jews in Amsterdam and deported them to concentration camps, the Hasenbergs, like every other Jewish family, lived in constant anxiety. One day Irene was in class when she heard the principal call out her name. She left the classroom and discovered her father had been arrested because he'd applied for a tram permit. Her mother had also been arrested. Irene and Werner were taken to a Jewish theater in the center of Amsterdam, from which all the seats had been removed. Hundreds of Jews were seated on the floor, which was covered with red carpet, and moans filled the stale air. Irene and Werner saw their parents and rushed to their side. The family stayed in the theater for three days, expecting to be deported at any time, but then they were released.

When they returned to their apartment, they had to break open the seals on their doors. Irene never knew why her family was released, but by then her father was working for the Joodse Raad, the Jewish Council, which had a small amount of influence. He worked with a team of people who went into the homes of arrested Jews, packed up their hastily left belongings, and shipped them to camps. Sometimes people were arrested on the street and went to camps with only the clothes on their backs.

The Hasenberg family knew the day would come when they, too, would be arrested. Night after night, the Wehrmacht, the Dutch equivalent of the Nazi SS, rolled into the Jewish section of Amsterdam in large trucks to round up more Jews in *razzias*—military raids. From loudspeakers on the trucks Nazis barked orders for the Jews to stop on the street. Other Nazis broke down doors. Irene remembers the screams of families pulled from the streets or out of houses and loaded into the trucks. John told his family their arrest was only a matter of time.

Gertrude packed rucksacks with clothes for all four of them, and a Gentile family offered to keep their photographs. For about a year, the Hasenbergs lived with the certainty that at any moment they would be taken.

On Sunday morning, June 20, 1943, the Nazis blocked off the Hasenbergs' neighborhood and began a house-to-house search. The day was hot, but all four of the Hasenbergs dressed in several layers of clothes. They grabbed their rucksacks and bags of food. They joined a crowd of hundreds of other Jews in the street and began the slow march to a large square, where they were loaded into trucks and taken to the train station. All Irene remembered of that walk is that it was hot and long. Her clothes were drenched with sweat.

About midday, they arrived at the station, and Irene and her family were loaded into a cattle car with sixty or so other people. Irene heard the snap of a lock being bolted. The cattle cars had no drinking water, and two buckets were for human waste. Everyone, even those old and sick, sat on luggage. Babies cried. The only light came from small slits. Then a whistle blew and the train jolted forward. With a mixture of shock and perverse relief, Irene thought that at long last what she had imagined as the worst had happened. In the crowded cattle car, she felt utterly terrified and humiliated.

After an eight-hour trip, the train stopped late at night at the Westerbork Transit Camp in the northeastern Netherlands. Everyone on the train was taken into a large room and told to take off all their clothes. They were inspected for lice, and anyone infested had all the hair shorn off his or her body. Irene gasped, as she had lived a sheltered life and had never seen anyone naked. She had seen only two movies: *Hansel and Gretel* and *Snow White*. Nothing had prepared her for what she saw that night: hundreds of naked bodies, young and old, with Nazi inspectors probing them for lice.

For the most part, the Nazis turned over the day-to-day running of the camp in Westerbork to the Jewish security service. Irene's mother was assigned to a sewing circle and her father did hard labor. The camp was built around a railroad track, and every Saturday long trains came into the center of Westerbork, and their arrival is one of Irene's most vivid memories. The trains, spanning the length of the camp, sat empty through Monday. Everywhere Irene walked in the camp, she saw the long, hideous cattle cars and was filled with a sense of doom.

At midnight on Mondays, the barracks leaders in Westerbork came in to each barrack, turned on all the lights, and read off the names of people who were scheduled for transport. Those whose names were called would be sent to their deaths in the Auschwitz or Theresien-stadt concentration camps. On those Mondays when Irene's family was not called, she lived in despair because she always knew someone on the list who was going the next day. Anne Frank and her family arrived in Westerbork in August 1944, fourteen months after Irene arrived. In September, the Franks' names were called.

The Nazis forced the Jews to decide which Jews would be sent to their deaths out of Westerbork and to live with the guilt. More than one hundred thousand Jews transported from Westerbork were killed in gas chambers in Auschwitz and Theresienstadt.

While in Westerbork, Irene contracted hepatitis and was hospi-talized for two weeks. The separation from her brother and parents was difficult. Many people around her in the hospital were dying. Some were demented—their angry, desperate screams frightened Irene.

Soon after their arrival in Westerbork in June 1943, the Hasenberg family had come close to being transferred to Auschwitz. A friend of John Hasenberg's, a man he served with during World War I, spot-ted the Hasenberg name on a train list to Auschwitz. The man had influence in camp and managed to get the Hasenbergs off the list.

Soon after, John received an unexpected piece of mail. In the envelope were four passports stamped with the magic word *Ecuador*. John and Gertrude stared at the falsified passports in disbelief. Not only had the broker kept his promise, somehow the mail had been forwarded from their home in Amsterdam to Westerbork. Immediately the status of the family changed; John realized they wouldn't be transferred to Auschwitz.

In February 1944, Irene and her family were transferred to Bergen-Belsen concentration camp, which was more crowded, and conditions were much worse. In Westerbork, primarily Dutch Jews administered the camp; in Bergen-Belsen, the SS ran the camp and meted out vicious punishment. The prisoners were crammed into smaller spaces than at Westerbork, and women and men had segregated barracks, which meant separation and uncertainty.

As the Russians approached Auschwitz, some of the prisoners there were transferred to Bergen-Belsen. Other transports came from Albania, Greece, and Hungary, which meant that prisoners in Bergen-Belsen had less food. At night in the barracks, the women would lie in the dark and describe recipes for their favorite foods— stuffed breast of veal, goulash, vegetables of all kinds, cakes and cookies. Each woman would try to outdo the others in these night-time fantasy feasts. During these nights, Irene thought to herself that there was no word to describe the physical pain of hunger. "True hunger is a painful, ever-present feeling that is impossible to comprehend," Irene said. "It's a gnawing, hollow feeling."

During the day, she cleaned the barracks and did the laundry. There was no soap, only cold water. When mothers left the barracks to go to work, Irene and other young teenagers cared for the smaller children. Werner did hard labor alongside his father.

Under conditions that were barely survivable, Irene and her family spent eleven months in Bergen-Belsen. "Every night I went to sleep hoping that I would wake up in the morning," Irene recalled. Finally, on January 21, 1945, after the Hasenberg family passed their medical examinations, they assembled at the center of the camp with a group of about three hundred other Jews in Bergen-Belsen who were on the list for exchange.

Near evening, a train flying a Red Cross flag rolled into camp. Irene and Werner steadied Gertrude as they walked up the steps into the heated train, John following behind. As the train moved slowly out of Bergen-Belsen, the Hasenbergs were silent. Irene stared out the window.

The train, headed for Switzerland, was forced to make numerous stops. Allied pilots had bombed many of the tracks and they had to be cleared. At times the train sat on the tracks for hours, unable to move. In the compartment, both Gertrude and John were in great physical pain. They struggled to stay upright in their seats. Werner and Irene, both suffering from malnutrition, did their best to take care of their parents.

On the second night of the four-day journey, John got up to go to the bathroom. He was too weak to walk by himself, so Irene walked with him.

"We're almost free now," she whispered.

"I'm not gonna make it," he replied.

That night, he fell asleep on Irene's shoulder, and sometime during the night he died. Irene shook him but there was no response. For several hours, she and Werner held him in their arms. Gertrude seemed confused, unable to comprehend what had happened. John was the first person to die on the train. Over the next few days, others from Bergen-Belsen, headed for exchange and freedom, died as well.

In the morning, a nurse came by and declared John dead. His body was wrapped in a blanket and left off at the next town on a bench near the train station. The indignity of it—their father left in a strange town with no funeral rites—did not yet penetrate Irene or Werner. After all they had endured, they were too numb, perhaps in shock.

When breakfast was distributed throughout the train, Irene and Werner heartily ate the first real meal they had eaten in more than a year. An acquaintance from Amsterdam, a man who knew their father, approached them to express his condolences for their father's death.

"How can you eat when your father has just died?" the man said.

Irene and Werner stared at him, unable to say a word. Both thought to themselves, "How could he speak to us like that?" With their father dead, they had to fight for their lives. They were literally starving and had to survive. They continued to eat their breakfast in silence.

The Red Cross train stopped in several camps to pick up Americans who were held in internment camps. The real Americans, as Irene thought of them, filed onto the train, some weeping with relief. The reality of the exchange was not yet clear to Irene. "It was like we were commodities," she said. "I didn't yet understand that my life would be saved."

On February 3, the train passed from Konstanz, Germany, across the border into Kreuzlingen, Switzerland. Swiss authorities boarded the train with food and water. Irene focused on her mother—watching her chest rise and fall—to make sure she was still alive.

Once the Swiss had checked off names for the exchange, the train continued to St. Gallen, Switzerland, where they disembarked. Irene slept in a barn on a bed of hay soiled with urine and feces, but at least there was food. Compared to Bergen-Belsen, the conditions were manageable. Werner and Gertrude were immediately admitted to a Swiss hospital. Werner's feet had been frostbitten, and he needed surgery to avoid gangrene. In Bergen-Belsen, he had stood too many hours in the cold in shoes too small for him during the daily roll calls.

Gertrude's condition was critical. Someone at the hospital called a priest to say prayers over her because they thought she was dying. An elderly Jew from the train told the doctors to stop the priest from praying, explaining that in Jewish tradition prayers aren't spoken until after someone has died.

In early February, the Swiss authorities, flooded with refugees and eager to be rid of them, put together the list of everyone—Americans, prisoners of war, and the Jews from Bergen-Belsen—who would return to America on the MS *Gripsholm*, the ship that had carried Ingrid and her family from America, which was scheduled to leave from Marseille on February 8.

The Swiss authorities placed Irene, now an official displaced person (DP), on the list for the train bound for Marseille. Her mother and brother, also DPs, were scheduled to stay behind in the hospital. In a year and a half in concentration camps, Irene had not been separated from her family. She told the authorities she couldn't leave her mother behind, who might not survive, and wouldn't travel to America without her older brother.

"Here in Switzerland we are free, right?" said Irene. "I won't go without my family."

But the Swiss gave her no choice. On the day the train left, Irene boarded with assurance that if she went on to Marseille, the Swiss would find a way to bring her back to her family in St. Gallen. It was a ploy to get her on the train. The moment she sat down, Irene regretted her decision and wished she had sought out a place to hide in St. Gallen.

The train was filled with Americans who had been trapped in Germany. Many had been housed in abandoned German army barracks and had subsisted on little food and lived in fear for their lives. However, compared to Irene, an emaciated concentration camp survivor, the Americans looked reasonably healthy and were naturally in good spirits on this day.

An American woman, horrified at the sight of the sickly and despondent Irene, sat beside her on the train. Irene explained that her mother and brother were in St. Gallen in the hospital and that she didn't know if she would ever see them again. The American woman picked up Irene and placed her on her lap. Even though she was fourteen, Irene sat and buried her face in the woman's shoulder. The woman rocked and hugged Irene as if she were an infant. The woman whispered to Irene that everything would be all right, that she would take Irene with her to America and care for her until her mother and brother could make their way to the United States as well. Irene relaxed in her arms.

A Red Cross worker walked down the aisle and delivered a Red Cross package to every passenger. Irene took her package. Then the American woman gave Irene her package. Now she had two and told the woman, "I'm in seventh heaven."

As the train neared Marseille, one of the Swiss authorities approached the woman and asked to speak to her. They left the compartment and moved to the back of the train. When the American woman returned to Irene, she was crying and said, "I can't take you to America. They won't let me." Irene felt confused but had no choice and accepted the news.

When the train came to a stop in Marseille, Irene saw the MS *Gripsholm* in the harbor. The stunning sight was more beautiful to Irene because the ship was Swedish and neutral. Next to the ship was a small Italian freighter, the *Città di Alessandria*.

When she disembarked the train, Irene was placed in line with other DPs from Bergen-Belsen. The Americans formed a separate line and boarded the MS *Gripsholm*, where champagne and a large buffet of good food waited. Irene and a group of approximately one hundred Jews from Bergen-Belsen boarded the freighter. Once on board, Irene was told that the freighter was bound for a United Nations Relief and Rehabilitation Administration camp near Algeria in North Africa. Irene had no idea where Algeria was on a map.

The first night at sea the cooks on the ship served platters of hamburgers, the first hamburgers Irene had seen since she'd left Amsterdam and entered Westerbork in June 1943. She ate more than one and became sick. All she could do was lie on the deck beneath the moon stitched into the dark sky. As the sides of the freighter were licked by waves, Irene vomited the hamburgers. She scolded herself for eating too much, too fast.

Later that night, she heard a door open and saw a waiter bring a tray of hamburgers on deck and dump them into the sea. She couldn't believe her eyes. After so many months of hunger, the waste of food seemed criminal to Irene. The ocean kept moving beneath her. The wind whipped up and darkness covered the moon and stars. She could smell the salt from the sea. Alone on the deck, with her father dead and her mother and brother far away in Switzerland, Irene cast her mind back to her childhood in Amsterdam and cried for all she had lost. Then she fell asleep, a lonely girl at sea, as the freighter took her to North Africa.

CHAPTER FOURTEEN

Under Fire

From the moment the Eiserloh family was transferred to Bregenz, they were outside the protection of the US government and the Swiss and under the authority of the German Reich. Step by step through the snow, the family made their way north on foot, headed for Idstein, Johanna's hometown. Cold was the immediate enemy, with temperatures well below freezing. Johanna tucked Guenther, a sickly infant, inside her coat. Ensi, only four, stayed close to her mother. Ingrid and Lothar followed in their father's footsteps.

After a few hours' walk, Mathias hitched a ride for the family in an open-air truck to the next railroad station. From the back of the truck, Lothar watched as they passed through villages heavily damaged by Allied bombing. Even at nine years old it was clear to Lothar that Germany had all but lost the war.

Only two weeks before, the German winter offensive to the west of Germany in Belgium and the Ardennes Forest in France, known to the Allies as the Battle of the Bulge, was finished and Germany's fate sealed. The battle began on December 16, 1944, when Germany opened fire with two thousand guns on American forces in the Ardennes Forest. The weather was bad and the attack came as a surprise to Allied forces. When Brigadier General Anthony McAuliffe was asked to surrender, he replied famously, "Nuts!" Meanwhile, General George S. Patton's Third Army turned north to attack the left flank of the Germans while British Field Marshal Bernard Montgomery attacked the right flank. In the battle the Germans lost one hundred thousand men and the Americans eighty-one thousand.

The complex endgame of the war was in play. In the early days of February, as Ingrid and her family trudged through the snow in Germany, they were invisible casualties of much larger forces. Given the official secrecy of the government's exchange program, few in America knew anything of the plight of families such as the Eiserlohs. In the face of the magnitude of the loss of American lives during the war against Japan and Germany, it is unlikely many would have cared.

On February 4, 1945, the three Allied leaders—FDR, Winston Churchill, and Joseph Stalin—gathered in Yalta on the Black Sea to plan the final defeat of Germany and Japan. Stalin, whose army controlled Poland and the Balkans and was advancing toward Berlin, had insisted that the meeting take place on his home turf. Only a few weeks earlier, on January 20, 1945, Roosevelt was sworn in for a historic fourth term. By then, FDR was a sick man. Determined to spare his strength, his inaugural address lasted only five minutes, the shortest in history.

Over seven days in Yalta, Roosevelt, Churchill, and Stalin haggled over reparations. Stalin wanted $10 billion, and both Churchill and Roosevelt held firm against his demands. By the end of the meeting, Roosevelt was physically spent but wrote to Eleanor that he was pleased with the negotiation: "Dearest Babs, We have wound up the conference—successfully I think. . . . I am a bit exhausted but really all right."

When Franklin returned to the White House on February 28, Eleanor was shocked by his appearance. Not even when he was stricken with polio had he ever looked so frail. The following day FDR gave an address to Congress and remained seated for the first time in his presidency. "I hope you will pardon me," he told the combined chambers. "It makes it a lot easier for me to have to carry about ten pounds of steel around the bottom of my legs." His eyes looked down at the podium. "It has been a long journey." His voice faltered. "I hope you will agree that it was a fruitful one."

Meanwhile, on the other side of the Atlantic, Ingrid and her family continued their hazardous journey. Everywhere the Eiserlohs traveled they saw evidence—fields rutted with bomb craters, trees felled, farmhouses in pieces—of the success of the Allied campaign. Food was difficult to find. During the first few days, Mathias traded small personal items—a few cigarettes, pieces of clothing—for hard bread and thin soup. "I began to feel as if my body was shutting down," recalled Ingrid. "I had no energy and it was hard to put one foot in front of the other." As a teenager, she was self-conscious about her body and struggled to stay clean. On the walks, she foraged for water and used handkerchiefs to wipe the grime from her body. When they stopped to sleep at night, she slept fully clothed. Many nights, air-raid sirens sounded and the family would rush to seek shelter in bunkers.

On and on they made their way on foot along damaged rail tracks. The trains kept no particular schedule. When the trains did pull into stations, German troops in full uniform, all headed for the Western Front, crowded onto the cars, leaving little room for civilians.

As a child in Strongsville, Ohio, Lothar had spent hours assembling model airplanes. From the touch of glue and paint on his hands, Lothar knew the intimate details of many American fighter planes—the P-61 Black Widow, a night cruiser; the P-38 Lightning, and the Navy's twin-engine F7F Tigercat. Day after day, he watched his listless mother, a shell of her former self, struggle with sickly Guenther. Her eyes stayed fixed on the ground. Slowly he began to comprehend the tragedy of his father's decision to repatriate.

At night Lothar eavesdropped on arguments between his parents. Johanna blamed Mathias for the financial pressures during the early years of the marriage, for not securing American citizenship for both of them, for not anticipating his arrest and internment and leaving the family defenseless. Lothar began to see his father through Johanna's eyes: as unreliable. Ingrid heard the arguments as well but sided with her father. "My mother constantly criticized my father," recalled Ingrid. "She saw herself as a victim." To Ingrid, Mathias was blameless.

As the journey north continued, Ingrid consigned the names of the towns they passed to memory. When the Eiserloh family arrived in Ulm, a small town situated on the Danube River, they saw their first glimpse of the near destruction of a town. Eighty-one percent of the city had been destroyed by British bombers in December 1944. The damage was from the square in front of the Muenster, the highest church spire in the world at the time, to the west as far as the train station. The Muenster was the only thing in sight virtually untouched, because bomber crews used the church as a major landmark that could be seen from great distances. From Ulm, they caught a train west to Stuttgart and straight north to Würzburg. Finally, in the first week of March 1945, they arrived in Frankfurt am Main, which had been flattened by Allied bombs. As they pulled into the station, Ingrid looked out the window. In the center of the medieval town, she saw industrial buildings reduced to rubble. The streets had holes large enough to drop a Volkswagen into.

When they arrived it was late evening, and everyone was filthy, hungry, and cold. While they stood on the street, a loud siren shrieked and Allied bombs fell from the sky. The Eiserloh family joined the stampede of people running for the nearest air-raid shelter. The shelter, deep in the earth, was dark, crowded, and unpleasant. Mathias and Johanna huddled with their children in a corner and tried to stay warm. Someone found powdered milk for Guenther. The hours passed slowly and no one slept except Lothar.

Later that night, Mathias nudged Lothar and said, "Let's go for a walk." Outside, Mathias began a panicky search for cigarettes. Lothar loathed his father's habit and avoided his hugs because Mathias reeked of cigarettes. His fingers, nostrils, and ears were stained yellow. That night Mathias had no money to buy cigarettes and nothing to barter, so he gathered partially smoked butts off the ground. When Mathias found one, he smoked it quickly and lowered his eyes in search of another. In the cold night, Lothar was angry with his father and frightened of Allied bombs, and exhaled his own bitterness.

The next morning, Lothar and the family left the shelter and returned to the train station in Frankfurt. They boarded a train for Idstein, a distance of about sixty kilometers, the final leg of the trip. Idstein was Johanna's hometown, where her parents still lived.

The train chugged out of the station at an even pace. About eight kilometers east of Idstein, in a small town called Neuhof, the train slowed to enter a tunnel. As it snaked its way through the tunnel to the other side, the conductor blew the whistle once. Then a second blast filled the air, and suddenly the train lurched forward and picked up speed. The passengers straightened in their seats. Outside the windows snowy mountains and forests whizzed by. Something was wrong and everyone on board knew it.

Then Ingrid heard the sound of airplanes above the train followed by blasts of machine-gun fire. Mathias moved to the end of the train and looked outside, with Ingrid following in rapid strides close behind. Eight American P-38s flew above them, each mounted with two four-barrel machine guns.

"Attack! Attack!" yelled the conductor in German.

Ensi watched the scene from the window seat; her mother, cradling Guenther, had the aisle seat. "Get down," ordered Johanna. "Get down." Ensi didn't move. Eyes opened wide, she strained to see the action, as machine-gun bullets hit the side of the train. Ensi heard a new round of *rat-a-tat* each time the planes made another pass overhead.

Johanna slapped Ensi's face and pushed her underneath the seat. Then Johanna reached up to an overhead rack, grabbed a suitcase, and placed it on top of the seat to further protect Ensi. "Keep your face down!" screamed Johanna. "Don't look up."

Mathias and Ingrid hurried back to their seats. He shoved both Ingrid and Lothar under their seats. "I'll smack you both if you move," Mathias said.

The train slowed and came to a stop. As the passengers cautiously emerged from beneath the seats, the conductor ordered everyone off the train. Mathias pointed to a ten-foot embankment on one side of the train that led into a grove of trees. He grabbed Guenther from Johanna and wrapped the child in a white blanket. "Let's go," he ordered.

All six of them hurried up the hill. Lothar took Ensi's hand and set a quick pace for the others. Mathias handed Guenther to Ingrid, who clutched the baby in her arms and scuttled up the hill, right behind Lothar.

When Ingrid looked over her shoulder, she saw her mother flat on the ground with Mathias crouched over her. Johanna had fallen, and Ingrid watched as Mathias dragged Johanna to her knees and then to her feet. Together they pushed up the hill.

At the top of the hill, Lothar positioned himself and Ensi beneath the branches of a small pine tree. Ingrid carried Guenther to join them. Most of the trees in the forest had been cut for fuel, but the black limbs of the pine trees were visible against the gray winter sky. The children watched as Mathias inched Johanna up the hill.

From this vantage point, they fixed their eyes on the train, stopped on the tracks, and the American planes that circled it. Mathias speculated to his wife and children that the purpose of the American mission must have been to seal the tunnel that led to Idstein.

The conductor blew the whistle to signal that the train was leaving. The Eiserlohs hurried down the hill and reboarded the train. Once the passengers were back on board, the battle continued. The American planes swooped down over the rails and flew low to the ground, their machine guns hitting to the right of the train and to the left. German soldiers returned the fire from two antiaircraft guns attached to the train—one gun on the last car, the other just behind the locomotive.

As Lothar and Ingrid watched from their seats, each saw a P-38 hit by German fire. The American pilot ejected from his plane with a parachute and landed in a tree, his body riddled with bullets. Then a second plane was hit and went down on the other side of the train. Ensi was on that side and watched as the plane plunged to the ground, leaving a spiraling trail of black smoke in the sky.

None of the German soldiers were hit, and the six remaining P-38s retreated. Though the battle was over, the atmosphere inside the train was pandemonium. The conductor walked through the train to check on the passengers. None were wounded or killed, and everyone settled back into their seats, shaken and confused.

Lothar looked at his mother, who appeared to be in a daze. When she spoke, she described her mixed emotions. She was relieved they were all alive, but remorseful for the two American pilots who were killed. "The irony of American fly boys shooting at my American-born children," she told him. "I'll never understand it."

Both Lothar and Ingrid were shaken from traveling between two distinct worlds: America and Germany. One part of them was still in Strongsville, Ohio, and Crystal City, Texas, and the other faced the reality that their lives had been saved by German soldiers firing on American pilots.

Two months after the Eiserloh family left Crystal City, they arrived in Idstein, a quaint town surrounded by meadows and rolling hills in a picturesque valley. They walked about a mile from the train depot and passed the town's landmark, a craggy, twelfth-century castle called the Hexenturm (Witches' Tower). Cobblestone streets, lined with houses that were centuries old, fed into the town square, with its fountain and a striking statue of a golden lion. When Ingrid lingered at the fountain, Johanna urged her to keep moving: "Just a little farther. It's just around the first street and above the row houses."

At last they arrived at the front door of the home of Johanna's parents. She expected a warm reunion for her and her children, who had never met their grandparents. While in Crystal City, Johanna had sent letters about their arrival, but none of the letters had arrived. That day her parents were stunned to see them. After an uncomfortable silence, Johanna's father awkwardly explained that Johanna and her family could stay a few days, but no longer. Like everyone else in Germany, Johanna's parents did not have enough food for themselves, much less a family of six from America that had turned up on their doorstep. For Johanna, the scene was like something from a frightening fairy tale: the cupboard was bare.

The three-story house had four bedrooms upstairs. The German government had conscripted three of the bedrooms as housing for wounded soldiers, and Johanna's parents occupied the fourth. Her father took the family to the basement, where he had a carpentry shop, and a shed for goats and pigs. He offered them a corner of the cellar as a temporary place to stay. All the pigs had been eaten, but there was a single goat. That night, Guenther had goat milk for dinner. Johanna and the rest of the family had what little was left of the stored canned goods from the summer before.

All of the family suffered from malnutrition. At five feet three inches, Ingrid weighed only seventy-five pounds. Johanna was gaunt and still weak from childbirth. Mathias, Lothar, and Ensi were half-starved as well.

Mathias and Johanna argued about where to go to find shelter. Mathias wanted to travel to his hometown of Plaidt, which was on the other side of the Rhine River, about sixty-four kilometers from Idstein. Mathias had inherited a small portion of his father's land and wanted to investigate how to claim it and eventually build a home there. Johanna thought they should look for a place of their own in Idstein. She urged him to stay in Idstein and help her with the immediate problem—finding food for their family. She had always held the small, drab village of Plaidt in disdain and did not want to settle there. In the long run, she told Mathias, it would be easier for him to find work in Idstein, which was larger and had more businesses. Besides, she wanted Ingrid and Lothar to enroll in school in Idstein.

Most of these arguments were waged in whispers, but that night the tension of many years erupted. In the presence of their wide-awake children, they yelled, screamed, and shoved each other. The quarrel lasted long into the night.

The next morning Mathias left the house and made his way on foot toward Plaidt. By that time, the Allies were nearing the Rhine, and close to the river, Mathias saw a line of olive-green German motorcycles. No German soldiers were nearby, and Mathias concluded that the motorcycles had been abandoned, perhaps by dead or wounded soldiers. Without considering the consequences, Mathias chose one of the motorcycles, mounted it, and rode to Plaidt.

When Mathias returned to Idstein a few days later, six SS officers knocked at the door of the home of his in-laws. Dressed in the traditional gray-green SS coats, they carried billy sticks. When they discovered Mathias in the cellar, they slammed him against the wall and, in full view of Johanna and the children, beat him repeatedly. In an effort to help his father, Lothar jumped on the back of one of the officers, who batted him off his shoulders like a fly.

Mathias was arrested on charges of stealing the motorcycle and taken to a nearby German prison camp, where he was interrogated as a suspected spy for the advancing American troops. A few days later, the SS officers returned and questioned Johanna about her own possible activities as a spy. While Johanna was cleared, she was not told where Mathias was incarcerated or when he would return.

Johanna found a small apartment near the train station with one large room and a window. She and the children settled there. By then, the American Army was on its way. Day and night Johanna and the children listened for air-raid sirens. When they heard them, they crossed the street from the apartment and took refuge in an underground shelter, where water dripped from the ceiling. Ingrid was careful to put on her shoes before climbing down the stairs. From the alleys, rats ran into the shelter as well and lived off the leavings of the humans. Ingrid was terrified of their bite.

In the shelter, the townspeople regarded Johanna and her children with suspicion. No one could comprehend why the Eiserloh family had returned to Germany. When Johanna explained about the family internment camp in Crystal City and the exchange two months before, they did not believe her. Night after night in the

Idstein shelter, Ingrid waited for the "all clear" and remembered the family bungalow in Crystal City where milk was delivered daily and where food was plentiful. Now the currents of history had shifted in an uncanny way. As he had been in Strongsville, Ohio, her father had again been arrested—this time by the Nazis in Idstein, Germany. For the second time during the war, Ingrid had lost her father. She could do nothing but wait for the Americans.

CHAPTER FIFTEEN

Into Algeria

Irene's journey across the Mediterranean to the port of Philippeville, a French colony formerly under the control of the Vichy regime located in the northeastern part of Algeria, took less than thirty hours. As the *Città de Alessandria*, the Italian freighter, neared the Algerian port, Irene watched seagulls dive overhead and blue water strike rocks near the shoreline. Even though it was still winter, the air was warm as sunshine poured from the sky.

At the dock, Irene was part of a group of fewer than one hundred Jews from the Bergen-Belsen concentration camp who were met by British representatives from Camp Jeanne d'Arc, a displaced-persons camp in Philippeville that was operated by the United Nations Relief and Rehabilitation Administration. The mission of the UNRRA was to provide assistance to European nations at the end of the war and to help refugees such as Irene who were liberated from Bergen-Belsen and other concentration camps.

The view outside the window of the bus that took Irene to the camp was of a healthier, brighter world than any she had seen since the dark days following the arrest of her family by the Nazis in Amsterdam in June 1943. Ahead of her were grassy hills with high ridges on both the east and west side of the roaring sea. Small houses, painted soothing shades of white and blue, rose gradually up the knolls. Among the houses were a few towering office buildings with red roofs. The road to the camp in Philippeville was lined with palms and a variety of fruit trees. Children zigzagged in happy packs on either side.

Despite the intense light and the beauty of surroundings, Irene's mind was fixed on the perils of the war. Even though she was now in Philippeville, the troubles in Europe did not feel far away. On the other side of the Mediterranean, her mother, Gertrude, and her brother, Werner, remained in a private hospital at St. Gallen, Switzerland. When last Irene saw her mother, Gertrude was near death. Was her mother conscious now, and if so, how was she bearing the uncertainty of not hearing any word from Irene? When would the war finally be over, and how would she be reunited with her brother and mother? All of these questions stirred squalls of sadness within Irene.

She'd never before been on her own. The task of learning to live without her family was so dark and heavy that she was in no mood to celebrate the sublime arrival of warm weather in early February in Philippeville. While she was warm and safe, she knew her mother and brother were still recuperating from serious injuries, their fates unknown.

The camp in Philippeville had a series of metal military barracks with rounded metal tops. While other children went with their parents to separate barracks, Irene was taken to a barrack for children who did not have parents or whose parents were too sick to take care of them. In other words, she was assigned to an orphans' barrack. Many of the parents of those children were desperately ill and were taken to a camp hospital. A variety of nationalities of UNRRA nurses and doctors worked in the hospital.

Irene was still skin and bones and pallid in contrast to the tanned British and American staff in the camp. "A British man was the director of the camp," recalled Irene. "They were very nice and showed a great deal of interest in me. I ate three meals a day in a dining room. Compared to the hell of Bergen-Belsen, it wasn't that bad, except I was so worried about my mother and my brother. I struggled to regain my strength and to keep going."

For Irene and the other children in camp, the days passed without structure. Every day they made their way to the beach and swam in the warm waters. Without the sight of Nazi arms raised in salute or the diet of bitter bread and watery soup, they slowly began to adapt to this sanctuary. They ate fresh fruit and vegetables and walked on paths lined with flowers.

But for Irene there was little peace. Although the UNRRA staff helped her send messages to her mother and brother in St. Gallen, these went unanswered. In the meantime, other unaccompanied refugee children in the barrack had successfully been reunited with their parents in small family units at the camp. Finally, only Irene and one other child, a seven-year-old boy from Poland named Vitek, were left in the orphans' barrack.

Though Irene felt sisterly toward Vitek, he was extremely troubled. Relief workers told Irene that Nazi guards had shot both of Vitek's parents in front of his eyes. Ugly, repetitive flashes of those deaths haunted Vitek while he was awake. At night in the barrack, Vitek flailed in his bed, unable to find rest. Irene rocked him until he dropped into sleep. Finally, a Polish family took him in and he was transferred.

Shortly after Vitek left the barrack, a German woman who was a friend of Irene's mother in Bergen-Belsen agreed that Irene could join her family. The woman and her husband had two children, a boy and a girl, and Irene stayed with them as she continued to await word from her own mother and brother.

Finally in March, a month after her arrival, Irene received word that both her mother and brother were alive in St. Gallen. She was extremely relieved, but while her brother's foot had healed, her mother was still critical. Both would have to stay in St. Gallen. The arrival of the first letter pulled Irene out of her slump, and she was soon corresponding regularly with her mother and brother. Irene took comfort in knowing that her mother was resting on clean sheets, under the care of nurses, and that she ate three good meals a day. However, in Philippeville, surrounded by the water and the seaside flora, Irene felt as lonely as a castaway.

By letters, they decided that the three of them—Gertrude, Werner, and Irene—would attempt to immigrate to the United States. Her mother had a cousin, Rose Kaplan, who'd gone to the United States from Germany in the 1930s. Rose and her husband, Hugo, owned a small carpet-cleaning business in New York and agreed to sponsor Irene and provide for her support. Without their sponsorship, Irene would not be considered for a visa. Relief workers in the camp set the process in motion. It took much longer than Irene had imagined.

One of the gravely ill patients in the Philippeville camp hospital was forty-three-year-old Sara Wolf, known by her friends and family by her Dutch name, Lien. Before the war, Irene's family and the Wolfs had known each other well in Amsterdam in the small, close-knit Jewish quarter. The Wolfs had two children, Jacob, pronounced Jaap by his Dutch family, and his sister, Marie, who was known as Mieke. The Wolf children were similar in ages to Werner and Irene. In Amsterdam, Werner and Jacob had attended the same school, and Marie, like Irene, had been acquainted with Anne Frank.

The path the two families had followed to Philippeville was also parallel. Both families were arrested in the summer of 1943, but a crucial difference between the legal statuses of the two families was that Henri Wolf, the father of Jacob and Marie, held an American birth certificate and American passport. Henri's parents had emigrated from Holland to New York in the late 1890s; Henri was born in Brooklyn in 1898.

At the time of his birth, his mother missed her family and preferred the tranquil environment of Holland to the chaotic life in New York. Henri's father did not want to return, which provoked a conflict, but in time Henri's father acquiesced to his wife's wishes and the family moved to Holland. He was careful to make sure that his own son, Henri, had an American birth certificate and an American passport in case Henri wanted to return to America.

When Henri was eight years old, he contracted a virus that left him disabled. "He became a dwarf," recalled Jacob, his son. "He stayed the same height that he was at eight for the rest of his life—never more than just over four feet tall." Despite his disability, Henri excelled in school and became a language teacher, offering instruction in French, German, and English. In Holland, he married Lien, and they had two children—Jacob in 1929 and Mieke in 1933. After the children were born, Henri made sure that they, too, acquired American citizenship. As the children of an American-born father, both children secured certificates of citizenship and American passports.

Like the Hasenberg family, the Wolfs, despite their papers, were crammed into a cattle car in June 1943 and transported to Westerbork, the transit camp for all the Jews from the Netherlands. Prior to his arrest, Henri had attempted to use his American passport and those of his children to get his family out of Amsterdam and back to the United States. By then, all requests for travel to America were denied because of visa restrictions. "The atmosphere of hate was such that the Germans took a dim view of our passports," said Jacob. "They didn't want any Jews to escape so they ignored our passports." Instead of sending the Wolf family to Auschwitz, the German authorities sent them to Bergen-Belsen, where they were classified as possible exchange Jews. They left Bergen-Belsen on the same train as Irene's family.

Jacob remembers the moment that the train from Bergen-Belsen clattered across the border from Konstanz, Germany, into the northeast corner of Switzerland and pulled into the station at Kruezlingen. Two large trains were parked side by side in the station. One train was filled with German POWs and the group from Crystal City, including the Eiserlohs, Ingrid's family. The other was packed with sick and dispirited Jews from Bergen-Belsen, including the Wolfs and Irene, her mother, and brother. Her father, John, had secured his family's freedom but died before making the short walk into freedom between those two trains.

The moods of the passengers on board the opposing trains were quite different. The Germans and German Americans, including

Ingrid and her siblings, were being deported from their home country into a war-torn and, for most, alien environment. In contrast, the Jewish families from Bergen-Belsen were being transported from imminent death to freedom and plenty. In the Eiserloh train, the people were anxious and afraid. When Jacob disembarked from the train from Bergen-Belsen and boarded the train from Kruezlingen to Marseille, he heard jubilant shouts from the crew and incoming passengers. "U-S-A! U-S-A!" they shouted. Relief workers covered Jacob's shivering body with warm blankets. His younger sister was blanketed as well. His mother, who had developed cancer in Bergen-Belsen, was so ill she could barely walk. Medical personnel rushed to take care of her. His father was handed a cup of strong, hot coffee. Henri and the two children settled into their seats in the Pullman car.

On the other side of the track, Jacob heard repeated shouts of "Heil Hitler!" from the passengers inside the train headed to Germany, including German POWs and civilians from Crystal City. He was a sixteen-year-old Jewish boy who since his deportation from Amsterdam had kept his eyes down and his fears squeezed into a tight ball. But at that moment the dreaded phrase *Heil Hitler* no longer held any power over Jacob. "I understood that my life was being saved," Jacob recalled. "At long last, I felt safe."

When the train arrived in Marseille, Jacob's momentary sense of safety was marred by a surprise turn of events. In the port stood the gleaming-white *Gripsholm*, the Swedish liner. Jacob's family joined the line of American prisoners of war and civilians who boarded the ship of freedom. On deck waiters served champagne. Buffet tables spread with poultry and fish dishes, savory vegetables, and sweet desserts waited in the banquet room.

While Jacob's family awaited their assignments, a pair of officials from the American consulate approached Henri and explained that he and his two children were welcome to stay on board and sail to America. All three of their passports were in order. But Sara, a Dutch citizen, would have to stay behind and be transported to the displaced-persons camp in Philippeville. She couldn't get an American visa because of the restrictions.

Jacob's eyes fixed on his father's tired face. Henri seemed to be concentrating all of his senses in an effort to weigh the unbearable choice that faced him. "You want me to leave my sick wife behind?" asked Henri, his voice a crackle of panic. "No, no, no. I can't do that."

As a dwarf, Henri routinely attracted attention. People stared at his shriveled legs and sharp bones. On that day, Jacob, who was five feet nine inches tall, towered over Henri by almost two feet. He watched his father straighten his spine and heard him give officials his answer, delivered in perfect English: "Take us all to Philippeville."

Officials escorted the whole family off the ship bound for America and they boarded the Italian freighter, the same ship that Irene was on. Upon arrival, they joined Irene at the camp in Philippeville. Jacob's mother was immediately taken to the camp hospital. Doctors explained to Henri that the renal cancer had spread and they could do nothing. Sara, forty-three years old, forcibly extracted by the Nazis from her home in Amsterdam, who had struggled to survive and keep her children alive in a concentration camp, was now incapacitated in a hospital bed in a distant country. Jacob and Marie visited her every day for two weeks. Henri never left her side.

One afternoon Henri returned to the barracks and told Jacob and Marie their mother had died. The next day Sara was buried in a Jewish section of the cemetery in Philippeville. All that Jacob remembers of the funeral is that the cemetery had a view of the sea. A Jewish family from Philippeville promised Henri that when he and his children returned to America, they would tend Sara's grave.

Given the larger political and global circumstances, that Irene and Jacob were still alive in Philippeville was exceptional. As the historians Richard Breitman and Allan J. Lichtman documented in *FDR and the Jews*, their 2013 history of American policy toward overseas Jews during World War II, during his first term as president Roosevelt put his New Deal policies ahead of the Jewish question in Europe. Prior to 1939, about 127,000 Jews had arrived in the United States as refugees, but 110,000 quota spaces were left unfilled. Immigration laws excluded people who might not be able to support themselves in the United States. This represented a political crisis for FDR, who was still managing bank failures and high unemployment rates. In the face of fierce isolationism, nativism, and anti-Semitism at home, Roosevelt concentrated on domestic affairs. To save more Jews, Roosevelt would have had to relax a US immigration system based on discriminatory quotas that had been legislated in 1924. Even a bill in Congress in 1939, supported by the Catholic Church and Jewish groups in America, that would have admitted ten thousand Jewish children from Europe failed to pass. Roosevelt did not intervene.

When Germany invaded Poland in September 1939, the possibility of escape for Jewish refugees trapped in Germany was for all practical purposes closed. At that point, the waiting list for German nationals seeking US visas numbered 310,000. The quotas for citizens of Hungary, Romania, and Poland were even smaller than for Germans. Most Jews from those countries were not even eligible to apply.

In the end, millions of Jews in Europe unknowingly faced a death sentence because of the visa restrictions. The most famous case is that of the family of Anne Frank. In 1941, the Frank family— Otto, Edith, Anne, and Margot—had not yet gone into hiding in Amsterdam. In an effort to secure an American visa, Otto contacted a friend, Nathan Straus Jr., whom Frank had met thirty-three years earlier. Straus had been put in charge of the New Deal's United States Housing Authority, which had an $800 million budget for public housing. When Straus, in a position of power in Washington, tried to secure visas for the Frank family, he was turned down. "The State Department," Breitman and Lichtman wrote, "had already cut off most visas to Jews."

By 1941, Roosevelt was in his third term and had adopted a more activist position with regard to the Jews. He announced that Nazi war criminals would be held accountable for the organized killings in concentration camps. He created the War Refugee Board, which brought together the Departments of War, Treasury, and State to help rescue Jewish remnants. He appointed Harrison, who had quit his position as INS commissioner in protest of the restricted visa policies of the United States, to the War Refugee Board.

On June 29, 1944, the War Refugee Board considered a proposal to bomb the rail lines to Auschwitz to slow down the deportation of Jews and to bomb the crematoriums and gas chambers there as well. Allied planes were already in the area—industrial complexes and oil refineries near Auschwitz had been bombed. The successful bombing would have destroyed the Nazi machinery of death. While prisoners would have been killed, the perpetrators would also have died. But the War Department opposed the plan for a variety of reasons. Those in charge of operations thought they had greater-priority military targets than the concentration camp, and the proposal was rejected. How successful it would have been is a matter of ongoing debate. The massacre of Jews in Auschwitz and in other camps continued. From early January 1945 until Soviet troops liberated Auschwitz on January 27, 1945, Nazi troops, in the final phase of genocide, murdered 250,000 additional Jews.

In the face of so much death, the handful of Jews spared in the January 1945 exchange, including Irene and Jacob, had defied overwhelming odds. Indeed, the chances of Irene and Jacob being hit by lightning were greater than their chances of escaping genocide. During negotiations between Berlin and Washington for the exchange, Irene was saved by her father's lucky ruse, the false passports from Ecuador. These had made her eligible for exchange for a German with a Latin American passport from Crystal City. The legitimate American passports of Henri, Jacob, and Marie Wolf were tickets to that family's salvation.

In November 1945 the Wolf family—Henri, Jacob, and Marie—were released from camp. They boarded a Liberty ship, one of the hastily built cargo ships that *Time* magazine called an "ugly duckling" because of its crude construction, and slowly made their way to the port of New York. For them it was truly a "Liberty ship," as Roosevelt had christened such vessels at the launch ceremony in 1941, where FDR citied Patrick Henry's 1775 speech: "Give me liberty or give me death." He predicted that the Liberty ships would bring freedom to Europe. Four years later Roosevelt's prediction had come true. The war in Europe had been won.

In less than two weeks, the ship carrying the Wolf family pulled into New York Harbor. "U-S-A!" said Jacob out loud. "U-S-A!" From the deck of the freighter Jacob saw the panoramic lines of skyscrapers, so straight they looked like soldiers standing at attention. At the pier, the Wolfs went through customs and were soon standing on a windy corner with crowds of harried people waiting for a bus. The air of freedom was electrifying.

The Wolfs went straight to a small apartment in Brooklyn that had been arranged for them by relief workers at the Philippeville camp, who had also arranged a job for Henri as a foreign-language teacher. In New York, Henri told Jacob and Marie they had three days to get accustomed to the neighborhood. On the fourth day, both Jacob and Marie enrolled at Eramus Hall High School, a celebrated school in Flatbush where such celebrities as the actress Mae West and the detective novelist Mickey Spillane had preceded them. Two weeks later, Jacob was playing soccer for Eramus Hall, where he was now known as Jack. For the Wolf family, liberty had arrived.

Meanwhile, Irene stayed in Philippeville waiting for her papers— and her own Liberty ship to America.

CHAPTER SIXTEEN

The All-American Camp

Information about the war was slow to reach the internees in Crystal City. Radios were not permitted, and newspapers and magazines were censored. The newsreels that most Americans watched rapt from their seats in movie theaters weren't permitted in Crystal City.

For internees the war was experienced in exile. The Buddhists in Crystal City understood it as a *bardo* state—a provisional period between their lives before their confinement, and the dream of freedom after the war. All through the war, trains kept bringing people to Crystal City and transporting others out of camp and on to Germany, Japan, and elsewhere. Life happened between the comings and goings of trains. By the spring of 1945, 153 babies were listed on the camp's birth records, including Guenther Eiserloh, Ingrid's baby brother, now in Idstein, Germany. Seventeen internees had died, including the two Japanese Peruvian girls who drowned and one German boy hit by a truck. School years started and stopped, children morphed into teenagers, loyalties shifted—all ways of passing transitional time inside the fence.

O'Rourke often said that he wanted the children in camp to have happy memories of Crystal City and grow up to be what he repeatedly called "good American citizens." There were happy memories— school plays, picnics, family gatherings—but the teenagers in camp knew the fence meant that they were regarded as criminals, that their government considered them, as well as their parents, dangerous. It meant they lived in a government cage.

Students in the Federal High School sometimes asked O'Rourke why their "enemy alien" parents were scapegoated by the government and why they, as American citizens, weren't free to come and go from camp. O'Rourke, a career Border Patrol agent with little flair for philosophy, had no satisfying answer. "You're victims of a lousy war," he told them. "You've got no choice but to make the best of it." Once O'Rourke told Jerre Mangione, the press aide to former INS commissioner Harrison, "My family is the people in this camp." This lonely, heartbreaking thing for a man to say indicated that O'Rourke felt exiled as well. If he could only keep the teenagers busy at work or school, he told Mangione, then "they'd all be a hell of a lot more relaxed."

On April 13, 1945, as newspaper hawkers all over the world shouted the headlines from street corners—"The president is dead!"—those trapped inside the barbed-wire fence in faraway Crystal City knew nothing of how Roosevelt had died in Warm Springs the previous day. A few days later, twenty-year-old Eb Fuhr learned of FDR's death from an armed guard who escorted Fuhr and other members of the ice crew into town to pick up a load of ice for delivery inside the camp. Over time, the relationship between the guard and the ice crew had grown relaxed, even friendly. Information about world events was about two weeks behind the curve on the grapevine inside the camp, but FDR's death was impossible for the guard to keep secret. Within hours, word of the momentous event—repeated by the ice crew—had spread to all those living inside the fence. Most of the internees had no context, no way to understand the impact of the death of the president. Eb hoped that it would shorten the war and hasten the closing of the camp. "We just wanted a change in status," he said. "The reaction in camp was pretty neutral. None of us knew what it meant for us."

In the Japanese section, Sumi and her friends were busy with end-of-the-school-year activities and worried about being forced to repatriate to Japan with their parents. "I don't have a strong memory of President Roosevelt's death," she recalled. "I assume there was sadness, but I can't say for sure. I know that I never heard any official news. It was all word of mouth, lots of it spoken in Japanese and therefore confusing."

In contrast, a few internees sent letters and telegrams to Eleanor in the White House. "Dear Mrs. Roosevelt," wrote Gongoro Nakamura, a Japanese internee. "In this hour of your deepest sorrow, I can find no better words than May God Bless you." Two German internees—Hans J. Brueckner and Werner Fertsch—wrote a more formal letter: "We, the undersigned, by means of these lines wish to express our deep and profound regret over the sudden and unexpected death of the President of the United States, Mr. Franklin D. Roosevelt. We feel this loss is so much heavier as the President was called in the midst of his work that he liked to do and which he felt he had to carry out for the future happiness and security of the great nation and the rest of the world."

If Eleanor Roosevelt read those letters, written by people arrested and indefinitely interned by the government for years in the desert of Texas, they must have struck her as deeply ironic.

Of course, the staff in Crystal City knew about the president's death. O'Rourke sent out a memorandum to all personnel after the news broke that any employee who wanted to take the day off in memory of Roosevelt was welcome to do so. Many stayed home and listened to broadcasts on the radio.

The morning of his death—Thursday, April 12—Roosevelt awoke at the Little White House in Warm Springs, Georgia, and complained of a slight headache. Later, he sat at a table and went through a large volume of mail. At about 1:00 p.m. the butler arrived to set the table for lunch. Shortly thereafter, Roosevelt complained of a terrific pain in the back of his head and collapsed. At 3:35 p.m. a doctor pronounced him dead of a massive cerebral hemorrhage.

To her regret, on the day Roosevelt died, Eleanor wasn't with him in Warm Springs. Instead, she was at the White House, preparing for the opening of the United Nations charter meeting in San Francisco, only two weeks away. Within a half hour after his death, Eleanor was given the news by phone at the White House. She phoned her daughter, Anna, and then sent a wire to their four sons, who were all serving in the armed forces: "Darlings: Father slipped away this afternoon. He did his job to the end as he would want you to do. Bless you. All our love. Mother."

Vice President Harry Truman was summoned to the White House, and Eleanor gave him the stunning news. Truman paused to collect himself, then asked, "Is there anything I can do for you?"

"Is there anything *we* can do for *you*?" responded Eleanor. "You are the one in trouble now."

Two hours later, she attended the swearing in of Vice President Harry Truman as president, then boarded an airplane for Warm Springs and arrived at the cottage at 11:25 p.m.

She immediately set to work with FDR's aides on the funeral arrangements. The following morning Eleanor and her entourage—secretaries, aides, and Secret Service—boarded a train in Warm Springs for the long funeral procession to Washington, DC. Roosevelt's casket was carried in a separate car. Hordes of people, many sobbing, lined the tracks. People were stunned by the news. Some carried posters of Roosevelt, head thrown back, a smile on his face, his strong, immutable character shining forth. When the train arrived in Washington, Roosevelt's casket was placed on a black caisson pulled by six white horses and taken to the White House. More than half a million people filled the streets.

All the commentators pronounced FDR's death ill timed. His first words as president twelve years before his death were "The only thing we have to fear is fear itself." In the intervening years, the country had faced many fears, including the Depression and the long war. But at the moment of his death, Berlin was about to fall. The successful Allied bombardment campaign signaled Japan's inevitable defeat. Victory was within reach but Roosevelt did not live to see it.

• • •

On a street corner in San Francisco in late February 1942, Shinko Fukuda, holding the package tied with string, and her daughter, Makiko, clutching a doll, were herded into a bus under armed military guard and transported to the Tanforan Assembly Center. The photo was taken by the renowned American photographer Dorothea Lange.

On the right, Shinko, who is pregnant, cradles her son Hiroshi and is surrounded by her other children and other women from the Konko Church in San Francisco. Ten weeks following Pearl Harbor, Shinko and her children, smiling and well dressed despite their uncertain future, were part of the roundup and removal of 120,000 Japanese, two-thirds of them American. Photo by Dorothea Lange.

Guards patrolling the perimeter of the Crystal City Internment Camp. From 1942 to 1948, the government imprisoned German, Japanese, and a few Italian "enemy aliens" and their families in this Texas town.

Inside the ten-foot-tall barbed-wire fence, Japanese American children play in the dust near the tiny cottages in the Japanese section of the camp.

A guard on horseback patrols the fence line of the 290-acre camp, a physical reminder to the internees of their twenty-four-hour surveillance and crippling confinement.

In 1942, the president and the first lady used this photograph of themselves seated together on a porch at the White House on their Christmas cards. By then, FDR's focus had shifted from the policies of the New Deal to the prosecution of the war. While Eleanor disagreed with his policies on internment, she reluctantly accepted them.

On November 6, 1942, Earl Harrison, the commissioner of the Immigration and Naturalization Service, traveled to Crystal City to consider the former migrant-labor camp as the site for the INS family internment camp. After World War II came to a close in Europe, he toured the Nazi concentration camps on President Truman's orders.

Behind the fence line and the guard tower was the Federal High School. Here, facing east, is the American School, which offered an accredited education. There were also Japanese and German Schools.

This is an aerial view of the camp, from the north. The swimming pool is visible in the upper lefthand quadrant.

In the summer of 1943, German internees dredged and leveled an existing reservoir and built a combination swimming pool for the internees and reservoir for irrigating the camp's vegetable gardens and citrus orchard.

In the summer of 1943, Harrison named a career Border Patrol agent, Joseph O'Rourke, shown here, as officer in charge of the camp in Crystal City. When O'Rourke arrived, he was a lonely bachelor, but as head of the camp he became popular with many of the children and teenagers.

Beauticians and barbers, all internees, at work in the German section. Internees labored in nearly every aspect of the building and running of the camp.

Johanna and Mathias Eiserloh were married on Christmas Eve 1923 and settled in Cleveland, Ohio.

When the Eiserloh family was reunited in the Crystal City Internment Camp in November 1943, camp officials took this family photograph. Six-year-old Lothar is on the left, Johanna next to him, then two-year-old Ensi, Ingrid standing behind, and Mathias on the right. A few months earlier, Ingrid, twelve years old, had permed her long red hair. "We were all trying to be brave and smile for the camera," she said of this photo. "In fact, we were devastated."

These German internees are seated at a table in the beer garden. They built the garden and were allowed to purchase one beer a day with camp scrip. The beer was made at the camp, and the one-beer-a-day rule was often violated.

Students of the German School lined up with their teacher in front of the school, located just inside the front gate.

This portrait of Sumi's family—the Utsushigawas—was taken in Los Angeles prior to her father's arrest at their apartment building in Little Tokyo. Her father, Tokiji, a photographer, and her mother, Nobu, seated to the right. Sumi, in the white dress with a white bow in her hair, stands between her two older sisters, Haruko and Yoshiko.

Japanese women—*issei*, or first-generation American immigrants—at work in the Sewing Project, a building that had seven power and foot-pedal sewing machines in operation from eight o'clock in the morning until ten o'clock at night. The women made clothes, mattress covers, curtains, uniforms for nurses and doctors, and unlikely items, such as typewriter covers.

YELL AND SONG LEADERS

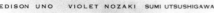

EDISON UNO   VIOLET NOZAKI   SUMI UTSUSHIGAWA

Here is Sumi as "A Good Scout!" in February 1944, standing on the grounds of the Japanese school. Both boys and girls participated in Japanese scouting programs at Crystal City.

The Federal High School in Crystal City operated like most American schools. It had regular classrooms, a spacious auditorium, athletic fields, and cheering squads. In 1944, Sumi, shown here with her friends, was one of the yell and song leaders.

In the summer of 1945, Earl Harrison (*the tall man, sixth from the left*) arrived in Bergen-Belsen concentration camp as President Truman's special envoy. Harrison appears with members of his delegation: Maurice Elgin of the American Jewish Joint Distribution Center (*extreme left*) and Dr. Joseph Schwartz (*fourth from left*), European director of the American Jewish Joint Distribution Center. On Harrison's right is Dr. Hadassah Bimko, survivor of Bergen-Belsen.

On December 8, 1945, a large group of Japanese and Japanese Americans from Crystal City boarded the SS *Matsonia* at the port of Seattle and sailed on rough waters to Japan, arriving on Christmas Day to a country devastated by war. "All of us teenagers from Crystal City experienced shock and disappointment," recalled Sumi Utsushigawa, who was among the American-born internees sent to Japan.

Alan Taniguchi, with his father, Isamu Taniguchi, an internee in Crystal City, in November 1985 at the dedication in Crystal City of a stone monument that memorialized the Japanese experience in what was described on the marker as a "World War II Concentration Camp." The monument was designed by Alan Taniguchi, a renowned Texas architect, and paid for largely by donations from former internees.

In Crystal City, the weather was sultry and hot and life settled into endeavors at normalcy. Eb and his ice crew worked overtime to keep iceboxes full. At Federal High School, fourteen students in the freshman class organized the Service Club and devoted themselves to volunteering. They worked in the school library, distributed school supplies, cleaned blackboards, and repaired desks. The Federal Elementary School published a newspaper every six weeks called the *Yehudi Express*. In 1938, the phrase "Who's Yehudi?" became popular slang for an invisible person when Yehudi Menuhin, a famous violinist, was a guest on the comedian Bob Hope's radio program. Another comedian on the show found the violinist's name side-splittingly funny and repetitively asked: "Who's Yehudi?" A hit song titled with the same question was released in 1941. According to Toni Tomita, who was on the staff of the newspaper in her sixth-grade year, the students chose the name as a gag, implying that the newspaper was written by people no one seemed to know. One of the stories reminded students that *Johnny Appleseed*, a book they'd studied in class, was an American classic because it told the tale of "unusual unselfishness in which Johnny Appleseed devoted most of his life to activities of service to his unknown as well as known friends."

The nights in Crystal City were a dreamlike mixture of the past and the present. Lights glowed from the bungalows. Sage was in bloom. Watermelons as large as basketballs grew on the ground. The scent of oranges, lemons, and plums was everywhere. The desert moon was so round and bright it looked like an anchor for the stars. At the Federal High School, Kathryn Goldsmith, Sumi's favorite teacher, directed seniors in a performance of *Night Owl*. Among the movie offerings in April was *Passport to Destiny*, a 1944 classic that stars Elsa Lanchester, who plays an English charlady who sneaks into Berlin with the idea of assassinating Hitler. The showing of that movie must have been uncomfortable for at least some of the German internees.

Every tennis and volleyball court and baseball diamond was crowded with players. American-style sports of all kinds—football, basketball, baseball—dominated the spring. Tate, the former football coach at Crystal City High School and now the superintendent of all the schools at the camp, organized two football teams at the Federal High School. The players on the two teams, all Japanese Americans, had nicknames. On the first team, "Porky" Akiyama played right tackle, and "Spider" Kumamoto was a tight end. On the second team, "Killer" Yonekura played left halfback, and "Stogie" Kanogawa, Yae's brother whose given name was Shoji, played fullback. Since no other Texas high school football team could enter the secret internment camp in Crystal City, Tate had no alternative but to create two teams within the camp.

When they tired of playing each other, the Japanese American players sought out the intramural German football team for scrimmage games and ran into two brick walls: the Fuhr brothers, Eb and his older brother Julius. By the spring of 1945, the Fuhr brothers had been in Crystal City for more than two years, and both were tall and strong. They had grown up in a mixed neighborhood in Cincinnati's West End and were accustomed to other ethnicities. Half of their high school was black. In high school, Eb had no real ambition other than to replace the great Ernie Lombardi as catcher for the Cincinnati Reds. He loved Lombardi. To escape the monotony in Crystal City, Eb played every kind of sport he could find: baseball, football, Ping-Pong, it made no difference to him. He and his brother were the only potential all-American football players in camp. Both were quick and nervy with their moves, impossible to outplay. "We thought we were fast," remembered Stogie Kanogawa. "But the Germans were in better shape, especially the Fuhr brothers, and really determined."

Like many others in camp that spring, Eb had a broken heart. His girlfriend, Millie Kesserlring, had been repatriated to Germany in January 1945, along with Ingrid's family and about 400 others. In the three months since her departure, Eb had received no word from her and presumed the relationship was at an end. Their breakup triggered memories of an earlier loss. When Eb was in high school in

Cincinnati, he had a steady girlfriend, a serious enough one that he had given her one of his lettered football sweaters. After his arrest, he left without telling his girlfriend good-bye and lamented the sudden loss of the relationship. When he arrived in Crystal City, he found many attractive girls, but Eb was determined not to repeat the loss of another girlfriend to the whims of the war.

"However, there was Millie Kesserlring from Albany, New York, rather well put together," recalled Eb. "Every evening we would walk the inside perimeter of the fence. She hated jazz. I loved Glenn Miller and Artie Shaw. Nonetheless, we really liked each other." Then Millie and her family left camp, bound for Germany, and Eb was again without a girlfriend.

In April, not long after FDR's death, Eb injured one of his fingers on an ice run. The wound became infected, and soon his hand swelled to the size of a small balloon. Eb, a tough, athletic young man, ignored the injury, but the pain increased and he reluctantly paid a visit to the camp hospital. When Dr. Martin took out a scalpel and drained the finger, Eb fainted onto the floor and had to be admitted to the hospital. His nurse, Barbara Minner, had lost her boyfriend in camp to the same repatriation that had separated Eb and Millie. That night Eb was the only patient in the ward, and about 8:00 p.m. Barbara brought Eb two freshly picked plums. Over the plums, they consoled each other about lost loves in Germany, and the following morning, Eb asked her to the movies.

The romance was on. Barbara liked jazz and loved to dance, especially the jitterbug. "It developed into a very intense love, which in the close facilities of the camp was quite restrictive," Eb recalled. Barbara's father was a German journalist who, prior to the war, had been employed by the German News Agency in New York City. When her father was arrested along with the German diplomatic corps, he refused repatriation because his wife was born in New York City, as were his two daughters. Barbara's mother didn't approve of Eb. Unlike the blond hair of many Germans, Eb's hair was dark and his face had sharp features. "She thought me too swarthy—possibly having some Latin blood or whatever," Eb said. Nonetheless, that spring the romance thrived.

Later in April, someone in Eb's circle of friends somehow slipped a radio into camp. Each night the radio was tuned to a station in San Antonio, which brought them nonstop news of the war in a way none of the boys had ever before heard. They learned that the Soviets had taken Berlin and that Mussolini was dead. On April 30 when Hitler and Eva Braun committed suicide in their bunker, Eb and his friends heard the news on the radio. All night the crackling voice on the radio kept repeating the news: Hitler was dead. Hunched over the small radio, Eb and his friends knew Germany's surrender was imminent and hoped it meant they would soon be free.

Adding to the sense of unreality in the camp was that since early January official-looking men from Philadelphia and Washington wearing business suits had been in and out of camp, carrying cameras, typewriters, and other equipment. Eb and the other internees realized that the men were at work on a motion picture about the Crystal City Internment Camp.

Mangione, Harrison's special assistant, had first suggested the idea of a film in 1943. Two years passed and nothing came of it. Then on January 19, 1945, O'Rourke received a letter from his friend Nick Collaer, the officer in charge of Crystal City and now acting assistant commissioner of the INS. With the war coming to a close Collaer told O'Rourke the time was right to make a film that placed Crystal City in the best possible light. "I believe that we can safely say that Crystal City is considered to be one of the best, if not the best, internment camp ever operated by any country and, because of the children of various races, there is a wealth of excellent pictorial material there," wrote Collaer in his letter from headquarters in Philadelphia.

His instructions were specific. He asked O'Rourke to request the Army to send pilot crews armed with 16 mm cameras to Crystal City to shoot film from the air, "preferably at about a forty-five degree angle in midmorning or midafternoon, when the shadows are long, to add to our collection of pictures."

The opening shot of the film was of the flag flying high over the entrance of the camp. Then came footage of the camp and the fence from the perspective of the guards in the watchtowers. The camera slowly panned to the front office, where O'Rourke held charge, followed by long shots of guards on horseback, patrolling the fence. The final shot in the opening sequence was of guards examining all cars entering and exiting the front gate. Security was the focus, the scenes establishing that this was an internment camp for civilian enemy aliens and their wives and children. Scene after scene showed that great care was taken to avoid infiltration of the camp by outsiders or any escape.

"Here is a party of women and children arriving in Crystal City," says Bern Barnard, a detention officer who narrated the film, over grainy shots of Japanese women, neatly dressed in hats, gloves, and crisp cotton dresses, and their children. Lines of other internees are there to greet them, and a band plays patriotic music. In a cheerful voice, Barnard then describes how Japanese internees, the majority of them wives and children born in America and who were American citizens, "lived, worked, and played" under "traditional American standards of decent and humane treatment" alongside German and German-American internees.

The carefully chosen shots confirmed the film's assertion: a shot of a family being taken to their living quarters and receiving articles of clothing supplied by the camp management; houses with close-ups of serene Japanese gardeners making the desert bloom with flower and vegetable gardens; German housewives in tiny kitchens preparing food with the family gathered around a table.

"It was important that normal conditions prevail in the camp, and to that end detainees are expected to do most of the work in connection with the operation of the camp," said the narrator. Then came a series of shots of internees at work in the carpentry shop making tables and benches; women in the sewing project making mattresses; internees receiving treatment at the hospital and the dental clinic; shots of the shoe shop, the beauty parlor, and the barbershop. The point was to prove that the internees—not workers hired by American taxpayers—did most of the work in camp.

For propaganda purposes, what had been a secret camp was now portrayed as a benign, even pleasant, experience for internees. The film obscured the reality of the prisoner exchange program—the trading of Germans, Japanese, and Americans as well—and the psychological trauma of internment. Moreover, the film presented Japanese and Germans in ethnically stereotyped ways that suggest that these people were happy, free agents in camp, instead of people held by their government against their will without being charged with or convicted of any crime.

In one peculiar sequence, the camera closes in on a large vegetable. "Those are radishes," says Barnard. "The Japanese boil and serve them as vegetables." Beefy Japanese men in loincloths are shown practicing sumo. "Here are cheering wrestlers, who are jostling and attacking each other while dressed in primitive sumo-style clothing."

The Germans are portrayed as caricatures of Nazis. The camera captured a shot of a German classroom with students standing stiffly next to their desks until their teacher enters and gives them permission to be seated. Another shot showed German students doing gymnastics under the strict tutelage of an instructor. "This is a German recreation center where Germans enjoy music furnished by their own orchestra," Barnard said. The film ends with a view of the American flag being slowly raised to the top of the pole.

Compared to the concentration camps in Germany where millions of Jews died or to the prisoner-of-war camps in Japan in which 140,000 Allied prisoners of war and civilians lived in appalling conditions, the Crystal City camp was undeniably far more humane. However, the film exaggerated the positives in Crystal City, concealing the harsh reality of isolation and confinement. Despite the favorable comparisons with German and Japanese camps, the film could not erase one stark truth: the internees at Crystal City were not free to leave, and there is no such thing as a happy internment camp.

However, the Crystal City film was not an outright fraud as was the infamous 1944 propaganda film made about the Theresienstadt "ghetto camp" that served as a transit center for Czechoslovakian Jews. In that film, Theresienstadt appears as a model Jewish settlement, described as a "spa town" where elderly Jews went to "retire." In the making of that film, Nazi propagandists built fake shops and cafés, designed to portray the concentration camp as a luxurious cultural center with its own orchestra, children's opera company, and vast library. The entire film was a charade. Over Theresienstadt's three-and-a-half-year history, more than 140,000 Jews were confined there in appalling conditions. Of that number, 90,000 were deported to concentration camps and certain death. A total of 33,000 died there, many of them due to malnutrition and sadistic treatment.

In April 1945, members of the 442nd Regimental Combat Team, made up entirely of Japanese American soldiers, liberated five thousand survivors from the Dachau concentration camp in southern Germany. Members of the 442nd fought in Italy, France, and Germany, and it became the most decorated unit of World War II. Many of the members of the fabled unit had parents and siblings in internment camps, including Crystal City. Yet in Crystal City, letters from members of the 442nd to their parents were censored. News of their accomplishments on the battlefields was officially suppressed. When the soldiers visited their parents in Crystal City, surveillance officers monitored all visits.

Ella Ohta, one of Sumi's closest friends, had a brother, Kenneth Hiroshi, who served in the 442nd. When Kenneth came to visit his family in the summer of 1944, he was stationed at Camp Shelby in Mississippi. He only had a one-day pass. "They wouldn't even let him come into the camp," remembered Ella. "We had to go through the gate to see him. The guards watched us closely. It was humiliating."

In May 1945, word spread in the German section of camp that Germany was at work on a "miracle weapon" that would win the war for Germany. On the Japanese side of the camp, Sumi's father and other issei elders continued to believe that Japan would fight until the death of every last soldier and would ultimately prevail.

That spring, families in folding chairs sat under the vast night sky, watching western movies projected on the big wall of Harrison Hall, as shooting stars flared overhead. Mountain lions roamed the sagebrush. At the Café Vaterland, Germans nervously gathered under a plaque that read COME WHAT MUST COME, TOMORROW IS ALSO A DAY, TODAY IS TODAY!

Then suddenly the war in Europe was over. On May 2, the Soviets accepted the unconditional surrender of the Berlin garrison, and the official German surrender occurred on May 8. On May 2, V-E Day, celebrations of the war's official end took place all over the United States—in Chicago, Los Angeles, and especially in New York's Times Square. Celebrations also took place in nearby San Antonio and in Dallas and Houston, but reactions in Crystal City were muted.

In an abundance of caution about potential negative reactions from internees loyal to Germany and Japan, O'Rourke made no official announcement. He wanted to keep peace in camp. However, the news flew quietly from person to person, bungalow to bungalow. In the German section, many refused to believe it was true. Eb and his friends were hopeful that after V-E Day, they would be released. Day after day, they waited for news that they would be paroled or—even better—that the camp in Crystal City would close, but there was silence. Their status did not change, and O'Rourke stayed mute.

On the evening of May 31, 1945, thirty-six Japanese Americans marched into Harrison Hall to the strains of "Pomp and Circumstance" and were given certificates of graduation by O'Rourke. These graduates were O'Rourke's greatest satisfaction. Two of them—Higo Harada and Harry Kawaguchi—were accepted at the University of Texas at Austin. Their graduation from the accredited Texas high school in the Crystal City Internment Camp was their ticket to the other side of the fence. O'Rourke and Tate wrote letters of recommendation for them. Both had decided on their majors: Higo was premed and Harry would study engineering.

Meanwhile, the war in the Pacific continued. On August 6, 1945, a twelve-man crew of Americans on a Boeing B-29 called the *Enola Gay* dropped an atomic bomb on Hiroshima. The blast obliterated everything within four square miles. About eighty thousand people were immediately killed and seventy thousand more wounded. Still, the Japanese did not surrender. Three days later, a second bomb, which killed forty thousand, was dropped on Nagasaki.

The following day, Emperor Hirohito surrendered. On August 15, Hirohito gave a short address in Tokyo, and for the first time the people of Japan heard the voice of their emperor on the radio. He urged the people to accept what he called the "unacceptable." He spoke in an indirect way of surrender—never using the word explicitly—which created confusion in Japan. The military was opposed to surrender, which they thought was dishonorable. Finally, on September 2, General Douglas MacArthur formally accepted the surrender on the deck of the USS *Missouri*, in Tokyo Bay.

In Crystal City, news continued to travel not by radio but by word of mouth, one internee to another. "I was in Crystal City when the United States dropped the bomb on Hiroshima and Nagasaki. I could hear grown men crying all over the camp, including my father," said Yae Kanogawa. "Many of them didn't believe Japan had lost the war. They thought it was just propaganda. They couldn't accept it. All of us kids in camp knew it was true and we were glad the war was over."

Everyone puzzled over what they heard, as different people in camp heard different versions of the event. Carmen Higa Mochizuki, one of the hundreds of Japanese Peruvians in camp, was a student in the Japanese School in Crystal City, trying to learn to speak Japanese. Her teacher announced in class that "the war was over" but did not say who won. Carmen's father insisted that Japan had won the war, not the United States. Her brother, who had previously been a journalist in Peru, knew that Japan had in fact lost. The father and son quarreled for days and then stopped speaking to each other. "That's what I remember about the end of the war," said Carmen.

"The big silence in our home and at school. No one was allowed to talk about it."

Ella Ohta was playing softball when someone ran onto the field and shouted, "The war is over! Japan has surrendered." The game stopped. Everyone on the field seemed stunned. Unlike many in camp, Ella's parents believed it to be true, and Ella felt relief.

From his bungalow in camp, Isamu Taniguchi tended trees and plants. He believed the news; indeed, it came as a revelation to him. "It was like watching the world come to an end," Taniguchi later wrote. "The radiation from atomic bombs, which started from flash and sound over Hiroshima and Nagasaki, shines in every corner of our skulls, flying over our heads with the humming sound, pressing us to act in repentance."

A few months earlier, as the war was drawing to a close, the War Relocation Authority announced its intention to close all internment camps by the end of 1945. Following the defeat of the Japanese, the INS began releasing inmates in internment camps who were considered nonthreatening, including many of the recent graduates of Crystal City's Federal High School. Others hoped to be freed soon. But on September 8, 1945, Truman issued a proclamation, No. 2355, which authorized the secretary of state to order the repatriation of all alien enemies. Also included was "any person who appears to be so clearly dangerous as to make his repatriation desirable." The issue of US born spouses and children was left unresolved, as was the issue of where the thousands of enemy aliens from Latin America and other foreign countries would be shipped. One by one other internment camps closed—Fort Lincoln in March 1945, Fort Stanton in November 1945—and those classified by the government as "dangerous deportees" were sent to Crystal City to await repatriation. Rather than close, Crystal City absorbed internees from other camps.

"After V-E Day and certainly after the Japanese surrendered, I thought we'd be released," said Eb. "But the war ended and nothing changed." Over the next few days, it became clear that most of those remaining in Crystal City—American as well as foreign-born—would likely be what the US government called "repatriated" internees, even though many were born in America, not Axis countries, and therefore could not by definition be repatriated. The fact that the US government used the word *repatriation* without irony implied that the Germans and Japanese interned in Crystal City, immigrants and native-born, were never fully considered Americans. A new wave of fear swept over the camp: the fear of involuntary transport to Germany or Japan.

The mood in Sumi's bungalow was sour. Only the day before, on August 14, 1945, she had turned seventeen. Her mother had made her a marble cake. Like Yae, Sumi had heard the sound of men crying all over camp and the disbelief of both women and men. "My father always said Japan would never surrender," Sumi said. He couldn't believe that Hirohito, whose official photograph had hung in the family's apartment in Los Angeles, would ever acknowledge defeat. Now, he told Sumi and her mother, Nobu, to prepare for their return to Japan.

CHAPTER SEVENTEEN

Shipped to Japan

During the fall of 1945, Sumi hoped that somehow the end of the war would mean that she could return to Los Angeles, where she had been born. As the days in Crystal City crept by with uncertainty, inside bungalow T-37-B Tokiji made plans to leave for Japan. In a letter to O'Rourke on September 17, 1945, Tokiji asked that the cameras the FBI had seized from his apartment on East First Street be returned to him. "The photographic business is the only profession I know," he wrote, and explained he intended to revive his career in Japan, even though by then he was sixty-eight years old. "I can earn my bread and butter by that profession alone." In the kitchen of the triplex, fifty-six-year-old Nobu went about her business with glacial calm as she, too, made plans to return to Japan.

It was midterm of Sumi's junior year. Her grades were good and she was the yell leader in a cheering squad at the Federal High School, and a popular member of a group of girls that nicknamed themselves the Big Six, which was her safe haven. Her friends understood her reluctance to leave Crystal City and her inability to defy her father.

On the morning of December 4, 1945, six hundred Japanese and Japanese Americans from Hawaii boarded special trains at the small station in Crystal City to return to the Hawaiian islands. Sumi said good-bye to some of her Hawaiian friends, who were happy to be going home. The following day Sumi, along with many others, would also board trains, but for Japan, not their home.

Never in the history of the small town of Crystal City had there been such a busy and chaotic scene as at the train station that morning. Trains lined the track for as far as the eye could see. Six hundred Japanese Peruvians, many who did not speak Japanese, and eighteen hundred Japanese and Japanese Americans, including Sumi, shuffled on board the trains, as if sleepwalking in a nightmare. Like Tokiji, many of the men on the trains believed that going back to Japan was better than the betrayal and humiliation of internment. Their children had no choice.

Though Sumi had long known this day was coming, it seemed inexplicable that she was once again on a train—leaving Crystal City with spasms of regret—and not bound for Los Angeles. Having avoided being exchanged on September 2, 1943, on the *Gripsholm* in New York harbor, Sumi was devastated to have been given yet another confusing government label: no longer *internee* but *repatriate*. Even though she wasn't yet on a ship to Japan, she felt an undertow of anxiety.

She wore a T-shirt that day, stuffed her fists in her pants pockets, and sat speechless on the hard seat beside Nobu. Whistles blew and the trains pulled out of the tiny station and headed west. She thought of all she'd seen and heard in Crystal City: the Popeye statue in town, the way some people said *howdy* and others *adios*, the wild cats that roamed the camp, the red ants, the hard work of fathers and mothers to build the camp, school graduations and weddings, sunsets and starry nights, come and gone.

INS regulations insisted that all trains be staffed with escorts. Sumi was disappointed that the escort in her car was a high school teacher who had given Sumi a difficult time. Just the week before, the teacher had asked her students, including Sumi, how many of them were repatriating to Japan. Sumi raised her hand. The teacher told Sumi since she was going back to Japan, it must mean she was disloyal to America. Sumi was outraged; nothing could have been further from the truth.

The first night on the train seemed endless. She stayed awake, listening to the rumbling of the train and the snores of her fellow passengers. Since Pearl Harbor, Sumi had come a long way—from Los

Angeles, to Heart Mountain Relocation Camp in Wyoming, to Ellis Island, and finally to Crystal City. With each move, Nobu reminded Sumi to practice *gaman*—the spirit of enduring what had to be endured. Now she was on a train to Seattle, Washington, where she would board a ship for Japan. She had an American birth certificate and her parents held a repatriation order to Japan. How would she survive in Japan? This was the context of her next lessons in *gaman*. Her status reflected so much that she had experienced: betrayal by her government, divided loyalties, incarceration, and now repatriation.

On the long journey, the teacher insisted that when the train traveled through cities, all the shades be lowered and the passenger car be dark. Sumi knew this drill; she'd been on INS trains before. Still, she was annoyed and repeatedly asked the teacher if, when the train passed through Los Angeles, Sumi might be able to raise the shades. "I just want one glimpse of my hometown," Sumi said.

The teacher made no promises. When the train neared Los Angeles, a teeming World War II metropolis with a distinct skyline, Sumi again asked the teacher to leave the shades up. Sumi wanted to see the city's iconic City Hall, located near her former home in Little Tokyo, and perhaps get a glimpse of the Pacific Ocean.

The teacher jerked the shades down and told Sumi not to raise them. For the first time since her father's arrest, Sumi cried. From her seat, she imagined the sights and smells of Little Tokyo and remembered her family's apartment on East First Street. Her mother placed her arm around Sumi's shoulder as if to say, *It'll be okay*.

It took six days to reach Seattle, and in the cars of the train people played cards and slept. Their clothes grew wrinkled and smelled stale. Occasionally rain whapped against the darkened windows. People shuffled to and from the dining cars as the escorts, including the teacher, patrolled the aisles. The murmur of three distinct languages—English, Japanese, and Spanish, by the Peruvians—created a strange background music for the trip.

On December 11, the train pulled into the port of Seattle, stopped, and the shades were raised. The train was crowded and it took many hours for everyone to disembark. When Sumi stepped outside, a blast of cold wind struck her in the face.

One by one the twenty-four hundred passengers—Japanese, Japanese Americans, and Peruvian Japanese—boarded the enormous ocean liner SS *Matsonia*, a former cruise ship that had been commissioned by the US government for troop transports and repatriations.

The distance from Seattle to the port of Yokosuka in Tokyo Bay across the Pacific Ocean was vast, almost forty-two hundred nautical miles. Like many of the others, Sumi had never sailed before. She and Nobu were assigned quarters belowdecks. They descended, step by step, into the entrails of the giant steamship on stairs without rails. Eventually they passed the level of the mess hall and walked down one more flight of stairs to a large room filled with bunks. The bunks, made of canvas and supported by long chains lashed to pipes, were stacked four high from the floor to the ceiling. To Sumi, the room seemed as deep and dark a place as she'd ever been.

Tokiji was assigned quarters on the top deck of the ship. During the day, passengers walked on the broad deck and watched the long hull of the ship cut a path of white foam through the dark waters of the Pacific. They kept a lookout for fish and birds and breathed in the crisp ocean air.

In the hold of the ship, many of the passengers suffered from seasickness. The great liner pitched, plunged, rolled, and tossed. What Sumi wouldn't have given for the flat, dusty desert of Texas and a simple bowl of rice from her mother's kitchen. "Food was the last thing we wanted," recalled Sumi. "It might have been wonderful if we could have disconnected feelings in the stomach from feelings in the head." Even though she had no appetite, Sumi was one of the lucky few on the lower deck who did not suffer from seasickness. Day after day in the hold, she brought tea and sympathy to one seasick friend from Crystal City to another.

At night, she stayed close to Nobu, who urged her daughter to rest and said, *"Shikata ga nai."* The phrase was as familiar to Sumi as Nobu's face and meant: "It cannot be helped."

Teenagers from Crystal City were all over the ship. Not far away from Sumi, Mas Okabe, who had been a fourteen-year-old freshman at the Federal High School in Crystal City, crowded together with his family: his father, mother, and three brothers. Before the war, his father was a farmer in Yolo, California, near Sacramento. Like Sumi's father, Mas Okabe's father was also convinced that Japan had won the war and that the news to the contrary was merely American propaganda. "My parents didn't discuss decisions with us," recalled Mas during an interview. "In Crystal City, I overheard them talking about going back to Japan. My father's word was the law. He said we were going and so we packed up. No questions asked."

During the voyage, Mas's mother was seasick and stayed in the hold of the ship, but Mas and his brothers spent most of the time on the top deck. "We were taught to make the best of things, and that's what we did," recalled Mas. "We played pickup ball on the deck and hide-and-seek. We watched for whales and dolphins." They had no idea what they would face when the ship docked in Japan, but they'd been living with uncertainty since the beginning of the war. "We knew that family was all we had," said Mas. "When you suffer together as a family, the bond grows stronger."

Carmen Higa Mochizuki, a Japanese Peruvian who'd been incarcerated in Crystal City for two years, was on the ship as well. Carmen stayed near the top deck with her mother and siblings. She saw little of her father, whose quarters were belowdecks. Her twenty-three-year-old brother was not with them on the voyage. After her father and brother quarreled in Crystal City, her brother joined about two hundred other Latin American internees from Crystal City who were paroled to Seabrook Farms in New Jersey, a large producer of canned and frozen vegetables. The wages at the factory were low—fifty cents an hour for starting pay—and the hours were long. In effect, the workers lived in bondage. However, as Carmen made the long voyage to Japan, she suspected that her brother's decision to stay in America was correct.

On December 22, fourteen days after the ship left Seattle, Christmas gifts from the American Friends Service Committee were delivered to the women and children. "There we were in the middle of the ocean," remembered Sumi. "The gifts arrived from the Quakers, a kerchief for my mother and a small doll for me. I couldn't believe it. They sent Christmas gifts to us in Heart Mountain as well. Now they sent them again. How in the world did those Quakers find us?" Even in the middle of the Pacific Ocean, the Quakers continued their support.

Two nights later, on Christmas Eve, the SS *Matsonia* approached the harbor at Yokosuka, not far from Tokyo. The liner could not make it to shore because the harbor was crowded with sunken Japanese ships.

The next morning, Christmas, it snowed. On the top deck of the *Matsonia*, Sumi huddled with Nobu under a thin wool blanket as neither she nor Nobu had coats. The icy wind ran over Sumi's skin. Barges were brought to take the repatriates to shore, and the nisei boys from the ship helped transport luggage from the ship to the barges and then to a warehouse on the dock. Sumi watched her mother climb down a ladder to a barge and made sure Nobu did not fall, then stepped onto the barge herself.

In addition to the barges that carried the repatriates, the bay was crammed with many sampans with flat bottoms, sharp sterns, and large bows. The Japanese boatmen pleaded with the passengers still on board the *Matsonia* to throw them fruit, candy, cigarettes—anything from America. The cries of the Japanese boatmen were the first indication for Sumi's father—and many of the other issei from Crystal City who were stubbornly loyal to Japan—that Japan had indeed lost the war.

One of the teachers from the Japanese School in Crystal City called out to a boatman who approached the ship. The two men, one an educated issei from America and the other an unassuming Japanese fisherman, had a conversation overheard by both Sumi and Carmen Higa Mochizuki. Both of the teenage girls were so surprised by the conversation that they later took notes about what they heard.

"Hey," said the boatman, "sell me some American tobacco, snacks, anything."

"Well, let me see," said the teacher from Crystal City. He searched his pockets, found an orange, and tossed it to the boatman.

"Thank you very much."

"Hey, did Japan win?"

"No, no, no. We lost."

"Ha ha!" the teacher said, unable to believe the truth. "Japan won, didn't it?"

"No," thundered the boatman, clearly exasperated. "Japan *really* lost."

"Quit kidding." A stricken shadow now crossed the teacher's face. "Japan would never lose. It surely won. I came because Japan won."

"Lost, lost," screamed the boatman. "You are a fool." The boatman threw the orange back to the teacher. "All of you on this ship"— the man shook his fist in the snowy air—"you're all stupid. Japan is a defeated country."

The barges took the repatriates from Crystal City up a narrow channel at the southern end of Tokyo Bay to the dock at Uraga. The wind blew hard and children in the barges cried. Sumi glanced at her father, Tokiji, and saw his jaw drop. His dark eyes looked surprised. He had expected to be greeted with Japan's Rising Sun flag and cries of victory. Instead, the boatman confirmed his worst fears: America had won. Slowly, the realization of his mistake began to sink in. "A part of my dad died that day on the barge," recalled Sumi. "Everything he'd believed in was suddenly gone."

On the dock, Sumi saw children from Saipan dressed in cotton dresses trembling in the cold. They had no warm clothes. In the distance, she saw clusters of Japanese men gathering driftwood to build fires.

Three rows of Japanese women dressed in white robes bowed deeply before the new arrivals from America. *"Sumimasen,"* they said. "I'm so sorry." Over and over the women prostrated themselves and murmured apologies. *"Makemashita,"* they cried. "We

255

lost." Tokiji stared at the lines of grieving women, offering their blatant laments.

Back in the United States, Associated Press photographs showed the arrival of the repatriates at Uraga. Over a photo of women and children aboard the *Matsonia*, a banner headline in the *San Antonio Evening News*, expressing the anti-Japanese bias of the times, read, "Japs Are Repatriated from Internment Camp in Texas." Another photograph in the newspaper showed a sick Japanese woman being carried on a stretcher from the ocean liner to the dock on Christmas Day. Other photos show the barges that carried Sumi and her family and all the others from Crystal City to shore.

From the dock, the repatriates were herded onto buses and driven three miles to the Uraga Evacuation Camp, formerly used as a Japanese naval barracks. Sumi and the others slept on straw floor mats on the second floor of a two-story wooden structure. The bathroom was on the first floor, and the stench from the toilets filled the air.

The barracks were dark, and Mas Okabe remembered that he used birthday candles to light his way to his mat. Across the barracks, Min Tajii, a slightly older teenager from Crystal City, also lit a candle and saw dead bodies stacked several feet high, as if they were wood. Min asked when the bodies would be removed and was told that nothing would happen until a truck became available to move them. Min stayed in the barracks for a week, and the truck never came. Sumi also saw the bodies and was told that due to a fuel shortage there weren't enough trucks to remove them.

When Sumi arrived, she was given a gray blanket that offered little protection from the cold. In the dark room she huddled with her parents and a few other families. That night they ate the husks of some grain, weak miso soup, tea, and a few tangerines. It was still Christmas and everyone shared memories of happier Christmases in the distant past. A few in the group sang Christmas carols, but Sumi was too cold and hungry to join in. On this long, silent Christmas night, Sumi wondered if she might freeze to death.

The next morning Sumi and the other repatriates formed lines outside near a group of tables. One by one, they were served break-fast: *karasu mugi*, a tasteless bowl of barley husks. For dinner, they ate *nuka dango*, a dumpling made from bran flour, also tasteless. For the following few days, Sumi subsisted on a few hard dump-lings, which stuck in her throat, and as much hot tea as she could find.

In the barracks, families gathered in groups according to where they planned to settle in Japan. For instance, Mas Okabe's family's destination was south of Uraga to a farm owned by his uncle near the city of Nagoya, a train ride of about 165 miles from the bar-racks. The Okabe family gathered with others trying to make their way south to small farming villages. In another corner of the bar-racks, Min Tajii, a teenager from California's Imperial Valley who had been interned in Crystal City for two years, sat with his father and other families and plotted a route to Hiroshima, more than four hundred miles away. The Tajii family feared what they would find; only four months earlier, Hiroshima had nearly been obliterated by an atomic bomb. Min's father had no idea whether any of his fam-ily were alive. Sumi and her parents had to make their way north to Sendai. Sumi's sisters were living with Nobu's oldest brother. Five other families from Crystal City also had relatives in Sendai and gathered to plan the 220-mile journey.

Seven days after their arrival in Uraga, Sumi, her parents, and the other five families from Crystal City left the barracks, each with a suitcase tied to his or her back. They took a truck to a streetcar that carried them to the train station. There, long lines of anxious people waited for trains that did not arrive on schedule and often didn't arrive at all. The atmosphere was utter chaos. Sumi and her friends spotted a cluster of American MPs, approached them, and struck up a conversation. The MPs, surprised that these were Jap-anese American teenagers from Crystal City who spoke English, offered to help them. The MPs asked a conductor to move enough passengers off a train to make space for them. "We didn't even have to buy a ticket," remembered Sumi. "We just boarded the train and headed for northern Japan." The gesture by the MPs, a small but significant act of kindness, was a reminder of home and that she was still a Japanese American, and that meant something to the MPs.

The windows of the train were broken and flurries of snow filled the car and soon melted in a circle around Sumi's feet. She and the others covered themselves in wool blankets. As the train passed Yokohama, Japan's second-largest city, Sumi saw with her own eyes the destruction left behind by the American attack on the city on May 29, 1945. In a daylight strike by the 468th Bombardment Group, five hundred Boeing B-29s dropped hundreds of incendiary bombs on the heart of Yokohama's industrial area. From the window, Sumi saw miles and miles of burned land and rubble. The snow added to the somber misery of the scene, which seemed incomprehensible to Sumi, who said, "It was something I couldn't take in. No camera could capture what I saw. No words can describe how disappointed I was not only in Japan but the reality of war itself."

Many tracks along the way had been bombed. Passengers, including Sumi and her parents, often had to stop, disembark, and make the long walk to the next station. They witnessed a confusing mixture of chaos and ordinary scenes. Children played on the roads, sometimes picking up cigarette butts to trade for rides. Old women lay dead in some of the train stations, and everywhere people were hungry and homeless. Yet in small towns, geishas performed traditional dances, and outside Buddhist temples, long lines of people formed, many chanting and sobbing. GIs lined up in front of churches as well.

When the train pulled into Ueno Station in Tokyo, it was filled with people who were not there to board trains but because the station had a roof and offered a place to sleep. People took mats from their backs and spread them on the floor to lie on and covered their bodies with newspapers, like sheets.

The train stopped several miles from the station in Sendai. Sumi and her family walked in the direction of Nobu's eldest brother's home. Prior to the outbreak of the war, the center of Sendai, located inland of the western Pacific Ocean, was filled with trees and plants and looked like a lush forest. On the day of their arrival, Sendai looked nothing as Nobu remembered it. The ancient architecture of the old city had been destroyed by American aerial bombardment.

On the edge of the city, Sumi's family walked through shattered rice paddies and fruit orchards and finally reached the home of Nobu's brother. Both of Sumi's older sisters were there. Nobu and Tokiji had not seen their older daughters in almost five years, and they greeted each other with relief and gratitude.

Nobu's brother and sister-in-law had little to offer but welcomed them. Nobu introduced her sister-in-law to Sumi as Aunt Tetsu, and Sumi and Tetsu soon formed a bond. Tetsu taught Reiki, an ancient Japanese healing technique, at Tohoku University in Sendai. The word *rei* in Japanese means "God's wisdom," and the word *ki* means "life force energy." Reiki practitioners lay hands on their subjects and use specific hand positions to restore energy and healing. Unlike many of her friends from Crystal City who were making their way across Japan, Sumi found an orderly and peaceful home, a balm for her exhaustion and trauma. For Sumi, Tetsu's mastery of Reiki was yet another example of *gaman*. "Reiki was a great practice of healing," recalled Sumi. "My aunt gave me a great gift. I didn't know it at the time, but Reiki would become a big part of my life."

More than three hundred miles from Sendai, Mas Okabe and his family had arrived at his uncle's farm near Nagoya, a large city that was the center of the Japanese aircraft industry and had been a target of repeated Allied bombing. One-fourth of Nagoya had been destroyed by the time Mas and his family arrived. The uncle was not happy to see his brother or his family. "There was nothing to eat and there was really no room for us," recalled Mas. "My brother and I found jobs in Tokyo shortly after we arrived. We left our parents behind and made our way to Tokyo." The separation from their parents was difficult for Mas and his brother. Neither of them was fluent in Japanese, and food was scarce in Tokyo as well.

"My brother and I worried about our parents day and night. It was just a terrible time."

Carmen Higa Mochizuki had never been to Japan. She was born in Peru and grew up speaking Spanish. Though she attended the Japanese School in Crystal City, nothing prepared her for the journey from the camp in Uraga to the birthplace of her parents. Their destination was the island of Okinawa, the scene of a battle that had lasted eighty-two days, the fiercest and bloodiest fight of the Pacific war. Some 287,000 American troops and 130,000 Japanese soldiers fought in the battle, code-named Operation Iceberg by the US Army. By the time Carmen and her family arrived six months after the battle ended, the island was a wasteland. An estimated one-quarter of its inhabitants, humiliated by defeat, committed suicide.

Carmen's family moved into a small house with her father's brother, his wife, and six children. Carmen was one of nine children in the house and conditions were miserable. Her aunt resented their arrival and took out her resentment on Carmen's mother, who spent long hours cleaning the house, doing laundry, and scavenging for food.

"There was no electricity and we all went hungry," recalled Carmen. "I remember that once, to get a pound of rice, I exchanged a pair of shoes. My mother exchanged a dress for a small number of sweet potatoes." Carmen's father, once a relatively happy farmer in Peru, was bitter and sad. He believed that when the war ended Japanese Peruvians would be allowed to return to Peru, but the country refused to readmit them, classifying them as "illegal aliens." "He could not understand how we could be considered illegal aliens when the Americans kidnapped us from Peru and brought us to Crystal City," said Carmen. "We did not come to America of our own free will."

The families from Crystal City who returned to Hiroshima and Nagasaki witnessed the worst of the devastation, among them Alice Nagao Nishimoto. Both of Alice's parents were born in Hiroshima. The Nagaos, her father's family, had a sake empire headquartered there. Like many of the other fathers in Crystal City, prior to his arrival in Japan Alice's father had believed Japan had won the war, and knew nothing about the dropping of atomic bombs on his hometown and Nagasaki.

Four months after the American atomic bomb exploded over the center of Hiroshima on August 6, 1945, killing thousands and flattening the city, Alice arrived in the city with her father, mother, and her six siblings. "My father put his hands over his eyes," recalled Alice. "All the buildings he remembered were gone—the Shima Hospital, the domed Hiroshima Prefectural Industrial Promotion Hall—had disappeared in seconds." As the family moved through the city, they found watches stopped at 8:15 a.m., the moment the bomb exploded. Outlines of incinerated bodies appeared on park benches. Alice didn't understand why so many people were bald and their blackened skin covered with horrific burns. The survivors of Hiroshima, who suffered from radiation sickness, moved through the city like living ghosts.

Her father's eldest brother, who ran the family business, survived, but his son, a physician, died of radiation poisoning. Alice and her family moved in with her uncle in the house where her father was born. Most of what the Nagao family owned was lost in the bombing. The sake factories were destroyed.

To find food, Alice's mother, along with other women, walked far from the city into the countryside, in search of farmers. She traded her wedding band for several bags of rice. After several weeks, Alice's family moved to a small house located near the ocean, owned by her uncle. The house lacked plumbing and electricity. Alice and her siblings scavenged for wood in the mountains behind the sea, using it for cooking as well as heating water for bathing in a large wooden tub. The nine people in the family took turns bathing. Her father, still treated as superior, went first, followed by the children, oldest to youngest. Alice's mother was always the last to bathe.

Her mother rationed the rice as if it were gold. Soon, they only had enough for one bowl of rice a day. "We were starving," Alice said. Eventually her father, once one of the most powerful Japanese-born businessmen in Peru, found a job working on the line of a canned-goods factory. The major benefit of the job was that he brought some of those canned goods home for his family.

The repatriation to Japan was a tragic event in the history of the Crystal City Internment Camp. The issei fathers who immigrated to the United States considered themselves victims of circumstances. In the anti-Japanese fervor in the United States after Pearl Harbor, they were perceived as enemies, arrested, and imprisoned. Once inside the fence at Crystal City, the pro-Japan sentiment of many of them, including Sumi's father, led them to the disastrous decisions to repatriate. That decision denied their children the opportunity to remain in the United States and live their lives as Americans. Instead, they—and their children—languished in postwar Japan. Repatriation also reflects the flaw in Roosevelt's decision to apply the terms of the US Alien and Sedition Acts to Japanese and German immigrants to the United States in the wake of Pearl Harbor. By arresting Tokiji, a photographer in Los Angeles who offered no discernible threat to the US war effort, as a "dangerous enemy alien" and holding him without charges behind barbed wire, targeting his family for secret exchange, the US government left him little choice but to take his chances in Japan. If he was not an "enemy" of America before the war, Tokiji—and many others in Crystal City— became an adversary as a result of his experiences.

As the months went by, the American-born children from Crystal City who were trapped in Japan were taunted as spies. While walking in Sendai, Sumi was regularly pelted with large stones. She spoke English. When clothing became available, she wore American clothes—skirts and crisp shirts. Once a young man from the university stopped her on the street and spit at her shoes. The old tomboy suddenly surfaced in Sumi, she couldn't stop herself. She gave him a swift punch in the jaw.

CHAPTER EIGHTEEN

Harrison's Second Act

The ferocity and global reach of World War II, which claimed more than 50 million lives, dwarfed the fate of individuals. When the war came to an end, millions more were uprooted from home. Inevitably, strangers became connected in unusual ways by the string of time that was the war. On June 22, 1945, as Ingrid Eiserloh and her family struggled to survive in Idstein, Germany, and Irene Hasenberg lived stateless in the camp in Philippeville, President Truman asked Earl Harrison to serve as a special envoy and conduct an inspection tour of Nazi concentration camps in Europe. Though none of the three knew it at the time, that summer their lives were entwined.

Harrison was the commissioner of the INS when Ingrid and her family were interned in Crystal City, one of the camps under his control. He signed the documents for the family's internment. When Harrison received Truman's call in the summer of 1945, he was enjoying his life as dean of the University of Pennsylvania law school. Truman explained that conditions in the former concentration camps, now called displaced-persons camps and operated by British and American military forces, were horrific. While military leaders assured Truman that the matter was under control, he asked Harrison to investigate the situation firsthand. Within a few days, Harrison was on his way to Germany, where Ingrid, an American, had been displaced. During the month of July, Harrison visited thirty DP camps in Germany and Austria. On July 23, 1945, only six months after Irene had left Bergen-Belsen concentration camp, Harrison arrived there.

The trip was formally instigated by the War Refugee Board, established by Roosevelt near the end of the war. In Executive Order 9417, Roosevelt defined the board's mission as "the immediate rescue and relief of the Jews of Europe and other victims of ongoing persecution." After Roosevelt died, John Pehle, executive director of the War Refugee Board, complained to Truman about reports of maltreatment of Jewish DPs.

In the summer of 1945, the policy of the US Army was that all DPs in the liberated camps would be treated the same. During this period, Germans, Poles, Ukrainians—Jews and non-Jews—lived alongside one another in camps. Even though the war was won, the Jews still lived in the same camps built by the Nazis—camps designed specifically for their persecution and extermination. Jewish refugees found themselves confined with former Nazis—SS men, Gestapo—and Nazi collaborators. The US Army had no system in place to identify Nazis from Jews, and no recognition that Jews were the primary targets of Nazi genocide and in need of protection. Moreover, repeated reports came of mistreatment of Jewish DPs by some military authorities, especially in Bavaria, where General George Patton's Third Army was in charge.

Most Americans knew nothing of these events. The first news reports about the horrors of the concentration camps came from reporters accompanying America's generals. The day after Roosevelt's death, three American generals—Patton, Dwight Eisenhower, and Omar Bradley—visited a subcamp of Buchenwald, where they saw piles of bodies, surrounded by torture devices. Patton's face drained of color and he became ill. In his official report, Eisenhower wrote, "We are told that the American soldier does not know what he was fighting for. Now, at least he will know what he is fighting against."

Three days later, Edward R. Murrow, the famed reporter, arrived in Buchenwald. Opening his radio broadcast, Murrow said in his gravelly voice, "There surged around me an evil-smelling stink, men and boys reached out to touch me. They were in rags and the remnants of uniforms. Death already had marked many of them, but they were smiling with their eyes. I looked out over the mass of men to the green fields beyond, where well-fed Germans were plowing." He described dead bodies so emaciated that people shot through the head did not bleed; children, with tattooed numbers, so thin their ribs showed through shirts. "I pray you to believe what I said about Buchenwald," said Murrow. "I have reported what I saw and heard, but only part of it. For most of it I have no words. If I have offended you by this mild account of Buchenwald, I am not in the least sorry."

On April 15, a combined British and Canadian unit of soldiers liberated Bergen-Belsen. Photos taken that day show scenes similar to those described in Murrow's broadcast. Stacks of dead bodies were everywhere. The living looked like human skeletons in striped pajamas. Other survivors curled in fetal positions in crowded dormitories. Signs were posted in camp, DUST SPREADS TYPHUS, as only the month before a typhus epidemic had swept through the camp, killing seventeen thousand prisoners. Thousands more died of typhoid fever. Only one month before, in March 1945, Anne Frank and her sister, Margot, had died, and their bodies were buried in a mass grave.

At home, pressure mounted on Truman to come to the aid of Holocaust survivors. In the US House, Jewish members delivered a formal protest of the treatment of Jewish survivors to the War Department. Jewish leaders also pressed Truman and the State Department to help Jewish survivors. Secretary of the Treasury Henry Morgenthau Jr. asked Truman to establish a cabinet-level committee to set new policies for the DP camps that would protect Jews. Truman rejected that proposal and instead decided to send Harrison to Germany to, as he put it in a letter to Harrison, "inquire into the condition and needs of displaced persons in Germany who may be stateless or non-repatriable, particularly Jews."

Well versed in immigration issues and closely connected to Jewish leaders, Harrison was a natural choice for the job. A month before Roosevelt died in Warm Springs, Georgia, on April 12, 1945, FDR appointed Harrison the US representative on the Intergovernmental Commission for Refugees, an organization responsible for the resettlement of millions of European refugees. This included Irene and the handful of other Jews from Bergen-Belsen who were freed as part of the January 1945 exchange between Germany and the United States, the same exchange that brought Ingrid's family to war-devastated Germany. By the time Harrison left Philadelphia for the tour of DP camps in Europe, Irene was stranded in Philippeville because of the limited number of visas allowed to Jews who wanted to immigrate to the United States. Her brother and mother were stateless in Switzerland. The resettlement dilemma of Irene's family was exactly the sort of problem that Harrison was sent to resolve.

Throughout his trips to the DP camps, Harrison took notes in a diary—notes filled with facts and figures, the names of people he saw, and carefully perceived details. For instance, when Harrison and his small delegation arrived in Bergen-Belsen on July 23, he saw Jews still dying of starvation, as available food was scarce. Most lived on a limited-calorie mix of watery soup, bread, and coffee. In his handwritten diary, Harrison described the bread as "black, wet and unappetizing" and noted of the food, "Need variety. Chocolate. Fruit."

Allied officials in charge said that since the camp had been liberated, thirty thousand Jews had died, most from starvation. One Army chaplain, an American rabbi, reported to Harrison that he personally had attended twenty-three thousand burials in the camp.

Harrison toured the facility with Josef Rosensaft, the elected leader of the Central Committee of Liberated Jews in Bergen-Belsen. Harrison noted that Rosensaft, the son of a scrap-metal dealer in Poland, was only thirty-three years old but looked much older as he weighed only seventy-eight pounds. Rosensaft and his wife, Hadassah, a physician, took Harrison to the Allied hospital, which had not been stocked with supplies and had nothing to treat the victims of malnutrition, typhus, and tuberculosis. The US military officers had allowed the hospital to continue to be staffed by German physicians—the same doctors who were there before liberation. "This is very objectionable to Jewish refugees," Rosensaft told Harrison.

Clothing was limited. Many of the refugees had no shoes and wore their old prison clothes or were issued old German SS uniforms. "It is questionable which clothing they hate the more," Harrison wrote. In a dormitory, he found people still stacked in cots and living in crowded conditions. "One loft, about 80 by 20, 85 people," he noted. Everywhere he noted small details of inhumanity: "Jews living in horse stalls, sick and well together."

He asked Rosensaft what the refugees most wanted. As Rosensaft and his wife talked, Harrison entered the answers in the diary:

1. Peace and quiet—live out remaining years.
2. Can't go back: anti-S [Semitism] parents killed, land soaked with Jewish blood.
3. People outside Europe too quiet about what has happened—nobody seems concerned.

Solution: Make effort to have doors of P [Palestine] and other countries open so we can find homes and be with relatives. Don't leave us in this bloody region.

Most offensive was the Allied policy of lumping the Jews by nationality—in other words, as Germans—which failed to take into consideration that they were the primary targets of Hitler's genocide. They were still treated as prisoners, not as free people. As Harrison noted in his diary, "Authorities won't recognize that Jews are in camp because they are Jews—seem to think they must have committed some offense."

Rosensaft told Harrison he was "disappointed in liberators," not only for the condition of the camp but because many of the Germans who worked at Bergen-Belsen during the war still held jobs there. Not much had changed. Jewish DPs were forced to do much of the manual labor. "If they refuse to work on the Jewish Sabbath," wrote Harrison, "they are punished." They were still under armed guard, not free to move at will around the camp. Given the circumstances, Harrison wrote he wasn't sure what "liberation really meant."

At the end of the long day in Bergen-Belsen, Harrison, dressed in an overcoat, white shirt, trousers, and a tie, posed for a photograph with a group that included Josef and Hadassah Rosensaft. He was the tallest person in the photo, and a worried smile creased his face. His empathy did not go unnoticed. A Jewish prisoner in Bergen-Belsen who met him that day later wrote that Harrison chain-smoked during their conversation and tears streamed down his face. "He was so shaken," wrote the survivor. Finally, Harrison asked, "But how did you survive and where do you take your strength from now?"

Harrison did not hide his despair. At his quarters later that night, he wrote in his diary, "Seldom have I been so depressed. I thought the lowest point had been reached at some of those spots in Munich. But today at Belsen. Only seven hours spent there but it seemed like a lifetime. And to think that I was told, quite officially, there was no need of my visiting Belsen because it had been burned down and no people left here. And then to come here and find a mere matter of 14,000 displaced people." Harrison had been misled by the American military and he knew it.

After Bergen-Belsen, Harrison traveled to Kaunitz DP camp. The camp housed several hundred survivors, mostly Jewish women from Hungary who had been transferred from Buchenwald concentration camp. He interviewed a twenty-three-year-old architecture student named Meredith, who explained that the women were housed in the village alongside German civilians. "I don't think Germans like us too much," she told him. "We are rather a trial to our commandant." Harrison noted in his diary, "Everybody well organized. Whole place run by people themselves." Meredith and others told Harrison that they did not want to stay in Germany. "All Hungarians want to go home," he wrote.

On August 3, 1945, only eleven days after his visit to Bergen-Belsen, Harrison submitted a draft report to Truman. In the report, he drew from his deep knowledge of immigration and refugee issues. He had overseen the registration of German, Italian, and Japanese citizens living in the United States in the run-up to the war. As director of the INS from 1942 to 1944, he'd established the camp in Crystal City and overseen other American internment camps. He was well schooled in the secrets of American internment—the arrests of immigrants born in Axis countries because of their nationalities; the prisoner exchange; the boredom of internees who lived under armed guard for indefinite periods. He'd resigned as INS commissioner as a protest of US immigration laws that discriminated against non-Europeans—Jews, Asians, Africans. Harrison also understood the difference between American internment and the Nazi genocide. Now he had Truman's ear. When he sat down to write his report for the president's eyes, Harrison did not hold back.

In direct, clear prose, his report indicted the American military. "As matters now stand, we appear to be treating the Jews as the Nazis treated them except that we do not exterminate them," wrote Harrison. "They are in concentration camps in large numbers under our military guard instead of S.S. troops. One is led to wonder whether the German people, seeing this, are not supposing that we are following or at least condoning Nazi policy." This was the essential message of his report: the treatment of the Jews by the American military was no better than that by the Nazis, except the Americans were not directly killing them.

The first paragraph describing the conditions of the camp set the firm tone for the remainder of the report: "Generally speaking, three months after V-E Day and even longer after the liberation of individual groups, many Jewish displaced persons and other possibly non-repatriables are living under guard behind barbed-wire fences, in camps of several descriptions (built by the Germans for slave-laborers and Jews), including some of the most notorious of the concentration camps, amidst crowded, frequently unsanitary and generally grim conditions, in complete idleness, with no opportunity, except surreptitiously, to communicate with the outside world, hoping for some word of encouragement and action in their behalf."

In a section on basic needs of Jewish DPs, he listed "clothing and shoes (most sorely needed), more varied and palatable diet, medicines, beds and mattresses, reading materials." Then he noted that clothing for the refugees was requisitioned from Germans and reported that the military had not compelled German civilians to give up a sufficient amount of clothing. "The internees feel particularly bitter about the state of their clothing when they see how well the German population is dressed. The German population today is still the best dressed in all of Europe."

Harrison's first recommendation to Truman was to abolish the nonsegregation policy of the military. During the war, Jews were singled out by the Nazis for genocide and, under the present policy, were still living alongside Germans who had tormented them. Harrison argued their persecution had earned them the chance to live separately in camps. "In the days immediately ahead, the Jews in Germany and Austria should have the first claim upon the conscience of the people of the United States and Great Britain and other personnel who represent them in work being done in Germany and Austria. The first and plainest need is a recognition of their actual status and by this I mean their status as Jews. Refusal to recognize the Jews as such has the effect, in this situation, of closing one's eyes to their former and more barbaric persecution."

The only real solution to the problem, Harrison argued, was the immediate evacuation to Palestine of those Jews who wanted to leave Europe. This was Harrison's second major recommendation— open immigration to Palestine. "To anyone who has visited the concentration camps and who has talked with the despairing survivors, it is nothing short of calamitous to contemplate that the gates of Palestine should be soon closed." He asked Truman to release one hundred thousand immigration certificates to Jewish DPs so that they could resettle in Palestine. In every camp, Harrison had asked

Jewish survivors where their first preference to go was, and in every camp the overwhelming answer was Palestine.

He also recommended that immigration laws in the United States be relaxed so that more Jews from Europe could obtain visas to America. This recommendation directly affected Irene in Philippeville, where she waited for her application to resettle in America to be granted.

Moreover, Harrison argued that the United States must force Germany to accept responsibility for the extermination of millions of Jews. "If it be true, as it seems to be widely conceded, that the German people at large do not have any sense of guilt with respect to the war and its causes and results, and if the policy is 'To convince the German people that they have suffered a total military defeat and that they cannot escape responsibility for what they have brought upon themselves,' then it is difficult to understand why so many displaced persons, particularly those who have so long been persecuted and whose repatriation or resettlement is likely to be delayed, should be compelled to live in crude, overcrowded camps while the German people in rural areas continue undisturbed in their homes." Harrison's reference to the policy regarding Germans was one of the principles agreed by the Soviet Union, Britain, and the United States during the Potsdam Conference in Berlin.

What became known as the Harrison Report was printed in its entirety in the *New York Times.* Truman's reaction was swift: he supported Harrison's recommendations. On August 31, Truman forwarded Harrison's report to Eisenhower, commander of US forces in Europe. In his letter, Truman told Eisenhower that he agreed with Harrison's recommendations and asked the general to make his own inspection tour and "clean up" the conditions in the camps. "I know you will agree with me that we have a particular responsibility toward these victims of persecution and tyranny who are in our zone," wrote Truman to Eisenhower. "We must make clear to the German people that we thoroughly abhor the Nazi policies of hatred and persecution. We have no better opportunity to demonstrate this than by the manner in which we ourselves actually treat the survivors remaining in Germany."

Eisenhower was furious. In a confidential message to Truman, Eisenhower agreed to tour the camps but minimized Harrison's findings: "It is possible, as you say, that some of my subordinates in the field are not carrying out my policies and any instances found will be promptly corrected." Instead, Eisenhower painted a brighter picture of conditions, arguing that no one representing "Jewish interests" had filed a formal complaint about US-controlled concentration camps. That belied the fact that the Harrison Report was one long indictment of the US military's management of the camps.

In conclusion, Eisenhower told Truman, "Mr. Harrison's report gives little regard to the problems faced, the real success attained in saving the lives of thousands of Jewish and other concentration camp victims and repatriating those who could and wished to be repatriated, and the progress made in two months to bring these unfortunates who remain under our jurisdiction from the depths of physical degeneration to a condition of health and essential comfort."

Patton's response was straightforwardly hostile and validated the charge that anti-Semitism was rife in the American military. In response to Harrison's criticism that Jews were living like prisoners, Patton defended the policy of not segregating Jews from other Germans and Europeans. He said that Jewish DPs "either never had any sense of decency or lost it during their internment by the Germans." He defended their still being under armed guard and opposed any "special treatment." Without the guards, Patton said the Jews would "spread over the country like locusts."

On October 17, 1945, the disagreement between Eisenhower and Harrison became public when the *New York Times* printed a copy of a letter Eisenhower sent to Truman after the general's inspection. Eisenhower wrote that since Harrison's visit in July, clothing and shoes had been made available for survivors, that medical services were "uniformly excellent," and that all of the camps were stocked with adequate rations, much of it from the Red Cross.

The following day, in a radio address from Philadelphia, Harrison countered Eisenhower's statement. He argued that Eisenhower's claim that Jews were transferred to better quarters was misleading. He suggested that the houses of German civilians should be requisitioned and Jews housed there. "What difference does it make what kind of camps they are living in?" he asked. "The point is that there shouldn't be any camps at all, but houses. Shifting them from one camp to another can hardly be said to be liberation."

The public embarrassment of Eisenhower and the Army prompted immediate improvements. In the remaining months of 1945, Jewish DPs were segregated in camps and were given preferences in employment. Many concentration camps were closed. Eisenhower created a position, "advisor on Jewish affairs," and named Simon H. Rifkind, a federal judge from the Southern District of New York, to the position. Rifkind arrived at Eisenhower's headquarters in Frankfurt on October 20, 1945.

In his diary, Harrison not only made notes of what he saw in the concentration camps but also described his general impressions of Germany that summer on his tour: "Food ration lines, no business being conducted, trucks and wagons with people and scant belongings, walking with bundles, many bicycles. Women working in fields. Broken bridges."

These were some of the same scenes, proof of the defeat of Germany, that Ingrid remembered seeing that summer, as she and her family settled into life in Idstein. She worked in the fields herself, gathering potatoes when she could find them. Her long red hair and American accent attracted attention.

"Hey, Fräulein," called the GIs who'd occupied the village by then. "What are you doing today?" Day by day, Ingrid seemed to close down emotionally, coming and going from the apartment by the train station, jumpy and distracted. An American citizen, she was mistaken for a German by American GIs.

Meanwhile, in Philippeville, Irene Hasenberg waited for one of those golden papers to arrive that would allow her to immigrate to America. By then, Irene was one of only twelve Jews from Bergen-Belsen in Philippeville. Finally, in December 1945, about three months after Truman received Harrison's report, the regulations relaxed and Irene received word that her papers were in order. In mid-December, she boarded a Liberty ship, filled with troops, bound for the United States. Ingrid, far away in Idstein, had no hope of returning to her homeland and no idea that her life was in any way connected to that of a Jewish woman named Irene.

PART FOUR

THE ROAD HOME

CHAPTER NINETEEN

After the War

Idstein, Germany

In May 1945, Ingrid Eiserloh's ten-year-old brother, Lothar, watched two regiments from the Second Armored Division of the US Army, nicknamed the Hell on Wheels division, roll into the streets of Idstein in bulky tanks. The battle for Idstein was over in a few minutes as the Germans did not put up a fight. At the sight of American occupiers, German soldiers ran through the streets—weapons down, hands over their heads—and surrendered.

The American tanks parked in the center of the city. Soldiers and civilians alike brought their weapons and handed them to Army tank commanders. Lothar watched in fascination as even the oldest men in the village brought their decrepit hunting rifles and added them to the pile. It took several days for the GIs to collect all the weapons in Idstein, a small city with a population of about five thousand. Within a week, the two regiments took over the school that Lothar and Ingrid attended and converted it into a mess hall.

The Allied nations—Britain, the United States, the Soviet Union, and France—carved up four zones of occupation in Germany. Fortunately for the Eiserloh family, Idstein was in the American zone, with its headquarters in nearby Frankfurt.

By then Germany had been battered by Allied forces. Food was almost nonexistent. The fields of farmers were destroyed and the rail system devastated. In large cities, streets pocked from American bombs were dusty with rubble. Perhaps in response to criticism in the Harrison Report, Eisenhower made sure German civilians were not coddled. He set the official ration for those living in the American zone at only 1,275 calories a day, much of it black bread. Like most families in Idstein, the Eiserlohs went hungry.

Johanna had not heard from Mathias since his arrest in March by the Gestapo on charges of being an American spy. She did not know if he was alive or dead. Prior to the American occupation, Johanna was taken in for questioning herself by German authorities and quickly released. She welcomed the arrival of the Americans.

On May 8, 1945, Ingrid turned fifteen, a confusing coming-of-age birthday. With her husband once again gone, Johanna was short-tempered and often critical of Ingrid for defending her father at every turn. Ingrid was an anomaly in the village, an American who spoke better English than German and was unaccustomed to the stringent rules in German schools. She shared a wooden desk with another girl, and the students rose when the teacher entered the room. More than once Ingrid's hands were rapped with a ruler because she was disobedient. With her blue-green eyes and copper hair, which fell down her skinny back, Ingrid stood out. She was treated like a scapegoat—hated by the Germans for being an American and banished from America for reasons she did not understand.

Johanna enrolled Ensi in kindergarten, and she, too, had a difficult time adjusting to the regimented system. The first week in school Ensi, traumatized by the events of the war, wet her pants in the schoolyard. In the presence of the other students, the teacher shouted and scolded Ensi, who cried inconsolably. The teacher sent for Johanna, who came right away and was told that Ensi would not be allowed to come to school until she was toilet trained.

At ten years old, Lothar had it easier. Johanna doted on him, her nickname for him being the Little Prince. While Ingrid avoided Johanna, Lothar was eager to please his mother. In Lothar's presence, Johanna's mood softened and she acted as though there were no place on earth she'd rather be.

When the US Army took over Lothar's school, one of the rooms was converted to a mess hall. Lothar and a few of his schoolmates went to the school in search of food and saw a long chow line of soldiers. One of the German boys asked the chief of the regiment for food.

"Get out of here, you little assholes," said the chief in English.

Lothar's German schoolmates skedaddled, but Lothar stayed behind. "Who are you calling assholes?" asked Lothar in English.

"Where did you learn English?" asked the chief.

"I'm from Strongsville, Ohio, near Cleveland."

The chief's jaw dropped. "I'm from Strongsville, too," he snapped. "Do you have an older sister named Ingrid who has reddish golden hair?"

"Yes, I sure do. She's here in Idstein."

The unlikely coincidence assured the Eiserloh family's survival. Lothar explained to the officer that his family had been interned in a camp in Texas and had recently been repatriated to Germany. He had papers to prove that he was an American citizen, born in Ohio. He explained that he and his family were starving and asked for help. On the spot, the chief of the regiment hired Lothar as a translator. With his small salary, Lothar was able to buy milk for Guenther, his baby brother, and provide rations for the family.

Eisenhower instituted a nonfraternization policy that forbade familiar contact between soldiers and occupied civilians, but the policy was loosely followed. In the case of Lothar, it was completely ignored. He was treated as a mascot. Within a week, Lothar had his own Army uniform, custom-made with pinstripes. Ingrid teased that he looked like Little Lord Fauntleroy.

Lothar did errands for the American GIs and made deliveries. One of his jobs was to go on regular patrol with the GIs, with one patrol at 7:00 a.m. and the other at 10:00 p.m. The soldiers drove around the countryside in half-tracks with three rubber wheels on each side and equipped with a small cannon. Lothar bounced in the backseat. "We'd see a house that was suitable for occupation," recalled Lothar. "My major ability was that I spoke both German and English. I would explain to the people that lived in the houses that they were being occupied."

In late May, another group of GIs on a search mission located Mathias Eiserloh locked in a small cell in a jail not far from Idstein. When the GIs arrived, he greeted them in English. After a thorough questioning, Mathias was released and he returned to his family. A condition of his release was that he had to undergo Eisenhower's denazification process, which required interviews about his activities during the war and a search of his file as an enemy alien in America. When the process was completed, Mathias was hired as a translator for the Army as well. The paradox was not lost on Mathias: the government that had imprisoned him—and his family—in Crystal City, then exchanged all six of them as ransom for US citizens in Germany, was now his employer and responsible for saving his family's life. "For the rest of his life, he talked about how the war was one long irony after another," said Lothar. "He'd shake his head. No way to figure it all out."

The Army moved the Eiserloh family into a small, two-room facility on the outskirts of town. Johanna, Ingrid, and Ensi didn't see much of either Mathias or Lothar, whose days were ordered to military precision by the Americans. Food was no longer a problem, and Mathias had access to all the American cigarettes he wanted. He used them to trade on the black market for clothes, liquor, and other scarce items. Ingrid's hollow cheeks filled out. Lothar grew taller and more muscular. Ensi and Guenther no longer cried from hunger, but Ensi did not gain weight and was lethargic. A military doctor diagnosed her with rickets, a consequence of not having been given enough milk since she'd left Crystal City. What milk the family had found on the journey from the United States had been given to Guenther, who was miraculously healthy, given his birth on the train from Crystal City and the journey into war.

One day a group of GIs asked Johanna if she knew how to make an apple pie. "Oh, yes, I do," she replied. Soon, the GIs stocked her tiny kitchen with flour, sugar, and Crisco. Suddenly, Johanna, with Ingrid's help, was in the pie business. "She made pies morning, noon, and night," recalled Lothar. "Apple pies, cherry, chocolate."

Next she offered to do laundry for the soldiers. Lothar collected the piles of dirty uniforms and provided soap. Johanna and Ingrid did the washing on old-fashioned washboards. The wash money, plus the pie money, allowed Johanna to buy household items and clothes. She put away whatever money was left to save for passage to America—if and when the Eiserlohs would be allowed to return.

The GIs invented nicknames for Lothar based on the sound of the last four letters of his name. Sometimes he was called Sweat Tar or Road Tar, depending on their moods. He did what they told him and enjoyed himself, and for him, the occupation was a lark. Many of the GIs had German girlfriends. Sometimes Lothar would deliver what the GIs called "Frau bait"—cigarettes, food, and olive-colored US Army blankets—to the girlfriends. The blankets were particularly popular. The women used them to make shirts and skirts. When Lothar delivered the blankets to the women, his nickname was Sweet Tar.

For a boy, this window into the boisterous world of men was an education. He was a wide-eyed innocent with an unpredictable father who was fresh from a German prison cell and with few prospects for future employment. Because of his connection to the GIs, Lothar provided for the family and became his mother's hero. The GIs were victors, infused with confidence and bright futures, and they bequeathed a healthy self-assurance to Lothar. Many were twenty or thirty years old, no longer freckled-faced boys but triumphant men who'd come into their prime during the war. Some were sensitive by nature and others vainglorious—an entire cast of characters with Lothar as a bit player, the useful kid from Ohio.

One character Lothar never forgot was a tall, strong Texan, predictably named Tex, in his forties who carried two ivory-handled pistols wherever he went. When Tex and his buddies visited local bars, Lothar would go along and translate for them. "Let's bring the little guy," Tex would say.

Lothar witnessed quarrels that broke out among hotheads and observed pennies paid for songs, dollars for women. One night Tex and Lothar went into a bar and Tex saw a GI splayed drunk on a couch. Tex drew his pistols, fired—and fortunately missed his target. The drunken GI charged Tex, brought him to the ground, and delivered blow after blow. Lothar headed for the door and went home.

In contrast, Ingrid's experience of the occupation was as unfortunate as Lothar's was privileged. With her good looks and ability to speak English, Ingrid found herself a victim of an environment in which the German girls were friendly and compliant with American soldiers, who expected the same from her. Wherever Ingrid went, the GIs stared at the pretty American girl with the long hair. When they picked up pies and laundry, they pleaded with Ingrid to go for rides in their jeeps or walks in the forest. Unsure of herself, Ingrid played along. In the middle of town was a bar frequented by GIs, and out of curiosity and a need for the kind of attention that Lothar received, Ingrid frequented it.

"In the beginning, it was fun. I went out on dates with a few of the soldiers. I thought of them as my protectors," recalled Ingrid. "They gave me rides in their jeeps. I asked them about what was happening in the States. I plotted my return to America. It was all pretty innocent—until it wasn't."

If Ingrid's relationship with her mother had been closer or if she'd had an older sister or close friend, perhaps she wouldn't have allowed herself to become vulnerable. Soon, one particular soldier followed her everywhere. On a sunny day in spring, while Ingrid was on a walk, she heard the sound of an approaching vehicle. The soldier pulled up in his jeep alongside her and opened the passenger door, and Ingrid got in and they went for a ride. When the soldier brought the jeep to a stop, Ingrid, sensing danger, jumped out and ran. He chased her, pulled her to the ground, and raped her. Ingrid debated reporting the soldier to his commanding officer, but didn't because she thought her mother might not believe her. She remembered that morning in 1942 when she had found her mother injured in bed. Johanna had never spoken of the incident. If Ingrid reported the soldier, Johanna would not want Ingrid to incur the public humiliation of a military trial. Rape was common during the occupation, and Ingrid decided to keep silent.

Eventually, she did disclose the rape to her mother and to Ensi and discussed it during interviews in my research for this book. "Ultimately, I decided it was just one more terrible event in the war," said Ingrid. "I was just a kid back then. I didn't want to make trouble for the soldier or for myself. I just tried to forget it. It was before the era of women's rights. I didn't think I had any."

What she did instead was to convince her parents to help her find a way back to America. Mathias wrote to his sister Klara, who lived near Los Angeles, and asked if she would serve as a legal guardian for both Ingrid and Lothar, his two oldest children. Johanna encouraged her children's return to the United States. She wanted to return herself, but Mathias decided his chances of getting a job as an engineer were better in Germany.

Klara agreed to serve as sponsor and guardian for Ingrid and Lothar, and they filled out the necessary paperwork. As a final step, both Ingrid and Lothar had to submit to a medical examination. Lothar passed with no trouble, but the physician found that Ingrid had gonorrhea. She did not tell him about the rape and he asked no questions. Instead, he gave her an injection of penicillin and some antibiotics for the voyage.

In July 1947, Ingrid, then seventeen, and Lothar, twelve, boarded a troopship, the SS *Ernie Pyle*, and made the voyage home to the United States, leaving behind their parents and two siblings. Lothar worked in the bar, serving drinks to the soldiers on their way home. Ingrid stayed in the female quarters of the ship. After a journey of two weeks, they arrived at Ellis Island and made their way by train to California, where for a while life in America was almost as hard as the life they'd left behind in Germany.

Philippeville, Algeria

In October 1945, as Ingrid and her family adjusted to life during the occupation in Idstein, the United Nations Relief and Rehabilitation Administration closed the DP camp in Philippeville where Irene lived. By the fall there weren't enough Jewish refugees left in the camp to justify its continued operation. The few remaining survivors, including Irene, were sent to a small hotel, where they waited for visas to America.

Many of the others returned to Europe, but Irene never considered returning to Germany or relocating in Palestine. "Our family had many relatives who had immigrated to the United States," recalled Irene. "We never thought of going anywhere else." Nonetheless, a voyage to America faced significant obstacles. Besides the visa problem, few Liberty ships made it to Algeria. Five months after the war in Europe ended, American soldiers were eager to get home for Christmas. Every available Liberty ship was filled with GIs, and spaces for refugees were rare.

From her mother's letters, Irene learned details of the Kaplans, her American sponsors. Rose and Hugo Kaplan had fled Mainz in the Rhineland of Germany in the 1930s as Hitler came to power, escaping just in time. They left with few possessions and settled in the Bronx in New York, where they worked in hotels, repairing carpet sweepers. Motorized vacuum cleaners were not yet common.

In Philippeville, Irene thought about what her life would be like in America, how she would fit into the Kaplan family, and where she would go to school. She wondered how long it would be before she was reunited with her mother and her brother. The shock of being separated from them after the exchange in Switzerland and the grief over the death of her father, John, on the train out of Bergen-Belsen left Irene with a dimmed sense of reality. She focused on one task at a time: gathering her papers, talking to the consul in Philippeville, and biding her time until she could get to America. Physically, she was stronger, her bones finally having some muscle, but the memory of starvation stayed with her, leaving her unsatisfied.

Most days she went to the ocean and took swimming lessons from a woman from Holland who had been in Bergen-Belsen with Irene and her family. The woman had a son, a little older than Irene, who was by then fifteen. She and the young man met every day at the beach, and as they talked and swam, their relationship grew into a romance, Irene's first. "We could relate to each other," recalled Irene. "We were both in Bergen-Belsen together. We talked a little about the camp—the last time I talked about it directly for many years."

Though she was in an oceanside paradise, her mind was still fixed on the horrors of the concentration camp. Moreover, paradise was empty of her family and her friends, except for this young man. They spent the days together, walking in the hills, swimming in the ocean, reading books, and taking meals. When he pressed Irene to marry him, Irene felt conflicted. She wasn't ready to marry anyone, but she also wasn't sure what awaited her in America. Weeks passed and the quandary persisted.

Finally, in November, three months after the public release of the Harrison Report and the subsequent relaxation on the release of American visas, Irene's visa arrived and she made her choice: she would go to America.

In late December 1945, a few seats opened on a Liberty ship bound for the United States. Twelve Jewish refugees from Bergen-Belsen, including Irene, were given passage on the ship, and one of the older refugees, Margaret Sussman, took Irene under her wing. Months earlier Margaret's husband and son had left Philippeville on a small all-male Liberty boat bound for the United States, but Margaret had worried about making the voyage on such a small boat and stayed behind. "Well, you and I will travel together," Margaret told Irene.

On the first Saturday afternoon in December, Irene, Margaret, and ten others left their hotel in taxis and drove through to the port of Bougie. A large truck packed with their luggage followed behind. As the caravan neared Bougie, the taxi that carried Irene and Margaret collided with the truck in the first mishap of the trip. The luggage spilled out of the truck, and Irene and Margaret were jostled but unharmed.

The Liberty ship took two weeks for the voyage, and the sea was rough. Many nights Margaret and Irene couldn't go to their shared cabin. As a safety measure, the ship's officers asked all the passengers to sit in the dining room. The pitching of the sea rattled the silverware from the drawers as people weaved and bobbed through the dining room.

Both Margaret and Irene were seasick, but Margaret found the strength to tend to Irene, bringing her tea and making sure she got fresh air. The two became close. "She became an adoptive mother to me," said Irene. "I hadn't seen my mother in a long time. I don't think I could have made the journey without Margaret."

On Christmas Eve 1945, the Liberty ship arrived in Baltimore. The weather was freezing and the harbor was frozen solid. The ship could not dock. The crew on board and the small cluster of refugees had no choice but to spend the night on board. The kitchen staff prepared a turkey dinner with dressing, vegetables, and dessert. The following morning, on Christmas, Irene and Margaret waited on the deck of the ship as small motorboats, equipped with ice cutters, arrived along both sides of the ship. One by one, the passengers were lowered into the boats and taken to the dock.

As no one was at the harbor to greet them, Margaret and Irene made their own way to the train station in Baltimore. From there, they boarded a train to New York and arrived at Grand Central Station, where Peter Sussman, Margaret's son, and the Kaplans waited for them.

With a great rush of relief, Irene joined the mass of strangers in the brightly lit station. Everywhere people were smiling; soldiers danced with reunited sweethearts. VICTORY signs left over from V-E Day celebrations still plastered the walls of platforms. The station was resplendent, with marble floors, a gigantic four-sided golden clock, and an American flag unfurled from the second-story balcony. A Salvation Army band played, and people threw pennies and nickels into donation buckets.

In the Kaplans' one-bedroom apartment in the Bronx, Irene slept on the couch in the living room with the Kaplans' only daughter, Lottie, who was a few years older than Irene. The Kaplans earned a modest living but provided Irene with food, clothing, and shoes and enrolled her in school. "They were very good to me," recalled Irene. "Parents couldn't have been better."

Shortly after Irene arrived, Rose and Hugo asked her not to talk about the war or her experiences in the concentration camp. "Now you must start a new life. You are in America. The past is behind you," they told her, as Irene remembered it. "You mustn't speak about it. You have to forget."

Irene was confused. The pressure to talk about the brutality of the years in camp weighed on her. It wasn't only the Kaplans who asked her to keep silent and to forget. Every Friday night, Irene and the Kaplans had dinner with other cousins in New York whose relatives had died in the Holocaust. One of Irene's mother's cousins had had two sisters in the Westerbork camp with Irene and her family. The sisters died in camp. "I thought they would want to hear what happened to their sisters," recalled Irene. "But they couldn't bear to listen. They all wanted to forget."

At the time, Irene resented the imposed silence. Later in her life, however, she wondered how much she would have been able to express if given the chance. Much of what had happened was unspeakable. "At the time I was at the point that I could have remembered all the terrible things that happened," recalled Irene in an interview. "Or I could get on with rebuilding my life. I don't think it would have been possible to do the two simultaneously."

Within a few weeks after her arrival, the Kaplans enrolled Irene in Walton High School in the Bronx. Having missed school for so many years, Irene was an eager student. She found part-time jobs and worked hard. "I began to tell myself that if I'd survived Bergen-Belsen, I could survive anything," said Irene. "I tried to focus not on what I'd lost, but what I had to gain. It was a struggle."

In those early months, what Irene wanted most was to reunite with what was left of her family. A group of relatives pooled resources to pay for the travel of her mother and brother to America. Werner was the first to arrive, in June 1946 on a ship that docked in Hoboken. The following month, Gertrude arrived on an airplane. She was still physically weak and chose to travel by airplane rather than risk seasickness on a long voyage by ship.

That summer after the war, New York was crowded with returning soldiers and immigrants, creating a housing shortage. Irene's mother tried to find an apartment but couldn't, so she rented furnished rooms in Manhattan for Irene and herself. Her brother lived with a cousin. It took three years for them to find an apartment to share, where they lived together for many years.

During those years, they rarely talked directly about all they had lost during the war. They focused on survival. Both Irene and Werner had jobs and both attended Queens College. When their experiences in Germany came up in conversation, it was often in an indirect way. For instance, at the sight of turnips, all three grimaced. They all knew why: they remembered the turnip soup in Bergen-Belsen.

Every January 23, the anniversary of Irene's father death on the train, they made a point of spending the day together. When they no longer shared an apartment, they called each other on that day. They never discussed John's death or mentioned why they called. Their shared loss went unsaid, but never unremembered.

Sendai, Japan

In January 1946, Sumi faced challenges in Sendai similar to those of Ingrid in Idstein and Irene in Philippeville: the reality of hunger and the desperation of navigating a world in constant violent rotation. Everywhere Sumi looked in Sendai, she saw scenes of struggle and defeat: shrines, temples, buildings, obliterated by American firebombs; the train station in rubble; farmers with hungry eyes and downcast expressions wandering through muddy fields, empty of rice.

The American occupation of Japan, which began on August 30, 1945, in Tokyo, was well under way in Sendai. A large American flag hung outside the military government headquarters established by troops from the Eighth Army. Through official news agencies, Japanese officials warned the population to avoid "unpleasant confrontations" and to act prudently, decorously, and with cooperation, "thereby displaying the true essence of the Yamato race." The people complied and the occupation went smoothly. Civilians and soldiers surrendered weapons. English instruction, which had been discouraged during the four years of war, was once again part of the curriculum in the Sendai schools. Japanese boys and men lined the sides of grim streets and bowed politely when American soldiers in jeeps passed by.

Everyone in her uncle's house, including Sumi, was hungry. The house was crowded with people and there was little rice. Sumi was skinny as a stick and could count her bony ribs with her fingers. One day she walked to the American military base in the center of town and applied for a job. Only seventeen years old, Sumi told an employment officer that she was an American. "I came to get a job," she told him.

"Can you type?" asked the officer. Sumi replied that she could and sat down at a desk in front of a typewriter and keyed a few paragraphs to prove her skills. She was hired on the spot and told the officer that she had two American-born sisters who could also type and interpret.

As Lothar helped save his family in Idstein by working for the American military, Sumi did the same. Her salary of fifteen hundred yen a month—about $100—helped her family survive. After she was hired, her two older sisters, Yoshiko and Haruko, got jobs at the base as well. They ate their meals at the mess hall and brought home food for their parents. "Three squares a day," Sumi recalled.

To relieve the food shortage in Sendai, the American military government brought in truckloads of cornmeal, rolled oats, and canned goods. At the headquarters, onions, potatoes, and meat were laid in store. On the streets, American GIs handed out chocolate bars, chewing gum, and candy to the local children. One day during an inspection of a delivery of a large supply of grain, Sumi noticed that the grain had been diluted with grass. She reported this fraud, the grain was sent back, and Sumi felt extraordinary pride: her work had impact.

One of the best parts of Sumi's job was that it allowed her to stay in touch with friends from Crystal City who'd been on the ship with her from Seattle and who were now working for the Americans at Haneda Air Base and in many other parts of Japan. The Japanese word *furusato* means "homeland," and Sumi and her compatriots embraced that concept, but without the emotional ties to Japan it suggests. That spring of 1946, Sumi and her friends from Crystal City began to plot their return to the United States. In letters and cables, they functioned as a community in exile—expatriates bound together by Crystal City.

For instance, Mas Okabe and his brother found jobs as typists at the Army Air Force base at Atsugi Airport, near Tokyo. General Douglas MacArthur had first set foot on Japanese soil there when he'd arrived to accept the emperor's formal surrender. Like Sumi, Mas and his brother were hired because they spoke both English and a small amount of Japanese. They sent money back to their parents. "It felt good to know they weren't starving," recalled Mas. "All of us kids from Crystal City kept up with each other in Japan. We watched out for each other. I think it's how we got through what was a difficult time." After a few months, Mas and his brother transferred to Haneda Air Base.

In Hiroshima, both Min Tajii and his father found work at the British headquarters located in the ruins of Kure, a former Japanese naval base. Like the others from Crystal City, Min was born in America, the son of a Japanese farmer in the Imperial Valley of California. At the camp in Crystal City, he was a pitcher for the baseball team. When he arrived in Hiroshima in January, Min realized it would be up to him to find a way to feed his parents and younger brother. His father was all but immobilized by the shock of Japan's defeat and the destruction of Hiroshima.

Not only British, but also soldiers from Australia and India occupied Hiroshima. Since he was hungry, Min applied for a job in the kitchen, run by an Australian sergeant. Min struck a deal: his father got a job as a cook, and Min's job was to interpret between the sergeant and his father. "You tell me what you want cooked," said Min. "My dad will cook it. I'll be your interpreter cook."

At the end of his shifts, Min took home large loaves of bread for his mother and other members of the family. He traded ration jars of jam and corned beef in cans for white rice. Like the others from Crystal City, Min saved his salary and planned his return to the United States.

Sumi worked at the military headquarters in Sendai for more than a year. During that time, both of her sisters married nisei soldiers, second-generation Japanese Americans, one brother-in-law headquartered in Sendai and the other in Tokyo. Finally, in the summer of 1947, Sumi spoke to her father and told him she wanted to return to America.

Sumi expected an argument, but Tokiji sat quietly with a serious expression. A space opened up between them, some immutable calm. Sumi explained that she wanted to finish high school in Los

Angeles. Tokiji nodded yes. The ship fare to California was about $300, and to her surprise Tokiji agreed to pay it.

In July 1947, Sumi left Japan on a troop ship, the SS *Marine Linx*, and entered the United States in Honolulu. Mas Okabe and Tosh Yonekura, another Crystal City internee, were also on the ship. When US customs officials checked her documents, they noted that she had traveled from an internment camp in Crystal City to Japan, which raised suspicions that she might be a danger to the United States. The officials threatened to detain her at Angel Island, a military prison, and send her back to Japan. After several hours, the situation was resolved and Sumi was released. Friends from Crystal City greeted Sumi, Mas, and Tosh in Honolulu.

She boarded another boat to San Francisco, stayed a week with friends who were her neighbors at Heart Mountain Relocation Camp, and at long last arrived in Los Angeles. It was the end of summer. The wind off the Pacific Ocean was warm and smelled briny. How many times during the years lost to the war had Sumi yearned to return to Los Angeles? Finally she was home.

Like New York, Los Angeles was filled with soldiers, and it was difficult to find a place to live. At last a friend from Crystal City helped Sumi find a place to live and a part-time job. She worked as a "schoolgirl" for the secretary of Harry Warner, president of Warner Bros. Studios, and enrolled at Fairfax High School to finish her senior year. In return for room and board, Sumi helped keep the woman's house and was given $20 a week. The secretary, whom Sumi knew as Mrs. Stern, was at the center of things in Hollywood. She and her husband treated Sumi well. Even though they were Jewish, they decorated an eight-foot Christmas tree for Sumi that year and put presents for her all around it. Though she missed her mother, the Sterns made it a happy Christmas.

By then, Sumi was well into her senior year at Fairfax High School, near the border of West Hollywood. She studied hard and in her free time went to movies and to restaurants with some of her friends from Crystal City who had also made it back to Los Angeles.

When she graduated from high school in Los Angeles, friends from Crystal City attended the ceremony. She wrote regularly to Nobu in Sendai, buoyant letters that did not conceal her happiness. "I was just so grateful to be home, to be an American citizen and not have to look over my shoulder," Sumi recalled.

CHAPTER TWENTY

Beyond the Barbed Wire

While Ingrid, Lothar, and Sumi were mired in the process of re-adjusting to life in the United States, others were still struggling to win their freedom. By August 1945, the machinery of internment, implemented during the run-up to the war in December 1941, was steadily being taken apart. Already many of the fifty-four internment camps operated by the US military and the thirty camps operated by the Immigration and Naturalization Service had shut down. The camp at Crystal City, the only family camp, was still open, but with a reduced population. That summer 2,548 Japanese, 756 Germans, and 12 Italian internees were left.

When O'Rourke arrived at the camp in September 1943, the job seemed clear. During wartime, the country had the right, arguably the imperative, to protect itself from suspected enemies. However, over the next two years, O'Rourke dealt with only a handful of internees who represented a real threat to US security. Most of those in Crystal City were caught up in a web of fear and intrigue not of their own making, especially the American-born children who made up the majority and whose loyalty to their country of birth was severely stressed by the humiliation of internment. At the start, O'Rourke thought of the camp in Crystal City as a humane project—a place where families were reunited. However, the undesirable aspects of family internment—the lack of freedom, the secret exchanges, and the forced repatriations—now outweighed the good.

By 1945 O'Rourke was forty-nine years old and had been remarried to a woman named Mary, a native of the West Texas town of Big Spring. They lived in a rock house just outside the barbed-wire fence in Crystal City, in close proximity to the internees on the other side of the fence. Sometimes Mary joined O'Rourke for the daily count of internees. He continued to be a melancholic drinker, and was still alienated from his only daughter. More than one of the young people who were interned in Crystal City—the ones who once thought of him as a Pied Piper—believed O'Rourke drank because he felt guilty over the internment of the American-born children in camp. At the end of the war, O'Rourke asked for a transfer to an easy desk job with the INS office in Kansas City, Missouri. He requested that the new job not involve internment, just routine immigration issues.

While he waited for a transfer, O'Rourke focused on winding down operations in Crystal City, which proved to be almost as challenging as opening the camp years before. During the summer of 1945, O'Rourke was at work on a report to INS headquarters in Washington about the history of the Crystal City camp and his reflections on the future of family internment. All that summer he and members of his staff labored over the report. In the historical narrative, O'Rourke described the opening in the fall of 1942, detailed rules and regulations, explained the operation of the schools, and highlighted camp activities.

He also described what he viewed as the source of the main problems in camp: the intense rivalry between the repatriates, whom he saw as loyal to the countries of their origin, and the nonrepatriates, who generally were loyal to the United States. "Although many of the nonrepatriates sympathized with the cause of their fatherland, a large number of this group evidenced a pro-American attitude," wrote O'Rourke. "This division of attitude was the basic cause of most differences among the internees, as the repatriates loudly blew the horn of loyalty to their home country and branded the others as traitors."

His tone was somber, even regretful: "Many discouragements

have been experienced and burdens have oftentimes seemed insurmountable." Given a chance, most of his employees made clear to O'Rourke they would never again work in an internment camp. "Admittedly, many mistakes have been made," said O'Rourke, "but we feel most have been corrected and that our operations have been consistent."

Finally, he offered advice. In the future, if the government decided to intern families of different nationalities, O'Rourke suggested creating separate camps for each nationality, rather than mixing Germans, Japanese, Italians, and other nationalities in one large camp. If that option proved too expensive, O'Rourke suggested strict segregation of nationalities into separate compounds within one large camp, which ironically was how Bergen-Belsen was organized in Germany. The problem with the mix of nationalities in Crystal City, O'Rourke noted, was that "they have very little in common and just are not compatible."

O'Rourke concluded that a family camp comprising enemy alien fathers who were involuntarily interned by the government and reunited with wives and children who were forced to volunteer for internment, was a flawed model and should not be repeated. The wives and children had volunteered under duress; they had lost their homes and had nowhere else to go. In effect, it was emotional blackmail. O'Rourke said he had watched "typical American boys and girls" develop deep feelings of betrayal by their government. Wives, too, became embittered. "We would caution extra careful consideration of evidence in the case of any woman, since our observation has formed the opinion that a woman, because of her usual emotional state, will generally develop an anti-American complex through internment, even if no such prior attitude existed."

His dry words, written as a bureaucratic duty, reflect the sentiments of a twentieth-century man, a career Border Patrol agent who year by year had observed the alienating effects of internment on women and children in Crystal City. His conclusion, preserved for posterity, was that the experiment of interning families of suspected nationalities—German, Japanese, Italians, and others—was a failure.

Nonetheless, near the end of the report O'Rourke could not resist an expression of sentiment for the majority of American-born children who had demonstrated loyalty to their country under the strains of internment. "This office greatly admires the children of interned parents who have weathered the storm of sentiment. We do not attempt to restrain our emotions when we see these children, many of whom are members of our military forces, visit their parents who are here as dangerous enemy aliens."

Even after the end of the war, internees were considered to be enemy aliens and continued to be repatriated, willingly or not. Many internees in Crystal City fought not to be deported. In June 1945, as O'Rourke was working on his report, a group of twenty-four Germans in Crystal City filed a lawsuit in opposition to the forced deportations. They argued that since the United States was no longer at war with Germany they could not be legally deported as enemy aliens. Though they ultimately lost the case in May 1946 in a hearing before the United States Court of Appeals in Washington, many other lawsuits by both German and Japanese internees challenged the constitutionality of their arrest and incarceration, an early indication of how blighted the legacy of American internment would become.

On September 8, 1945, Truman issued Proclamation 2655, which required any enemy alien considered dangerous to be repatriated, willingly or not. The first person in Crystal City deported under Truman's ruling was Fritz Kuhn, the American leader of the German Bund. In September 1945, the same month O'Rourke's report was delivered to the Alien Control Central Office, Kuhn boarded the *Antioch Victory* and sailed to Germany. O'Rourke was not unhappy about that as Kuhn had been a troublemaker in Crystal City.

But Truman's edict posed problems for the Department of Justice, the INS, and O'Rourke. How was O'Rourke to separate the "dangerous" internees in Crystal City from those who were not dangerous? What was the status of American-born wives and children? Were they to be deported as well? American military commanders in occupied Japan and Germany made clear that German and Japanese deportees from America weren't wanted; the local populations mistrusted them, and the military commanders already had their hands full. Nonetheless, O'Rourke was instructed by the INS commissioner Carusi to release internees that he thought were not dangerous, ship out those who had agreed to repatriate before the war was over, many of whom were now having second thoughts, and deport as many as possible to locations outside the United States.

O'Rourke's mandate from Washington was to encourage resistant deportees to end their fight. As an incentive for Japanese and German internees to leave camp, O'Rourke decided to close the German and Japanese schools, announcing the closure on January 24, 1946, in a brusque memorandum: "Since the necessity or desirability of this program no longer exists, these schools will be discontinued." By then, O'Rourke had the freedom to close the schools no matter what the parents thought. At the end of the war, Spain and Switzerland had withdrawn as the protecting powers for Japanese and German internees in Crystal City, so the internees had no "neutral power" to whom they could register their complaints. The German and Japanese camp schools were closed, and the few remaining German and Japanese students were transferred to the American schools.

Attorney General Tom Clark appointed O'Rourke chairman of a special hearing board in Crystal City to review the cases of internees, and decide if they should stay in Crystal City or be deported. In April 1946, hearings were held under tight security in crowded quarters. Transcripts were compiled.

One example was the case of Karl Eppeler, a forty-eight-year-old man born in Germany who had lived in the United States for twenty-three years, most of it in New York City. In 1930, Eppeler became a naturalized citizen, but his American citizenship was revoked in 1942 when the FBI arrested him as an enemy alien. His wife, a citizen of the United States, followed him to Crystal City. In July 1945, Eppeler had been placed on the list of repatriates to Germany and initially agreed to go. Now he had changed his mind and wanted to stay in the United States.

"Why did you change your mind?" O'Rourke asked moments after convening the hearing in his office.

"Well, the news that transpired during the last year or so brought my wife to the point where she just would not come along," replied Eppeler. "In all fairness, I must say she's right."

Eppeler also worried he would not be able to support himself and his wife in Germany: "I have been away from Germany for almost twenty-three years—I have no money. I see only one way to keep out of trouble in the future and to make a living in the future, and that is by becoming self-sufficient, and the only way I can see that is right here."

"Were you ever a member of the Nazi Party?" O'Rourke asked.

"No." Eppeler admitted that he'd belonged to the Bund from 1937 until its dissolution in 1941. His membership in the Bund was the reason his citizenship was revoked after he was arrested.

O'Rourke asked why Eppeler decided to become a naturalized citizen, and he replied, "I realized that I was going to stay here. I was married here and had quite a few friends and ties. To me that was the only logical way."

"You were a citizen. That citizenship was revoked and you were interned. Do you think you could live in this country and have respect for it after the way your case has developed? Have you formed any bitterness?"

Eppeler acknowledged his anger but explained it was harmless. "I don't think being mad is the same as bitterness. Don't you think a man who is born in this country sometimes has a gripe against the government—or a disagreement?"

"Don't you wish one side or another would win?" asked O'Rourke, pressing Eppeler to declare loyalty to either Germany or to the United States.

"I quit wishing long ago. I guess I am sort of a fatalist about this question."

In his written findings on Eppeler's hearing, dated August 26, 1946, O'Rourke noted that Eppeler's conduct in Crystal City had been satisfactory and his wife's US citizenship was a factor in his behalf and he gave Eppeler the benefit of the doubt. After three long years as officer in charge, O'Rourke still was capable of empathy. O'Rourke recommended that Eppeler's request to stay in the United States be granted and that he be paroled.

The Department of Justice rejected O'Rourke's suggestion. "I am troubled by your recommendation of release," wrote Thomas N. Cooley, one of Clark's assistants. Cooley did not believe that Eppeler's wife's American citizenship was reason enough to justify their release. Eppeler and his wife were involuntarily deported to Germany.

While internees like Eppeler were coming to terms with the decisions made for their future as the result of the hearings that O'Rourke conducted, other, younger internees were looking to the future they hoped to shape for themselves. In June 1946, only six students, the last graduating class of the Federal High School, walked across the stage of Harrison Hall and received their diplomas. The valedictorian of the class of 1946 was Barbara Minner, the only German in the six-person class. Barbara was the girlfriend of Eb Fuhr, whose family was also still interned in camp. Barbara and her family were not in danger of deportation and were scheduled for parole to New York not long after her graduation.

Barbara rehearsed her valedictorian's speech with Eb. He was in the audience on graduation night when Barbara stood behind the podium and delivered a thoughtful reflection on the hardships of confinement as well as her hopes for the future. "The graduation marks the climax in our lives; it is as though we, like wanderers through life, have reached a peak, a hill on which we can rest and look back upon the journey which has brought us to this point," said Barbara. "True enough, school and home life in recent years have not been the usual kind. But an internment camp has become a home to us and a camp school has furnished us with the educational structure for the future. But certainly these peculiarities, these very extraordinary circumstances, which have tinged our everyday lives could not change the educational ideals which school and home have inculcated in us."

The history of America is the history of overcoming hardships and that was never more true than during World War II. Despite what Barbara called "peculiarities," she emerged that night as a strong voice of American optimism. After four years of internment, Barbara and her parents had little future ahead of them in New York. Nonetheless, Barbara encouraged her classmates to recognize the strength they had acquired from the difficulties of internment in Crystal City. "Always along the way we have been able to meet the challenge of unfamiliar situations with confidence and the wise and patient guidance of parents and teachers," she said. "What they have given us thus far will be the backbone of the spiritual and mental life which lies ahead of us."

O'Rourke had always evinced a concern and affection for the young people in the camp, and Barbara Minner's inspiring speech must have given him a sense of accomplishment in his efforts to create educational opportunities for them. But not all stories ended so well as Barbara Minner's. Beyond the strategic and legal issues O'Rourke had to deal with in the process of phasing out the camp, there were profound emotional challenges involving individual cases.

Among the most tragic situations was the case of the Fukuda family from San Francisco. By the spring of 1946, the memorandum that O'Rourke had presented to Fukuda when the imposing Konko minister had arrived in Crystal City in January 1944, forbidding Fukuda from holding positions of power in camp, had long since been set aside. Fukuda had since served as principal of the Japanese School, worked as a printer and a projectionist, and delivered ice. To the remaining Japanese in camp, Fukuda had become unofficially known as the mayor of Crystal City.

Fukuda now faced a difficult war on two fronts: a legal battle to avoid deportation to Japan, and the medical crisis of his son Yoshiro. It had been almost two years since Yoshiro had been diagnosed with chronic kidney disease, and the ten-year-old boy had survived crisis after crisis. During the winter and spring of 1945, the camp newspaper carried a story about Yoshiro's need for transfusions, and many people had donated blood. On January 17, 1945, an abscessed tooth was pulled to remove an infection from the boy's body. On May 1945, Dr. Martin had performed a tonsillectomy for the same reason. Yoshiro was given large doses of vitamins.

In August 1945, Yoshiro returned to the Fukudas' bungalow, number 26 in the T section of camp. He weighed only forty-eight pounds. On Dr. Martin's orders, the boy ate a high-protein diet of meat, eggs, and fish. At dawn, the family carried him outside so that he could watch the sunrise. They gave him sponge baths, and when he complained of stomach pain they applied a hot-water bottle.

Nothing seemed to help. In Dr. Martin's case notes, he reported after a visit to the bungalow that Yoshiro "slept long periods" and was "very listless." He gave him a shot of penicillin and asked how he was feeling. "No complaints," responded Yoshiro. Though Dr. Martin warned Fukuda and his wife, Shinko, that Yoshiro's condition was critical, the family held out hope for many more months.

On March 11, 1946, Fukuda received a deportation order signed by Clark, the attorney general. Fukuda was not surprised. He had never hidden his personal loyalty to Japan. He was the embodiment of *Yamato Damashi*—faithfulness to the Japanese spirit and homeland. However, Fukuda continued his fight to stay in America. His children were all Americans, and he wanted to fulfill his mission to spread the Konko faith in America. He insisted that he was not— and never had been—a threat to America.

With his deportation order in hand, Fukuda went to O'Rourke and asked for help in gaining a reprieve. O'Rourke told Fukuda that he knew him to be a "good husband and father," but he could do nothing to keep him from being deported to Japan. The government's file on him was long and, in O'Rourke's words, "very unfavorable."

The following month, on April 26, 1946, Yoshiro caught a cold that escalated to pneumonia. Three days later, he returned to the camp hospital. Early the next morning, Yoshiro woke, asked the orderly for his father, and then lapsed into a coma. He died several days later, at 9:15 a.m. on May 1.

Shortly after the boy's death, O'Rourke came to Yoshiro's bedside, where Fukuda stood beside Dr. Martin. O'Rourke looked at Yoshiro's still body and his swollen face and told Fukuda how sorry he was for the loss. With three grown men standing over the bed of a small boy, it must have been difficult to distinguish the degrees of sorrow: that of the preacher from Japan whose God had taken his son, of the doctor who could not cure his patient's disease, or of the officer in charge who could not spare an American-born child the indignity of death behind a barbed-wire fence.

Two days later, a funeral was held for Yoshiro at Manifold Mortuary in Crystal City. Prior to the funeral, a photograph was taken in front of Harrison Hall of Fukuda, dressed in a dark suit; Shinko; their remaining six children; and a group of about thirty friends. The crowd of mourners stood behind large sprays of carnations. About 7:00 p.m. the group left the camp in several cars under armed guard and drove the short distance to the mortuary. Other drivers pulled to the side of the road, as is the custom in Texas, to allow the funeral caravan to pass. After a brief service, Fukuda left his son's body at the mortuary to be cremated and he and the others returned to camp.

When the ashes arrived, Fukuda kept them in his bungalow, with the intention of distributing them in San Francisco, if the family ever gained its release. One of the things that Fukuda grieved over the most was that his younger children—Yoshiro, now dead; another son, Hiroshi; Koichi, who had been born at the Tanforan Assembly Center; and Makiko, his only daughter—had no memories of San Francisco. "Instead of the beautiful greenery of Frisco, they have grown up behind the barbed wire and under the watch tower for so many years," he wrote. "To lose such a child as Yoshiro was indeed a major tragedy for my family."

On August 8, 1946, three months after Yoshiro's death, Fukuda sat down in his bungalow and wrote a formal petition for release from internment to the attorney general. Fukuda's tone was penitent: "I might have done many mistakes in my conduct and speech in the past which might have been taken to be too strong pro-Japanese. Now I understand that I should have been more careful to live in the foreign country, especially for the sake of my children who are all American citizens. It may be too late to wake up but please excuse me for all my faults in the past and release me to be able to educate my children at the public schools of San Francisco, which reopen at the end of August."

The petition was denied. Shortly afterward, Fukuda's two oldest sons—Michisuke, fifteen, and Nobusuke, fourteen—asked to be paroled from Crystal City so that they could return to San Francisco and resume their educations. O'Rourke approved the release, and on September 10, 1946, both of the older sons left Crystal City and returned to San Francisco. "It was difficult to leave our parents," recalled Nobusuke, "but my father wanted us to go back. We were behind in our education and needed to catch up."

Fukuda and fourteen other Japanese internees sought the help of Wayne Collins, a persistent defense lawyer in San Francisco who had become the national champion of Japanese internees. Collins filed a habeas corpus petition in federal court in Del Rio, Texas, not far from Crystal City, asking that all fifteen Japanese men be released on parole on the grounds that their internment was unconstitutional. The lawsuit bought Fukuda and the others time.

Meanwhile, Fukuda resumed his duties in the camp. He worked to find a way to keep the Japanese Peruvians who were in Crystal City from being deported to Japan. The government of Peru had refused to accept the Japanese immigrants back in the country, and many had already been exiled to Japan. "I no longer desired to leave behind in the camp those who were less fortunate," Fukuda wrote. "I wrote letters and petitions to the government requesting improvements in camp conditions. As a prison needs a religious minister, the camp needed me."

By then, large numbers of internees had been issued parole papers and had left camp. Each person who left was given instructions to report to the district director of the INS within twenty-four hours after their arrival in the city of their choice. Young men were required to notify draft boards. There were also odd new arrivals. In July 31, 1946, a group of three hundred Indonesian sailors was removed from a Dutch ship by immigration officers in New York and sent to Crystal City under "protective custody." The sailors, all of whom were Muslims, were prisoners and segregated in a deserted portion of the camp, isolated from the others in camp. They followed their religious customs, maintained their diet, and did hard labor in the camp, taking down abandoned Victory Huts and repairing roads, for which they were not paid. The camp at Crystal City was no longer a family camp, but the only internment camp still functioning as an incarceration facility for problem prisoners.

For the other internees, everyday life became more intolerable. The private kitchens in bungalows were no longer allowed. Everyone was required to eat in a main mess hall in the center of camp. Shinko, Fukuda's wife, was bedridden after Yoshiro's death with grief and illness. Her friends and remaining children had to bring her meals to her. In the camp hospital, three Japanese Peruvians were admitted with tuberculosis, which triggered a wave of fear throughout the camp and overwhelmed Dr. Martin and his small staff.

In early January 1947, O'Rourke received a telegram from headquarters, reassigning him as deputy operations director of the INS office in Kansas City, Missouri. The job in Kansas City offered freedom from the isolation of Crystal City and a significant pay raise to $9,560, more than $2,000 higher than what he then received. O'Rourke and Mary left Crystal City on January 31, 1947. He drove his Studebaker into town, past the statue of Popeye, and sped onto a two-lane highway headed for San Antonio and then, dust in his rearview mirror, drove north toward Kansas City.

With Mary in the passenger seat, O'Rourke followed the old Chisholm Trail that was used by cowboys in the nineteenth century to drive cattle from Texas to market in Kansas City. Arriving there on February 4, 1947, O'Rourke reported for work in his new, less complicated job.

L. T. McCollister, the former operations officer who replaced O'Rourke as acting officer in charge in Crystal City, faced a dilemma: he was under orders to close the camp by 1948 and had no solution for the Japanese, Japanese Peruvians, or Germans who were still there.

In Crystal City, only 108 Germans were left, including Eb Fuhr, his brother Julius, and his parents Carl and Anna. The Fuhr brothers worked on a crew that disassembled buildings in the Japanese section. The prefabricated Victory Huts were made of panel sections bolted together in sequence. After the huts were dismantled, the Fuhr brothers took them to nearby Border Patrol stations, where the Victory Huts were refitted with roofs. Border Patrol agents used them to house aliens arrested for illegally crossing the border from Mexico.

The Fuhr family was scheduled for deportation, but was still fighting to stay in the United States. By then, more than two hundred habeas corpus lawsuits had been filed by German internees, including the Fuhrs, to set aside deportations. The argument in these cases was the same advanced by Collins for the Japanese—that is, their homeland, in this case Germany, was no longer an enemy of the United States and thus German citizens could not be classified as enemy aliens. In late 1946, all of the lawsuits were consolidated into one case, the Schlueter case. A federal court judge in New York ruled against the plaintiffs and affirmed Truman's order. On January 3, 1947, the *New York Times* reported that, based on the court's decision, seven hundred Germans, including the Fuhr family, would immediately be deported.

In April the Fuhr family was ordered to Ellis Island for deportation. They took a train to New York, and arrived at Ellis Island, where Eb and his family were confined with 207 other German deportees in one massive room. Eb recalled that the confinement on Ellis Island was worse than at Crystal City. "We did a lot of talking and card playing and mostly a lot of waiting," he said. "In Crystal City, we worked outside. In Ellis Island, we had little exercise. It was crowded and the atmosphere was tense." Once a week, however, Barbara, his sweetheart from Crystal City, visited him at Ellis Island, and in the presence of armed guards, the couple planned their future.

Suddenly, on July 24, 1947, the US Senate passed a bill that called for an end to all deportations at Ellis Island. Two months later, the attorney general began granting releases to those in custody on Ellis Island, two and a half years after Germany surrendered. In mid-September new hearings were held for the prisoners. Eb, who remembered his hearing in Cincinnati, when his interrogator asked irrational questions about Nazi submarines coming up the Ohio River, wondered what he would be asked on Ellis Island. He entered the hearing room with dread. "From the first moment, I knew this one was different," recalled Eb. "They weren't looking for reasons to keep me there. The questions were fair." The hearing lasted only ten minutes.

When he walked out of the room, his brother Julius was waiting for his own hearing. "Don't worry," said Eb. "We're out of here. This is all over."

Two weeks later, the Fuhr family were handed release orders from Ellis Island and told their train tickets to Cincinnati would be given to them the following morning. The Fuhr brothers asked if they could leave immediately. The official said yes, and their parents told their sons they would stay and wait for the tickets. Carl and Anna Fuhr understood: Eb and Julius couldn't bear internment one minute longer. Within a half hour, both of them were on the Liberty Ferry to New York City.

Eb called Barbara from a pay phone in Battery Park, and she hurried to meet him. Eb was seventeen when he was interned and twenty-two when he was released. "No one can appreciate the intense terror of government power and the despair of hopelessness that we felt behind that barbed-wire fence," Eb said. "By the same token, no one can appreciate the thrilling sense of freedom I felt when it was over."

A year after his release, Eb and Barbara were married. In a photograph taken that day, Barbara, slender and dressed in a shiny white satin dress, and Eb, in a dark suit, rush arm-in-arm out of the church together. Eb's dark hair is slicked back and his face creased by a wide grin.

In the summer of 1947, while the Fuhrs were in the process of winning their freedom, the struggle was still on for the few remaining internees in Crystal City. Collins, Fukuda's attorney, had filed several lawsuits in California to stop the deportations of the Japanese Peruvians in an effort to delay their removal. Finally the INS in Washington, DC, settled on a solution—if the Japanese Peruvians in Crystal City found US sponsors who would secure jobs for them and a place to live, they could be paroled, not deported.

Fukuda told McCollister that the Konko Church in San Francisco would sponsor the remaining Japanese Peruvians. On September 22, 1947, McCollister received a letter from a leader in Fukuda's church, assuring him that church members would house the Japanese Peruvians, find them jobs, and comply with any other governmental requirements of sponsorship. Meanwhile, the lawsuit in Del Rio involving Fukuda and fourteen other plaintiffs remained unresolved. The strategy of delay had worked. McCollister agreed to release Fukuda and the other plaintiffs into the custody of Collins and they were all paroled.

At long last, on September 25, 1947, Fukuda, Shinko, and their four younger children—Saburo, Makiko, Hiroshi, and Koichi—left Crystal City. Others paroled that day, including the Japanese Peruvians, and the fourteen other plaintiffs in the Collins lawsuit, departed the camp in a bus. As a sign of respect for the loss of Yoshiro, Fukuda and his family were transported to the train station in a passenger car provided by McCollister. For Fukuda, the departure was bittersweet. Of his internment, Fukuda wrote, "I might have done many mistakes in the past, but five and a half years of confinement and misfortune may be enough to punish my faults."

Those paroled boarded a train and were given their own Pullman car. As the train pounded the rails, Fukuda reflected on all he and many others had lost: he was destitute, weary from confinement, uncertain about his ability to propagate his faith, and felt guilty that his arrest had inadvertently cost Yoshiro his life. All of the rest of his life, Fukuda considered Yoshiro a victim of internment.

The train trip took three days. When Fukuda arrived in his old neighborhood in San Francisco, Japantown had completely changed. After the Japanese had been evacuated in 1942, new African American arrivals from the American South moved in. In months Japantown became San Francisco's Harlem. The Konko church on Bush Street had been converted to a twelve-unit apartment building occupied by black families. During a meeting with tenants, Fukuda explained that he and many other church members had been interned because of their race and asked the families to relocate. To his surprise, every one of the black families agreed, found new places to live, and the property was restored as a Konko church. Seven days after his return, Fukuda held a religious service in the church.

On February 27, 1948, the camp in Crystal City officially closed, five years and three months after it opened. Radio Station KYZQ— Crystal City's station—was dismantled. The flag was taken down. The barbed-wire fence was removed, as were the guard towers. From its inception through June 30, 1945, Crystal City interned 4,751 enemy aliens and their families. Records were not kept after 1945, but in the remaining three years more than a thousand additional internees were received and later paroled, repatriated, or deported. In all, approximately six thousand American citizens and immigrants from other countries—ordinary people—endured confinement because of an overzealous government, widespread public fear of traitors, and a game of barter: "our" internees in America for "their" internees in Axis countries.

The fundamental questions of citizenship, the status of aliens—indeed the definition of who is and who is not an American—are perennial. The travesty in Crystal City, as O'Rourke implied in his report, is that in the effort to win the war that threatened the existence of the country, these and other constitutional questions were set aside. The heart of the problem was found in a provision of the Alien Enemies Act. Anyone of German, Japanese, or Italian ancestry, regardless of citizenship, was viewed as a perceived enemy. The cost to civil liberties was high. No one knew that better O'Rourke, Harrison, and others who worked in the camp and whose persistence and sense of fair play somewhat mitigated the injustice—except of course to the internees themselves, whose lives were torn asunder.

CHAPTER TWENTY-ONE

The Train from Crystal City

The men, women, and children of Crystal City were unsure what would happen to them after the war, but as with many of the "greatest generation," they imagined that the next chapters of their lives would be better. Few of them, however, lived lives unmarked by Crystal City. Many carried the weight and suffering of the memory of their years of internment with them for the rest of their lives.

The small white house in Castro Valley, California, fifteen miles from Oakland, where Sumi lives is on a cul-de-sac and shaded by a large magnolia tree in the front yard. Inside the front door the living room's wooden floor is scrubbed clean. Hanging from rails on two doors in the living room are two banners, emblazoned with CRYSTAL CITY INTERNMENT CAMP. From the kitchen, eighty-four-year-old Sumi steps through the folds of the Crystal City banner and emerges with a slight stoop. Her hair, which she wore in thick, dark pigtails as a teenager in Crystal City, is now grayed and cut short, like a silver bowl around her head. Her clear brown eyes, which for years have appraised the world coolly, now give the guarded expression of perhaps having seen too much.

"It was wartime," Sumi said as she sat at her kitchen table, a large bowl of blueberries in front of her. "I was very angry that they arrested my father, that we lost everything, and that I was sent to Japan. It was humiliating. But let's face it: Mama was right. War doesn't make any sense." More than six decades after the end of World War II, Sumi remains haunted by certain euphemisms: *evac-*

uation, which was in reality forced removal from her home; *internment*, which she experienced as prison.

After her graduation from Fairfax High School in Los Angeles in the summer of 1948, survival was her first priority. Two local colleges offered Sumi art scholarships, but she was undecided about her next step. Into this vacuum stepped Kiyo Shimatsu, a returning veteran from the famed all–Japanese American 442nd Regimental Combat Team.

Prior to the war, Kiyo's father and Sumi's father were friends. The fathers were from the same prefecture of Japan and knew each other in California. Both Sumi and Kiyo were interned at the same time at the relocation camp in Heart Mountain, Wyoming. While in Heart Mountain, Kiyo enlisted in the 442nd and served in both Italy and Germany. After the war, Kiyo returned to California and sought out Sumi in Los Angeles. Within a few months, he asked her to marry him. As was the custom of nisei children, Sumi wrote to her parents in Japan and asked for permission. Her father immediately gave his unqualified permission, but her mother, Nobu, had an intuition that Kiyo was "unlucky" and urged Sumi to delay the engagement.

Nonetheless, just past her twentieth birthday, Sumi married Kiyo in a small ceremony in a Christian church. She walked down the aisle in a long silk gown loaned to her by Mrs. Stern, her former employer. "I know Kiyo loved me, but I think the reason I decided to marry him wasn't love. It was security," recalled Sumi as she sat at her kitchen table. "I wanted to find a place where I could feel a part of a family again, instead of working for someone else."

They settled in Los Angeles, where Sumi graduated from the Los Angeles College of Chiropractic and opened her own practice. Before that, Sumi worked nights at a Security National Bank as a check sorter. They had six children: Robin, Derick, Nicola, Dion, Paula, and Lukas. By the 1950s, Kiyo had contacts with various film and television producers in Hollywood. A few of those producers hired Sumi's children as extras and gave them bit parts in various films, including Elvis Presley's *Blue Hawaii*, John Ford's *Seven Women*, and ironically Jeffrey Hunter's World War II film, *Hell to Eternity.*

In 1953, Tokiji and Nobu returned from Japan and settled in Los Angeles. For the first time since Pearl Harbor, Sumi felt secure. Her parents lived close by and she had her own large, busy family. Like other suburban American women during the 1950s, Sumi managed multiple roles: wife, mother, and her own chiropractic practice.

Years passed and Nobu's hunch about Kiyo proved true. In 1969, at the age of forty-seven, Kiyo suffered his first heart attack. Three years later, Kiyo died of a heart attack, and Sumi became the sole support for her six children. She continued to work at her chiropractic practice and built it into a thriving business. Her main clients were the skycaps and baggage handlers who worked at Los Angeles International Airport and, as a consequence of their physically demanding jobs, suffered from chronic back and shoulder pain. In addition to chiropractic remedies, Sumi offered her clients the kind of Reiki therapy that her aunt Tetsu had taught her during the difficult days in Japan after the war. Sumi practiced until she was seventy. She attributed her success to the ancient values of her parents. "I had the inherited spirit of *gaman* from my issei parents," she recalled. "Their perseverance was my greatest gift."

Crystal City was never far from Sumi's mind, or those of her parents. When her father was in his nineties, Sumi said that he often placed his clothes and personal items from his drawers—his billfold, keys, and pocket change—inside his pillowcase. It was a flashback to his internment, when he stored those items the same way. When Sumi or one of her older sisters asked him what he was doing, Tokiji became agitated and told them that he might be moved to another camp. "It was difficult to watch," recalled Sumi. "He never wanted to be caged in another camp."

In 1980, Sumi attended the first reunion of friends from Crystal City in Los Angeles and surrounding cities, held at Knotts Berry Farm, a theme park in Southern California. Thirty-seven years after

315

her arrival in Crystal City, Sumi reconnected with many of those friends who shared the stigma and suffering of internment. Many had never talked about their experiences. Over several hours, they shared memories of school days, daily counts, family dinners in the bungalows, and the lingering, injurious effects of the war. A bond of support was formed. After the reunion, Sumi started a newsletter called the *Crystal City Chatter*, which she published from her home—at first she wrote it on an IBM typewriter and later on a computer. In time, the *Chatter's* mailing list grew to more than two thousand, and it is now the main source of connection among the nisei survivors of Crystal City, providing notices of birthdays and deaths, plans for future reunions, and ongoing news of internment issues.

In 1985, a granite monument designed by Alan Taniguchi, former dean of the school of architecture at the University of Texas, was placed in Crystal City under the marker CRYSTAL CITY CONCENTRATION CAMP. An inscription on the monument read in part, "This marker is situated on an original site of a two-family cottage as a reminder that the injustices and humiliations suffered here as a result of hysteria, racism and discrimination never happen again." Taniguchi's marker referenced only the Japanese experience in the camp. The Germans and Italians from North America and Latin America who were interned in Crystal City were not mentioned, even though their experiences in camp were virtually the same. Thirty-seven years after the closing of the camp, the intense rivalries between the German and Japanese internees continued to hold sway.

In November 1997, Sumi returned to Crystal City with sixty former Japanese internees to celebrate the fiftieth anniversary of the closing of the camp. The reunion was well timed. During the 1960s, Mexican Americans in Crystal City had organized against the racially exclusionary politics they suffered under Anglo-minority political and educational control. Jose Angel Gutierrez, one of the founders of the Chicano political party La Raza Unida, was elected county judge in 1970, and it was Gutierrez who had encouraged

Taniguchi to design the granite marker. After fifty years, the ghosts of all that had happened during the war in Crystal City were ready to be confronted.

City Manager Miguel Delgado and a coterie of other city officials met Sumi and the others at the San Antonio Airport. On the bus ride, sixty-five-year-old Toni Tomita, interned in camp as a nine-year-old in 1942, led the group in the "Shojodan," a Girl Scout song. Seven miles from Crystal City, an official police escort joined the former internees, now treated as VIPs. Sumi and Toni stared out the window; both had knots in their stomach as they remembered the fear of their original bus ride into the camp in Crystal City. Instead of the hateful signs and anti-Jap jeers they had received during the war, the streets of Crystal City that day were lined with smiling spectators.

A parade was staged in their honor. The high school band marched, beauty queens waved from floats, and students from the Benito Juarez Elementary School depicted the well-known Japanese story *Sadako and the Thousand Paper Cranes*, with predominantly Mexican American students dressed as origami cranes.

Finally the internees, many in their seventies and eighties and three participants in their nineties, arrived on a grassy field where the camp once stood. None of the 694 buildings that had once dotted the landscape remained. On the footprint of the former camp were several public schools, built by the Crystal City school district. Taniguchi's granite monument was the only testimony to what the Japanese had experienced. Sadness descended on the group when they walked to the site where the 250-foot-wide circular swimming pool once was the center of social activity in camp. They paused to pay silent tribute to the two Japanese Peruvians girls who had drowned in the pool. In a nearby city cemetery, the graves of other internees who'd died in the camp, many of them German, were unmarked.

Waves of melancholy swept over Sumi and the others as they searched for a deeper understanding of how they and their parents found the resilience to endure imprisonment in an American internment camp. "I wanted to come back because I wanted to remember," recalled Sumi. "For fifty years I carried the weight of the war on my shoulders. The reunion brought resolution. We had all survived and were still together. I felt lighter."

During the ceremony at the abandoned camp site, the city manager gave all of the Japanese Americans symbolic keys to the city. Sumi offered the best line: "I wish I had this key when I was in the camp. Maybe I could have gotten out of here."

Many more reunions followed the first one in Crystal City. Every May for the last several years, Sumi and a group of thirty or more of her Crystal City friends from Los Angeles have taken an eight-hour bus trip to the California Hotel, a down-at-the-heels hotel in the old part of Las Vegas, located far from the expensive, glittering hotels on the famous Strip. The bus ride to Las Vegas is a sunny, nonstop social scene. People play cards and bingo. Mas Okabe, who made the trip to Japan in 1945 with Sumi, pours the wine. Toni Tomita passes cookies. Inside the hotel, the casino is shopworn, but no one seems to mind. The casino has it all: blackjack, poker, keno. They look forward to the Hawaiian lunches, the oxtail soup, and juicy rib-eye steaks, to say nothing of shared memories as survivors of Crystal City.

At the reunion in May 2012, Sumi stood hunched over a slot machine. On her head, she wore a Mickey Mouse cap with a generous visor that shielded her eyes. One of her daughters, Paula, stood nearby. All of Sumi's six children have college degrees and live in California. Nobu, her mother, died at eighty, and her father, Tom, died at ninety-seven. Over the *cha-ching* sounds of the slot machines, Sumi remembered her parents: "I was lucky enough to be brought up by the right parents. They suffered during the war more than I did and learned to be strong. Now I'm an old woman, and a tough cookie."

Upon Fukuda's return to San Francisco on September 29, 1947, he confronted the task of rebuilding his church on Bush Street and starting Konko churches elsewhere in America. Soon, he dispatched ministers that founded Konko churches in Fresno, Sacramento, San Jose, and other cities. Of the fourteen existing Konko churches in America, Fukuda had a direct hand in the formation of ten.

Despite all that he endured during the war, Fukuda became a US citizen in 1951. Six years later, Fukuda wrote a personal petition to President Eisenhower asking for redress and compensation of losses for Japanese and Japanese Americans interned during World War II. In the conclusion of his petition to Eisenhower, Fukuda wrote, "I am proud to be an American. I wish to hear the voice of conscience in this country, which stands on the principles of liberty, equality, justice and brotherly love." He never received a response from Eisenhower and died of a heart attack in San Francisco on December 6, 1957.

His wife, Shinko, became head minister at the church, and all of his six surviving children took his death hard. Makiko, his only daughter, took the loss the hardest. All her life she'd tried to please her father, to make good grades, and perhaps earn the kind of attention and love Fukuda felt in Crystal City for his dying son, Yoshiro. During church services, Makiko, a flashy dresser, would sit in the back row and during her father's long-winded sermons call out in English, "Time to wrap it up!"

On a cold night on November 8, 1961, Makiko, who had by then been married for a year, took a walk toward the Golden Gate Bridge. Makiko, who years before as a small child had tugged at her mother's dark coat while posing for a photograph for Dorothea Lange, climbed onto a railing, jumped into the icy water, and died. In interviews, Makiko's surviving brothers—Nobusuke, Saburo, Koichi, and Hiroshi—said that the family never knew the exact motive for Makiko's suicide. However, they noted numerous studies that indicate that many nisei who were incarcerated at a young age, as the Fukuda children had been, suffered lingering feelings of betrayal by their government, shame, and depression that extended well past the war. According to her brothers, Makiko fit that pattern. They consider her death a ripple effect from the war.

319

Shinko continued to serve as minister of the Konko Church until her death on April 3, 1972. At sunrise that morning, she got off a bus on Geary Street and was struck by a driver who was blinded by the sun. Shinko was sixty-six. "Both of our parents lived their lives practicing *gaman*—patience and resilience," said Nobusuke, the second-born son. "They never wasted anything—not food, time, or anger. Instead, they waited for things to work out." Today, the Konko Church, in which the Fukuda sons remain active, serves about one hundred families in Japantown.

Neither Fukuda nor Shinko lived to see the nation's official attempt at redress. Fukuda's petition was filed thirty-one years before President Ronald Reagan formally apologized on August 10, 1988, for the mass incarceration of Japanese and Japanese Americans. Congress appropriated $37 million for restitution, and Japanese American survivors were awarded $20,000 per person.

In June 1996, a class-action suit was filed in federal district court in Los Angeles on behalf of the twenty-two hundred Latin Americans of Japanese descent who were deported to the United States during World War II and were forcibly interned on the orders of FDR. Many of those who filed the suit, including Carmen Mochizuki and Alice Nishimoto, were former Crystal City internees.

The lawsuit requested the same redress that Japanese Americans received under the Civil Liberties Act of 1988, signed by Reagan: a formal apology and $20,000 in reparations. The Justice Department, under President Bill Clinton, argued that the Japanese taken from Latin America were not citizens upon their arrival on US soil and entered the country as illegal immigrants. "The argument was as bizarre as it was false," said Carmen. "After all, we were abducted by the American military, brought here on American ships, and many Japanese Peruvians from Crystal City were used as hostages in prisoner exchanges." The lawsuit, *Carmen Mochizuki v. the United States of America*, was settled with a formal apology from the government and $5,000 per person for Japanese Latin American survivors, $15,000 less than Japanese Americans received.

• • •

The postwar paths of US officials involved in the fraught history of internment at Crystal City were variously impacted. Some stayed silent about their part while others formally recanted.

After the war, Joseph O'Rourke continued his contact with some of the internees from Crystal City. After Fukuda became a citizen, O'Rourke traveled to San Francisco and had dinner with him and other former issei internees at Yamato Restaurant in Japantown. By then O'Rourke was director of the INS office in Kansas City, a job he held until his retirement. He and Mary, his second wife, then moved to Dallas, where they settled in a midcentury home on McFarlin Boulevard in University Park, a tree-lined neighborhood not far from downtown.

O'Rourke died at sixty-two on April 5, 1959, of a heart attack. A funeral mass was held at a small Catholic chapel in Dallas. Though his daughter, Joan, was listed as a survivor, they never reconciled, and she did not attend the funeral. O'Rourke is buried in Restland Cemetery.

During the postwar period, Harrison, a lawyer and civic leader in Philadelphia, devoted himself to civil rights issues. He continued to press his proposal for the settlement of Jews in Palestine. Historians have credited the Harrison Report as having laid the groundwork for US support for the state of Israel. In 1946, Harrison testified on behalf of Heman Marion Sweatt, a black student who was denied admission to the University of Texas Law School.

Harrison left no record of what he thought about the efficacy of the Crystal City Internment Camp. His son Barton speculated his father would most likely have been conflicted. "I think that he would have been comfortable and proud of the fact that the camp was mixed nationalities and reunited families. He would have been in favor of that and proud of the accomplishment," said Barton. "I'm not sure he would have supported the trades, especially of American children, but he would probably have concluded that it was his job to run the camp and the State Department's job to handle the exchanges."

On July 28, 1955, while on a trip to a remote camp operated by Quakers in the Adirondacks, Harrison suffered a heart attack and died at the age of fifty-six. His funeral was held at Race Street Meeting House in Philadelphia. His three sons—Paul, Barton, and Earl—were in college or graduate school at the time of his death. Paul later became a surgeon. Barton followed his father as a Philadelphia lawyer. After graduation from Yale Divinity School, Earl became headmaster of Westtown School in Philadelphia and later head of the Sidwell Friends School in Washington, DC. "We used to joke that all we needed was one more brother—an undertaker—and together we'd be able to take care of any family situation," Barton recalled.

As attorney general, Francis Biddle acquiesced to Franklin Roosevelt's decision to intern Japanese, German, and Italian immigrants in the United States, but regretted his part in the internment for the rest of his life. In his autobiography, Biddle wrote that the program was "ill-advised, unnecessary and unnecessarily cruel."

After Roosevelt died, Truman appointed Biddle as the leading American judge at the International Military Tribunal at Nuremberg. As Biddle sat in court, lawyers for Nazi war criminals attempted to justify their concentration camps by pointing out that the United States operated internment camps. In addition, the German lawyers invoked US Supreme Court decisions, including the pivotal 1944 case *Korematsu v. the United States*, in which Hugo Black, the liberal leader of the court, writing for the six-to-three majority, legalized the American camps in disregard of the Bill of Rights.

Tom Clark, Biddle's successor as attorney general, later publicly apologized for his part in the internment. On December 7, 1941, he became civilian coordinator of the evacuation of the Japanese from the West Coast. Truman later named him to the Supreme Court. After his resignation from the Court in 1967, Clark purged his conscience. "I have made a lot of mistakes in my life. One is my part in the evacuation of the Japanese from California in 1942. . . . I don't think that served any purpose at all. . . . We picked them up and put them in concentration camps. That's the truth of the matter. And as I look back on it—although at the time I argued the case—I am amazed that the Supreme Court ever approved it."

On May 8, 1945, V-E Day, Eleanor Roosevelt listened to the radio as Truman, Churchill, and Stalin announced the surrender of Germany. Later, she confessed to a friend, "It was sad Franklin couldn't have announced it." In December 1945, Truman telephoned Eleanor in New York and asked her to serve as a member of the American delegation to the first United Nations General Assembly in London. Eleanor debated the offer for several days, but finally accepted the position.

During her highly public second career as a leader in the United Nations, Eleanor devoted the next twenty years of her life to human rights for Jews in Europe, and for blacks and women in the United States. At the time of her death on November 7, 1962, she was consistently voted in international polls as "the most admired person in the world."

Upon his deportation to Germany on September 11, 1945, Fritz Kuhn, formerly the leader of the Bund in America, returned a defeated man to a defeated country. He was imprisoned at the infamous Hohenasperg Prison, located near Stuttgart, for more than a year. Upon his release, Kuhn moved to Munich and lived with his wife, Elsa, and their two children, Walter and Waltraut, in a poor neighborhood. "He will now, like other Germans, have to live on 1,275 calories per day," gloated one newspaper account.

When Kuhn died at fifty-five on December 14, 1951, the *New York Times* described him as "a poor and obscure chemist, unheralded and unsung."

In contrast, Bert Shepard, the young P-38 pilot who repatriated to America during the exchange that included the Eiserloh family, returned wounded but unbowed. Shepard lost his leg when his plane was gunned down near Berlin, but while a prisoner of war he trained himself to walk with an artificial leg. Prior to the war, Shepard, a left-handed pitcher, played in the minor leagues. During the long, difficult days in a POW camp, Shepard continued to practice his pitching.

When he returned to the United States in late January 1945, Shepard went out for spring training, and the Washington Senators hired him as a pitching coach. On August 4, 1945, only seven months after Shepard left Germany, he was on the field when the Senators played game two of a fourth consecutive doubleheader against the Red Sox. In the fourth inning, the Senators trailed the Red Sox 14–2. The manager of the Senators made the call to the bullpen for Shepard to enter the game in relief with the bases loaded and two outs. Shepard took the mound, threw a few warm-up pitches, and then struck out his first batter, ending the inning with the bases loaded. He pitched five and a half innings of impressive relief, allowing three hits and one run. While the Red Sox won the game 15–4, the crowd went wild for Shepard, a hero in baseball as well as in World War II. Instead of a laurel, they crowned Shepard, the first man with an artificial leg to pitch in a major league game, with a standing ovation and wholehearted applause.

After Eb Fuhr married his Crystal City sweetheart, Barbara, in 1948, the couple moved to the Midwest. Barbara worked as a secretary and put Eb through college and an MBA program at Ohio State University in Columbus. After graduation, he was hired as a salesman for the Shell Oil Company and had a successful business career. He applied for citizenship, but because he had been interned in Crystal City, the process took seven years. No one could understand why he was interned. Finally in 1955 he was naturalized. After he retired from the Shell Oil Company he began to speak in public about his experience and that of other Germans in Crystal City. Although the abuse of the rights of the Japanese and Japanese Americans has been well documented, Eb was angry that the consequences of the government's internment of more than ten thousand German and German American civilians had never been acknowledged. "This shameful chapter in American history did not just happen to the

Japanese," he said. "I was a kid when I was arrested. I hadn't done anything wrong. Our family, one of the last to leave Crystal City, paid a very heavy price. All ethnicities, including Germans, who were wrongly held as prisoners deserve redress." After fifty-six years of marriage, Barbara, who shared his frustration over the government's refusal to make amends, died in 2004.

After the Civil Liberties Act that granted reparations to the Japanese was passed in 1988, Arthur Jacobs, a German American who was in Crystal City with Fuhr, filed a class-action lawsuit. Jacobs charged the act ignored German and German American enemy aliens and their families who had been treated the same in Crystal City. The Jacobs lawsuit contended that Germans were discriminated against on the basis of their ethnicity as Germans and as children of Germans. The US Court of Appeals in Washington, DC, turned down Jacobs's lawsuit on the grounds that the Japanese were detained on the basis of their race, while Germans were detained in smaller numbers based on potential security risks. Since then, numerous bills have been filed in Congress calling for the establishment of a commission to review the treatment of Germans and German Americans who were interned, but none of the bills have passed. Like Fuhr and the Eiserloh family, Jacobs continues to press for the US government to acknowledge the internment of German immigrants and their children between 1941 and 1948.

The world into which Ingrid was dragged with her loved ones on January 8, 1942, the date of her father's arrest, engulfed her. While Johanna, her mother, Lothar, her brother, and Ensi, her sister, found ways over the years to redeem the past, the other three members of the family—Ingrid; her father, Mathias; and her younger brother, Guenther, never did. For those three, the calamity never ended.

When Ingrid and Lothar returned to the United States in 1947, under the guardianship of Mathias's sister, they settled in the Los Angeles area. At seventeen, Ingrid briefly enrolled as a high school junior in Reseda, a community in Los Angeles, but was too far behind in her studies to excel and dropped out. Her early dream of studying music vanished. Instead, she worked as a housekeeper for two families in Beverly Hills. In her spare time, she rode horses in Reseda and in time purchased a mare named Dolly, who had a star on her forehead. One of her friends in the riding group introduced her to Mack Leetham, a twenty-one-year-old private in the Army. They married when Ingrid was only nineteen years old.

On November 15, 1948, Mathias Eiserloh, who was still in Germany, filed the first of many applications for a reentry visa from the Immigration and Naturalization Service for himself, Johanna, and the two younger children, Ensi and Guenther. The request was repeatedly denied.

After graduating from Van Nuys High School in Los Angeles, Lothar joined the US Air Force. Given his success with the American GIs in Idstein, the choice of a military career seemed inevitable. He trained as a pilot and in 1955 was granted a top-security clearance to receive nuclear-weapons training. Perhaps because of Lothar's valued status, his parents and two younger siblings were finally granted visas and returned to the United States later in 1955.

When they arrived at Ingrid's home, it had been almost nine years since they had last seen each other. By then, Ingrid had two daughters: Diana, five years old, and Debbie, a one-year-old. Ingrid later had a son, Darrell. "When Dad got out of the car, I was startled by how thin he was," recalled Ingrid. "Then Mom, Ensi, and Guenther got out, and I grabbed her and we were all crying and laughing at the same time."

By then, Mathias was sixty years old and could not find work as a civil engineer. He took a low-paying job as a draftsman at a bridge company near Los Angeles and purchased a small tract home about fifty miles from Ingrid's home. Two years later, he and Johanna purchased a coffee shop in downtown Los Angeles, but the restaurant failed. Johanna took odd jobs as a maid in a small hotel and as a seamstress. At family gatherings, no one talked about what had happened during the war. However, Mathias was anxious and always looking over his shoulder. He didn't want to be reminded of the past. "By then," recalled Lothar, "my father was a broken man."

One evening in 1960, Mathias went to a corner grocery store to buy cigarettes and groceries. He had a heart attack, collapsed, and died in the store at age sixty-five. Ingrid, Lothar, and Ensi scraped together the money to cover the cost of their father's funeral. By then, Ensi had graduated from high school and worked odd jobs. She had hoped to go to college, but instead secured a real-estate license and went to work full-time.

Life was not kind to Guenther, who was born on the train from Crystal City to Jersey City in January 1945 as his family headed to Germany. After he graduated from high school, he enlisted in the Navy but neglected to follow orders and was discharged. At the age of twenty-three, he was an ironworker in New Jersey, earning union wages. Returning home late one night, Guenther failed to negotiate a traffic circle; his car jumped the curb and hit a tree head-on, and Guenther was instantly killed.

On November 19, 1961, a year after Mathias's death, Johanna became a US citizen. Her citizenship, according to Ensi, was a partial absolution from her family's mistreatment during the war. However, Ensi said Johanna found it a bitter pill to swallow when she read newspaper articles about the Japanese internment with no mention of the Germans who were also interned. "That's what brought my mother to tears," recalled Ensi. "It made her feel invisible—like a nonentity—as far as the internment saga goes."

At eighty-nine Johanna developed Alzheimer's disease. Ensi, who took care of her, was grateful for her mother's loss of long-term memory because she no longer remembered the trauma of the war. In time, she forgot she was ever married to Mathias. "One day she picked up a signed photograph of Ronald Reagan and his wife, Nancy, that had been sent to her because my mom was a Reagan volunteer," recalled Ensi. "She looked at it, pointed to Nancy, and asked, 'What's that woman doing with my husband?'" Johanna died in January 1997 at ninety-five years of age.

Ingrid and her mother never fully reconciled their differences. By the time Johanna died, Ingrid had had three children and was divorced from her husband. To support her children, she'd worked as a waitress and eventually remarried, but divorced again. Ensi also had multiple marriages and has one son, Kevin. "I harbored a deep, lingering sorrow about my German roots and the memories of what happened to our family," Ensi said. "It crippled me for years." Eventually she became a fervent Christian, which has brought her a measure of peace. She lives with her son in an apartment in Anaheim, California.

The only member of the family who flourished was Lothar. He met his wife, Carole, at UCLA in Los Angeles and was married in August 1959. Later, he graduated from San Francisco State University with a degree in political science. Carole earned both a bachelor's and a master's degree in education and worked for many years as a teacher. Over their long marriage, they have raised two sons, Eric and Kris, and divide their time between San Francisco and Maui, where they own several residential properties. "My father would sometimes ask me, 'Why did this happen to us?'" said Lothar. "I couldn't give him an answer. It destroyed a lot of my family. All I knew was that from the moment I left Germany, I was on my own. It was my job to stay alive, build and maintain my own family."

Like many internees, Ingrid did not often talk of her experiences during World War II. A few times she ventured to tell friends what had happened to her family in Crystal City and in Germany, and they found it hard to believe. Her fear of the government's power increased with age, and she, like her father, lived her later years constantly looking over her shoulder. The sign on Ingrid's bedroom door in Honolulu said a lot about what she thought of government surveillance: "If you can't afford a doctor, go to an airport—you'll get a free X-ray and a breast exam, and if you mention Al Qaeda, you'll get a free colonoscopy."

Yet over two years, Ingrid sat for long interviews for this book. We pored over government documents—her father's FBI file, her family's files from Crystal City, and the January 1945 exchange—establishing a sequence of events. "I'd like to make some sense of all this," she said.

Prior to an interview with Ingrid in August 2013, I found at the Holocaust Memorial Museum in Washington, DC, a document prepared by the Nazis' Central Registry of Jews that listed two hundred names of Jews in Bergen-Belsen who were slated for exchange in January 1945, when Ingrid and her family were traded into Germany. I had not yet told Ingrid about Irene Hasenberg, whose name was number thirty-eight on the list, but that day on the back porch I handed Ingrid the list and pointed to Irene's name.

"What is this?" asked Ingrid. "What does it mean?"

I explained that she and Irene were part of the same exchange and told her some of Irene's story: how her family, all German, secured the false passports from Ecuador prior to their arrest by the Nazis; the unspeakable conditions in Bergen-Belsen; and the tragic death of her father, John, on the train before the exchange took place.

Ingrid's eyes widened and her frail body began to shake. Slowly, she absorbed the ramifications of the document. During a negotiated exchange in which Germans in America were supposed to be traded for Americans in Germany, Ingrid, born in America, was traded for Irene, born in Germany. With an index finger, Ingrid traced the names of the Hasenberg family on the list: John, Gertrude, Werner, and Irene. After a silence, Ingrid's hands flew to her mouth and tears fell down her face. "This changes everything," she said. "It means our family's sacrifice was worth something. It wasn't for nothing. Something good came from it. Irene, her brother, and her mother made it out."

Two months later, I visited Irene in her home in Ann Arbor, Michigan, and told her about Ingrid and her family. A small woman with blue eyes, short gray hair, and a string of pearls around her neck, Irene sat at her dining-room table and shook her head in surprise. "I had no idea that American-born children were part of the exchange," she said. "It's dreadful. What on earth was Roosevelt thinking?" She asked questions about Ingrid's siblings and how her parents had weathered the war. When I explained that Ingrid did not often talk about the war, Irene smiled and said she understood.

After arriving in the United States, it was years before Irene spoke about her past. She was too busy trying to build a new life. She graduated from Queens College in New York in 1953 and went on to earn a doctorate in economics from Duke University. While at Duke, she met her future husband, Charles Butter, who was pursuing a doctorate in psychology. In time, both became professors at the University of Michigan; Irene taught public health and Butter taught psychology and neuroscience. They had two children, Pamela and Noah. When Pamela was in junior high school, she prepared a report on the Holocaust and asked Irene to speak at her school. It was the first time Irene had spoken publicly about her experience, and after that speech she continued to speak out. In 1991, she and her brother returned to Germany and visited Bergen-Belsen and found their father's grave. Eleven years ago, she and five other Holocaust survivors, all women, in Ann Arbor began meeting with six Arab women in an effort to bridge their political and cultural differences. "It's a work of peace. We so-called enemies meet and listen to one another," said Irene. "How else can we learn from our mistakes?"

Irene and Ingrid both wanted to meet each other to share experiences, much as Irene's group in Ann Arbor explored their different perspectives. However, time ran out. For most of 2013, Ingrid suffered from diverticulitis. Unable to keep food down, her weight dropped to seventy pounds. On December 7, 2013, in a hospital not far from Pearl Harbor in Honolulu, exactly seventy-two years to the day after the attack that ignited the war, Ingrid died, without the apology that she deserved from the government.

Acknowledgments

This book would not have been possible without the generosity of many people, especially the many survivors of the Crystal City Internment Camp who gave of their time and memories and whose names are listed in the bibliography. Their passion for sharing their stories—and the stories of their parents—motivated me every step along the way.

In particular, I am grateful for Ingrid, Ensi, and Lothar Eiserloh and deeply regret that Ingrid died near the end of the research. She wanted so much for the story to be told. I owe an enormous debt to Irene Hasenberg Butter, who shared her experience as a survivor of Bergen-Belsen concentration camp as well as her own memories of the January 1945 exchange. Grateful appreciation as well to Sumi Utsushigawa Shimatsu not only for her family's story, but for introducing me to many of her friends who are former internees in Crystal City.

Although the seeds for this book were planted years ago, I want to acknowledge that the inspiration in 2011 for pursuing it came from Evan Taniguchi, the son of Alan Taniguchi; Richard Santos, a historian who died in February 2013; the persistence of two friends, Sherry Kafka Wagner and Therese McDevitt, who shared initial research; and the ongoing counsel of Dr. Kay Schanzer.

A number of people and institutions advanced my work. William Creech, archivist at the National Archives in Washington, DC, was a patient tutor as I made my way through the boxes of Record

Group 85 and gained access to the Special FBI files of key characters. Thanks as well to Vincent Slatt, archivist at the Holocaust Memorial Museum, for directing me to the critical list of exchange Jews from Bergen-Belsen and the papers of Earl Harrison. I am indebted to the Texas Historical Commission and specifically to William A. McWhorter, who shared his own research at National Archives 2 in College Park. At the Institute of Texan Cultures in San Antonio, Tom Shelton helped me locate photographs of the camp and oral histories of the internees and staff. Thanks as well to the dedicated staff of the Japanese American National Museum in Los Angeles, where Yae Aihara, one of the children from the camp, continues to volunteer as a docent. I am grateful to Chester Rosson, a former colleague at *Texas Monthly*, for fact-checking the sections on Germany, and to Cecily Fergeson, an intern who served as a reader and helped gather photographs. Special thanks to William and Cecil Scanlan for their friendship and patience throughout this process.

While interned at Crystal City, Sumi had what she called the Big Six, a trusted group that became her friends for life. While writing this book, I had a version of my own Big Six, friends whose cheerful company lightened what was often a formidable task. Mariana Aitches Davis, a retired history professor, read many versions of this book and made helpful suggestions and edits. Mimi Swartz, an executive editor at *Texas Monthly*, served as a sounding board for ideas through the entire process. Jan Braun helped with research and the organization of materials. Joanie Brooks solved technical problems, and Adelle Brewer provided encouragement and feedback.

In addition, there was also the Big Five. My agent, Amy Hughes, crusaded for this book from its earliest beginnings until its publication. I was fortunate to have Colin Harrison as my editor. At every stage of the project, Colin made excellent suggestions and a number of significant changes that greatly enhanced my work. By complete coincidence, I learned when I was well into the research that Earl Harrison, an important character in the book, was Colin's grandfather. That bit of synchronicity—which could have driven us apart—

only served to deepen his passion for the project, and for that I am grateful. At Scribner, I also owe thanks to Katrina Diaz, Colin's editorial assistant, for her own reading of the manuscript and her help in putting the pieces together. Thanks as well to Steve Boldt, copyeditor, and Laura Wise, production editor.

Finally, there is the Big One. My husband, Lucky Russell, supported my decision to do this project and was at my side through the four years that it took to accomplish. Even though this book is dedicated to my mentor, Maury Maverick Jr., a large part of the work, as is everything in my life, was made possible by Lucky.

Sources and Notes

Rather than offer readers the standard bibliography, I believe an annotated description of my sources, broken down by chapter, provides the most comprehensive picture of the research and the reporting conducted for all of the sections and chapters of the book. While this approach results in some repetition among chapter summaries, it compensates for that in clarity and transparency.

This book is a work of both historical documentation and of memory—the memories of the main and secondary characters. Pertinent aspects of World War II were gleaned from numerous books, essays, and newspaper articles, and the documentation of internment came from a wealth of sources, including primary documents pulled from the National Archives and Records Administration and other institutions and organizations. While the documents formed the spine of the book—providing chronology and context—the heart of the research came from extensive interviews with survivors of the Crystal City Internment Camp and others affected by the camp.

Generally speaking, sources are cited in full only on their first appearance. The individual citations that follow each chapter summary are mostly limited to quotations, dates and figures, and unique facts.

My personal scenes—in Crystal City, Texas; Los Angeles and San Francisco, California; Ann Arbor, Michigan; Las Vegas, Nevada; and Honolulu, Hawaii—took place during 2011 to 2014 on reporting trips to conduct first-person interviews. The scenes did not all take place in the order they appear.

Abbreviations

CC50   Crystal City 50th Anniversary Reunion Album
ER   FBI file of Eleanor Roosevelt
FK   FBI file of Fritz Kuhn

SOURCES AND NOTES

HNCC   Historical Narrative of the Crystal City Internment Camp,
National Archives 1, Record Group 85, Box 1
ME   FBI file of Mathias Eiserloh
NA1   National Archives in Washington, DC
NA2   National Archives in College Park, MD
SF-E   Special File of Mathias Eiserloh
SF-F   Special File of Yoshiaki Fukuda
SF-U   Special File of Tokiji Utsushigawa
SWPD   Special War Problems Division
YF   FBI file of Yoshiaki Fukuda

Preface

The use of trains as the central symbol of the book and of the war is both literal, as trains were the main source of transport, and figurative, as the book describes the train of events that begins in Crystal City and continues well beyond the gates of the camp.

To clarify, some of the internees arrived at the small train station in Crystal City, while others arrived at the somewhat larger station in Uvalde and were taken by bus to the internment camp.

I have used the number six thousand as the approximate number of all internees who were incarcerated at Crystal City during its six-year operation. The precise number is not known. Records from the National Archives indicate that personnel in Crystal City stopped keeping precise counts of internees on June 30, 1945. On that date, the officer in charge at Crystal City had received 4,751 internees. The camp continued to exist until its official closing on February 27, 1948, and during that time new internees arrived. After consultation with William McWhorter, the coordinator of military sites at the Texas Historical Commission, who has done important research about the camp in Crystal City, I settled on the number six thousand, which I believe to be a conservative estimate. After the war ended, the traffic in and out of the camp continued.

xv   And then there were the trains: HNCC.
xvi   Sumi Utsushigawa: Author interview, May 24, 2011, Los Angeles.
xvi   Paul Grayber: Telephone interview, June 2011.
xvii   The popular history: Arnold Krammer, *Undue Process: The Untold Story of America's German Alien Internees* (Rowman & Littlefield, 1997), 33–34.

SOURCES AND NOTES

xvii Virtually unknown: Carmen Higa Mochizuki, author interview, May 24, 2011, Los Angeles.

xviii In Crystal City, Isamu: Biographical notes and an essay by Isamu Taniguchi, "Essay on Atomic War and Peace," generously provided by Evan Taniguchi.

xix Living now in Honolulu: Ingrid Eiserloh, author interview, February 12, 2012, and multiple other interviews.

Chapter One: New Enemies

The stories of the arrests of the fathers of two primary characters—Ingrid Eiserloh and Sumi Utsushigawa—were drawn primarily from interviews with both women. At the time of the first interviews, Ingrid was eighty-one and Sumi was eighty-two. Both women had clear recollections of the events preceding the arrests of their fathers and what followed.

Documentation of the arrest of Mathias Eiserloh, including biographical information, time of arrest, case file number, and items taken from his home came directly from Eiserloh's FBI file, supplied by Ensi Eiserloh, Ingrid's sister. Ensi Eiserloh petitioned the FBI for her father's file near the end of 2000 and obtained the file in January 2001.

The documentation of the case of Tokiji Utsushigawa, Sumi's father, was more complicated. According to my correspondence on January 18, 2013, with the Records Management Division of the FBI, Utsushigawa's FBI file was destroyed on December 28, 1979, thirty-seven years after his arrest, under the supervision of the archives.

With Sumi's signed consent, I filed a request to NA1 for release of Utsushigawa's Special File, kept by the War Relocation Authority, a division of the Department of Justice during World War II. With the signed consent of Ensi Eiserloh, I also filed a request for Mathias Eiserloh's Special File. Both files were received and information from them is used in this chapter.

To get a sense of the aftermath of the attack on Pearl Harbor, I toured Pearl Harbor in Honolulu and made two trips to the Japanese American National Museum, where I viewed photos of Japantown taken in the days after the attack. I drew heavily on images from *Only What We Could Carry*, a remarkable collection of photographs, poems, newspaper articles, and private diaries, edited by Lawson Fusao Inada, published in 2000 by Heyday Books. In addition, I reviewed the front pages of many American newspapers on December 8, 1941, including the *New York Times*, the *Honolulu Star-Bulletin*, the *Los Angeles Times*, and the *Cleveland Plain Dealer*.

3 Ingrid Eiserloh's world: Author interview and ME.

4 Even in tiny Strongsville: Full Pearl Harbor Casualty List, www.uswest virginia.org.

4 *Cleveland Plain Dealer:* Front page of the Monday, December 8, 1941, edition.

5 In 1936, President Franklin D. Roosevelt: Athan Theoharis, *The Boss: J. Edgar Hoover and the Great American Inquisition* (New York: Temple University Press, 1988), 183.

6 That year, 1941, Christmas: Author interview, Lothar Eiserloh, February 17, 2011.

6 Two FBI agents: ME.

8 Ingrid left the garage: Author interview, Ingrid Eiserloh.

9 the morning of December 7: Sumi Utsushigawa, author interview, May 2011 and many other subsequent interviews.

10 JAP HUNTING LICENSE: *People's World*, January 9, 1942. Other newspaper accounts: "Japanazis or Japaryans," *San Francisco Chronicle*, January 7, 1942; "Alien Hysteria Mostly Imaginary," *San Francisco Chronicle*, February 6, 1942. These newspaper stories were reprinted in *Only What We Could Carry*, 11–23.

11 Within two hours of the bombing: Author interview and SF-U.

13 Sumi's father's first name: SF-U.

15 In the three months: Author interview and SF-U.

Chapter Two: Eleanor vs. Franklin

My account of the conflict between Franklin and Eleanor Roosevelt over the internment of German, Japanese, and Italian immigrants drew from numerous biographies of the Roosevelts. Particularly helpful for an understanding of their disagreements during the war was Doris Kearns Goodwin's renowned book *No Ordinary Time: Franklin & Eleanor Roosevelt: The Home Front in World War II* (New York: Simon & Schuster, 1994).

Kenneth S. Davis's *FDR: The War President* (New York: Random House, 2000) helped provide context for larger events of the war through Roosevelt's eyes. *Traitor to His Class: The Privileged Life and Radical Presidency of Franklin Delano Roosevelt*, by H. W. Brands, a fellow Texan, was brilliantly readable, and offered further insight into how Roosevelt prosecuted the war. *FDR: A Centenary Remembrance* (New York: Viking Press, 1982), published on the hundredth anniversary of Roosevelt's death, by Joseph Alsop, the celebrated journalist and columnist, offered personal details of both Eleanor and FDR.

Alsop's prose was so evocative I could almost hear FDR's voice as I read the famous line "The only thing we have to fear is fear itself."

The best secondary sources for Hoover's role in executing the internment policies were found in Athan Theoharis's *The Boss: J. Edgar Hoover and the Great American Inquisition* (New York: Temple University Press, 1988), particularly chapters 8 and 9, and Curt Gentry's *J. Edgar Hoover: The Man and the Secrets* (New York: W. W. Norton, 2001). Both Theoharis and Gentry relied on FBI memorandums and government correspondence. In addition, a chilling secondary source was FBI case file 62-62735, the four-thousand-page file that the FBI maintained on Eleanor Roosevelt from the 1940s until the end of her life.

In this chapter, those with direct experience of the Crystal City camp—internees and children of internees—provided invaluable information. As an example, John Eric Schmitz, a history professor at Northern Virginia Community College, is the son of John Schmitz, who was interned in Crystal City for three years with his family. While a doctoral student at American University in Washington in 2007, John Eric Schmitz wrote a 638-page dissertation about the internment of German, Italian, and Japanese Americans during World War II. For my research, Schmitz generously shared his thesis, which cites numerous secondary sources and a wealth of archival documents. I have noted the use of his sources below.

19 Neither Ingrid nor Sumi: Kearns Goodwin, 295–96; and Davis, 714.

20 "Let's be honest": Kearns Goodwin, 296.

21 Dressed in a miner's clothes: Alsop, 129.

22 Even in the aftermath: Kearns Goodwin, 296–97.

22 Although history would later prove her right: Brands, 697.

23 California's attorney general, Earl Warren: Brands, 657; Francis Biddle, *In Brief Authority* (New York: Doubleday, 1961), 214.

23 Later, Dewitt: Stetson Conn, *Guarding the United States and Its Outposts* (Washington: Center of Military History, 2000), as cited in Schmitz, 358.

24 Their fears: Joseph E. Persico, *Roosevelt's Secret War: FDR and World War II Sabotage* (New York: Random House, 2002), and the Black Tom incident cited in Schmitz, 43.

25 On February 15, 1933: Brands, 279.

25 But it wasn't just Roosevelt: Headlines cited in Schmitz, 96.

26 On that day, Roosevelt called Hoover: Gentry, 205; and Theoharis, *Boss*, 172.

27 On August 24: Theoharis, *Spying on America*, cited in Schmitz, 107.

27 By the end of the year: ER.

27 Eleanor made no secret: Gentry, 288–306.
28 On September 1, 1939: P. Scott Corbett, *Quiet Passages* (Kent, OH: Kent State University Press, 1978), chapter 1, "The Rules of War and the Special Division."
29 In September 1941: Max Paul Friedman, *Nazis & Good Neighbors* (Cambridge, England: Cambridge University Press, 2003), 1.
30 On Sunday, December 7, 1941: Biddle, 50–53; and Kearns Goodwin, 292–94.
31 At noon the following day: Kearns Goodwin, 295.
31 Prior to Pearl Harbor: Letter from Eleanor Roosevelt to Francis Biddle, November 5, 1941; and Biddle to Eleanor, NA2, RG 60.
32 Three days later: Mangione, 319–20; and Biddle, 53.
33 "Please tell the President": February 2, 1942, James H. Rowe Jr. Papers, Assistant to the Attorney General Files, Enemy Control Unit, Box 33, NA2.
34 When the novelist: Hazel Rowley, *Franklin and Eleanor* (New York: Picador, 2010), 257.

Chapter Three: Strangers in a Small Texas Town

Since I live in San Antonio, I am familiar with the terrain and history of South Texas. I made several reporting trips to Crystal City. The tiny train station is in ruins. The small public library, located next to City Hall on E. Dimmit Street, has a few files about the camp. For years, no official acknowledgment was made of its role in World War II. However, on November 11, 2011, McWhorter, of the Texas Historical Commission, installed eight panels on the site that describe where the internees lived, the repatriation process, and camp life. A group of more than twenty-five former internees, Germans and German Americans, returned to the site for the dedication. During interviews over two days, many of the former children of the camp provided useful perspectives of the campsite as it was seventy years ago.

While documents from the National Archives provided a chronology for the site selection of Crystal City, I owe a particular debt to J. Barton Harrison, the son of Earl Harrison, for his insight into how his father approached complex problems. In a delightful interview at his home in Philadelphia, Barton described his father's unflagging work ethic and political savvy. He generously shared some of Harrison's letters and documents and newspaper accounts of his career. Barton also explained the importance of Jerre Mangione, an Italian American who was special assistant to Harrison and a frequent guest in the Harrison household. Barton directed me to Mangione's memoir, *An Ethnic at Large* (New York: G. P. Putman's Sons, Syracuse University Press edition, 2001). Mangione was a brilliant observer of human behavior, and I have shamelessly milked his memoir for key moments in the lives of both Harrison and O'Rourke.

In the early days of my research, I found little information about O'Rourke, officer in charge of Crystal City. Many of the internees I interviewed remembered him as good-natured, but offered few concrete details. In August 2012, I petitioned the INS for his personnel file, which provided biographical information as well as his work history. Through records on Ancestry.com, I located O'Rourke's granddaughter Pamela Smith, who lives in Philadelphia, not far from Barton Harrison's home. Though Smith never met her grandfather, her mother, Joan, told her many stories about O'Rourke. The characterization of O'Rourke as a lonely man who was a melancholic drinker came from Pamela and was confirmed by former internees. His granddaughter generously shared photographs of O'Rourke.

35 in a place so strange: HNCC.

35 Sixty-five million: *Texas Almanac*, 2010–11, 30–41.

36 One hundred and twenty: Hugh Hemphill, *The Railroad of San Antonio and South Central Texas* (San Antonio: Maverick Publishing Company, 2006), 72–73.

37 The train: Ibid., 74.

37 Twelve years later: Author interview, Jose Angel Gutierrez, July 29, 2012; and description from Jose Angel Gutierrez, *The Making of a Civil Rights Leader* (Houston: Arte Publico Press, University of Houston, 2005).

37 From his house: Author interview, Barton Harrison, August 4, 2012; and details from an essay by Lewis M. Stevens, "The Life and Character of Earl G. Harrison," *University of Pennsylvania Law Review*, March 1956.

38 In 1938: Friedman, 1–8.

39 Once the Latin Americans: Mangione, 322.

40 In the wake: Earl Harrison, *Officers Handbook: A Guide for Proper Conduct and Relationships with Aliens and the General Public*, NA1, RG85, Box 1, entry file 276.

40 With Harrison: Paul F. Clark, "Those Other Camps: An Oral History Analysis of Japanese Alien Internment During World War II" (thesis, California State University, Fullerton, April 25, 1980), Clark's interview with Amy Stannard, 119–35.

41 "We began": Ibid., 124.

42 "We hated": Author interview, Gutierrez.

42 It wasn't only rock-ribbed Texas: Norman Moss, *19 Weeks: America, Britain, and the Fateful Summer of 1940* (New York: Houghton Mifflin, 2003), 243.

42 At that time: Marian Jean Barber, "How the Irish, Germans, and Czechs Became Anglo: Race and Identity in the Texas-Mexico Borderlands" (dissertation, University of Texas at Austin, May 2010), 324–28.

43 Surveying the site: HNCC, 1.

43 The land itself: Author interview, Gutierrez.

44 Harrison had many practical issues: HNCC, 3–5.

44 A precedent existed: Friedman, 142–43.

45 In Crystal City: HNCC, 3.

45 Harrison's trip: Stevens, 592.

45 He was born: Ibid., and author interview, J. Barton Harrison.

46 The heroine in the play: Stevens, 593.

47 Biddle agonized over the passage: Biddle, 110.

48 It was a grim sell: Mangione, 271.

49 Convinced that aliens: Ibid.

50 To honor Harrison: Ibid., 275–80.

52 Harrison was praised: Biddle, 112.

53 When Biddle became attorney general: Ibid., 113.

53 "Dear Earl": This Biddle letter and Harrison's response provided by J. Barton Harrison, as were all of the newspaper articles.

54 "Dear Joe": Biddle, 114.

54 thirty-five German families: HNCC, 1–6.

55 He, his wife, and three children: Collaer to Earl Harrison, December 21, 1942, NA1, RG85, Box 1.

55 Before leaving Ellis Island and Tennessee: HNCC, 6; and memo to Harrison, NA1, RG85, Box 1.

56 Both the internees and Collaer's staff: Telephone interview with Christine Collaer Kite in April 2012; and "Reconnecting to Father's 'Mistake' as Fort Missoula Commandant," *Missoulian*, June 29, 2010.

56 Little by little: NA1, RG85, Box 2.

56 A tall man with wavy hair: O'Rourke's INS personnel file, obtained from the US Department of Justice.

57 O'Rourke was lonely: Author interview, Pam Smith, August 12, 2012; and US census data, 1920, Joseph L. O'Rourke and Loretta M. O'Rourke.

57 One night: Mangione, 331–34.

58 "Effective this date, the auditorium": Administrative order no. 9 from O'Rourke, NA1, RG85, Box 1.

58 Harrison paid: Mangione, 332.

Chapter Four: Internment Without Trial

Most of the material in this chapter was derived from personal interviews. Over multiple interviews, the three living children of Mathias and Johanna Eiserloh—Ingrid, Lothar, and Ensi—entrusted me with their stories, many of them painful, and I am grateful to them. The reporting of the travails of the family required back-and-forth checking among the three.

When the three offered differing views, I referenced the primary documents—Eiserloh's FBI file and his Special File—and then considered the views of each to arrive at the truth. For instance, the attack on Johanna is drawn from the perspective of Ingrid and Lothar, who had memories of the event. Ensi's perspective was useful as well. Although she was an infant in 1942, she later discussed the episode with her mother.

61 On the morning: Author interview, Ingrid Eiserloh.

62 After Ingrid: ME.

62 According to one State Department memo: SWPD, RG59, Box 129.

63 In her first effort: ME.

63 One day Ingrid: Author interview, Ingrid Eiserloh.

64 The FBI file: ME; and author interview, Lothar Eiserloh.

65 "Americans love swimming pools": Lothar Eiserloh.

66 The morning: Author interview, Ingrid Eiserloh.

67 Later, Johanna: Ingrid and Lothar Eiserloh, separate interviews.

68 Meanwhile, Mathias: ME.

70 While in Idstein: Author interview, Ensi Eiserloh.

77 During the war, Roosevelt: SWPD, Box 70, NA2, RG59, as cited by Schmitz, 617.

77 On March 4, 1942: SF-E.

79 By the time: Ingrid Eiserloh.

79 While his wife and children: Friedman, 140–42; and Krammer, *Undue Process*, 137–38.

80 The report on Mathias at Stringtown: ME and Jacobs and Fallon, *Documents*.

80 In his book: Friedman, 141.

81 On April 8, 1943: SF-E.

SOURCES AND NOTES

Chapter Five: A Family Reunion

Mathias Eiserloh's FBI file provided solid footing for this chapter. The many details of Eiserloh's status changes were documented, as were Johanna's petition to the government for "voluntary internment" in Crystal City and for repatriation.

83 July 8, 1943: ME.
83 From her hard: Ingrid Eiserloh.
84 Finally Johanna: ME.
84 Prior to the trip: ME. Eleanor Neff's letter was mailed from the Cuyahoga County Relief Bureau in Cleveland to the INS on June 2, 1943.
86 Ingrid remembered that: Ingrid Eiserloh.
87 As Johanna: ME.
87 The camp at Kenedy: Texas State Historical Association, "Kenedy Alien Detention Camp."
88 Johanna had also filed: ME.
88 Mathias was not: Ibid.
88 The reunion: ME, memo on July 5, 1943, from Ivan Williams, officer in charge of the camp in Kenedy to the chief liaison officer in Crystal City.
89 At the entrance: Lothar Eiserloh.
90 Three hundred and seventy-five Germans: HNCC, 5.
91 Dr. Symmes F. Oliver: The section on Oliver draws from Louis Fiset, "Medical Care for Interned Enemy Aliens: A Role for the US Public Health Service in World War II," *American Journal of Public Health*, October 2003.

Chapter Six: The Hot Summer of '43

My account of the troubles in the German section drew heavily from my own research at the National Archives, as well as a large collection of internment documents collected by Arthur D. Jacobs, a former internee who now lives in Tempe, Arizona, a retired major in the US Air Force. Jacobs was born in America and was interned in Crystal City as a twelve-year-old boy with his family. He and his family were exchanged into Germany in 1945. His memoir, *The Prison Called Hohenasperg* (USA: Universal Publishers, 1999), describes his wartime experience. Jacobs has worked for many years with Joseph E. Fallon, his coeditor, to produce a five-volume index of documents titled *World*

344

War Two Experience: The Internment of German-Americans. This index, which continues to be updated, is an invaluable resource.

During the summer of 1943, as Jacobs's documents and others reveal, camp officials struggled to distinguish German internees who held patriotic feelings for Germany but were not a security threat to America from Germans who were Nazis. According to Jacobs and Eb Fuhr, a principal character in this chapter, by that summer the term *Nazi* had become synonymous with *German.* For a variety of reasons—Germans had never been a minority in the United States, their anger at the FBI for their arrest and internment—many German nationals were hardened and labeled troublemakers by O'Rourke and his staff.

I appreciate Jacobs, Fuhr, and other German internees for offering their perspectives.

93 Only three months before: NA1, RG85, Box 27.

93 "We believe": Complaint letter to Collaer, NA1, RG85, Box 28.

94 In response: Collaer to Harrison, NA1, RG85, Box 27.

94 The Japanese: HNCC, 7–8.

95 At the time of the flag: Author interview, Dr. Heidi von Leszcynski, November 11, 2011.

95 Upon arrival: NA1, RG85, Box 27.

96 In June 1943: FK.

96 The Jacobis: NA1, RG85, Box 58; and Jacobs and Fallon.

97 Despite Kuhn's: FK.

98 What the presidency: FK. Given the dramatic nature of the extortion attempt of Helena Rubinstein, the following additional details are offered: On March 9, 1942, an agent in New York filed a report about an informant who claimed he acted under orders from Kuhn, a prisoner at Dannemora, to extort Rubinstein. The informant was a former prisoner with Kuhn who had recently been released. On April 16, 1942, agents filed a second report that described the interview with Rubinstein in her apartment.

100 In Crystal City: FK.

101 Eberhard E. Fuhr: Author interview, Eb Fuhr; as well as Fuhr's account in Stephen Fox, *America's Invisible Gulag* (New York: Peter Lang Publishing, 2000), 51–56, 257–61.

104 A confidential memo: "Circular to All Officers and Employees," NA1, RG85, Box 1.

104 O'Rourke's task: HNCC, 5.

105 As a productive: Texas Historical Commission, Crystal City.

105 However, Johanna: Author interview, Ensi Eiserloh.

106 One afternoon, Ingrid and Lothar: Author interviews.

107 Provisions of the Third Geneva Convention: NA1, RG85, Box 6.

108 "Selling these employees": HNCC, 5.

109 "No living thing": Mangione, 329.

109 In August: NA1, RG85, Box 6.

Chapter Seven: "Be Patient"

Contextual knowledge of how the Eiserloh and other families weathered the continuing conflicts in Crystal City emerged from primary documents at the National Archives and interviews. This chapter owes a particular debt to chapter 19, "Nazis and Troublemakers in the Internee Camps," in Krammer, *Undue Process.*

111 One of: HNCC, 24.

111 All through: Author interview, Ingrid Eiserloh.

112 Kazuko Shimahara; Karen Riley, *Schools Behind Barbed Wire* (Lanham, MD: Rowman & Littlefield, 2002), 58.

112 on September 7, 1943: HNCC, 25; and interviews with Ingrid and Lothar Eiserloh.

113 By October: FK.

114 By December: NA1, RG85, Box 3.

114 "Imitation Dictator": Ibid.

115 That fall: "Be Patient," Harrison, *Officers' Handbook,* 18.

115 Kuhn was number 68: NA2, SWPD, RG59, Box 69, as cited by Schmitz, 519.

115 *Das Lager:* Jacobs and Fallon, *Documents.*

116 O'Rourke wrote: NA1, RG85, Box 3.

116 The May 6, 1944: Jacobs and Fallon.

117 Kreuzner threatened: NA1, RG85, Box 17.

117 Mathias once went: Ibid.

118 Only forty-nine years old: O'Rourke's INS personnel file.

118 His strategy: HNCC, 9.

119 At first, Fujii: Ibid., 17.

Chapter Eight: To Be or Not to Be an American

A small group of academics have focused on the infamous work of the Special Division within the Department of State, which negotiated exchanges between the United States and Japan and the United States and Germany. My baseline for understanding the complexities of the exchanges from Crystal City came from two books.

The first, *Quiet Passages: The Exchange of Civilians Between the United States and Japan During the Second World War* (Kent, OH: Kent University Press, 1987), is by P. Scott Corbett, a professor of history at Ventura College in California. This book, which relied on primary documents of the Special Division, tells the story from the point of view of the United States. At the time, the diplomatic records of Japan were not yet available to researchers. More than ten years later, Bruce Elleman, an associate professor at the US Naval War College, found new documentation in Tokyo. His book, *Japanese-American Civilian Prisoner Exchanges and Detention Camps, 1941–45* (New York: Routledge, 2006), utilized primary documentation from both American and Japanese sources.

For the section on the American School, I relied on primary documents from the National Archives, a 1979 oral history of R. C. Tate, superintendent of schools. In addition, Karen Riley's first-rate book about the three schools in Crystal City, *Schools Behind Barbed Wire: The Untold Story of Wartime Internment and the Children of Arrested Enemy Aliens* (Lanham, MD: Rowman & Littlefield, 2002), provided useful description of curricular and extracurricular activities, and insight into Tate, the teachers, and the students.

In addition to the thanks I owe to Sumi Utsushigawa for hours of interviews, I'm also grateful to her for sharing hundreds of copies of the *Crystal City Chatter*, a newsletter she has published from her home since 1980. Over the years, many internees in the camp have contributed primary documents and recorded their memories of internment in the *Chatter*. The issues of the newsletter provided irreplaceable insight into the lives of the children of the camp.

121 While fifteen-year-old: Author interview, Sumi Utsushigawa.
122 At the New Jersey harbor: Corbett, 93; and Elleman, 146.
123 During the first: Corbett, 68.
123 Given the success: Elleman, 146–55; and Corbett, 72–95.
125 To their surprise: Author interview, Sumi Utsushigawa.
126 Not far away: Author interview, Yae Aihara, March 23, 2011; and Densho Digital Archives, Japanese American Legacy Project, http://denso.org.

127 As the train: Yoji J. Matsushima, *Crystal City Chatter* 28 (December 1995).

127 In Heart Mountain: Author interview, Sumi Utsushigawa; and video-taped interview conducted by Leslie Burns in November 1997, deposited at the Institute of Texan Cultures.

130 Somewhere in Mississippi: Author interview, Sumi Utsushigawa; and Matshushima, *Crystal City Chatter.*

131 When the train stopped: Videotaped interview, Shoji Kanogawa, 1997, UTSA.

132 That first night: HNCC, 10.

133 It often: Ibid., 26.

133 By the time: Riley, 47; and State Department of Education, Summer School Report, 1945, NA1, RG85, Box 65.

134 R. C. (Robert Clyde): Riley, 44; Thomas Walls's interview with Tate, February 21, 1979, UTSA, Institute of Texan Cultures; and HNCC, 25–30.

135 Over time: HNCC, 26.

136 "Yet the attitude": Tate interview with Walls.

136 Some Japanese American students: Tai Uyeshima's essay "The First Concentration Camp: Crystal City, Texas," CC50, 26.

136 The September 1943: Ibid., 43.

137 From time to time: Author interview, Sumi Utsushigawa; and Riley, 105.

137 Like the other nisei: SF-U.

Chapter Nine: Yes-Yes, No-No

Fortunately, much useful documentation of the Japanese and Japanese American experience of internment is available. Useful interviews of both the Uno family and the Taniguchi family and other now-deceased Japanese and Japanese American internees have been collected by universities, the Japanese American National Museum in Los Angeles, National Japanese American Society in San Francisco, and elsewhere. Particularly useful here were the Taniguchi family interviews, as well as the collection edited by Lawson Fusao Inada, *Only What We Could Carry: The Japanese American Internment Experience* (Berkeley, CA: Heyday Books, 2000).

139 After Pearl Harbor: Entire text of Roosevelt's memo, *Only What We Could Carry*, 341.

139 The key word: Michi Weglyn, *Years of Infamy* (New York: Morrow Quill Paperbacks, 1976), 136.

140 Mary Tsukamoto: Ibid., 141.

141 In Crystal City, the battle: Kay Uno Kanedo, 2010, Denso Digital Archives.

141 When war broke out: Yuji Ichioka, "The Meaning of Loyalty: The Case of Kazumaro Buddy Uno," *Amerasia Journal* 23 (3) (1997): 47–59.

142 Kay Uno, the youngest: Kay Uno, "Pearl Harbor Remembered," *Only What We Could Carry*, 31.

144 As Ernie felt: Letter from Stanley to Robert Uno, April 26, 1944, NA1, RG85, Box 190.

144 When Stanley wrote the letter: Essay by Edison Uno, CC50, 23.

145 The family: Interview with Izumi Taniguchi, March 2000, by Nancy Taniguchi for the Japanese American Historical Collection (JACL), archived at California State University, Fresno, 2–17.

148 On April 23, 1943: Weglyn, 219.

148 "Everything is": Kearns Goodwin, 428.

149 In March 1943: *Only What We Could Carry*, 263.

149 While in Gila River: Taniguchi interview, 15–21.

151 Isamu and Sadayo: Alan Taniguchi, biographical summary of his parents, September 1995.

151 In a speech: Biddle, "Democracy and Racial Minorities," December 14, 1943.

Chapter Ten: A Test of Faith

My account of the life of Yoshiaki Fukuda drew from his FBI file, which was heavily redacted, and his Special File, which contained many notations of his activities before and after his internment. In addition, Fukuda's memoir, *My Six Years of Internment: An Issei's Struggle for Justice*, published by the Konko Church of San Francisco in 1957, is a striking account that links his personal history with the political and religious events of his times. More than any other book that I have read about the experience of issei men during American internment, Fukuda's memoir reveals their cultural values and the agonies of divided loyalty.

For an understanding of the Konko faith, founded in 1859 in Japan and which Fukuda brought to America in 1930, I am grateful to the Reverend Joanne Tolosa, the head minister of the Konko Church in San Francisco, who welcomed me there on several occasions and helped me understand the basic tenets of the faith. In addition, two other Konko ministers—the Reverend

SOURCES AND NOTES

Masato Kawahatsu in San Francisco and the Reverend Alfred Tsuyuki in Los Angeles—illuminated aspects of the faith. The Konko religion was originally a Shinto sect but established its independence in 1859. However, anyone associated with the Shinto religion, a cornerstone for Japanese culture, was immediately arrested and interned by FBI agents in 1941.

I would like to express my appreciation to Fukuda's four living sons—Nobusuke, Saburo, Hiroshi, and Koichi—who provided personal papers, religious tracts written by Fukuda, documents from Japan, and photographs taken during their internment.

153 All he could see: NA1, RG85, Box 50, and Fukuda, *My Six Years*, 22.

153 In his seat: Author interview, Nobusuke Fukuda, April 29, 2011, San Francisco.

154 "I came": Fukuda, *My Six Years*, 40.

154 "The Issei": Essay by Nobusuke Fukuda, *Discover Nikkei*, May 8, 2008.

155 In Missoula and Lordsburg: Fukuda, *My Six Years*, 68.

156 At 1:30 a.m. on January 27, 1944: NA1, RG85.

156 O'Rourke approached: Fukuda, memoir, 22.

157 Fukuda was born: Ibid., 122; and author interviews with Fukuda's four sons Nobusuke, Saburo, Hiroshi, and Koichi.

157 Three years: The description of the send-off was found in an unpublished biography of Fukuda written in 1967 by Masayuki Fukibayashi, a schoolmate of Fukuda's in Japan.

158 On December 7: YF; Fukuda memoir, 7.

158 On Monday, December 8: *San Francisco Call-Bulletin*.

159 Fukuda and the others: YF.

159 Her title: Ibid., and essay by the Reverend Fumio Matsui, 1981, 50th Anniversary, Konko Church, San Francisco.

159 At his hearing: YF.

160 The Konko religion: Author interview, the Reverend J. L. Tolosa, head minister, Konko Church, San Francisco.

161 A tall, lean: Author interview, Nobusuke Fukuda.

162 Shinko stayed: Fukuda, *My Six Years*, 49.

163 During Fukuda's: Ibid., 52.

164 In Crystal City: SF-F.

164 Despite the order: Ibid.

165 On February 14: Ibid.

166 A report from the Red Cross: March 6, 1944, memo from Harrison to O'Rourke, NA1, RG85, Box 6.

166 On the morning of November: Fukuda, *My Six Years*, 55–62.

SOURCES AND NOTES

Chapter Eleven: The Birds Are Crying

As the flag controversy in the German section in the summer of 1943 illus-trates the anger of German immigrant fathers, who realized the government—not them—controlled the lives of their children, two key events described in this chapter about the summer of 1944 revealed the helplessness of issei fathers.

When I first heard the accounts of what the Japanese American children in the camp refer to as the "prom disaster," I didn't understand why such a small event had such extraordinary consequences. After interviews with doz-ens of former internees, now elderly men and women, I began to recognize that the prom was yet another line in the sand: if the students said yes to the prom, it meant yes to America, and no to their issei parents. Again, the issue was loyalty.

This chapter relies on interviews with both German American and Japa-nese American internees. All of those interviewed vividly remembered the day that the two Japanese Peruvians drowned in the camp swimming pool. The account in this chapter is a compilation of the memories of many internees.

On the day in August 2012 when I stood in the reading room of the National Archives in Washington, DC, and pulled out the May 1944 love letters described in this chapter, I grasped the utter isolation of internment. The secret notes from the unhappily married Japanese American woman to her lover in Denver were written in tiny script and hidden beneath the letters' postage stamps and discovered by camp censors. I elected not to use the names of the lovers. One line in particular became the central metaphor for the trag-edies of that summer: "The birds are crying, too."

169 In any other: HNCC, 27.
170 The battle: Letter from Fujii to O'Rourke, NA1, RG85, Box 3; and the prom incident also covered in Riley, 150–52.
170 O'Rourke's answer: Letter from O'Rourke to Willard Kelly, INS, NA1, RG85, Box 4.
171 At school: Author interview, Sumi Utsushigawa Shimatsu.
171 Sumi's friend: Author interview, Yae Kanogawa Aihara; and Aihara's interview with the Densho Visual History Collection.
172 Nevertheless, on May 26, 1944: Ibid.
173 Yae's teacher: This incident was also described by Yae's brother Stogie Kanogawa in his videotaped interview with Leslie Burns, UTSA.
173 The following day: Letters from censor found at NA1, RG85, Box 3.

174   She was not alone: Ibid.

174   Maruko Okazaki: Ibid.

175   In May 1944: NA1, RG85, Box 17.

176   While O'Rourke: Author interview, J. Barton Harrison.

176   When in 1943: *Washington Post*, July 20, 1944.

176   "The only other": Ibid.

176   On July 20, 1944: *New York Times*.

177   "Hats off": *Washington Post*, July 24, 1944.

177   A Japanese internee: Toriu's note generously provided by Barton Harrison.

178   In August 1944 the hospital: NA1, RG85, Box 3; HNCC, 20–24; and also described in *Alien Enemy Detention Facility* (16mm camp film of Crystal City, Texas).

178   All that changed: The account of the deaths of the two girls was drawn from author interviews with Ty Nakamura, Alice Nishimoto, Sumi Utsushigawa, and Toni Tomita. The account from Bessie Masuda was found in an oral history, Texas Historical Commission. Medical records of their death, NA1, RG85, Box 50.

Chapter Twelve: Trade Bait

Interviews with Ingrid, Ensi, and Lothar Eiserloh, as well as other children from Crystal City who made the voyage from the port of New Jersey to the port of Marseille, formed the foundation of this chapter. The interviews with Bernard Levermann and Elizabeth Lechner, known as Suzy, confirmed the experience of the Eiserloh children. In addition, the Graber family story, located on the German American Internee Coalition website, provided additional insight into the particulars of the exchange.

Additional details came from chapter 20, "To Germany," of Stephen Fox's book *America's Invisible Gulag: A Biography of German American Internment & Exclusion in World War II* (New York: Peter Lang, 2000), and from records in the special FBI file of Mathias Eiserloh.

183   As good-bye ceremonies: Author interview, Ingrid Eiserloh.

184   Near the end: Krammer, *Undue Process*, 146.

185   The January 1945: Fox, 236–46.

185   Even on the morning: Letter from Mangels to his superior, January 9, 1945, ME.

186   Customs agents: Author interviews, Ingrid and Ensi Eiserloh.

186 On December 29: Fox, 237.

186 Finally, the day of reckoning: SF-E, memo from Martin to O'Rourke.

187 All day: Mangels letter, ME.

187 "It was": Author interview, Lothar Eiserloh.

187 Security was: Krammer, *Undue Process*, 147.

188 By morning: Martin's memo to O'Rourke, SF-E.

188 "Don't take": Author interview, Ingrid Eiserloh, confirmed by Ensi Eiserloh.

189 In his written report: SF-E.

189 The trains: Krammer, *Undue Process*, 147.

190 Johanna and Guenther: Author interview, Ensi Eiserloh.

191 Meanwhile, Lothar: Author interview, Lothar Eiserloh; and description of the ship taken from *M.S. Gripsholm: The FBI Files*, 100-124687, Section 7.

191 As the ship: Author interviews, Ingrid and Ensi Eiserloh.

192 "If the ship": Author interview, Lothar Eiserloh.

192 Once inside: Fox, 238.

192 One of Lothar's: Ibid., 243–44. Like the Eiserloh children, in Ruth Becker's account to Fox and to this author she described the voyage over, the net of mines, and the lack of food in Marseille.

193 "You're making": Author interviews, Ingrid and Lothar Eiserloh.

193 The passengers: Author interviews, Bernard Levermann and Elizabeth Lechner; and the Graber family story, found on the German American Internee Coalition website, http://www.gaic.info.

194 Bert Shepard: Fox, 253–54.

194 Mathias needed: Author interview, Ingrid Eiserloh.

Chapter Thirteen: The False Passports

Irene Hasenberg's incredible story had its beginning for me in a list of names I found in the archives of the United States Holocaust Memorial Museum in Washington, DC. An archivist had led me to this list when I asked how I might locate names of Jews who could have been exchanged. The museum had obtained the list directly from Nazi archives: the Centraal Registratiebureau voor Joden recorded the names of Jewish prisoners at Bergen-Belsen concentration camp who were released in January 1945. A detailed accounting, it records full names, birth dates, birthplaces, and nationalities. Of the 190 persons listed, I was able at first to locate only one survivor: Irene Hasenberg. I later found a second survivor, Jacob Wolf.

On June 12, 2013, I traveled to the home of Irene Hasenberg (Butter) in Ann Arbor, Michigan. It was the birthday of Anne Frank, who was a friend of Irene's in Amsterdam. Our intensive interview in Ann Arbor has been augmented by subsequent telephone conversations. Her generous narrative is the basis for this chapter. Also consulted was Irene's lengthy interview of September 22, 1986, for the Voice/Vision Holocaust Survivor Oral History Archive, deposited at the University of Michigan, Dearborn.

Important for an understanding of US government policies regarding Jews during World War II was one book in particular: Richard Breitman and Allan J. Lichtman's *FDR and the Jews* (Cambridge, MA: Belknap Press, 2013). Breitman and Lichtman offer a nuanced examination of Roosevelt's response to the Jewish question. They conclude that he was a consummate politician who also acted at times to rescue Jews. This finding sheds light on how the exchange of Jews at Bergen-Belsen for German American internees such as Ingrid Eiserloh could even have taken place, considering how contrary it seems to the stated goals of exchanging US German residents for Americans behind enemy lines in Germany.

197 On the morning: Author interview with Irene Hasenberg, June 12, 2013. Other aspects of her family's story recounted throughout this chapter come from this interview.

198 856 quota: Stephen Fox, *Inside the Roundup of German Americans During World War II: The Past as Prologue* (Bloomington, IN: iUniverse, 2005).

Chapter Fourteen: Under Fire

The narrative of the Eiserlohs' repatriation from Crystal City to Germany is a compilation of the memories of the three surviving Eiserloh children: Ingrid, Lothar, and Ensi. They generously shared their experiences and thus enabled a clear picture of what that trauma entailed.

213 the moment: Author interviews, Ingrid and Lothar Eiserloh.

213 Only two weeks: Cawthorne, 176–77.

214 On February 4: Brands, 793–802.

214 Over seven days: Rowley, 273.

214 When Franklin: Ibid., 286.

215 Meanwhile: The rest of this chapter is based on extensive interviews with Ingrid, Lothar, and Ensi Eiserloh.

Chapter Fifteen: Into Algeria

A crucial addition in this chapter is the testimony of Jacob Wolf, whose name also appears on the list of exchanges from Bergen-Belsen. Irene Hasenberg Butter graciously put me in touch with Wolf, who lived in Brooklyn, New York. Wolf provided the majority of the material regarding his family and his experience of the exchange, although Irene also remembered key information.

A secondary source that provided useful historical context is Richard Breitman and Allan J. Lichtman's *FDR and the Jews* (Cambridge, MA: Belknap Press, 2013).

223 Irene's journey: Author interview with Irene Hasenberg Butter, June 12, 2013. Irene's memories of the events, people, places, and her feelings about the time in Philippeville are my source for her experience there.

226 One of the gravely ill: Author interview with Jacob Wolf, October 13, 2013, and Centraal Registratiebureau voor Joden (list of exchangees from Bergen-Belsen).

227 Two large trains: Interviews with Irene Hasenberg Butter, Ingrid Eiserloh, and Jacob Wolf. Also in Fox, *America's Invisible Gulag*, 254.

228 On the other side: Author interview, Jacob Wolf.

230 Prior to 1939: Ira Katznelson, "Failure to Rescue: How FDR Hurt Jewish Would-Be Immigrants," *New Republic*, July 6, 2013.

230 Even a bill: Breitman and Lichtman, 148–51.

230 In the end: Ibid., 179.

230 By 1941: Ibid., chapter 13, "The War Refugee Board," 262–75.

231 On June 29, 1944: Ibid., 287.

231 In November 1945: Author interview, Jacob Wolf.

Chapter Sixteen: The All-American Camp

The story of how the prisoners inside the Crystal City camp lived under a veil of censorship and surveillance could not have been told without the generosity of former internees such as Eb Fuhr and Sumi Utsushigawa, who shared their memories with me. Their experiences shed light on how isolated and constrained the lives of internees were, and how difficult it was for them to stay connected with news and family from the world outside the fence, during the war and even after it was over. Materials in the National Archives were also invaluable in fleshing out this chapter, especially for creating the context of the camp and the actions of authorities.

233 By the spring: HNCC, 23–24.

234 Students: Mangione, 333.

234 On April 13, 1945: Author interview, Eb Fuhr.

234 In the Japanese section: Author interview, Sumi Utsushigawa.

235 In contrast: NA1, RG85, Box 38.

235 Of course: Ibid.

235 The morning, Brands, 815–18; and Rowley, 281–85.

237 In Crystal City: NA1, RG85, Box 46.

237 At the Federal High: CC50, 50; NA1, RG85, Box 49.

237 In 1938, the phrase: Wikipedia, and author interview, Toni Tanita previously fixed.

237 The nights: Author interview, Sumi Utsushigawa.

237 *Night Owl*: CC50, 50.

237 Every tennis: Ibid., 57.

238 When they tired: Author interview, Eb Fuhr; Fox, 257–61; and Jacobs and Fallon.

240 Mangione: Mangione to O'Rourke October 27, 1943, and Collaer to O'Rourke, January 19, 1945, NA1, RG85, Box 1; and the film *Alien Enemy Detention Facility.*

243 1944 propaganda film: Steven Spielberg Film and Video Archive, United States Holocaust Memorial Museum.

243 In April 1945: Fusao, *Only What We Could Carry*, 377–87; and Junichi Suzuki, *442: Live with Honor, Die with Dignity.*

243 Ella Ohta: Author interview, Ella Ohta Tomita.

243 In May 1945: Author interviews, Eb Fuhr and Sumi Utsushigawa.

244 On the evening: CC50, 50–53.

245 Meanwhile, the war: Cawthorne, 214–17.

245 In Crystal City: Author interviews, Yae Kanogawa Aihara and Carmen Higa Mochizuki.

246 From his bungalow: Isamu Taniguchi, "Essay on Atomic War and Peace," unpublished.

246 "After V-E Day": Author interview, Eb Fuhr.

247 The mood: Author interview, Sumi Utsushigawa.

Chapter Seventeen: Shipped to Japan

This chapter offers a glimpse into the complex repercussions of the government's repatriation policy. Interviews with the Japanese Americans who were forced, oftentimes by their fathers' decisions, to go to Japan reveal the tragic effects on the lives of individuals and entire families. Tensions developed between fathers and their children. Parents who believed Japan had won the war suffered shock and regret upon arriving in Japan. Since their children were unfamiliar with Japan, having been born elsewhere, their adjustment to a new country was intensified by the poverty, social devastation, and psychological trauma of a defeated nation. The American-born children considered themselves American. Some, like Carmen Higa Mochizuki, a Peruvian, had to learn a completely new language. Even worse, the "repatriates" were resented by their new countrymen and suspected of being spies.

The testimonies of these child internees about their feelings and about their family's experiences weave the central thread throughout this chapter: divided loyalties, divided families, divided lives.

249 During the fall: SF-U.
249 It was midterm: Author interview, Sumi Utsushigawa.
249 On the morning: CC50, excerpts from Walls, 21.
250 Six hundred: Ibid.
250 Though Sumi: Author interview, Sumi Utsushigawa.
253 Teenagers from Crystal City: Author interview, Mas Okabe.
253 Carmen Higa Mochizuki: Author interview, Carmen Higa Mochizuki.
253 On December 22: Author interview, Sumi Utsushigawa.
254 One of the teachers: CC50, 76, article by Sumi Utsushigawa, which includes the dialogue between the schoolteacher from Crystal City and the Japanese boatman.
255 The barges: Ibid.
256 Back in the United States: CC50, 75, Associated Press photos of the arrival of Crystal City repatriates to Uraga, Japan, printed in CC50 with permission of Roy Kubo.
256 The barracks: Author interview, Mas Okabe.
257 The next morning: Author interviews with Okabe, Sumi Utsushigawa, and Min Tajaii.
258 The windows: The description of Yokohama was taken from a website that describes details of the attack with photographs from the National Archives, http://www.468thbombgroup.org.

258 the snow: Author interview, Sumi Utsushigawa.

259 More than three hundred: Author interview, Mas Okabe.

260 She was born in Peru: Author interview, Carmen Higa Mochizuki.

260 Their destination: Cawthorne, 212–13.

260 The families: Author interview, Alice Nagao Nishimoto.

262 As the months: Author interview, Sumi Utsushigawa.

Chapter Eighteen: Harrison's Second Act

My account of Harrison's special mission to Europe drew from the Earl G. Harrison paper collection, donated by Harrison's family in August 1994 to the United States Holocaust Memorial Museum in Washington, DC. Vincent Slatt, an archivist at the museum, directed me to the digitized version of Harrison's extraordinary diary of his survey of displaced-persons camps in July and August of 1945. The file also contains a recording of Harrison's radio address in October 1945 in response to Eisenhower's criticism.

An understanding of the personal implications of Harrison's trip emerged from secondary sources, including the previously cited article by Lewis Stevens, printed in the *University of Pennsylvania Law Review* in 1956, and a transcript of Harry Reicher's speech at the Truman Presidential Museum and Library in 2012. Barton Harrison, Earl Harrison's son, directed me to those sources.

263 Harrison was the: "The United States and the Holocaust: Postwar American Response to the Holocaust," *Holocaust Encyclopedia*, United States Holocaust Memorial Museum, Washington, DC.

264 The trip: "War Refugee Board: Background and Establishment," *Holocaust Encyclopedia*, United States Holocaust Memorial Museum, Washington, DC.

264 Roosevelt's death: "Buchenwald: History," Jewish Virtual Library.

264 Three days later: Transcript of Murrow's broadcast found at https://www .jewishvirtuallibrary.org/jsource/Holocaust/murrow.html. It can also be viewed on YouTube.

265 On April 15: Cawthorne, 200; and Murrow transcript.

265 Truman rejected: Truman to Eisenhower, August 31, 1945, United States Holocaust Memorial Museum, Washington, DC.

266 Throughout his trips: Harrison's diary, United States Holocaust Memorial Museum, Washington, DC, RG-10.088, accession no. 1994.A.0079.

266 Harrison toured the facility: According to Harrison's diary notes, he

arrived in Bergen-Belsen on July 23, 1945, and met Rosensaft and his wife, Hadassah.

267 He asked: Harrison's diary, July 24, 1945.

267 At the end: Harry Reicher, "The Post-Holocaust World and President Harry S. Truman: The Harrison Report and Immigration Law and Policy" (transcript of a speech at the Truman Presidential Museum and Library, Kansas City, MO, July 10, 2002), 12.

267 Harrison did not: Harrison's diary, July 24, 1945.

267 After Bergen-Belsen: Ibid.

268 On August 3, 1945, United States Holocaust Memorial Museum, archives, Washington, DC.

272 In a confidential message: Eisenhower to Truman, Jewish Virtual Library.

272 Patton's response: United States Holocaust Memorial Museum, archives, Washington, DC.

272 On October 17, 1945: *New York Times*, October 17, 1945.

273 The following day: *New York Times*, October 18, 1945.

273 The public embarrassment: Angelika Konigseder and Juliane Wetzel, *Waiting for Hope: Jewish Displaced Persons in Post War Germany* (Evanston, IL: Northwestern University Press, 2001), 35.

Chapter Nineteen: After the War

The postwar struggles of displaced persons described in this chapter were provided in interviews with survivors of the Crystal City repatriation, as well as with Irene Hasenberg. The circuitous journeys of Ingrid and Lothar Eiserloh, Irene Hasenberg, and Sumi Utsushigawa to America testify to their incredible determination to rebuild their lives. As Americans displaced by the repatriation policy of the US government, Ingrid, Lothar, and Sumi were determined to get back to their homeland. For Irene, America would be where she would reunite with her mother and brother, secure an education, and build a remarkable life.

277 In May 1945: Author interview, Lothar Eiserloh.

278 Eisenhower made: Victor Gollancz, *In Darkest Germany* (London: Gollancz, 1947), 116.

278 On May 8: Author interviews, Ingrid and Ensi Eiserloh.

279 When the US Army: Author interview, Lothar Eiserloh.

279 Eisenhower instituted: Gollancz, 125–26.

280 In late May: SF-E.

280 The Army: Author interviews, Ingrid, Lothar, and Ensi Eiserloh.

282 In contrast, Ingrid's: Author interview, Ingrid Eiserloh; details confirmed by Ensi Eiserloh.

283 and they filled out: SF-E.

284 In October 1945: Author interview, Irene Hasenberg.

289 In January 1946: Author interview, Sumi Utsushigawa.

290 For instance: Author interview, Mas Okabe.

291 In Hiroshima: Author interview, Min Tajii.

292 In July 1947: Author interview, Sumi Utsushigawa.

Chapter Twenty: Beyond the Barbed Wire

Several sources were important in composing this account of the difficulties faced by the administration as well as the remaining internees at Crystal City in the last stage of the camp's existence. As always, interviews with internees and family members were invaluable. Much material from the Reverend Yoshiaki Fukuda's memoir, *My Six Years of Internment*, made its way into this chapter. Also useful was the INS personnel file of O'Rourke and records about the camp in the National Archives. Arnold Krammer's book *Undue Process: The Untold Story of America's German Alien Internees* (London: Rowman & Littlefield, 1997) provided contextual information.

295 By August 1945: NA2, RG59, Box 70.

295 By 1945: O'Rourke's INS personnel file, Department of Justice; and interviews with former internees.

296 He also described: HNCC, 30.

297 Finally, he offered: Ibid., 31.

298 On September 8: NA1, RG85, Box 21; and Krammer, 151.

299 O'Rourke's mandate: NA1, RG85, Box 46.

299 One example: NA1, RG85, Box 25.

301 The Department of Justice: Ibid.

301 While internees like Eppeler: Author interview, Eb Fuhr; and Riley, 121–22.

302 Nonetheless, Barbara encouraged: Riley, 121.

302 Among the most tragic: Fukuda, *My Six Years*, forward by Isao Goto, head minister, Konko Church of Gardena, California, and 63.

303 Fukuda now: The case notes of Dr. Martin found in SF-F.

303 On March 11: SF-F, and Fukuda, *My Six Years*, 62–63.

304 The following month: Ibid., 59–62.

304 Two days later: SF-F.

305 On August 8, 1946: Ibid.

305 The petition: Author interview, Nobusuke Fukuda.

306 By then: NA1, RG27; and author interview, Eb Fuhr.

306 For the other: SF-F.

306 In early January: O'Rourke's INS personnel file.

307 L. T. McCollister: Fukuda, *My Six Years*, 62–68.

307 In Crystal City: Author interview, Eb Fuhr; and *New York Times*, January 3, 1947.

308 In April: Author interview, Eb Fuhr; and Krammer, 159.

309 Fukuda told: SF-F.

310 On February 27, 1948: NA2, RG59, Box 70.

Chapter Twenty-one: The Train from Crystal City

To extend the narrative past the closing of the camp in 1948, I revisited major characters and described what, if any, meaning they made of their experiences during the war. I relied on interviews with Sumi, the Fukuda children, Carmen Mochizuki, Ingrid, Ensi, Lothar, Eb Fuhr, Irene, and others.

Secondary sources, previously cited, provided information for US government figures. As examples of losers and winners, I used newspaper clippings, primarily from the *New York Times*, to describe Kuhn's unhappy ending and Shepard's triumphant postwar life.

In my research, I was struck by how many of the US officials responsible for the camp died of heart attacks, a common cause of death, but perhaps exacerbated by the strain—and perhaps guilt—of their participation in this bleak period in American history.

313 The small, white: Author interview, Sumi Utsushigawa.

316 In 1985: Taniguchi papers provided by Evan Taniguchi; and author visit to site of monument.

316 In November: Author interviews, Sumi Utsushigawa and Jose Angel Gutierrez.

317 City Manager: Author interview, Tomoko Tomita.

317 A parade: John MacCormack, *San Antonio Express-News*, November 9, 1997; and *Crystal City Chatter*, issue 38, December 1997.

318 Many more reunions: Author interviews, Tomoko Tomita, Mas Okabe, and Sumi Utsushigawa.

318 Upon Fukuda's: Fukuda, *My Six Years*, 74.

319 His wife, Shinko: Author interviews, Nobusuke, Saburo, Hiroshi, and Koichi Fukuda.

320 In June 1996: Author interviews, Carmen Mochizuki and Alice Nishimoto; and Campaign for Justice, Nikkei for Civil Rights and Redress, February 2008, http://www.ncrr-la.org.

321 After the war: Hisao Inouye, *Crystal City Chatter*, January 1988.

321 O'Rourke died: Death notice found on Ancestry.com; and obituary, *Dallas Morning News*, April 6, 1959.

321 During the postwar: Author interview, Barton Harrison.

322 As attorney general: Biddle, 212; and Weglyn, 291. Also *San Antonio Express-News* column by Maury Maverick Jr., December 29, 1985.

322 Tom Clark: Weglyn, 114.

323 On May 8, 1945: Kearns Goodwin, 620.

323 Upon his deportation: Jacobs and Fallon.

323 In contrast: Richard Goldstein, "Bert Shepard, 87, an Inspirational Amputee, Dies," *New York Times*, June 20, 2008.

324 After Eb Fuhr: Author interview, Eb Fuhr; and Jacobs and Fallon, *Documents*.

325 The world: Author interviews, Ingrid, Lothar, and Ensi Eiserloh.

329 Two months later: Author interview, Irene Hasenberg.

Bibliography

Books

Alvarez, Elizabeth Cruce, ed. *Texas Almanac, 2010–2011*. Denton: Texas State Historical Association, 2010.

Asahina, Robert. *Just Americans: How Japanese Americans Won a War at Home and Abroad*. New York: Gotham Books, 2006.

Biddle, Francis. *In Brief Authority*. New York: Doubleday, 1962.

Brands, H. W. *Traitor to His Class*. New York: Anchor Books, 2009.

Breitman, Richard, and Allan J. Lichtman. *FDR and the Jews*. Cambridge, MA: Belknap Press, 2013.

Cawthorne, Nigel. *World at War: The Compelling Guide to World War II*. Sywell, England: Igloo Books, 2012.

Christgau, John. *Enemies: World War II Alien Internment*. Lincoln: University of Nebraska Press, 1985; 2009.

Cook, Blanche Wiesen. *Eleanor Roosevelt: Volume One, 1884–1933*. New York: Viking, 1992.

Corbett, P. Scott. *Quiet Passages: The Exchange of Civilians Between the United States and Japan During the Second World War*. Kent, OH: Kent University Press, 1987.

Crystal City 50th Anniversary Reunion Album. Monterey, CA: October 8–10, 1993.

Davis, Kenneth. *FDR: The War President, 1940–1943*. New York: Random House, 2000.

Donald, Heidi Gurcke. *We Were Not the Enemy: Remembering the United States' Latin-American Civilian Internment Program of World War II*. New York: Universe, 2006.

Elleman, Bruce. *Japanese-American Civilian Prisoner Exchanges and Detention Camps, 1941–1945*. New York: Routledge, 2006.

BIBLIOGRAPHY

Fox, Stephen. *America's Invisible Gulag: A Biography of German American Internment & Exclusion in World War II.* New York: Peter Lang, 2000.

Frankl, Viktor. *Man's Search for Meaning: An Introduction to Logotherapy.* 3rd ed. New York: Simon & Schuster, 1984.

Friedman, Max Paul. *Nazis & Good Neighbors: The United States Campaign Against the Germans of Latin America in World War II.* Cambridge, England: Cambridge University Press, 2003.

Fukuda, Reverend Yoshiaki. *Life with Faith: Being a Konko Believer.* San Francisco, CA: Konko Church of San Francisco, 2007.

———. *My Six Years of Internment: An Issei's Struggle for Justice.* San Francisco, CA: Konko Church of San Francisco, 1957.

Gollancz, Victor. *In Darkest Germany.* London: Gollancz, 1947.

Gutierrez, Jose Angel. *The Making of Civil Rights Leader Jose Angel Gutierrez.* Houston: Arte Publico Press, 2005.

Hemphill, John. *The Railroads of San Antonio and South Central Texas.* San Antonio: Maverick Publishing, 2005.

Higashide, Seiichi. *Adios to Tears: The Memoirs of a Japanese-Peruvian Internee in U.S. Concentration Camps.* Seattle: University of Washington Press, 1993.

Howard, John. *Concentration Camps on the Home Front: Japanese Americans in the House of Jim Crow.* Chicago: University of Chicago Press, 2008.

Inada, Lawson Fusao, ed. *Only What We Could Carry: The Japanese American Internment Experience.* Berkeley, CA: Heyday Books, 2000.

Jacobs, Arthur D. *The Prison Called Hohenasperg: An American Boy Betrayed by His Government During World War II.* USA: Universal Publishers, 1999.

Jacobs, Arthur D., and Joseph E. Fallon. *World War Two Experience: The Internment of German-Americans*, a five-volume index of documents accessed as Jacobs and Fallon, *Documents.*

Kearns Goodwin, Doris. *No Ordinary Time: Franklin & Eleanor Roosevelt: The Home Front in World War II.* New York: Simon & Schuster, 1994.

Konigseder, Angelika, and Juliane Wetzel. *Waiting for Hope: Jewish Displaced Persons in Post War Germany.* Evanston, IL: Northwestern University Press, 2001.

Krammer, Arnold. *Nazi Prisoners of War in America.* Pbk. ed. Lanham, MD: Scarborough House, 1992.

———. *Undue Process: The Untold Story of America's German Alien Internees.* London: Rowman & Littlefield, 1997.

Krauter, Anneliese "Lee." *From the Heart's Closet: A Young Girl's World War II Story.* McCordsville, IN: Schatzi Press, 2005.

Mangione, Jerre. *An Ethnic at Large.* New York: G. P. Putnam's Sons; Syracuse, NY: Syracuse University Press edition, 2001.

BIBLIOGRAPHY

Masterson, Daniel M., with Sayaka Funada-Classen. *The Japanese in Latin America*. Urbana: University of Illinois Press, 2004.

Moss, Norman. *19 Weeks: America, Britain, and the Fateful Summer of 1940*. New York: Houghton Mifflin, 2003.

Riley, Karen L. *Schools Behind Barbed Wire: The Untold Story of Wartime Internment and the Children of Arrested Enemy Aliens*. Lanham, MD: Rowman & Littlefield, 2002.

Rowley, Hazel. *Franklin & Eleanor: An Extraordinary Marriage*. New York: Farrar, Straus & Giroux, 2010.

Takaki, Ronald. *A Different Mirror: A History of Multicultural America*. Toronto: Little, Brown, 1993.

Tateishi, John. *And Justice for All: An Oral History of the Japanese American Detention Camps*. New York: Random House, 1984.

Theoharis, Athan G. *The Boss: J. Edgar Hoover and the Great American Inquisition*. New York: Temple University Press, 1988.

Walls, Thomas K. *The Japanese Texans*. San Antonio: University of Texas Institute of Texan Cultures at San Antonio, 1987.

Weglyn, Michi. *Years of Infamy: The Untold Story of America's Concentration Camps*. New York: Morrow Quill Paperlocks, 1976.

Articles and Essays

Fiset, Louis. "Medical Care for Interned Enemy Aliens: A Role for the US Public Health Service in World War II." *American Journal of Public Health* 93 (10) (October 2003): 1644–54.

Fukuda, Nobusuke. "Enduring Communities: An Issei's Six Years of Internment: His Struggle for Justice." *Discover Nikkei*, May 8, 2008.

Ichioka, Yuji. "The Meaning of Loyalty: The Case of Kazumaro Buddy Uno." *Amerasia Journal* 23 (3) (1997): 45–71.

Katznelson, Ira. "Failure to Rescue: How FDR Hurt Jewish Would-Be Immigrants." *New Republic*, July 6, 2013.

Matsui, Reverend Fumio. "The Present Head Minister." 50th Anniversary Konko Church of San Francisco, 1981.

Maverick, Maury. "Crystal City." *San Antonio Express-News*, December 29, 1985.

Stevens, Lewis. "The Life and Character of Earl G. Harrison." *University of Pennsylvania Law Review* 104 (5) (March 1956): 591–602.

Zuckerman, Laurence. "FDR's Jewish Problem." *Nation*, July 17, 2013.

BIBLIOGRAPHY

Theses and Dissertations

Barber, Marian Jean. "How the Irish, Germans, and Czechs Became Anglo: Race and Identity in the Texas-Mexico Borderlands." Dissertation, University of Texas at Austin, May 2010.

Clark, Paul Frederick. "Those Other Camps: An Oral History Analysis of Japanese Alien Enemy Internment During World War II." Thesis, California State University, Fullerton, April 25, 1980.

Schmitz, John Eric. "Enemies Among Us: The Relocation, Internment, and Repatriation of German, Italian, and Japanese Amerians During the Second World War." Dissertation, American University, Washington, DC, 2007.

Newspapers

Cleveland Plain Dealer
Honolulu Star-Bulletin
Laredo Morning Times
Missoulian
New York Times
San Antonio Evening News
San Antonio Express-News
San Francisco Call-Bulletin
San Jose Mercury News
Washington Post

Government Documents

FBI files
National Archives 1 (Washington, DC)
National Archives 2 (College Park, MD)

Archival Materials

Burns, Leslie. Videotaped interviews. University of Texas at San Antonio, Institute of Texan Cultures, 1997–98:

BIBLIOGRAPHY

Yae Ahiara
Sei Dyo
Miyo Eshita
Betty Fly
Cheiko Kamisatu
Stogie Kanogawa
Hide Kasai
Lucy Lunz
Carmen Higa Mochizuki
Roy Muraoka
Alice Nishimoto
Derick Shimatsu
Sumi Utsushigawa Shimatsu
Toni Tomita
S. Yamaguchi

Oral histories. University of Texas at San Antonio, Institute of Texan Cultures:

Mona Bizzell Baskin, office employee, 1979
George Ferris, guard, 1979
John Schmitz, 2007
R. C. Tate, superintendent of the camp's schools, 1979
Margaret N. Williams, secretary, 1979

Centraal Registratiebureau voor Joden 23, Jan Luikenstraat, Eindhoven (list of names of exchangees from Bergen-Belsen). Archives of the United States Holocaust Memorial Museum, Washington, DC.

Crain, Suzanne Wright. Videotaped interviews of Isamu Taniguchi.

Crystal City Chatter. Newsletter published by Sumi Utsushigawa Shimatsu from 1980 to the present.

First National Reunion of Crystal City's World War II Internment Camp Families, November 8–10, 2002. Booklet, a project of the Zavala County Historical Commission.

Fukibayashi, Masayuki. Unpublished biography of Fukuda, 1967.

Harrison, Earl. Diary. Donated August 1994, United States Holocaust Memorial Museum, Washington, DC. RG-10.088, accession no. 1994.A.0079.

Here, in America?: Immigrants as "the Enemy" During WWII and Today. Report of the Assembly on Wartime Relocation and Internment of Civilians, April 8–9, 2005, San Francisco, California. San Francisco, CA: National Japanese American Historical Society, 2006.

BIBLIOGRAPHY

M.S. Gripsholm: The FBI Files. Washington, DC: FBI Files, 2009. 100-124687, Section 7.

Reicher, Harry. "The Post-Holocaust World and President Harry S. Truman: The Harrison Report and Immigration Law and Policy." Edited transcript of presentation made in the course "Aftermath of the Holocaust: Truman and the Post-War World." Conducted by the Midwest Center for Holocaust Education and the Truman Presidential Museum and Library, Kansas City, MO, July 10, 2002. 1–25.

Interviews

Yae Aihara, Los Angeles

Ejii Ayabe, San Francisco

Ruth Becker, Charlotte, North Carolina

Irene Hasenberg Butter, Ann Arbor, Michigan

Michael Camarillo, Crystal City

Arthur Contag, Quito, Ecuador

Suzanne Wright Crain, San Antonio, Texas

Karen Ebel, New London, New Hampshire

Ensi Eiserloh, Anaheim, California

Ingrid Eiserloh, Honolulu

Lothar Eiserloh, Honolulu and San Francisco

Eberhard Fuhr, Chicago

Rose and Tetsuro Fujii, Sebastopol, California

Koichi Fukuda, San Francisco

Nob Fukuda, San Francisco

Saburo Fukuda, San Francisco

Paul Grayber, Bend, Oregon

Jose Angel Gutierrez, Arlington, Texas

J. Barton Harrison, Rosemont, Pennsylvania

Arthur Jacobs, Tempe, Arizona

Lori Lechner Johnston, Sedona, Arizona

Reverend Masato Kawahatsu, San Francisco

Suzy Lechner Kvammen, Newport Beach, California

Heidi Kolb Leszczynski, Frankfurt, Germany

Bernard Levermann, Euless, Texas

Charles McCollister, Simi Valley, California

Carmen Higa Mochizuki, Los Angeles and Las Vegas

Roy Muraoka, Chula Vista, California

BIBLIOGRAPHY

Tony "Kaz" Naganuma, San Francisco
Alice Nishimoto, Las Vegas
Mas Okabe, Las Vegas
Sid Okazaki, Los Angeles and Las Vegas
Zeke Romero, Crystal City
Peter Sakai, San Antonio, Texas
Richard Santos, Crystal City
Sumi Utsushigawa Shimatsu, Los Angeles and Las Vegas
Pam Smith, Philadelphia
Min Tajii, Las Vegas
Ben Takeuchi, Las Vegas
Evan Taniguchi, Austin
Joanne Tolosa, San Francisco
Ella Tomita, Honolulu
Toni Tomita, Los Angeles and Las Vegas
Sigrid Banzhaf Toye, Santa Barbara, California
Reverend Alfred Tsuyuki, Los Angeles
Werner Ulrich, Mt. Sinai, New York
Johanna Wartermann Howell, Garland, Texas
Al Wohlpart, Oak Ridge, Tennessee
Jacob Wolf, New York City

Documentaries

Alien Enemy Detention Facility. Crystal City, Texas. 16 mm black-and-white camp film.
Hattendorf, Linda. *The Cats of Mirikitani.* Arthouse Films, 2003.
Hidden Internment: The Art Shibayama Story. Peek Media in association with the Japanese Peruvian Oral History Project, 2004.
Reverend Yoshiaki Fukuda, 50th Year Memorial Service. Produced by Konko Church, San Francisco, 2007.
Suzuki, Junichi. *442: Live with Honor, Die with Dignity.* UTB Pictures and Film Voice, 2010.

Online Resources

Crystal City Internment Camp, 1945. http://www.youtube.com/watch?v =WRfSHgdh2UA

BIBLIOGRAPHY

German American Internee Coalition. http://www.gaic.info

Japanese American Legacy Project. http://denso.org

Jewish Virtual Library. http://www.jewishvirtuallibrary.org/jsource/Holocaust
/murrow.html

National Archives. http://www.468thbombgroup.org

Pearl Harbor Casualty List. http://www.usvirginia.org

US Holocaust Memorial Museum. http://www.ushmm.org

Index

INDEX

Photograph Credits

Page

1   Top and bottom: courtesy of the Fukuda family.

2   All photographs are courtesy of UTSA's Institute of Texan Cultures.

3   Top: courtesy of the Franklin D. Roosevelt Presidential Library. Bottom: courtesy of J. Barton Harrison.

4   All photographs are courtesy of UTSA's Institute of Texan Cultures.

5   Top: courtesy of Pamela Smith. Bottom: courtesy of UTSA's Institute of Texan Cultures.

6   Top left: courtesy of Ensila Eiserloh Bennett. Top right: courtesy of Diana Foster. Middle and bottom: courtesy of UTSA's Institute of Texan Cultures.

7   Top left: courtesy of Sumi Shimatsu. Top right: courtesy of UTSA's Institute of Texan Cultures. Bottom left and right: courtesy of Sumi Shimatsu.

8   Top: courtesy of UTSA's Institute of Texan Cultures. Middle: courtesy of Sumi Shimatsu. Bottom: courtesy of UTSA's Institute of Texan Cultures.

About the Author

Jan Jarboe Russell is a former Nieman Fellow and a contributing editor for *Texas Monthly*, and has written for the *San Antonio Express-News*, the *New York Times, Slate*, and other magazines. She is the author of *Lady Bird: A Biography of Mrs. Johnson* (Scribner, 1999) and has also compiled and edited *They Lived to Tell the Tale* (Lyons Press, 2007). She lives in San Antonio, Texas, with her husband, Dr. Lewis F. Russell Jr.